English Domestic Architecture

KENT HOUSES

Anthony Quiney

Frontispiece. Smarden: Kent at its most characteristic, with Hartnup House, a medieval house remodelled in 1671 by Dr Matthew Hartnup for his third wife Joanna Newenden, and, down the lane, the tower of St Michael's church.

Opposite. Franks, Horton Kirby: The classical entrance doorway of Lancelot Bathurst's house of 1591.

English Domestic Architecture

KENT HOUSES

Anthony Quiney

Antique Collectors' Club

ISBN 1 85149 153 8

British Library Cataloguing-in-Publication Data
A catalogue record for this book is available from the British Library.

Printed in England
by the Antique Collectors' Club Ltd., Woodbridge, Suffolk
on Consort Royal Silk paper
supplied by the Donside Paper Company, Aberdeen, Scotland

THE ANTIQUE COLLECTORS' CLUB

The Antique Collectors' Club was formed in 1966 and now has a five figure membership spread throughout the world. It publishes the only independently run monthly antiques magazine *Antique Collecting* which caters for those collectors who are interested in widening their knowledge of antiques, both by greater awareness of quality and by discussion of the factors which influence the price that is likely to be asked. The Antique Collectors' Club pioneered the provision of information on prices for collectors and the magazine still leads in the provision of detailed articles on a variety of subjects.

It was in response to the enormous demand for information on 'what to pay' that the price guide series was introduced in 1968 with the first edition of *The Price Guide to Antique Furniture* (completely revised, 1978 and 1989), a book which broke new ground by illustrating the more common types of antique furniture, the sort that collectors could buy in shops and at auctions rather than the rare museum pieces which had previously been used (and still to a large extent are used) to make up the limited amount of illustrations in books published by commercial publishers. Many other price guides have followed, all copiously illustrated, and greatly appreciated by collectors for the valuable information they contain, quite apart from prices. The Antique Collectors' Club also publishes other books on antiques, including horology and art reference works, and a full book list is available.

Club membership, which is open to all collectors, costs £19.50 per annum. Members receive free of charge *Antique Collecting,* the Club's magazine (published ten times a year), which contains well-illustrated articles dealing with the practical aspects of collecting not normally dealt with by magazines. Prices, features of value, investment potential, fakes and forgeries are all given prominence in the magazine.

Among other facilities available to members are private buying and selling facilities, the longest list of 'For Sales' of any antiques magazine, an annual ceramics conference and the opportunity to meet other collectors at their local antique collectors' clubs. There are over eighty in Britain and more than a dozen overseas. Members may also buy the Club's publications at special pre-publication prices.

As its motto implies, the Club is an organisation designed to help collectors get the most out of their hobby: it is informal and friendly and gives enormous enjoyment to all concerned.

For Collectors — By Collectors — About Collecting

The Antique Collectors' Club, 5 Church Street, Woodbridge, Suffolk

In memory of my mother, Marion Quiney

CONTENTS

Preface and Acknowledgements

One of the best things in life is doing something you have always wanted to do. It is even better when someone asks you to do this before the idea has entered your head. This happened to me when John Steel suggested that I write a book about the houses of Kent. I had written about a number of specific houses already and about houses generally as well: now I could combine both pursuits in the best of ways. Kent had always appealed to me for very special qualities not found in other English counties; and it is also the first county I remember visiting outside my native south-east London.

In 1938, at the time of the Munich crisis, I was evacuated to a small cottage on the fringes of Edenbridge, Cowden and Hever. Every evening my mother pushed me to Hever station to meet my father coming back from work in London. Unlike the suburbs I knew, this mile-long journey was a miracle, not just for its trees and fields, but for the way the houses were hidden from view until a momentary glimpse revealed their existence.

After the war, I often returned to Kent, particularly on long rambling car journeys with my mother. 'Let's see where this goes' she would say, abruptly turning off the main road, and plunging mapless into the secret web of lanes which cover the whole landscape. We would then drive along, by guesswork, passing countless old brick and timber houses, tightly embraced by the endless woodland. Later, I learned how they came to be built, but not until I started this book did I realise just how remarkable their story really is.

Happily, since my mother had set this flame burning in the first instance, I was able to share this experience with her. She came on many of my journeys of discovery, parish by parish, during the last year of her life, and helped me by keeping an eye on one side of the road while I watched the other, as well as attempting to navigate with, by now, heavily annotated maps. Although she was crippled by arthritis, she nevertheless saw all kinds of houses and kept up with my developing ideas. For her gift of enquiry and exploration, as well as for many others reasons, I dedicate this book to her memory.

Another reason for my pleasure in writing this book is more academic. History is not just an exploration of the past for its own sake. It is a mirror reflecting the present from a standpoint which nullifies the effects of immediacy. Seen this way, I believe that Kent produced a society during the later Middle Ages which more closely reached an ideal than any other county could manage at that time, or any other period has been able to achieve since then on quite the same scale. Affluence and equitabilty reduced poverty in a unique way which is worth pondering, and, as the following pages demonstrate, changed the landscape for good.

This achievement is no argument for conservatism. Today's standards are different. In any case, the changes of the eighteenth and nineteenth centuries eroded that state of affairs. If any moral can be drawn from Kent's example, it is to decry the social stratification of other counties: Durham, for instance, during the heyday of the prince-bishops, or the wealthy northern half of Norfolk during the oligarchical rule of the eighteenth and nineteenth centuries. Perhaps Kent provides an argument against the ordering of much of society even today. Its generally benevolent social hierarchy is now lost, but maybe its ideals are not beyond emulation.

To return to mundane matters and definitions, when I first visited Kent it had different boundaries from today's. Kent, here, is the county included within the boundaries last defined when part of the north-west of the county was removed to form the Greater London Boroughs of Bexley and Bromley in 1965. Already in 1889 another slice of the north-west had been taken to form the County of London's Metropolitan Boroughs of Deptford, Greenwich, Lewisham and Woolwich, but a small section of Sussex was given up at the same time so that all the built-up part of Tunbridge Wells should lie within Kent. These boundaries determine whether a parish is included in the Gazetteer. Significant houses which were built in the older Kent, outside these boundaries, for instance Wickham Court (in Bromley, Greater London, since 1965) and Charlton House (in Greenwich, County of London, since 1889) are included in the opening chapters (though not the Gazetteer) because they are too important in the context of Kent to be omitted.

Parishes in the present Kent are, nevertheless, only included in the Gazetteer if they contain significant houses within the context of this book. By house I mean an individual building principally used as a private dwelling by a single family. This definition excludes a number of related buildings such as castles, palaces, inns, lodgings and flats. Even so, I have not entirely omitted these: the boundaries between them and houses are vague, and their development and the development of houses are too close for a rigid adherence to definitions. The residence within Eynsford Castle, therefore, has a place here, but Dover Castle does not. The Archbishop's Palaces at Canterbury, Charing, Knole (Sevenoaks), and Otford are all mentioned, since these were princely houses and, as such, set the standard for much that followed them. Another vague area is where houses have been converted to other uses (for example Hemsted to become part of Benenden School), and where other buildings have been converted to domestic use (countless oast-houses and barns, most of them with little sympathy for their original form).

So far as significance is concerned, I have given pride of place to historic houses. No other county has so many houses which have been statutorily listed for their architectural or historic interest, so I have to choose between them. I have included large numbers of houses which were built by medieval yeomen because of their remarkable size and age. This weight of numbers is one of Kent's wonders. I have included later houses again largely on the basis of their contribution to this county's unique qualities, although, increasingly, I have had to consider national rather than local qualities as century succeeds century, and increasingly exclude fine houses as a result. I have to admit that my selection is often subjective, never statistical, and, at times, probably accidental — if the sun shone on a house, it is more likely to be here than one in the shade. I have also tried to be fair to what is typical of the last three centuries, but only by looking for good exemplars.

Books of this kind are never their author's unaided work. This one would have been impossible without much help from others. My principal guide was John Newman, both through his two volumes on Kent in the *Buildings of England* series, and in person through discussion and visits, starting in 1975 with a tour of east Kent, organised by the Society of Architectural Historians, and culminating memorably just before publication at Cobham Hall. His published comments, parish by parish, have been so ingrained into my thoughts that I have not given specific references to *North East and East Kent* and *West Kent and the Weald* in my text because these would appear in every paragraph, if not every sentence. Nevertheless, I fully acknowledge this greatest of all debts.

Accompanying him as a guide at Cobham Hall was Tim Tatton-Brown, formerly of the Canterbury Archaeological Trust; he and his colleagues through their *Reports* have again provided me with an insight which I could not have obtained unaided. I am greatly indebted to their published surveys for several of my figures. I owe a similar debt to Sarah Pearson and her colleagues in the Ashford branch of the Royal Commission on the Historical Monuments of England. Their work on the medieval houses of Kent has not yet reached publication, but I am grateful to them for being able to use their surveys for Figures 10, 21, 35, 53 and 59. I similarly wish to remember the late Stuart Rigold, also of the RCHM(E), who discssed the halls of Kent with me twenty years ago; his cryptic comments were always worth deciphering, and his surveys have again been invaluable. Jane Wade and her students opened my eyes to what lies behind the modest walls of Brook's houses; Figures 69, 70, 78 and 79 are redrawn from their surveys made for the Vernacular Research Unit, Canterbury School of Architecture, by Tayo Aluko and David Rea, Nicholas Hobbs and Mark Storey, and Jennifer Brett and David Hopps, and published in *Traditional Kent Buildings* 5 (1986) by the Kent Institute of Art and Design. Several more figures are based on other people's published surveys and records, and this debt I gratefully acknowledge: I could never have done the work myself.

I have had great help from many other friends and acquaintances, particularly Jill Allibone, who was my guide at Penshurst and Leigh, as well as to the works of George Devey and Anthony Salvin; Mitzi Quirk, who showed me her conversions of oast-houses in the Weald; Jayne Semple, who answered all my questions about Plaxtol; Dorothy Phillips and the Royal Archaeological Institute, who made a visit to Mereworth Castle possible; Anthony Emery, who showed me Nettlestead Place; and E.W. Parkin of the Kent Archaeological Society, who discussed Cobb's Hall, Aldington, and other early sixteenth century houses with me. I should like to thank both Malcolm Airs and Andor Gomme for the help they have given me here, as so often before. I owe another debt to many of my students, particularly Paul Slane, who studied Wealden houses, Bob Blower, who studied Ashford New Town, and Jean-Paul Abbyad, who studied Mote Park at Maidstone.

Without the help of numerous house-owners (and occasionally their dogs) I could never have started. I should like to single out Michael Coombes who showed me the house he designed for himself at Biddenden as well as many other houses there, old and new, and also Mr and Mrs Vaughan who showed me Bumpit at Lynsted and discussed recusancy in Kent with me. Finally I must thank Primrose Elliott, my editor, who found the countless mistakes in my text of the embarrassing sort academic writers are particularly prone to making.

Finally, I would always welcome comments from readers, particularly where I have made mistakes or allowed glaring omissions to occur.

NOTES ON DRAWINGS

The scales represent 15ft. at the top divided into 5ft. units, and 5m at the bottom divided into 1m units, unless marked otherwise.

The following abbreviations have been used in some of the plans to denote the functions of rooms

b	bedroom	k	kitchen
C	great chamber	lr	living-room
c	chamber	p	parlour
ch	chapel	s	service room
cp	cross passage or screens passage	sb	smoke bay
d	dining-room	sc	solar or upper chamber
e	entry lobby, vestibule or hall	sh	shop or workshop
g	garderobe or closet	st	stairway
gh	ground-floor or floored hall	u	undercroft
H	open hall	uh	upper hall

Chapter 1

The County and its Builders

'Kent, sir' says Jingle in *Pickwick Papers* (1836-41), 'everybody knows Kent — apples, cherries, hops and women.' Dickens had spent much of his boyhood around Rochester, and stayed in many of the coastal resorts before he went to live at Gadshill, near Higham, where he died in 1870. He understood Kent well. He made Chatham, Broadstairs, Cobham and Rochester echo with the footsteps of David Copperfield, Nicholas Nickleby, Mr Trotman and Betsey Trotwood, as well as Pickwick and Jingle.

While Jingle could talk knowingly about the essential Kent, it was a unique combination of topography and social custom which had given Kent its special distinction. These had let Kent's wealth be spread more equitably than in any other English county and given Kent's peasants their chance. In the Middle Ages they became affluent and called themselves yeomen. They built countless substantial houses. Thousands are still standing, even though many — perhaps most — are more than five hundred years old. Nowhere else in England did the peasantry do so well, if their houses are anything to judge by. A number of gentlemen and the occasional lord built grander houses in Kent, but these, like their large estates, are exceptional, not the rule.

Most yeomen built their houses in the tangled patchwork of ancient coppices and enclosures which undulate across the downland into the Weald (Colour Plate 1). This is a secret landscape, as the experienced traveller Celia Fiennes recorded in 1697:

> ...when I turned off the road to Maidstone I travell'd through lanes and woods which were very fine but hid the sight of the Country about, being so close that it was the privatest Road I have travell'd...

That web of lanes has hardly changed, and the scale of the countryside is still small. Just occasionally, a break in this landscape reveals dramatic contrasts:

> ...about 10 mile short of Maidstone you ascend a very steep hill which discovers the whole Country at one view 40 mile off... which shew the variety of grounds intermixt with each other and lesser hills and plaines and rivers... at one view (Morris 1984, 124 and 128).

It is only around Thanet in north-east Kent and on Romney Marsh in the south that the landscape becomes open in every direction. But even there the small houses dotted about appear to be wrapped up in their own solitude.

Geography and topography

The origin of the yeomanry's wealth lay in Kent's natural resources and, more particularly, how they came to be exploited. In essence, Kent is no better endowed than many other English counties (Figure 1). The rich farmland of the northern and eastern downland is more than counterbalanced by the dry sandy heaths of the chartland to the south-west and the dank, soggy clays of the Weald along Kent's south-western boundary with Sussex. Nevertheless, rising populations could exploit both of these infertile districts at a time in the Middle Ages when people elsewhere in the country faced land-hunger, poverty and starvation.

Geographically, Kent was well placed for success. It lies like a broad peninsula jutting eastwards towards Continental Europe between the Thames estuary and the English Channel. The Continent has always been a source of ideas and trade for Kent,

Colour Plate 1. Harts Heath Farm and, in the background, Husheath Manor, Staplehurst, two ancient enclosures on the edge of the High Weald, complete with their timber-framed houses.

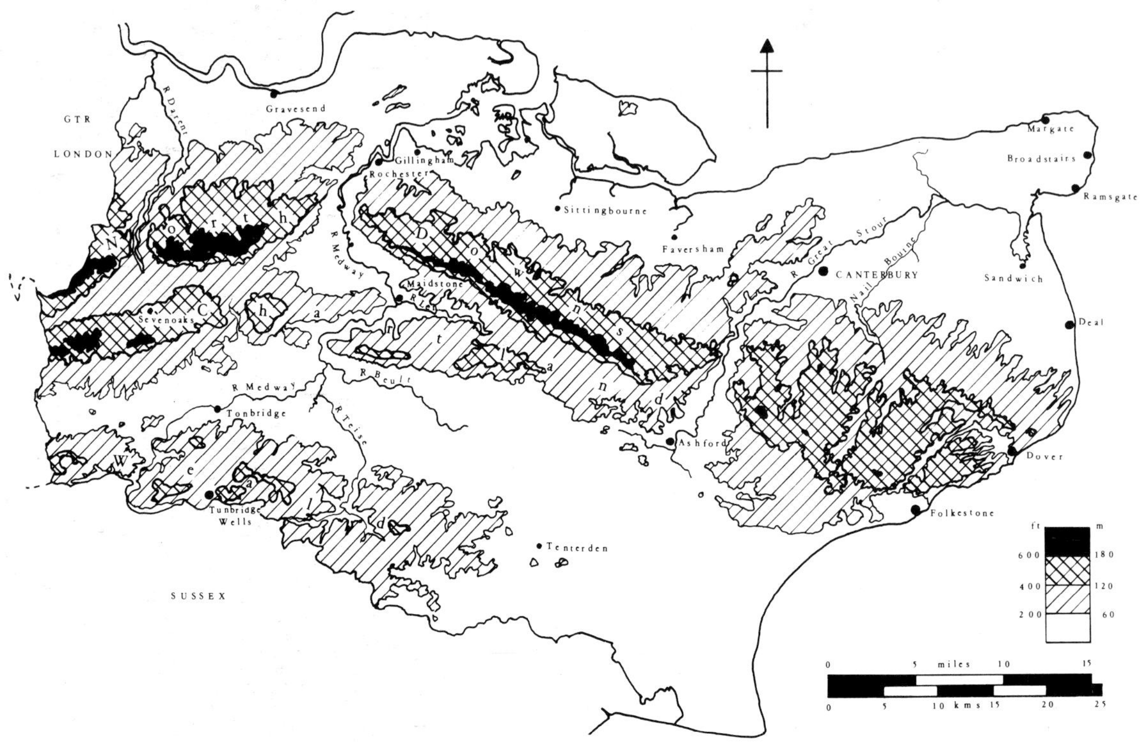

Figure 1. Kent. Relief, rivers and principal towns; the boundaries with Sussex and Surrey are those established in 1889, and with London in 1965.

Colour Plate 2. Maidstone Palace, set beside the Medway and dating back at least to the 1320s, although most of what is visible belongs to rebuilding campaigns between the 16th century and 1909.

but seldom was of overwhelming importance. The narrow waters between the Channel and the North Sea were an obvious route for invaders — the Belgae fleeing the advance of Rome, the Romans themselves, and, later, the Anglo-Saxon migrants who started the conversion of Roman Britain into the England of today; but the sea was also a clear-cut frontier. There is no doubt where Kent starts. The indented coastline offered numerous havens for ships, and, by the Middle Ages, these encouraged trade more than invasion. Inland, Kent was seldom a marching ground for soldiers. Lacking the open plains of the Midlands, it was topographically unsuited to warfare. It was little affected by the clash of arms during the Norman Conquest, the Wars of the Roses and the Civil War.

Reinforcing the natural barrier of the sea along the north coast were the marshes of the Thames estuary, the Isle of Sheppey, and the Wantsum dividing Thanet from the mainland. These made excellent pasture for cattle and sheep — as the name Sheppey implies — and Romney Marsh on the south coast was better still. Across the south-west side of the county, from Tenterden westwards to Cowden, the low sandstone hills of the Weald formed another natural barrier, dividing Kent from Sussex. The region takes its name from the old Germanic word *Wald,* meaning wood, and it was less the height of these hills than the impenetrable woodland encouraged by the the dense quaggy clay soils on their surface which made so effective a boundary.

The Weald dips downwards in a north-easterly direction towards a series of heavy clay vales running diagonally across the county. These served cattle well, but put grain at a disadvantage. The vales start close to Romney Marsh and the shingle beaches of Dungeness, pointing out into the Channel, and continue all the way to Edenbridge near the western boundary with the county of Surrey. North of these, a scarp running from Hythe on the Channel coast to Crockham Hill on the Surrey border marks the edge of the narrow band of overlying Greensand hills which carry the dry and infertile chartland, itself dipping in a northerly direction to an increasingly widening fertile vale running discontinuously between Folkestone and Westerham. A further scarp starting between Folkestone and Dover marks the beginning of the chalk downland, the newest of Kent's geological formations, which continues all the way to Biggin Hill on the southern fringes of London. Chalk gives Kent the White Cliffs of Dover and forms the bastions of North and South Foreland before it too dips northwards towards the Thames Estuary. Here it is overlain with tertiary deposits and alluvial drifts of shingle, and, more importantly for the county's wealth, clays and silts, which provide the best soils in the county for corn.

Roman Kent

This was the most prized land of all, and it attracted the earliest settlers. It also attracted the Romans, who needed British corn to feed their armies on the Rhine. When anarchy followed the death of the tribal King Cunobelin (Shakespeare's Cymbeline) shortly before AD 43, this supply was threatened, so the Romans invaded. Their landing point, traditionally, is said to be near Richborough at the southern end of Pegwell Bay. Richborough, *Rutupiae* to the Romans, became an important port. Today, the site is marked by a fort, designed to defend the coast against Saxon raiders. A more indelible mark left by the Romans on the county is the strategic Watling Street, which ran from Canterbury (their *Durovernum Cantiacorum),* where it immediately crossed the Great Stour, by way of an important crossing of the Medway at Rochester *(Durobriva),* to London. Roads also led to Richborough, and to naval ports at Dover *(Dubris)* and Lympne *(Lemanis).* So Canterbury was established as the centre of Kent.

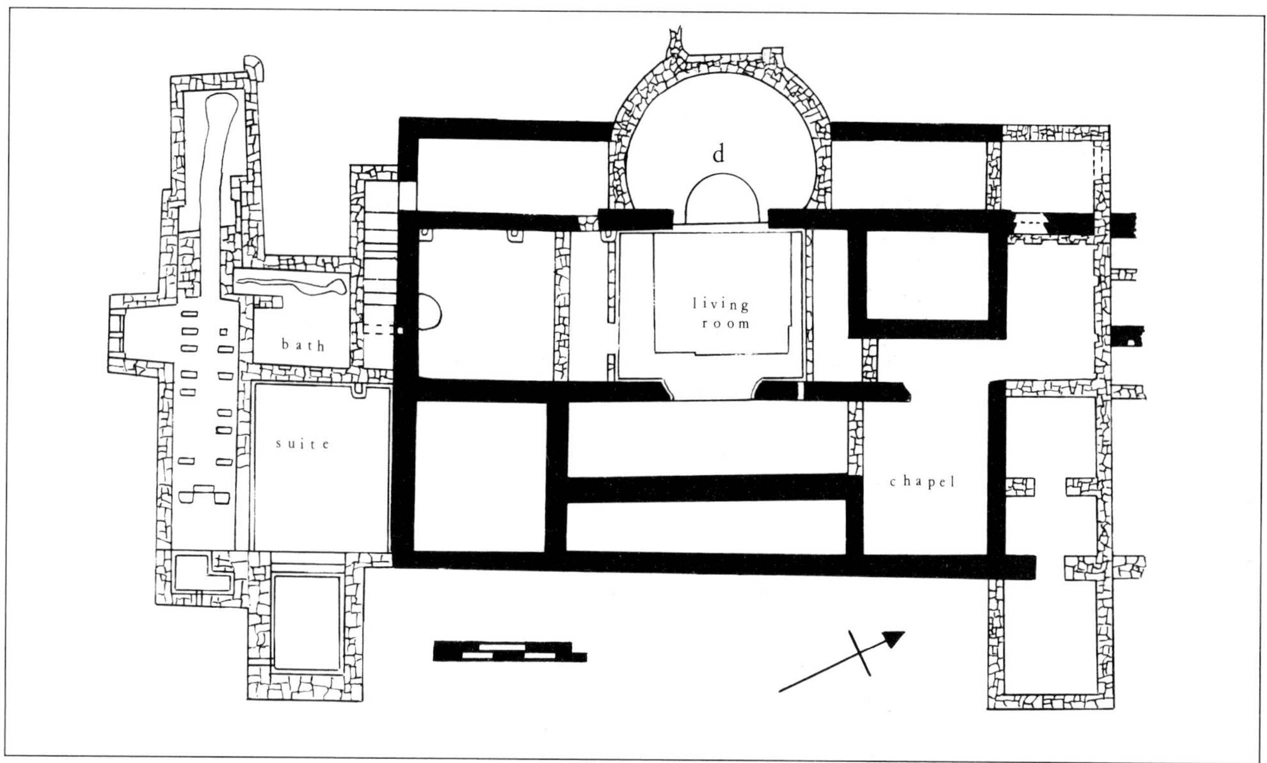

Figure 2. Lullingstone Roman Villa. Ground plan in Period IV (mid 4th century), showing the main living accommodation in the centre, an extensive suite of baths on the left, and rooms on the right which included, unusually, a Christian chapel; the earlier work is shown solid and the most recent work in notional masonry. (After Meates 1980.)

Other signs of how much the Romans needed Kent's rural wealth are the remains of their villas, which were densely concentrated in the Darent and Medway valleys and along Watling Street. The heavy clay soils of the high Weald were so densely wooded that, despite the exploitation of its iron resources, it remained sparsely inhabited.

The choice of a site for a villa was determined by the need for flat ground, shelter from prevailing winds, a good water supply and fertile soil. Vitruvius, the one Roman architect whose writings have survived, paid great attention to the ideal qualities required by building sites (*De Architectura,* Bks. 1, 5 and 6), but ideals are seldom reality: villas are not always placed where one would expect. The landscape of lowland Britain was already full when the Romans arrived, and, though they were conquerors, they came to terms with the natives and their land boundaries. Villas had to rise where they could, and natural determinants were on no more than equal terms with man-made ones. Human whim, supernatural prompting, or a spectacular view might make the final choice. This was equally true of a later age.

Water was so important that Vitruvius devoted a whole book to it (*De Architectura,* Bk. 8). The bath epitomises Roman bodily luxury, and many Romans and Romanised Britons made a fetish of water, dedicating shrines and temples at their villas to the spirits who brought it springing from the hillsides. The rippling waters of the River Darent at Lullingstone surely meant more than refreshment for cattle and a convenient route to the Thames and to markets in London and Rochester (Figure 2). They can hardly have left unaffected a people whose culture made poetry of the countryside.

A major advantage of the villa's rectangular form over the round form of building, which had been ubiquitous in Celtic Britain, was that openings for doorways or

Colour Plate 3. Court Lodge, Mersham, Christ Church Priory's manor house and great barn, with the parish church close by; the other side of the house appears in Colour Plate 59.

Colour Plate 4. Ightham Mote. Started about 1340, with a hall, chapel and gatehouse, these buildings were progressively extended over the next two centuries until they enclosed a small courtyard.

Colour Plate 5. Hamden, Smarden. Although modernised and encased in brick, much of the timber frame of the original mid-14th century house still remains (see Figure 14).

Colour Plate 6. Stone Street, Cranbrook, with Union Mill of 1814 dominating a view of typical weatherboarded houses.

windows could easily be made in the walls without imperilling the structure, and a rectangular building allowed infinite variation since it could be subdivided into rooms and extended to serve both usage and appearance. The villa's standard of finish was another innovation. Walls were often smoothly plastered and sometimes decorated outside with red patterning on a white ground, and with all kinds of schemes of geometrical and figurative decoration inside. Lullingstone was decorated with painted friezes and water nymphs, while Christian figures and symbols were a less usual touch. Carved reliefs and architectural features like columns, pilasters, entablatures and finials all added a new distinction, while paved floors and glazed windows commonly gave comfort. These are only less remarkable when compared with luxurious suites of baths, under-floor heating by hypocausts, and lavish mosaic floors. Nothing like this would be seen again for over a thousand years.

The foundation of the Kingdom of Kent and the advent of Christianity

The collapse of Roman rule in 410 and the culture and economy that went with it caused a deadly break in British history. It ended an unrivalled civilisation, one that was to survive only in the imagination to inspire future generations. Pagan prehistory and the imported civilisation of Rome imposed on it belong to an irretrievable past, while the new order brought by the sword of invaders and, soon, the steadying hand of the Christian Church stretches in an increasingly comprehensible way to the present.

Politically the Britons and their Celtic version of Roman rule survived for a good century and a half, comparatively peacefully until the 440s, thereafter with increasing bloodshed. Needing military help, the British leader Vortigern made the fateful decision about 430 to enlist Saxon mercenaries against the invading Picts and Scots. This was successful for a while, but the price was to give north-east Kent to their leader, Hengest. Eventually he rebelled and founded a separate kingdom, named after the *Cantiae,* its ancient British inhabitants. The *Anglo-Saxon Chronicle* for 473 records that the Britons of Kent 'fled from the English like fire', though British communities apparently survived in the Medway valley at least until the seventh century. *Durovernum* fell to pieces, eventually to be rebuilt as the new Canterbury. Archaeological evidence shows Hengest's mercenaries building sordid *Grubenhaüser,* the common Anglo-Saxon form of sunken-featured building which, like Iron Age round houses, could be set to any use. Yet, if fire and pillage swept into many corners of England, they did not reach everywhere, particularly in Kent (Hawkes 1969).

From the time of Hengest's founding of the kingdom, Kent enjoyed special privileges. The Laws of Ethelbert contain the first reference to a class of Anglo-Saxon freemen living in the county, the so-called ceorls. This vaguely defined group stood between the king and his noble eorls or thegns on the one hand, and several classes of half-free laets and serfs on the other. They were the ancestors of the yeomen of later years, and evidence that Kent did not suffer the steep decline that afflicted the rest of England.

Indeed it enjoyed some prosperity. The rich agricultural land around the North Downs encouraged settlement; the proximity of the sea abetted by navigable rivers and the short crossing to France fostered trade. Nowhere did Roman standards of wealth revive more quickly. One consequence was Ethelbert's marriage to the Frankish Princess Bertha, an otherwise inexplicable tie between this very small kingdom and a very large one overseas. A second consequence, closely linked, was the choice of Kent for Augustine's mission of 597. The resulting monasteries at Reculver and

Minster show Kent's acceptance of Christianity, but they also show the Church involving itself in revived trade; and other monasteries headed by Canterbury's Christ Church Priory were to become great promoters of agriculture. Kent was a special case in the new England, and was to remain so after it had been absorbed into the kingdom of Wessex in the eighth century.

One way in which order was brought to the settlement of the land was through the establishment of manors. In Kent, as elsewhere in England, they may owe their existence to grants of land made by the king to his nobles in return for loyal support. Similarly, the peasantry received a share of the land and the protection of the manorial lord in return for rendering services, sometimes military, usually agricultural (Aston 1958). Vortigern's grant to Hengest and the Saxon mercenaries of part of Kent in return for military aid may be a forerunner of the system, but military service was eventually less essential than working the land. Political and economic stablity went hand in hand.

While the terms of the grants varied, generally half a manor's land was granted to tenants, half remained as demesne land for the use of the lord. King Ine's laws of the 690s recognised this form of land settlement in Wessex, and it seems to have been widespread in southern England, including Kent. When manorial estates were formed, the demesne and tenanted land was distributed in a readily comprehensible form. A manor and a parish consisting of a village settlement together with its surrounding lands and clearly established boundaries were probably one and the same. But manors soon became so varied in size and character that, by the time of the Domesday Survey in 1086, land was the only thing they had in common (Maitland 1897, Essay 1, Ch. 6). In Kent some manors owned land far away from the parish centre in the wilderness of the Weald. Moreover, Kent's ancient form of inheritance played havoc with the ownership of its lands, as it was passed down from hand to hand. After a lapse of some centuries, a parish might contain several manors or parts of them, and, similarly, a large manor might have lands in several parishes.

Manorial lords were not drawn from the secular nobility alone, particularly in Kent. Ultimately this was of great significance to the growing prosperity of the yeomanry. The continuance of the Church as an institution depended on more than piety: wealth was imperative. This involved it in worldly affairs just as deeply as it involved lay institutions. The Church took on a prominent secular role through its various foundations and eventually through its princes and lords as the owners of numerous manors. Old Kent of the first Saxon settlement, that is to say the rich cornland of the north and east including Thanet, was divided into manors, mostly owned by the monasteries. Many laymen gave their manors to the Church as acts of piety or atonement, and this included the English kings. They saw political as well as spiritual advantages in granting land to the Church. There were economic advantages too, for the Church soon outshone the temporal nobility in its ability to exploit the agricultural potential of the land.

The most overt sign of the profit this brought is the architectural splendour of Kent's cathedrals, monasteries and churches. Christ Church, Canterbury, at once a priory and the seat of the first prince of the Church, was sustained by manorial estates on the fertile land of north-east Kent, and others as far away as West Sussex and Middlesex. One of the richest estates, on the fertile hills of Aldington overlooking Romney Marsh, was given to Christ Church by Queen Ediva in 961, and it eventually included lands scattered in the neighbouring parishes of Lympne and Stowting, and on the marsh itself. By the time of the Domesday Survey, this was the most densely

Colour Plate 7. Archbishop Bourchier's Palace of Knole, Sevenoaks, begun soon after 1456, with his great gatehouse and flanking ranges, finished with shaped gables added by Sackville after 1603.

Colour Plate 8. Houses of the 17th and 18th centuries in Bank Street, Maidstone.

Colour Plate 9. Market Place and the Guildhall of 1574 framing a view of Court Street, Faversham.

Colour Plate 10. The entrance range of Sissinghurst Castle, with Sir John Baker's entrance and one of the flanking towers of about 1535, built in brick, with diagonally laid courses of tumbled brickwork to form the gable slopes.

populated part of all Kent and employed as many or more plough-teams per square mile as anywhere else in the country. The first architectural expression of this wealth in the Saxon cathedral at Canterbury was eclipsed by its successor, but future generations used the cathedral's wealth on the estates themselves to build palaces (Colour Plate 2), manor houses and barns. Many fragments of these survive today.

Free peasantry and gavelkind

In Kent inheritance was commonly by a partible system, known as gavelkind, whereby land was equally distributed among all sons, not simply the eldest, if a man died intestate. Wills reflected this custom too. Even houses and their contents were sometimes divided between two heirs. The advantage of this form of inheritance over primogeniture was that eldest heirs were not better endowed than younger ones and, being no better able to seek equally well-endowed heiresses, were less likely to continue accruing wealth, generation by generation. To build up an estate meant effort and judgement, not the luck of being born first.

Over the years, the consequences of both this inevitable division and the economic success or failure of tenants fragmented the manor and complicated everyone's role within it. This process was partly balanced by men of wealth, power or determination consolidating their position by absorbing parcels of manorial land whenever they could. Nevertheless, the equitable role of gavelkind came into play, ensuring that wealth could not easily be concentrated and leave a few people in positions of overweening economic power, and the remainder in poverty.

The social organisation of the manor came to be reflected in the very fields where its wealth was created. The open field system was possibly brought by the immigrants from Germany, where it was of great antiquity. Tacitus referred to communal cultivation of shared fields in German villages, and rotation between cropping and fallow in circumstances where there was plenty of land for all *(Germania,* Ch. 26); but it may have been the upturn in population that brought it into existence in England and allowed villagers to hold a share of the land through ownership or lease of strips in what became known as common or open fields. The system required a high degree of social agreement, but it offered the advantages of co-operation, mutual security and a share of the village's assets.

Only in the aftermath of the Conquest is the open field system clearly recognisable, and then mainly in the Midlands where it was widely practised (Gray 1915, 450-509). For a while it was well established on the cornland owned by the monasteries in northern Kent and Thanet, but less so elsewhere and hardly at all in the pastoral Weald. Gavelkind probably undermined the stability needed for the system to work efficiently, and this had an effect on settlement patterns.

A consequence of adopting the open field system was that the peasantry's houses had to be grouped closely together in compact villages. They are widespread, and decidedly the rule where there were open fields devoted to growing grain, and can still be seen in St Peter's at Broadstairs, in St Nicholas at Wade and in Ringwould. All the villagers' homes were concentrated into a single nucleus, hemmed in by the common fields. The buildings were crowded together and built on small crofts, the individually owned parcels of land which, together with the streets and lanes, and perhaps a village green, the parish church, manor house and a few other buildings, made up the nucleus. In the later Middle Ages the system decayed, allowing houses to be built wherever land was enclosed to form individual farms. Where pastoral farming was dominant, notably the Weald, nucleated villages owed their existence to

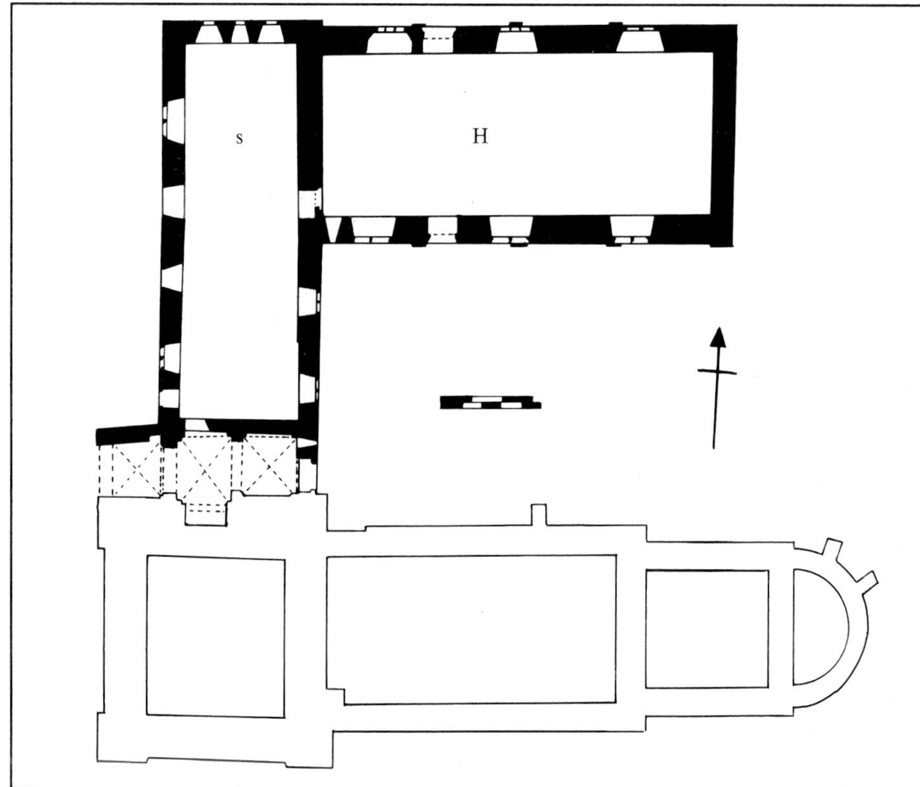

Figure 3. Minster-in-Thanet, Minster Grange. Plan of former grange of St Augustine's, showing outline of demolished church forming south range of courtyard, early 12th century west range, which comprised service accommodation with chambers for the brethren in its upper storey, and the rather later hall range across the north side of the courtyard; Abbot Hunden extensively refurbished the buildings about 1413, providing new fenestration and hall roof. A nearby aisled barn and brewery completed the establishment. The surviving buildings were incorporated into an abbey in the 1930s. (After Kipps 1929.)

other causes, for instance as centres of trade, and they were never the sole places of habitation within a parish. So, by the end of the Middle Ages, nearly all parishes contained a number of scattered farmsteads and hamlets built on the individual enclosures that so attracted Celia Fiennes, as well as a clearly defined centre.

The Middle Ages

The thirteenth century saw the climax of the Middle Ages. The beginnings of the expansion are dimly perceptible before the Conquest. The comparatively settled conditions of the late Saxon period reduced mortality and allowed the population to rise; more hands in the fields reaped greater harvests. The expansion of both agriculture and the population it fed fostered trade. This led to the circulation of money and the foundation of new towns in the seventh and eighth centuries. Canterbury, the new capital, flourished as the centre of Christianity in southern England, but also as a centre of trade. The new port of Sandwich, a possession of Christ Church Priory, succeeded the now silted-up harbour of Richborough and grew fat on the export of wool. This regeneration showed how far agriculture was able to produce marketable surpluses.

After the Conquest this continued at a greater pace, thanks to the Norman settlement (Postan 1944). Much rural wealth was the creation of religious institutions, newly revived after the Conquest or freshly created. Since their arrival in 597, the Benedictines had led the way. They received fresh impetus after the reforms of Archbishop Dunstan in the tenth century, and again after William's reorganisation following the Conquest. They founded numerous granges on their manors, which usually comprised a group of farm buildings, usually a large barn, and some accommodation, often scanty, occasionally grand. The manor of Minster-in-Thanet, which King Cnut gave to the Benedictines of St Augustine's at Canterbury early in the eleventh century, became the wealthiest of their possessions (Figure 3). During the twelfth century they built a grand hall there, forming the north range of a courtyard,

Colour Plate 11. The garden front of Clanricarde's Somerhill, Tonbridge, which was finished about 1613.

with chambers for the brethren in the west range, and, exceptionally, a chapel in the south; beyond to the north-east was a large barn, the agricultural centre of the enterprise (Kipps 1929). Many small manorial granges took the form of a barn overlooking a house, possibly with a chapel; otherwise the monks who ran them would have to use a parish church, which often lay nearby. These arrangements are particularly common in Kent, Mersham (Colour Plate 3) and Brook remaining classic examples to this day.

Kent did well from the events of 1066. It submitted to William and was never devastated by conquest. William gave Kent to his half-brother Odo of Bayeux, Earl of Kent, to rule, but Odo plotted against the king and was disgraced. In 1070 Kent received Lanfranc as Archbishop of Canterbury. He championed Kentish liberties against Odo and ensured the county's future wealth.

Lanfranc had every interest in a prosperous Kent. He became its greatest landlord. He divided the Christ Church estates, giving one part to the Priory and taking the other for himself, including the rich Aldington. This arrangement was in both their interests, and it well served the other religious houses, St Augustine's and St Radegund's, Faversham and Rochester; but a man of Odo's power would have been another matter. The large number of freemen in Kent, as well as the institutional landholders, had a common interest in not being subject to Norman overlords, and gavelkind ensured that however rich a man might become, this would not be a stepping stone leading a single heir to inordinate power.

This was of the utmost importance for the future. The manorial system never came

Colour Plate 12. Scotney Castle, Lamberhurst, showing the late 14th century tower of Roger Ashburnham's fortified house, and, beside it, part of the rebuilding works done for the Darrells in the 1630s.

to be exploited by over-powerful secular lords, as it was in other counties, and only a very few manors remained firmly in the hands of powerful families for any length of time. Among those who did leave a significant mark on Kent were the Crevecoeurs: Hugh de Crevecoeur and his descendants were responsible for the early works at Leeds Castle during the twelfth and thirteenth centuries, before it passed into royal hands, and Robert de Crevecoeur founded the Priory for Augustinian canons at Leeds in 1119. Another exception were the various owners of Ightham Mote, who built its picturesque manor house, at once a rarity in Kent and small and modest to match its poor heathy chartland site (Colour Plate 4). The de Penchesters' rather more fertile manor of Penshurst is another example, but it was more the recipient of wealth than the provider when Sir John de Pulteney purchased it and started to build his country seat here in 1341 (Colour Plate 28): he was a draper and merchant in the City of London, four times Lord Mayor, founder of a chantry, a college and a friary, and already the builder of a princely house in the City. By today's standards, he was a millionaire many times over, and it was this wealth rather than anything extracted from his manorial estate which gave Kent its finest surviving hall.

Although there were other dominating manorial landlords among Kent's laity, the main beneficiaries were individual yeomen, whether they were descended from the ancient ceorls or were tenants of ecclesiastical manors with favourable leases. The rich cornland of north and east Kent was soon densely settled, but in the Weald Kent had a reservoir of land, albeit poor, wooded and inaccessible, that freemen could colonise as the population expanded. Apart from the old Roman road from London that ran eastwards along the back of the downs to Dover, most roads were originally droveways that meandered southward to the summer pastures of the Weald. Here, early settlers established 'denns' and 'hursts', clearings where they tended swine and, later, cattle. These became permanent, not as nucleated villages, but as single farmsteads or widespread groups of them, set in the narrow, secret lanes which Celia Fiennes found in the Weald four hundred years later. The soil may have been poor, but there was enough for all who would colonise it and set up a cattle station free of manorial restriction. Just such people were the Hamdens. The family was recorded in Wye at the end of the thirteenth century, but one of them colonised a part of the Weald near Smarden soon afterwards (Colour Plate 5). This meant clearing the woodland to form a small farm complete with a number of little fields for grazing and for growing grain for bread and cattlefeed, and digging ponds, both for watering the cattle and for keeping fish. A farm like this exactly matched the labour which a family of five or six could provide. By 1361 they were rich enough for John Hamden to endow the parish of Smarden with the almost princely sum of six shillings per annum, and he or his father had probably already built the splendid hall-house which still bears their name (Rigold 1967).

There were markets and a demand for goods as close as Canterbury and as far as Calais. Enterprise was encouraged by the turnover of land that resulted from the continual splitting brought about by gavelkind, and by the ability to diversify through combining farming with industries like tanning and weaving. Seventy or eighty acres were quite enough to keep a household in some luxury, and pay for the construction of a house beyond the dreams of the peasantry anywhere else in England.

Towns

Trade required markets beyond those in the ancient towns of the early settlement. The Domesday Survey of 1086 recorded eight boroughs in Kent: the former Roman towns

Plate 1. Tenterden at the end of the 19th century, with the grand tower of St. Mildred's church overlooking the wide High Street.

of Canterbury, Dover, and Rochester, and Sandwich, Fordwich, Seasalter, Hythe and Romney. Few others joined them before the fourteenth century; Faversham was chartered in 1252, but Ashford, Maidstone and Tonbridge were of little consequence. Edward III gave Cranbrook (Colour Plate 6), Smarden and Tenterden charters in 1332, recognition of the growing importance of the Weald. They all retain wide streets where markets were held, but only Tenterden's seems credible today (Plate 1), and Smarden has declined into no more than a small village. Nevertheless, Canterbury remained the only town of national significance, and even it dropped from eleventh place (just after Oxford and way behind leaders such as York, Norwich and Lincoln) to sixteenth (after Hereford) between the later twelfth century and 1388, when the Lay Subsidy (a form of tax) required heads to be counted. Canterbury's population then began to rise again and had more than reversed its position on the eve of the sixteenth-century Reformation, overtaking York and Lincoln to become eighth in the league.

Trade also required capital. Completely outside the ordinary run of society were the Jews. They came to England with the Conqueror because he needed their business prowess. He and his successors protected them, but treated them as personal possessions by taxing them more heavily than ordinary people. Jews were still able to flourish in these peculiar circumstances. They were forbidden to enter trade or craft guilds, since these required their members to swear an oath to the Holy Trinity, but there was a chink in this wall of restrictions: because canon law forbade Christians to lend money at interest, Jews were able to exploit this by oiling trade with their capital and charging very high rates of interest. They provided the capital equally for building cathedrals and waging war, as well as for engaging in the more profitable processes of trade, and all this so successfully that they controlled a large proportion of the country's coinage. This made them at once popular because they were so useful and despicable because they were so rich. They protected themselves and their property from common envy by building strong houses of stone, as the house of Jacob the Jew in High Street, Canterbury, once testified. During Henry II's reign they reached a peak of wealth and influence, but after his death in 1189 a century of persecution

Colour Plate 13. Basing, Cowden, the timber-framed house built by the yeoman ironmaster Richard Knight and his wife Elizabeth in the 1590s, roofed with Wealden sandstone tiles and later hung with vermilion wall tiles.

Colour Plate 14. The former Chiddingstone Workhouse at Somerden Green, which bears the date 1601.

Colour Plate 15. The Pantiles, Tunbridge Wells, designed for company and diversion, where it became harder to lose a reputation once people started to prefer the seaside in the 19th century.

Colour Plate 16. The Paragon, Ramsgate, a terrace well suited to guests looking for propriety.

Plate 2. The flint, timber and stucco of High Street, Sandwich, a medley of five hundred years' building.

began which finally concluded with Edward I's expulsion of them in 1290. By then, foreign merchants and even Christian moneylenders had learnt from the Jews and largely taken away their business.

The principal Kentish boroughs were ports engaged in both fishing and trade. In the middle of the twelfth century a number of them challenged the power of the Church, and, by claiming ancient privileges granted by the Crown in return for naval service, they established the right to govern themselves as the Cinque Ports. Sandwich was by far the largest of these (Plate 2); the remaining four were Dover, which served passengers crossing the Channel, and Hythe, New Romney, and Hastings, the latter in East Sussex. Attached to each of these were a number of subsidiary ports or Limbs. All of them were able to act in their own interest with great freedom, particularly after Edward I gave them a charter in 1278. This enabled them to trade freely, a cause of great envy elsewhere which led to the occasional sea battle. The loss of Normandy to the French in 1204 gave the Cinque Ports added strategic importance, and the excuse to raid the French coast and engage in general piracy. Eventually, the tables were turned on them: the French grew stronger, sacking Sandwich in 1216 and attacking twice again before a party of four thousand Frenchmen landed behind the town, breached its defences, murdered the mayor and left half of it in flames. The other enemy was nature. Silt had blocked most of the harbours by the seventeenth century, and left Sandwich with the small jetty that remains today. Deal took its trade, leaving only Dover of the original five eventually to build on its past.

Agriculture, industry, trade and enough land to colonise gave the people of Kent exceptional wealth, and their customs spread it widely among them. Few peasants elsewhere in England had this freedom. The thirteenth century brought many of them to a desperate plight (Postan 1966, Titow 1969), particularly in the Midlands, and many people had to squeeze in where they could. The low wages, high grain prices and agricultural profits of the thirteenth century fulfilled the promise of the Norman Conquest, but outside Kent the rich often became very rich indeed and the poor became destitute or starved.

During the second decade of the fourteenth century, economic expansion faltered, and by the 1340s the old conditions of rising grain prices and cheap labour had been reversed. Here and there land was even dropping out of cultivation. A difficult harvest in 1314 caused by a cold, wet summer was followed in 1315 by incessant rain from the middle of spring to the end of the summer. Rot claimed the harvest and starvation scattered corpses all round Europe. This upset the balance of labour, production, prices and trade by entering full graveyards and empty granges into the account. In 1324-6, only a few years after Canterbury Cathedral Priory's wool production had reached a peak, floods struck its sheep pastures on the marshes of Thanet. Drowning and disease so ravaged the flocks that their numbers never recovered. Inundation became a continual threat to herds and flocks alike. Though fine summers in the 1320s refilled granges, the climate began a long decline with lowering temperatures and greater summer rainfall (Lucas 1930).

On top of this natural disruption came the first skirmishes of the Hundred Years War with France. Trade was upset, and poor European silver production aggravated the decline. By the 1340s grain prices had fallen to a half and even a third of their peak about 1320. The population stopped rising and probably started to fall as a consequence of famine and uncertain food supplies. This brought a rise in wages and reduced profits from grain. The Church, whose income had relied on this profit, tried to maintain it by increasing rents. Rather than work its estates itself, it put them out to farm. Before these changes resolved into a new pattern, there came the plague: it would liberate the peasant — in this world or another.

The later Middle Ages and prosperous yeomen

The Black Death was the great turning point of the Middle Ages. It first struck in 1348, leap-frogging from port to port until, a year later, it mouldered away with the corpses it had claimed. Some places survived unscathed. Deaths in Cowden do not seem to have risen above average during the plague years. Elsewhere half a parish might be smitten. Overall, England lost a third of her population, perhaps more. The survivors had to bear further visitations. The plague returned in 1361-2, in 1369 and 1374; between 1361 and 1485, thirty more years saw fresh outbreaks. Only by the end of the fifteenth century was the calamitous fall in the population arrested at perhaps half its level on the eve of the plague.

Arable farming was put at a disadvantage. The labour on which it depended became harder to find and increasingly expensive to keep. The demand for grain dropped with fewer mouths clamouring for bread, so prices fell into a downward spiral. This favoured pastoral farming, which needed less labour, and redressed the balance lost to grain in the thirteenth century. If there were any winners, they were the yeomen who had recently colonised the Weald.

The Black Death was an economic catastrophe for manorial landlords. The difficulties of the past three decades were aggravated beyond endurance. Their surviving peasants demanded wages rather than what they regarded as too little land and tenuous feudal rights in return for their services. Now they hoped to pay a just rent for as much land as they could afford. The difficulty for manorial lords was that rents fell below what they needed to pay the higher wages.

The Peasants' Revolt of 1381 was sparked off in Kent by the threat of a new poll tax, one that would be levied on rich and poor alike, but afflict them differently. Poverty did not drive Kent's tenants and land-holding yeomen into mute subservience. They knew freedom and affluence, so the strongest reasons for their uprising were economic grievances and a sense of social deprivation. The hedgerow preacher John Ball's appeal to the equality of those first farmers Adam and Eve was not lost on anyone: 'Who was then a gentleman?'; yet the gentlemen of England gained the upper hand and Ball, Wat Tyler and many of their followers paid with their lives.

Nevertheless, a period of unrivalled prosperity began for the yeomen of Kent. Industries such as weaving, iron smelting and tanning brought prosperity and people to the Weald and supplemented the profits of the already established patterns of agriculture. This was nearly as true of those yeomen elsewhere in Kent who were subject to its greatest lord, the Archbishop of Canterbury. Increasingly archbishops leased out their manors, usually for short but renewable periods, and rents, paid in money rather than in kind, were often low. Thanet became a land of yeoman farmers, and other parts of Kent's arable land joined the hursts and denns of the Weald in offering a largely unrestricted base for peasant agriculture (Baker 1964-5, du Boulay 1958, 1962, 1964-5).

One such peasant was Henry Bayly. His farmland at Boughbeech in the northern part of the parish of Chiddingstone was part of the manor of Sundridge, and owed allegiance to the Honour of Otford, a possession of the archbishop. Through the complications of Kent's manorial system, this was in the hands of the de Clintons in the fourteenth and fifteenth centuries, so it was to them that Bayly paid the almost nominal rent of ninepence and one hen per quarter, and a rental of about 1420 shows it reduced to threepence per quarter and 'hens 10 eggs' at Michaelmas. He did well enough from his arable and pasture (as well as low rent) to build the hall and service wing of a large farmhouse which for long bore his name (Slane 1984).

While successive archbishops withdrew from agriculture, they still enjoyed travelling from manor to manor along a triangular route from Canterbury to Bognor in West Sussex, up to Harrow in Middlesex, and then back to Canterbury, not to bring spiritual blessing, but to live off their produce and cast a secular eye over the fields, the farm buildings and the accounts. This led them to build more residences on their estates or to modernise old palaces; in the last decades of the Middle Ages they enjoyed an Indian summer, and built vast new palaces at Knole (Colour Plate 7) and Otford (du Boulay 1966, 238).

The yeomanry was best able to prosper when it could combine farming with industry (Thirsk 1961). Weaving was the outstanding route to success. Wool exports were little affected by the Black Death, since sheep farming made small demands on labour. Despite faltering in the plague years, trade was soon back to normal. Then a gradual decline in the export of raw wool set in, as increasing numbers of English weavers purchased it instead. The Hundred Years War quickened the process, mainly because it disrupted imports of cloth. The resulting demand for English cloth and the

Plate 3. Biddenden, photographed at the end of the 19th century, with its sweep of weatherboarded and tile-hung houses.

imposition of duties on imports transformed weaving. It quickly became a domestic craft and soon a rural industry. Weaving centres did not flourish so much on the cornland of northern Kent, where large herds of sheep commonly grazed on fallow fields, or on the sheep pastures of the coastal marshes, but in the cattle-rearing pasture land of the Weald, which had a plentiful water supply. Water was essential for cleansing the cloth and turning fulling mills, as it was for watering the cattle. The Weald was rich in deposits of fuller's earth too, so washing and finishing presented no problem. Moreover, the land was generally owned by family farmers and the self-employed who had the time after tending their herds to give to organising a home industry. The delivery of wool from the North and South Downs, from Romney Marsh and Thanet was hardly difficult, and all that remained was to set up looms. Soon they were in every Wealden farmhouse.

From Biddenden to Cowden, iron works dotted the south-west border parishes, and added their profit to the profits of weaving. This brought a new agricultural and mercantile class into being, one that distinguishes the late Middle Ages from the era before the Black Death. Its prosperity still indelibly marks Kent, mainly because it never lasted long enough to be transformed by the Industrial Revolution and therefore obliterate its past. Biddenden (Plate 3), Cranbrook, Headcorn and Smarden, and dozens of other small townships and villages are direct evidence of the labours of men and women in weaving and other diverse industries and the wealth they won from it, and so are the almost countless surviving houses which they built on the proceeds.

This combination of farming and industry together with the free ownership of enough land rather than extensive tracts of particularly fertile land made the yeomen here and, indeed, in most of Kent the richest in England. With about a million acres (405,000 hectares) in the county and a population of about 100,000 early in the sixteenth century, a household of seven or eight could, theoretically, own some 75 acres (30 hectares). The equitability of Kent's society meant that many families, probably a majority, were in fact in possession of this amount of land, and it was more than adequate to keep them in affluence. The Lay Subsidies of 1524-5 show their wealth as the highest and the most evenly distributed of any rural area in England (Sheail 1972).

Only Dungeness, Romney Marsh and the Wealden heights north-west of the future Tunbridge Wells fell below the highest concentrations of wealth, and even they were no lower than the average for the richer parts of England. The reason for a lower level of wealth in that part of the Weald was because an unusually large number of gentleman iron-masters owned the land there, rather than yeomen, and secular landed estates were prevalent. By the standards of Kent, there were fewer yeomen and more labourers, and ultimately lower overall levels of wealth. The Weald of Sussex was relatively poorer still, notwithstanding its flourishing iron-smelting industry, and for the same reason: the land here was owned by even fewer wealthy men and the iron was in the hands of yet smaller numbers of masters. These causes drove up the number of poor labourers.

Kent, meanwhile, was living up to the promise of a thousand years and would continue to do so. The old tag expresses it all.

A knight of Cales [Cadiz]
A gentleman of Wales,
A laird of the North Countree;
A yeoman of Kent
With his yearly rent
Will buy them out, all three.

Prosperity under the Tudors

When Henry VIII succeeded to the throne in 1509, the prosperity which had filled yeomen's purses since the later fourteenth century was visible all over Kent in their houses. The ending of the Wars of the Roses and the Tudor succession in 1485 brought yet more opportunities for making money: an astute eye for political chance, a crafty pen in practice at law, and a nose for trade could lead to fabulous riches. Life in Kent's few towns, now joined by Maidstone, which at last began to flourish, gained new attractions.

The Wars of the Roses had not greatly affected the county, but the plague was still a constant threat. Even so, with a little luck one might enjoy the fruits of wealth, and effort and innovation went unstinted into tending and plucking them. Crops from north Kent and cattle from the Weald, all red and 'counted the largest breed in England', as Defoe recalled them (Rogers 1971, 131), went up to London and added to Kent's substance. Hides were a secondary source of wealth on Wealden farms, since they had the necessary supplies of water and oak bark needed for tanning. Cattle were again in great demand in the weaving and the iron industry as beasts of burden, as well as sources of food and clothing.

An important cause of prosperity was the great Tudor price rise. Yeomen did well from this: their rents and other outgoings were often fixed; the prices they charged could rise. When they employed labourers they paid wages that lagged behind price rises and, similarly, when they invested in new buildings they paid lagging wages to the craftsmen who built them (Airs 1975, 182-91).

Apart from the profit to be made in agriculture through the workings of inflation, the rising demands of the sixteenth century encouraged farming in other ways. The number of small market towns serving all the needs of numerous localities declined as larger regional centres took their place. The change freed farmers from having to produce all the goods needed in their immediate vicinity, and instead they could produce what best suited their fields, with the aim of sending it to a large market where it might be distributed to any part of the land.

Canterbury grew accordingly. It remained the only inland market town in east Kent. Its population reached about 5,000 by 1600, although this was only a third of

Plate 4. The chamber block of Charing Palace, begun in the late 13th century in flint, and extended in brick by Archbishop Morton at the end of the 15th century, and altered yet again about 1586 after it had passed out of the archbishops' hands.

what a really large town like Norwich could show. Maidstone (Colour Plate 8) got its chance, and joined Canterbury as a town of more than local importance. Faversham (Colour Plate 9) and the fishing villages of the north coast specialised in oysters, a luxury which found a growing market in London. Similarly, Folkestone became the centre of a mackerel and herring fishery. Some of the small harbours along the Thames, for instance Woolwich and Deptford, took on new importance when Henry VIII developed them as naval ports. The traditional enemy was France, and Henry's Reformation of the Church had to be defended against the Pope's allies. Ultimately it was France again, particularly in the person of Napoleon, which caused Chatham and Sheerness to develop as naval garrisons.

The Dissolution of the Monasteries in 1536 and 1539 was a mixed blessing for Kent. The Church and the yeomanry had established a working relationship which suited both of them. Within the space of a few months the Crown grabbed a thousand years of accumulated wealth. These pickings it offered to those whose loyalty it prized. Yeomen might gain from increased access to former monastic land, but they could not stop rich outsiders moving in. St Augustine's manor at Pluckley passed to the St Legers and then to the Derings, who made themselves masters of the estate, took the profits and, in the 1630s, built a large house on the proceeds. The Crown failed to profit, because, needing political support, it used land as a bribe, and let middlemen fleece it. The old monastic estates soon melted away (Kerridge 1953-4). Archbishop Cranmer similarly depleted the archiepiscopal estates to ensure his survival. He gave his palace at Charing (Plate 4) to Henry VIII, who leased it out, and Charles I finally sold its decayed remains at far less than their relative value in 1540. The Palace of Knole fell into royal hands, and Elizabeth I eventually granted it to the Sackvilles, who transformed it. Despite the aggrandisement of new men, this plunder of the ecclesiastical estates left the yeomanry fairly unscathed, at least by national standards.

By contrast, Kent gained in great measure from the influx of a different class of new people, the Protestant refugees from the Netherlands. The first large immigration followed the Emperor Charles V's attempts to suppress the Reformation, but it was after Elizabeth's accession in 1558 that England became so attractive a haven. The

Plate 5. Filmer's Charlton Court at East Sutton, where work stopped in 1612 leaving just one range of a larger planned house.

Duke of Alva's Council of Blood and continual terror after 1567 sent Lowlanders to their boats and the easy coastal route to Sandwich, Deal and Dover. Thousands of these immigrants were skilled craftsmen, and they brought new life to Sandwich, where they were allocated St Peter's Church. Many moved on to Canterbury, Maidstone and, eventually, London. The refugees augmented the profits of Canterbury's trade by introducing silk-weaving to the town, and this luxury helped to continue its prosperity long after the Reformation had reduced the wealth of the Church.

Industry and new markets

Kent still remained largely rural, and it was in the countryside that its industries were to flourish for a good century and a half. The iron industry had been founded in the Weald before the Roman occupation. Its revival during the Middle Ages was briefly checked by the plague. Then, under the Tudors, it had its heyday, sharing the market with the Forest of Dean. Much of its production of cast iron went into the manufacture of cannon for Continental wars.

Because of the high capital expenditure needed for its furnaces and forges, these became the business of richer families. Before the Black Death, the Culpepers of Bedgebury had an interest in the South Frith iron works on the fringes of Kilndown and Hawkhurst, and some three centuries later were to build a large brick house at Bedgebury Park. The Streatfeilds of Chiddingstone were another ancient family involved in iron; they built High Street House (now called Chiddingstone Castle) from its profits. In much the same way the Bakers of Sissinghurst built their large new house (Colour Plate 10), although they had the benefit of earnings at court as well. Richard, 4th Earl of Clanricarde, invested heavily in the iron industry and leased out a furnace and forge together with seven cottages for the workmen at South Frith, all enabling him to build Somerhill (Colour Plate 11) at Tonbridge. The Darells of Lamberhurst altered Scotney Castle (Colour Plate 12), and the Filmers of East Sutton (Plate 5) started two houses, all on the proceeds of the iron industry (Melling 1961).

Smaller iron masters put their profits into the construction of simpler houses, such as the yeoman Richard Knight and his wife Elizabeth were building in Cowden in the 1590s (Colour Plate 13). Another iron master, Richard Tichborne, followed them in 1607 when he built Crippenden (Leveson-Gower 1895), but anonymity shrouds the names of many other builders of ordinary houses in the parishes of the high Weald with names associated with the iron industry such as Furnace Farm, Forge Farm and Gun Farm.

One of Kent's oldest industries was paper-making. Wood and rags were readily available raw materials, and water supplies for power and washing were plentiful. The paper industry particularly favoured the waters of the Darent and Medway and some of its tributaries. Maidstone did well from this. Hayle Mill, the lowest mill in the Loose valley, still operates on water power. Turkey Mill, part of which again survives, started life as a fulling mill in the valley of the River Len, but was converted to paper-making towards the end of the seventeenth century.

With all this rural wealth, there was one town, a city in reality, which increasingly dominated Kent — London. With its 250,000 inhabitants, it became the hub of Kent's universe. It was on the doorstep and easily reached by water. From the time of the Reformation onwards, it exported its fashions and imported Kent's produce in an ever increasing flood.

Fruit and hops

Fruit and garden produce originally went to the capital from abroad, notably from the Netherlands, but in the sixteenth century, especially in the last decade or two, immigrants set up orchards and market gardens to serve the metropolis, as a commentator noted in 1652.

> In Queen Elizabeth's time we had not only our Gardiners ware from Holland, but also Cherries from Flanders; Apples from France; Saffron, Licorish from Spain; Hopps from the Low-countreys... whereas now... the Licorish, Saffron, Cherries, Apples, Peares, Hopps, Cabages of England are the best in the world (Fisher 1935).

Kent did not supply quite all of these, but it took a large slice of what was to be a very profitable market. This needed capital for investment in trees and plants which took some years to bear fruit, and it needed expertise. The yeomen had capital in plenty, and immigrants supplied the rest. They set up market gardens on the low-lying hinterland of Sandwich, and, together with their compatriots who went into business as clothworkers in the town, gave it a modest prosperity after Deal took much of its trade as a port.

The cornland of northern Kent was just as well suited to growing fruit as grain. In 1533 Henry VIII's Fruiterer Richard Harrys is said to have cultivated the first English cherries here, and he built a house at Teynham which, appropriately, he called Newgardens. Fruit growing expanded so rapidly in the sixteenth century that already in 1570 the historian William Lambarde was calling the thirty parishes between Rainham and Blean Wood 'the Cherrie gardein, and Apple orcharde of Kent' (1970, 222). The deep ragstone soils around Maidstone and in the adjacent vales were good for apples, and they flourished too. Wealden farms made apples and pears into cider and perry, as there was no other way that all the fruit could be consumed, but this was never as widespread as in such counties as Herefordshire and Somerset, because fresh fruit could so easily be sent to London. By 1600, as Defoe recorded over a century later, yeomen were sending 'Kentish pippins, runnets, &c. which come up as the cherries do, whole hoy-loads at a time to the wharf, called the Three Cranes, in London; which is the greatest pippin market perhaps in the world' (Rogers 1971, 131).

Hops, like apples, were widely grown in the vales too, as Jingle was to say. (Apples and women had reached Kent long beforehand, though not together.) Hops became a profitable supplement to older forms of agriculture. Immigrant Flemish weavers had brought hops to England in the fourteenth century and grew them in a small way to flavour their beer. They were not cultivated widely, since they also needed a heavy capital investment, mainly because the hop bines were cultivated on an expensive tripod of wooden poles and took some years to mature. William Caxton, who knew Germany and the Low Countries from experience, summarised the position: 'Ale of England; Byre of Alemayne'; and that was that for the fifteenth century.

In the sixteenth century brewers at last realised that hops could replace wormwood as a preservative to stop the liquor from souring as ale was prone to do, and also that they allowed economies in malted barley. From the 1520s hop-growing became popular, eventually with new strains that could be grown on the North Downs as well. This led the sixteenth-century agricultural doggerelist Thomas Tusser to write:

> Turkeys, Heresy, Hops and Beer
> Came into England all in one year.
>
> *(Five Hundred Points of Good Husbandry)*

That was supposedly the year 1526, but it was wrong on all counts.

Plate 6. Hennikers, Sutton Valence, a late 14th century hall-house, its timber frame now concealed by tile-hanging, together with the 19th century oast built on to its left-hand end.

The first extensive cultivation was in the Wealden vales around Maidstone. A hop garden at Little Chart claims to be England's oldest. There was plenty of money here to invest and there was ready access by water to the market that grew up in Southwark, still recorded by the name Hopton Street. The 'Mother of Hop Grounds' soon had many daughters.

The self-appointed expert Reynolde Scot modelled his hop-growing at Smeeth on practice he had observed at Poperinge, the centre of the Flemish hop industry, and wrote about it in his book *A Perfite Platforme of a Hoppe Garden* of 1574, but he was probably recording what was already widespread in Kent.

Hops must be dried and then tightly packed to preserve them. This was usually done on an open floor: 'If you have no oste' wrote Scot, 'drye them in a loft as open to the ayre as may be...' This was not entirely satisfactory: 'few men have room enough in their houses to contain a great multitude of hops, so that the dust that will arise shall empair them...' It was better by far to dry hops over a kiln or oast. Some yeomen therefore added oasts to their farmhouses; an old house at Crundale had an oast built into one corner, and, about 1814, a hop kiln was recorded inside Starvenden Farm at Cranbrook, 'by which means in the season for drying hops, the house is very liable to take fire...' (Melling 1965, 41, 51). To this day, Hennikers at Sutton Valence has an oast which once contained a pair of kilns built against its south end (Plate 6).

Hop-drying remained in the hands of the farmers who grew them, until this century. Separate oasts came into ever greater use and by the early eighteenth century there was probably one on half the farms in the Kent hop country. This greatly benefited Wealden yeomen. During the eighteenth century, smelting slowly declined in the Weald in the face of a growing northern iron industry which had the advantage of coal; and this released charcoal for the oasts. The weaving industry declined even more rapidly through competition from the West Country and Yorkshire, leaving it a shadow of its former self after the Civil War. By the early eighteenth century, according to Defoe, there were hardly ten clothiers left among 1,500 freeholders in Cranbrook, Tenterden, Goudhurst and other Wealden townships, but by then hops had given a special character to the whole landscape and helped to maintain wealth instead. Here was an alternative investment that produced handsome profits.

Between 1540 and 1640 London grew into an enormous market for food. 'London will be all England' James I had despaired. It had come to dominate Kent's markets, even while Maidstone gained in importance and older market towns such as Ashford and Faversham prospered. In the sixty years before the Civil War London's consumption of cereals imported round the coast increased five and a half times. Nearly eighty per cent came from Kent in 1579-80, but, though Kent's exports to London increased over four times, its proportion of London's imports had dropped to sixty per cent on the eve of the war as other, more distant suppliers built up their trade. Hops and fruit had allowed Kent, nevertheless, to move from everyday necessities into luxuries, and these were less prone to fluctuations in price.

Recusancy, the Civil War and the Restoration

The Civil War was not the disaster for Kent that it was for some Midland counties, where five years of strife led to a real decline in prosperity. Even so, Kent was not untroubled. The Elizabethan Settlement had left the county with its share of recusants. The Ropers, for instance, were one ancient family to adhere to the old religion: a William Roper had married Thomas More's daughter, and his brother Christopher was the builder of Lynsted Lodge; later generations, not surprisingly, gave their support to the Stuarts. They were joined in this by another local family, the Hugessons. Mostly Kent took a moderate line, hoping for compromise between King and Parliament, but as attitudes hardened, the moderates tended to favour the King. Parliament quickly stifled this potential opposition by occupying the county. Neverthless, there was an ineffective revolt in 1643, and in 1648 the Ropers and Hugessons joined a second, but it was easily put down by General Fairfax at the so-called Battle of Maidstone. There was little loss of life, material damage was slight, and fines rather than executions ended the matter.

For Kent, the Restoration was simply that: wealth and possessions were quickly restored to the recusants, and the yeomen went from strength to strength. In 1697 Celia Fiennes described the farmers and remaining clothiers as 'a sort of yeomanly Gentry, about 2 or 3 or 400£ a year and eate and drink well and live comfortably and hospitably...', comments which Daniel Defoe could echo a generation later.

> These clothiers and farmers... for the plainness of their appearance, are called the gray coats of Kent; but are so considerable, that who ever they vote for is always sure to carry it, and therefore the gentlemen are very careful to preserve their interest among them (Morris 1984, 124 and 128; Rogers 1971, 132-3).

It is no wonder that Defoe admired the 'gray coats of Kent'. Their dress implied a certain puritanism; they were not gentry, nor did they ostentatiously flaunt their wealth, yet wealth was already clear enough in their houses. They built the substance of a golden world.

Depression and newcomers

By the start of the eighteenth century, unlike in earlier ages, agriculture had overcome the crisis of supply of the late sixteenth century caused by the rising population. Instead of too many people seeking too little food, production generally rose enough to satisfy everyone's needs and food was efficiently distributed to them. Moreover, there was a potential for great expansion. By 1620 the nation was seldom faced with the old horrors, but, instead, with a new one, strangely familiar today, a mountain

Plate 7. The Old Workhouse, Brenchley, no longer clearly demonstrating the comparative poverty which afflicted some parishes in the Weald.

of food. 'Plentie hath made us poore' wrote John Chamberlain: 'We are here in a straunge case to complaine of plentie, but so yt is that corne beareth so lowe a price that tenants and farmers are very backward to paye theyre rents; and in many places plead disabilitie' (Fisher 1935). There was a second crisis in the 1670s. Prices collapsed once more and stayed depressed until 1750.

One obvious way to maintain profits was through improvement and greater efficiency, but this inevitably led to higher production. The other way was to invest in new products. Kent did both, and maintained its wealth during a period of economic stagnation. None the less, the agriculture and industry which had sustained the yeomanry between the fourteenth and seventeenth centuries were not to be so sure a money-spinner in the depressed markets of the eighteenth century. They soldiered on, still the backbone of the county, but innovation increasingly needed large amounts of capital if it should succeed. This originated higher in society and stayed there.

The custom of gavelkind had declined so far that some of the county's old yeomanly families had seen one line's wealth accumulate with the generations, while the remainder of the family struggled to keep up their old station. This created a class of gentry out of old families such as the Culpepers and Honywoods, Knatchbulls, Tokes and Derings. They were joined by newcomers to the county who were more and more able to exploit Kent's resources, particularly now that the Church had been stripped of its power and the Crown had passed on so much of its lands to the rich and influential.

The changes also increased poverty, especially among labourers. Despite the generally equitable spread of wealth in Kent, poverty neither was nor could be totally absent. The depression of the eighteenth century aggravated it, and it bit harder still in the early nineteenth century. The Church had once cared for the poor, but the Dissolution had left individual parishes to cope however they would. Realising that poverty might be caused as much by failure to find work as by a lack of inclination to work, many parishes purchased raw materials such as hemp, flax and wool, and set their poor to work them. This was supposed to reduce the evils of begging and the cost to the parish of supporting its poor. Often this process was undertaken in a house especially purchased or built for the purpose. The workhouse system was enshrined in the Poor Law Act of 1601, and it remained in being until the Act of 1834 made a fresh attempt to ameliorate the heavy burden of poverty on parish funds.

The earliest evidence of the workhouse system is in Wealden parishes where iron allowed wealth to become concentrated in a few hands and where hired labourers were a necessity. The medieval Court House beside Hawkhurst church once served as the parish workhouse, and there is a seventeenth-century house at Brenchley which, again, served as a workhouse (Plate 7). Perhaps the oldest of Kent's workhouses, specially built as such, is at Chiddingstone. What the Streatfeilds did not own here was largely in the hands of the neighbouring Hever estate or the Sydneys of Penshurst, so the landless population was high and poverty common. A house at Somerden Green (Colour Plate 14), inscribed with the date 1601 in modern numerals, was built as the parish workhouse, although the inscription is more likely to refer to the year of the Elizabethan Poor Law than the year of building.

The need to increase efficiency or change to those products that were in the greatest demand was, even so, less onerous in Kent than in many other counties, and helped to keep poverty at bay. Fruit and hops were ideal products for these circumstances and remained so during the turbulent years of the Industrial Revolution. By the eighteenth century hops had spread to practically all Kent. Hop gardens had appeared around Canterbury within living memory, according to Defoe, and already covered nearly 6,000 acres (2,428 hectares). In the nineteenth century the amount of land given over to hop growing was to double and, despite several years of blighted crops, reached a maximum of 46,600 acres (18,860 hectares) in 1878. There were several good reasons for this. London provided a ready market and, being close, hops could be rushed there to catch the best prices. The East End had a large labour supply for the three weeks of picking, while cattle provided the plentiful manure that hungry hop bines needed. Indeed some farmers would countenance a loss on their herds because well-manured hops would tip the balance back into profit. The development of the oast-house gave the yeomen of Kent an efficient means of drying their hops, and the landscape its most picturesque symbol of continuing prosperity.

The increasing political power of the landowning class after the Restoration led to the oligarchical governments of the Hanoverians. They looked after their own interests, both in the counties where they had their country seats and in those towns where they developed highly profitable estates as England became increasingly urbanised. This affected Kent less than most other counties, so strong were its traditions. Even so, Folkestone as well as six other manors and twenty-four farms had belonged to the Desbouveries since 1697; this London family was not looking for a country retreat but a profitable investment in a small fishing town. With that security they could occupy themselves in politics, in the army and at law, and their income left the county. Penshurst had belonged to the Sydneys for a long time, and Cobham was Darnley's; they acted as landlords everywhere, offering employment, but taking the

Plate 8. A pair of estate cottages at Pluckley, with the round-headed 'lucky' windows which are the trade mark of houses on the Dering estate.

profits. The Bridges family turned Goodnestone into an estate village, and labourers' cottages here and in a few other villages, such as Leigh and Pluckley, exemplify the desire of wealthy landowners to improve the conditions of the poor in a visible way, rather than to remove the causes of poverty (Plate 8).

Just as landed power caused poverty by concentrating wealth in the hands of the landlord, it also encouraged class division. This owed much to France, where society was far more divided than in England. Now it provided a model for fashionable gentility. So, as the eighteenth century progressed, society became increasingly stratified, even in Kent. The old household structure in which the head lived together with his family of kin, servants and farmhands or apprentices as the head of a hierarchical though egalitarian unit faded away before a division that gave the head, his wife and children their separate lives and the servants theirs. This division was visible in all kinds of ways, even in the planning of the house. The levelling effects of gavelkind faded before primogeniture, at the same time as strict entail institutionalised aristocratic estates, causing them to be passed intact from heir to heir. The real losers were the smaller landholders and the cottagers, who could no longer scrape much of a living while market prices were depressed and rents stayed high. They gave up their land and became labourers or migrated to the towns.

The rich, meanwhile, put their money into industry, as well as land. The boom in publishing books and journals brought new demands for paper in the late seventeenth century, and this continued in the eighteenth century at an ever increasing pace. Kent played a large part in filling this demand, if only to satisfy the needs of London's chattering classes. Turkey Mill was rebuilt in 1739 by Richard Harris before it passed by marriage into the hands of the Whatman family. James Whatman senior and James his son made it the largest of all paper mills, its fine papers the most renowned. Size was not all; the small Hamptons Mill at West Peckham, which was built or rebuilt about 1740, gave the Dalison family the wealth, albeit through leasing it, with which they eventually rebuilt their house, also called Hamptons (Melling 1961, 114-17) (Plate 9).

Spas and the seaside

Meanwhile, as goods went up to London, so Londoners came down to Kent, for pleasure as well as work, and in ever greater numbers. The capital came to dominate Kent, not just as a market, but as a source of fashion and as a place from which the

Plate 9. Hampton's, West Peckham; the house has been extended by a further block on the right-hand side.

fashionable fled in search of recreation. Right at the start of the seventeenth century Kent satisfied this new demand in an unexpected way.

The courtier Dudley, 3rd Baron North, enjoyed a dissipated life. Maybe in 1606, just possibly in 1615 or 1616, he went for a rest cure to Eridge Castle, the seat of his friend Lord Abergavenny, set in the dense woodland of the East Sussex Weald. Riding home to London, he suddenly noticed 'the shining mineral scum' and 'ochreous' sediment of the chalybeate springs which soon gave Tunbridge Wells its fame. In 1630 Queen Henrietta Maria recuperated from giving birth to the future Charles II by taking the waters here for six weeks — and living in a tent. This feat of endurance attracted visitors, who soon flocked to the spa and, even more, to The Walk (later The Pantiles), laid out in 1638 as a promenade (Colour Plate 15). At first, visitors stayed elsewhere, and the first public buildings were built beside the spring only after the Restoration, to be followed by a chapel in 1676. Celia Fiennes drank the waters 'many years with great advantage' in the 1690s, and enjoyed The Walk: 'there are two large Coffee houses for Tea Chocolate etc., and two roomes for the Lottery and Hazard board'; there were other attractions too — bowls, dancing, music — and, of course, it was conveniently close to London. So Tunbridge Wells was made 'very comodious by the many good buildings all about it and 2 or 3 mile round, which are Lodgings for the Company that drinke the waters, and they have encreased their buildings so much that makes them very cheape' (Morris 1984, 125-7).

The waters attracted all sorts, as Defoe remarked:

> ... the coming to the Wells to drink the water is a mere matter of custom: some drink, more do not, and few drink physically. But company and diversion is in short the main business of the place; and those people who have nothing to do any where else, seem to be the only people who have any thing to do at Tunbridge.

Defoe found the Wells full of 'fops, fools, beaux, and the like', who could enjoy the place as long as they had money. Anticipating Jingle, he was bowled over by the women: 'The ladies that appear here, are indeed the glory of the place'; but to make acquaintances was another matter:

> ... if a gentleman desires to be more intimate, and enter into any acquaintance in particular, he must do it by proper application, not by ordinary meeting on the walks, for the ladies will ask no gentlemen there, to go off the walks, or invite any one to their lodgings, except it be a sort of ladies of whom I am not now speaking.

Plate 10. Marine Parade, Folkestone, begun in 1848 to catch the new railway trade.

In short, it could be a difficult place for a lady, who 'for want of good conduct may as soon shipwreck her character as in any part of England', such was the constant outpouring of tittle-tattle, along with the tea and coffee, emanating from The Walk (Rogers 1971, 141-3). A century later, it was no better. In 1823 William Cobbett called Tunbridge Wells a little toadstool 'created entirely by the gamble' (1912, 222); but that was on the eve of John Ward's Calverley Park estate. From then on, gentility ruled, and indeed a certain crustiness set in, giving Tunbridge Wells a notoriety of a different kind.

A very different form of recreation began in the old established fishing port of Margate. Experts had advocated sea-bathing in the later seventeenth century, but this became popular only with Dr Richard Russell's declaration in 1754 that drinking large quantities of sea water and bathing before dawn, preferably in winter, were beneficial to health. Modesty, as well as health, was an issue. Happily, the previous year, a local Quaker called Benjamin Beale had invented the bathing machine. It took the form of an enclosed wagon, open at one end for discreet embarkation from the sandy beach; it was pulled into the sea by horse and turned round so that the bather could make an equally discreet descent into the waves to bathe in a small pool sheltered from prying eyes beneath a large umbrella. In this way the modestly inclined could take to the waters with the strictest delicacy for a much more bracing cure than any on offer at Tunbridge Wells.

The great advantage of Margate was its sandy beach, and this was equally true of the other Thanet resorts, Broadstairs and Ramsgate; moreover, Thanet has the sunniest and driest climate in all Kent, so it was the best place to enjoy the seaside. Margate was well served by the old Thames sailing hoys, which brought visitors from London. They, like the visitors to Tunbridge Wells, were often of the improper sort, looking for pleasure rather than a cure, and that is how Margate progressed. Ramsgate (Colour Plate 16), by distinction, enjoyed royal patronage, and, while Jane Austen viewed it askance, it attracted the young Princess Victoria as well as the nobility. The future queen went to Broadstairs too (Colour Plate 17), although it was Charles Dickens who gave this resort lasting fame.

When the French Wars curtailed the Grand Tour of Europe, Kent's coastal resorts came into their own. Dover, Folkestone, Sandgate and Hythe joined their number, the visitors being augmented by the military garrisons stationed to counter the threat of invasion. The Desbouveries, progressively Viscounts Folkestone and Earls of Radnor, developed Folkestone to meet the new demands. Terrace after terrace of

Plate 11. Central Parade, Herne Bay, built in the 1830s with a series of stuccoed bays offering a northerly prospect of the sea.

houses went up, principally after the arrival of the South Eastern Railway in 1843 (Plate 10).

A few other coastal towns owed their existence to the fashion for bathing and seaside holidays, for instance Herne Bay, which was laid out with terraces and villas in the 1830s (Plate 11), but Kent's seaside resorts were eventually overtaken by those on the South Coast, which grew steadily after the Prince Regent popularised Brighton in the 1780s. The topography of many of Kent's resorts did not allow long marine parades. Instead, estates of holiday houses and bungalows were developed at Herne Bay, St Margaret's Bay and Sandwich Bay (Plate 12). After the First World War, the resorts experienced their first difficulties with the onset of the great depression. Even so, the construction of small houses continued. There was a revival of seaside holidays after the Second World War with renewed prosperity, but in the 1960s inflation and cheap foreign travel reduced their attraction once more and Thanet's resorts started to look extremely forlorn. As improved health gave people longer lives, they gained a new lease of life, becoming places of retirement.

The Industrial Revolution

After 1750 the population began to increase dramatically. The old England, which for some two thousand years had had a population that could be measured in a few million — probably never more than five or six — was rapidly left behind. By 1801 there were already over nine million people living in England and Wales, and this number was to grow fivefold.

Generally, the growth was linked to changes brought about by the Industrial Revolution. Kent, which had had a comparatively high rural population commensurate with its wealth, was still largely an agricultural county, and increased its numbers fairly slowly. Nevertheless, the next century and a half saw its population exceed 1½ million before Greater London took away its north-western corner. This immense change was most strongly felt in Kent's towns, but the rural labouring population rose as well. Most families of labourers suffered periods of intense poverty which touched the large numbers of remaining yeoman far more lightly. Most yeomen remained in possession of their land and could continue to farm it.

Nevertheless, there were changes in agriculture as well as industry. Efficiency increased in the century after 1750 so much that output per acre rose by nearly fifty per cent, and those who were responsible for this were able to profit from the new

Plate 12. The wide open garden front of White Hall at Sandwich Bay, set between two even more wide open golf courses just behind the sea wall.

demand. Employment in agriculture continued to rise until well into the nineteenth century, although the proportion of the population employed in this way started a long decline.

Essential to this increased production were the first major improvements to Kent's roads. The eighteenth-century Turnpike Acts turned several winding lanes into a number of modern roads, including the A28 from Margate to Hastings via Canterbury, Ashford and Tenterden, as well as improving the old Roman Watling Street between London, Canterbury and Dover. Small toll houses were built along the new turnpikes, and some of these can still be found at Biddenden, Bridge (Colour Plate 18), Charing, Cranbrook, Sheldwich and Whitstable. Another improvement was the toll bridge at Sandwich; built in 1773, and replaced by a swing bridge in 1892, it is served by a modern toll house built into the sixteenth-century Barbican, and this gives the town its most famous view.

As the eighteenth century gave way to the nineteenth, the increasing pace of change forced a new, hard world out of the old. The idyll of rustic life was only for those who could pay for it. These people were, as always, the landowners. Labourers had to learn new ways, particularly mobility. The old Elizabethan Poor Law, which attempted to keep paupers dependent on the parish of their birth, was abandoned, allowing labourers to range the country in search of the best wages, while seasonal migrations served the needs of hopping and fruit-picking, and, of course, the harvest. Londoners might come to Kent for pleasure, but others came for work.

Meanwhile, a number of yeomen succumbed to the harshness of the age, particularly in parishes like Pluckley where large landowners demanded rent, regardless of the paucity of agricultural profits. The yeomen had no recourse but to sell up and join the labouring classes. Many a proud and ancient farmhouse was subdivided and tenanted by the landless. Where it had accommodated a yeoman and his family of half a dozen in six rooms, now it might accommodate three or four larger families of labourers with all the prettiness of bucolic charm — and all the squalor of decay. That was the fate of Dowle Cottage at Pluckley (Colour Plate 19). It had been built early in the fifteenth century by a free yeoman, and now became no more than one of several houses on the Dering estate which were split up and filled with subservient labourers, three families of them in this case. A few labourers built small cottages on waste land beside the road, such as one lying beside the old Roman road at Lydden (Plate 13). For homeless labourers who failed to find a master, there was the road or the workhouse and its overseer:

And every village owns its tyrants now,
And parish-slaves must live as parish-kings allow.
(John Clare, *The Village Minstrel,* 1819-21)

Plate 13. Wayside cottages built on waste land hard by the old Roman Canterbury-Dover road at Lydden.

Plate 14. One of the converted Martello Towers at Hythe.

New workhouses went up in Kent right through the eighteenth century. Cudham workhouse was built in 1731 on similar lines to Chiddingstone workhouse; Bexley workhouse followed in 1789.

Between 1793 and 1815, the French Wars at last brought back good profits to Kent's farms. They also brought a new sort of activity all along the coast. This was the construction of 'barracks, magazines, martello-towers, catamarans, and all the excuses for lavish expenditure, which the war for the Bourbons gave rise to', as the radical William Cobbett recorded. 'Chatham has had some monstrous *wens* stuck on it...', and it became Kent's prime naval port until its recent closure. 'Hythe is half *barracks;* the hills are covered with barracks; and barracks most expensive, most squandering...' *(Rural Rides,* 1912, 41-2, 237). None, happily, was put to the test of invasion. Many of the Martello towers survive along Kent's south coast, thanks to their solid construction, which was designed to resist cannon fire. They are solitary monuments, close to the beach, but a few at Hythe have been converted for domestic use (Plate 14).

The end of the French Wars at Waterloo in 1815 removed this expenditure at a stroke, and brought renewed industrial and agricultural depression, with all the suffering of a fresh bout of poverty to Kent's albeit small numbers of tenant farmers and landless labourers. In 1821 Cobbett could justifiably single out Sir Edward Knatchbull of Mersham-le-Hatch as one of the causes. Here was a landowner who could see:

> no more of these sufferings than if he were a baby. How should he? Not very bright by nature; never listening but to one side of the question; being a man who wants high rents to be paid to him; not gifted with much light, and that little having to strive against prejudice, false shame, and self interest, what wonder is there that he should not see things in their true light? *(Rural Rides,* 1912, 46)

As MP for Kent, he opposed reform of the Corn Laws, since he profited from high grain prices while his labourers went hungry.

Again, low wages and high rents became the lot of the landless. Unemployment stalked the fields, and meant the workhouse. Here the old haphazard benevolence gave way to a new harshness as overseers of the poor tried to stem the drain on their

Colour Plate 17. Broadstairs on a day when the sea was too rough for discreet bathing, and even entry to the 16th century harbour needed careful seamanship.

Colour Plate 18. The former tollhouse at Bridge, now by-passed by yet more road improvements.

Colour Plate 19. Dowle Cottage, Pluckley, a 15th century yeoman's hall-house with typical Kentish framing, which fell on hard times and housed three families of labourers who worked on the Dering estate until the house was sold and restored after the Second World War.

Colour Plate 20. Great Maythem, Rolvenden, the small house of 1721 which Lutyens rebuilt and greatly enlarged for H.J. Tennant in 1907-09.

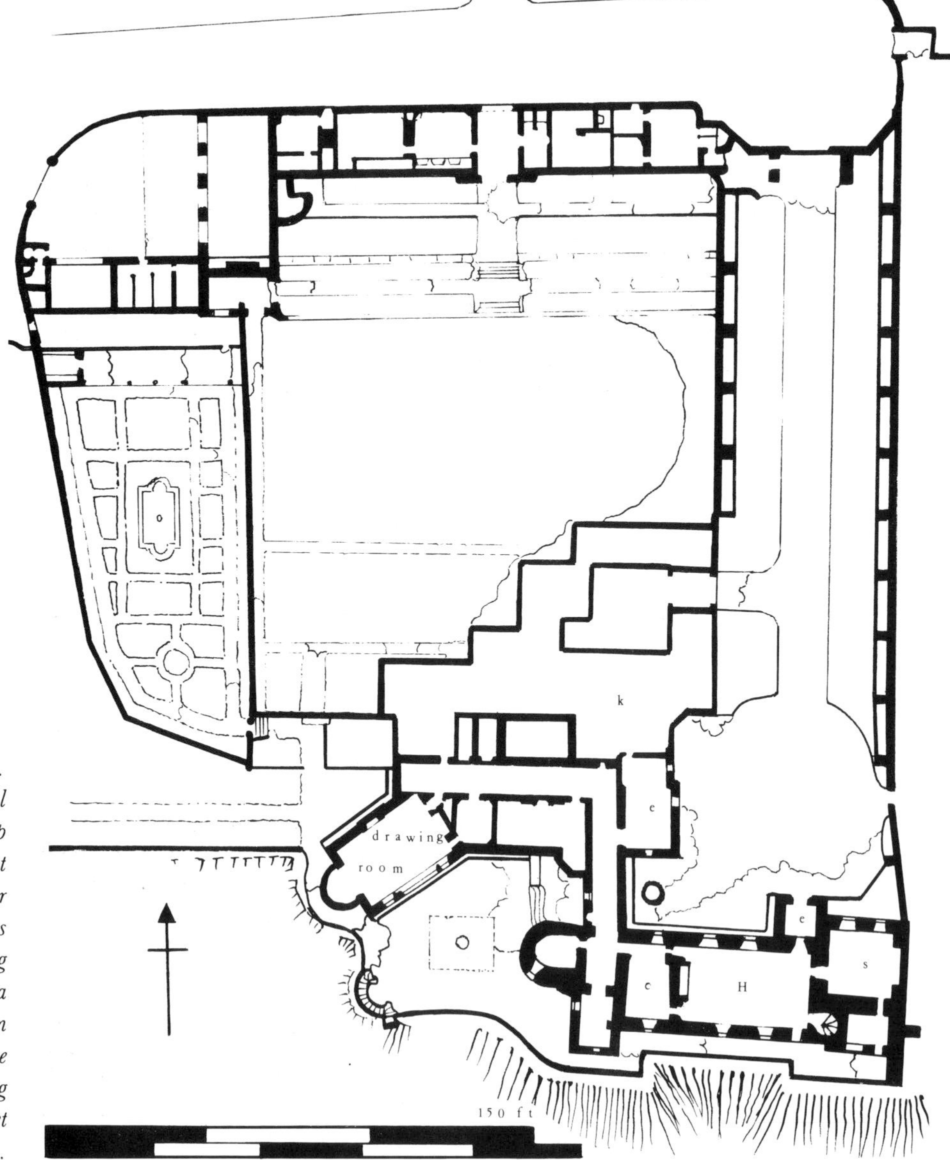

Figure 4. Lympne Castle. Plan, showing the medieval castle built on the hilltop overlooking Romney Marsh at the south of the site, with Sir Robert Lorimer's additions for F.J. Tennant extending northwards to include a drawing room, a large kitchen complex and an extensive service and garage range along the northern boundary, all set in terraced gardens.

resources. Groups of parishes were enabled to form unions for the purpose of administering the Poor Law more effectively and economically. Following the Poor Law Amendment Act of 1834 groups of ten Kent parishes formed unions. They disposed of their old parish workhouses, which were then used as ordinary houses, and constructed new prison-like buildings from the proceeds, which served the poor of the whole union. Their appearance was designed to deter, since poverty was believed to be a consequence of individual failing, not economic circumstance. Charity has seldom looked so grim.

Despite depression, Kent kept a valuable share of the London market. The farms that suffered least were committed to cattle and those that did best of all had their capital in other things as well. Here, domestic industry was less and less a help, as process after process fell before the low costs of mass production in factories; but fruit and hops, though expensive for newcomers because they needed a heavy capital investment to set them up, took the edge off the depression. Kent was able to keep itself on what by now was a traditional combination of crops and stock. These fulfilled the needs of an insatiable market, and so the county retained its great numbers of independent small yeoman farmers for whom affluence was second nature.

By 1830 the overproduction of wheat stemming from the Napoleonic Wars was at last absorbed by the rising population. The agricultural economy picked up over the next decade, and by 1850 it was so thoroughly mended, despite the repeal of the Corn Laws in 1846, that the years up to 1870 became a golden age of high farming. This put a seal of success on the middle of Queen Victoria's reign in all kinds of ways (Thompson 1968).

Because it was harder to import cattle than grain, the increasing demand for meat caused cattle prices to rise relatively and so cattle farmers' profits. Again, this helped Kent: real wages consequently rose, and a high proportion of Kent's yeoman farms survived. Few of them employed outside labour, and most still occupied less than 100 acres (40 hectares). Small herds of cattle provided not so much profits on their own account as through the manure that brought hops and cherries to a market that could not have enough of them.

The depression that hit farming after the fine harvest of 1872 is a tale of woe too close to modern experience for comfort. At last grain could be cheaply imported from the United States and this opened the floodgates. Once again, Kent withstood these changing fortunes better than most other counties could do. The Cockney labourer, brought up on bread and cheese and a pint of beer, kept up demand and extended his tastes. While barley for beer was substituted for wheat for bread in Kent's fields, the London market for fresh fruit and vegetables was augmented by a new demand from canneries and jam factories. Even after the Great War, renewed agricultural depression did not obliterate fruit and hop production as it did wheat.

Transport, war and the twentieth century

Although the Industrial Revolution largely passed Kent by, it did not leave Kent utterly untouched. The profits of industry made elsewhere in England were spent in the county when the lawyer and MP Gathorne Hardy inherited his father's wealth made from a Staffordshire ironworks and, in 1859-62, built Hemsted House at Benenden (now Benenden School). In the first decade of the twentieth century the two sons of the chemical manufacturer Sir Charles Tennant, F. J. Tennant and H. J. Tennant, rebuilt, respectively, Lympne Castle (Figure 4) and Great Maythem at Rolvenden (Colour Plate 20), again with inherited money which in this case originated in Glasgow.

Local profits from industry also encouraged building, though on a less splendid scale. Large breweries run on the lines of factories sustained workers in Maidstone and Faversham by satisfying their pockets as well as their thirsts, and most towns in Kent followed suit. Streets of small terraced houses appeared all round their edges. Some old forms of manufacturing continued and needed new factories. Paper-making, unlike weaving and iron-smelting, survived and was progressively industrialised. Large mills sprang up on the Medway. To serve their workers, speculative housing turned villages like Aylesford, Ditton, East Malling and Snodland into small towns or extended them far beyond their original bounds. When the Bowater Paper Mill was built on the empty marshes overlooking the Swale, a model village was built at Kemsley in 1925-6 for its labour force (Plate 15).

It was in transportation that the Revolution played its greatest role in Kent. Most of the old ports were improved. Broadstairs had served ocean-going ships since the

Colour Plate 21. Preston Hall, Aylesford, designed by John Thomas and built for Edward Ladd Betts in 1850, now living on in leaner times as a hospital.

sixteenth century, but here the harbour remained much as it had been (Colour Plate 17). At Ramsgate, a diving bell was employed in 1750 to construct new piers to shelter the harbour. These enclosed too little water, and low tide delayed anchorage for several hours. Nevertheless, it was an advance, and the harbour is still popular. In 1809, soon after the French invasion scare, Thomas Telford constructed a new harbour at Folkestone, and it served the British Expeditionary Force in the First World War.

This and the port at Dover were the prizes which encouraged the largest new industry in Kent, the railway. It changed the county in a way which had not previously been achieved since the Roman era, and it is changing Kent still. The Canterbury and Whitstable Railway of 1830 was a false start, but from 1834 the line from London progressively stretched eastwards by way of Ashford, reaching Folkestone in 1843 and Dover early in the next year. The South Eastern Railway, as it called itself after 1836, had the basis of its network complete by 1851, the year in which it established its principal engineering works in the centre of its system at Ashford. Here it built a new town for its engineers and other staff. The company had a competitor in the London Chatham and Dover Railway; this company took a long time pressing along a more northerly route to the Channel ports, and only reached Dover in 1860. Thereafter, much squabbling between the two companies was finally resolved by their merger in 1899, but, eventually, there was a great advantage in the duplication of lines when the Luftwaffe bombed them during the Second World War.

Colour Plate 22. Tonbridge Castle. Beyond the massive gatehouse of about 1300 is the house built into the castle walls which became Samuel Beazley's country residence.

Plate 15. Staggered terraces of neo-Georgian houses at Kemsley, built in 1925-6 for the workers at the nearby paper mill.

Plate 16. A curving street of semi-detached houses built for the miners of Chislet Colliery at Hersden.

Kent reaped its rewards long before that in speedy transport for its perishable fruit and other goods, as well as in a new source of employment, on a large scale at Ashford, and on a small scale everywhere the railways reached. Railway money went into grand houses as well. The railway contractor E. L. Betts built Preston Hall at Aylesford in 1850 (Colour Plate 21), and Samuel Beazley, architect to the South Eastern Railway, set up house at Tonbridge Castle (Colour Plate 22). The railway was heavily involved with cross-channel traffic and owned several packet-boats. Business was so good that in 1909 a fine new harbour was constructed at Dover; with extension, it has become the busiest international port in the country, and regained a pre-eminence which it last knew in Roman times.

The railway brought another new industry into existence. The Channel Tunnel had been a dream for many years before the South Eastern Railway undertook test borings near Shakespeare's Cliff. The project was abortive, but in 1882 the borings led to the discovery of the Kent coalfield. The seams lay at great depth and were difficult to reach; only one train-load of coal was ever dispatched from here. That was as late as 1912, six years after Tilmanstone Colliery had opened; by the outbreak of the Great War, it had been joined by successful pits at Snowdon, Betteshanger and Chislet. The railway took the steaming coal and more went to the paper mills of the Medway valley and the new cement works on the Thames estuary; the larger coal supplied the homes of east Kent. Several estates of houses were built for the miners, particularly at Aylesham, Elvington and Hersden (Plate 16), but the immigrant miners preferred to live in the Thanet towns, and in Dover, Deal and Canterbury.

In the 1960s the Kent coalfield fell on hard times, and is now little more than a scar on the land. This and the failure of the Thanet resorts to attract holidaymakers has reduced the prosperity of Kent north-east of the Canterbury-Dover road. Too distant from London and rather off the beaten track, its farming subdued by hasty urbanisation, it lacks the appearance of well-being so evident elsewhere in the county, despite the arrival of light industry.

Traditional qualities have continued to serve Kent better. Its particular combination of natural beauty and local affluence made it especially popular among cosmopolitans looking for a convenient retreat from London. When the law of strict entail was abandoned in the 1880s, so threatening the way old estates could be handed down, father to son, newcomers arrived, attracted by Kent's beauty and heritage.

Plate 17. The terrace of Sir Philip Sassoon's Port Lympne, overlooking Romney Marsh and the distant English Channel.

Plate 18. Chartwell, seen from near the studio and the walled garden where Churchill practised his skills as a bricklayer as well as a landscape painter.

Ancient chivalry and particularly its associations with Anne Boleyn made Hever Castle irresistible to the American landowner and diplomat William Waldorf Astor (Colour Plate 23). The splendid panorama of sea and marsh added an extra quality to F.J. Tennant's enjoyment of Lympne Castle. It similarly gave Sir Philip Sassoon the best of sites for Port Lympne (Plate 17). H.G. Wells' Spade House at Sandgate (Colour Plate 24) has the further advantage of distant views of the French coastline, and the sweeping inland panorama of the Weald attracted Winston Churchill to Chartwell on the scarp above Westerham (Plate 18). In a different vein, the architect Sir Herbert Baker went to live at Owletts, a farmhouse which the yeoman Bonham Hayes had built at Cobham in 1683-4; Baker made one or two small additions to the house, and, more importantly, restored a number of medieval yeomen's houses nearby. This has now reached the proportions of big business: with legislation to promote the conservation of historic buildings, Kent's past has increasingly captured people's imagination, leaving some farmhouses almost more 'medieval' as a result of restoration than they had been in the Middle Ages.

Kent today

All these new inhabitants found privacy. Nevertheless, the railway brought London closer to Kent as its suburbs leapfrogged down the railway lines. In 1889 the County of London Act removed what had once been the Thames-side fishing villages of Deptford, Greenwich and Woolwich from the county of Kent, and also their hinterland as far south as Lewisham and Eltham. Even then, the metropolis was extending its tentacles further outwards along new railway lines and continued to do this along the by-pass roads which came with motorised traffic after the Great War. The old village of Bexley was transformed into a suburb of semi-detached houses (Quiney 1986), and, with a little more discretion, so was Bromley. Only the establishment of the Green Belt in 1938 impeded this headlong rush into the Kent countryside.

Colour Plate 23. Hever Castle. Originally built by Sir John de Cobham in the 1380s, it was restored by William Waldorf Astor in 1903-07.

Eventually, new boundaries were established in 1965, giving Bexley and Bromley to Greater London. Meanwhile, similar expansion affected all of Kent's towns, and several villages as well, until the requirements of Town and Country Planning applied the brakes. By then, Kent was experiencing national changes, and the houses which resulted were indistinguishable from those built anywhere else.

One effect of the Great War and the agricultural depression which followed it was to reduce the cost of land just when reformers wanted improved housing for the poor. This encouraged the construction of the housing estates serving the new industries, just as it also encouraged speculators, who offered small houses for sale at low prices with readily available mortgages to attract newly-weds. These houses were irresistible to many couples earning as little as £4 a week. Another group to cash in on this demand were farmers who, rather than selling whole fields to speculators, sold small plots of land adjacent to their lanes to veterans of the Great War. These men and many others with the spirit of adventure established smallholdings in the hope of a better life than they could have in the London slums. They built large numbers of little roadside houses on the fringes of villages such as Biddenden (Plate 19), Charing and Cranbrook. With rather more order, the British Legion built an entire settlement of bungalows for veterans at Aylesford (Plate 20).

War was not forgotten. The newly formed Royal Air Force developed aerodromes in Kent for the protection of London in the event of another conflict. Ordered suburban streets of simple but neat Georgian houses provided married quarters at Biggin Hill, Manston, Hawkinge, West Malling, Eastchurch and Lympne, long

Colour Plate 24. Spade House, Sandgate, H.G. Wells' house, which Voysey designed for him as a retreat in the 1890s and extended in 1903 at the nearer end, now an old people's nursing home.

Plate 19. One of the homes for heroes built at Biddenden beside the Benenden Road on land once belonging to Little Randolph's Farm.

Plate 20. Some of the bungalows of the Preston Hall Colony built at Aylesford in 1923.

before their pilots achieved renown in the Battle of Britain (Plate 21).

Many of these RAF stations have now closed, and their married quarters have been sold as the demand for houses continues to rise. Despite planning laws, many new houses have been built in a haphazard way on all kinds of available plots, and the estates of houses developed by speculative builders on the edges of towns and villages are not necessarily more cohesive visually. There are some notable exceptions. When the London County Council built its Stangrove Park estate at Edenbridge about 1960 to rehouse some of the capital's overspill population, the layout of the weatherboarded and tilehung terraces set among tree-lined open spaces gave it a recognisably traditional atmosphere (Plate 22). Possibly it was a certain self-consciousness as well as the speed of construction and settlement which denied it the life of a real village. A determined attempt later in the 1960s to instil quality in terms of both amenity and appearance with the building of a garden suburb at New Ash Green should have been entirely successful, but it ran into financial difficulties. Even in its modified form, New Ash Green is still the most successful speculative housing in Kent (Plate 23).

The main difficulty is that communities cannot be easily created simply by building houses. Kent's great asset was and still is its vast number of individual houses, built within the seclusion of their own small enclosures. They sheltered a community based on common social values and the affluence to support them, not on the ideals of planners, so it is no wonder that they remain popular.

Because Kent's farming was typically small in scale and seldom employed large numbers of labourers, it has suffered less from the agricultural mechanisation of post-war years. Even so, many farms have been joined together into large units, often when institutional landowners purchased them. This has caused many yeoman farmhouses to be divorced from their land and sold to newcomers with money made in London and motor cars allowing them to enjoy rural homes.

The yeomen of Kent have their descendants, but the houses which served their local affluence are now common property. Their social values have changed beyond recognition. With well over a million people living in Kent, it could hardly be otherwise. Kent is brimming with all kinds of people rich enough to afford to live there.

With these people have come new businesses and industries. The north-east apart, Kent is becoming the victim of its own success. The attractions of south-east England — its climate, its resources, its proximity to London's wealth and even more so to the Continent's — are bringing further changes which are compounded by the construction of the Channel Tunnel. This has demanded ever more houses and all the services required by modern life to go with them from sewers to shops. It would be

Plate 21. RAF Quarters at West Malling, still bearing traces of green and brown camouflage paint.

Plate 22. The weatherboarded terraces of cottages on the London County Council's Stangrove Park estate at Edenbridge.

Plate 23. Scandinavian modernism, replete with the landscaping typical of all Span estates, set in the woodland of Kent's downland at New Ash Green.

the hardest of ironies if this wealth ultimately heaped disaster on the first corner of England to discover how to live with wealth on equitable terms.

Equitability, indeed, must take on a new meaning if the balance of people and natural resources is to be maintained in Kent. Most newcomers, unaware of Kent's distinguished past, are equally unaware of this need. Those who enjoy Kent for what it was as well as what it is are united by their admiration for its unique combination of seclusion and convenience, still preserved in a secret landscape of the utmost beauty, just as Celia Fiennes found it. How these qualities can be successfully defended against the ravages of the modern world is not clear, but, without them, there would be no Kent for future generations to enjoy.

Chapter 2

MATERIALS, CONSTRUCTION AND DESIGN

A quick journey across Kent shows that this is a county of timber and brick, not stone (Clifton-Taylor 1972, 32 *et passim;* 1983). Most roofs are covered by clay tiles, not thatch or stone, and, when their timbers are not exposed, the walls are often hung with tiles as well. Accordingly, Kent's houses glow red, orange and vermilion in a green landscape. Maybe they do not have the instant appeal of the honey-hued walls and stone-flagged roofs of Cotswold villages or the endearingly overhanging thatch of the West Country, but the quality of their brickwork is unsurpassed. The timber-framing is hardly less excellent, despite being standardised and fairly plain, even dour when compared with the showy decoration of the western Midlands.

Stone

Like all the counties in south-east England and East Anglia, Kent is not well endowed with building stone. Yet there could be less of it, and it could be worse in quality. In flint Kent has one of the hardest and least destructible of all stones, and this appears in many of its oldest houses — those that date from the twelfth and thirteenth centuries. Kent has a form of limestone called Kentish Rag which is found in such abundance in the stratum of Lower Greensand that it was already being widely exported in Roman times, even though it is neither easy to work nor durable. Kent also has one truly excellent stone, a fine-grained Wealden sandstone, which gives a special quality to the nineteenth-century villas of Calverley Park at Tunbridge Wells.

Geologically, Kent lies on three main strata of Cretaceous rock with intervening layers of gault and clay (Figure 5). These tilt upwards in a southerly direction to be exposed by erosion, thus forming the hills of the Weald, the chartland and the North Downs. The rest of the land is covered with tertiary deposits and extensive tracts of alluvium. Together these form the backbone of Kent's landscape; they produce its building stones, and the soils they carry provide yet more building materials.

The oldest and lowest of these Cretaceous strata, the Hastings beds, come to the surface along the heights of the Weald. Great rocks of this brownish or yellowish-grey sandstone can be seen at Tunbridge Wells, and several Wealden lanes have cut their way through this stone to form deep banks, often held together by the gnarled roots of ancient trees. Wealden sandstone comes from the quarry, sometimes as very large blocks, usually fine-grained and streaked with yellow and deep brown; its durability varies too, but it can last well and be finely carved. Small quarries gave Scotney Castle its mellow ashlar in the fourteenth century (Colour Plate 12), and its Victorian successor its crisply detailed walls in 1840. Robert Adam's Brasted Place is again built from Hastings beds sandstone (Colour Plate 87); it had to be transported some distance, but no other stone in Kent could be worked into this splendid neo-classical display. A special quarry at Tunbridge Wells was opened for Decimus Burton's villas, and its characteristically brown seams are known as Calverley sandstone (Colour Plate 25). Some seams are so well layered that they can be split to make heavy roof tiles, such as can be seen at Stanfords End, Edenbridge, and at Cowden (Colour Plate 13). Like the walling stone taken from the Hastings beds, these are better known in Sussex; so far as Kent is concerned, the difficult terrain of the Weald, which impeded transportation, as well as the ready supplies of timber for framing and clay for bricks have kept the Hastings beds out of the limelight, for all their fine seams.

Colour Plate 25. One of Decimus Burton's italianate villas in Calverley Park, Tunbridge Wells, built from the local Calverley sandstone in the 1830s with a characteristic bay window, low-pitched slate roof and a prominent veranda.

Colour Plate 26. Starkey Castle Farm, Wouldham, built in the later 14th century from ragstone and flint, with an open hall to the right of the entrance and service rooms and a solar to the left.

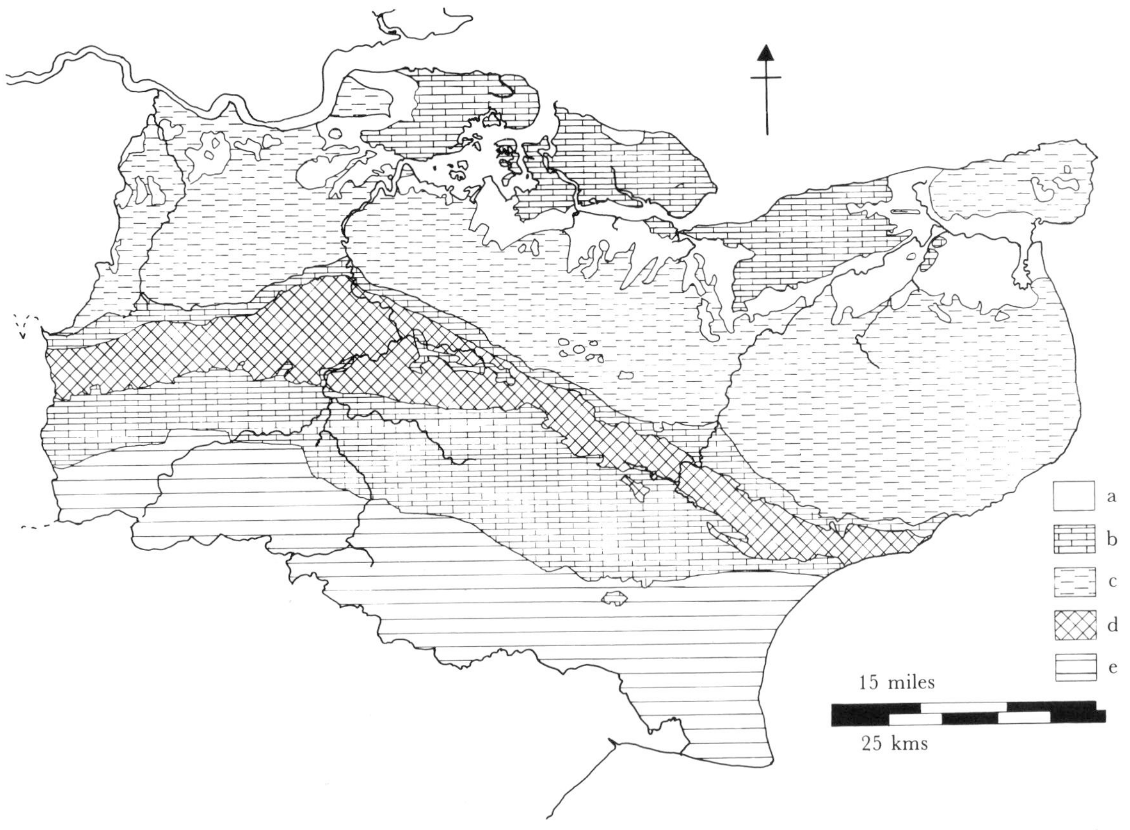

Figure 5. Kent. Geology: (a) Tertiary gravels and sands; (b) clays, mainly Tertiary London clay, Cretaceous Upper Greensand (Gault) and Wealden Clay; (c) Chalk; (d) Lower Greensand; (e) Hastings Beds. Overlying soils are not shown.

Plate 24. The purpose of the galletting at Old Soar, Plaxtol, seems to be no more than to save mortar by filling gaps between the blocks of ragstone masonry. Later generations turned this to decorative use by filling all the joints with galletting, sometimes using a contrasting stone such as flint.

Overlying the Hastings beds is a layer of Wealden clay, which at once provided the raw material of bricks and the heavy waterlogged soils which so favoured the growth of oak trees. Lying above this is a thin layer of Lower Greensand. It forms the more southerly of the two scarps which run across the landscape from north-west to south-east, and it carries the poor soils of the chartland. Westerham, Sevenoaks, Maidstone, Ashford and Hythe are all built on the dip-slope of the Greensand, and its building stones are much in evidence in these towns. They are extremely variable in colour, ranging in hue from pale grey and light buff to a dark purple-brown or murky green, depending on how much iron or glauconite is present, and, again, they are sometimes attractively streaked. Most Lower Greensand is neither durable nor easy to work. Often small chips of stone were set into the binding mortar between the roughly shaped blocks, both to economise in the amount of mortar needed to fill the large gaps and to decorate the surface of the wall (Plate 24). This method of laying stone, which was called galletting, was used at Dover Castle in the middle of the twelfth century, again at Old Soar a century later (Colour Plate 52), and often thereafter. Flint walls were also galletted on occasion. Despite the unsatisfactory qualities of Lower Greensand, it provides a light grey, coarse and brittle form of limestone known as Kentish Rag. This was quarried during the Roman period, and was exported as far as London right into Victorian times. The most prolific quarry was at Boughton Monchelsea, where the Loose valley cuts through the Greensand and exposes abundant seams of passable building stone. Ragstone was used almost everywhere in Kent outside the Weald, and, although it may easily flake away when attacked by frost, the walls of such imposing houses as Starkey Castle Farm at Wouldham (Colour Plate 26) and Boughton Malherbe Place (Colour Plate 50) were built of it, not to mention countless cheap cottages in a later age.

A thin layer of Upper Greensand or Gault lies above the Lower Greensand, and this provided clay for bricks, but no building stones. Rising above it is the dramatic scarp of the North Downs, breaking across the landscape from the Surrey border to the coast. It is formed of the commonest and most recent of all southern England's geological strata, chalk. It is soft and pervious, qualities which give the Downs their lovely rolling shape, but not ones prized by the mason. Even in its hardest form, clunch, chalk needs a harder stone to protect its edges when used for building. Because of the abundant supplies of ragstone and, of course, of timber and brick, chalk was seldom used to build Kent's houses. Nevertheless, it was burnt to produce the lime used in their daub and mortar, and, more recently, it has been quarried as the principal ingredient in the manufacture of cement.

Found in the upper strata of chalk in a union of opposites is flint. As hard as chalk is soft, flint was prized from the earliest prehistoric times for making cutting tools. In building it could be used just as it was found, in small knobbly lumps (Colour Plate 53) or as cobbles pounded round by the sea (Colour Plate 91), and bound with mortar. It could be split or knapped to make a flatter surface, characterised by its shiny, perceptibly translucent blackness, and even shaped into roughly square blocks (Colour Plate 27). Used like this, it could be set in alternate bands with ragstone or in squares with blocks of stone to produce an attractive chequerwork pattern. The sixteenth-century refacing of the northern ranges of Hall Place at Bexley (now Greater London) was executed in a chequerwork of flint and chalk, a wonderful re-assemblage of two contrasting materials so strangely joined by nature.

All these stones belong to the Cretaceous formations. Above them are a few insignificant Tertiary deposits and the alluvium of the Thames estuary and the coastal marshes. These, by and large, provided no building stones, but plenty of clay for bricks as well as sand and gravel for mortar and concrete.

Demonstrably, Kent has been better served by nature than its neighbours across the Thames, particularly Essex, which has hardly any building stone at all. Nevertheless, good stone was expensive: it was in short supply and it taxed local transport to the limit. Poor stone was abundant, but its ability to last was not necessarily greater than that of other materials. For all this, Kent's stones were crisp and colourful when new, and gave an element of status to every building raised in them. Such qualities prompted the importation of Quarr stone from the Isle of Wight in the Middle Ages, and, more importantly, Caen stone from Normandy, although these fine Jurassic limestones were principally reserved for the decorative parts of churches because of their high cost.

Timber

Kent has a variety of soils on which trees can grow. These include the thin dry soils directly eroded from the chalk of the Downs, the sandy acid heaths of the chartland, and the cold deep clays of the Weald. Luckily for agriculture, rich mixtures of clay and marl cover the eastern downland and some of the vales, fertile silts fill the river valleys and estuaries, and some coastal marshland. Only the pebbly shores and some gravelly heaths are really inimical to trees. The clay soils of the Weald and the eastern part of the Thames basin gave the oak perfect conditions in which to flourish. Oak became the most important of trees for building. Its hardness and durability, and its resistance to warping and splitting were highly prized. Other trees were to play their part in building too. Elm was used where its greater length was an advantage, and, since it lasts well when totally submerged in water, it was useful for piled foundations beneath the water table. Ash could serve a multitude of roles. Sweet-chestnut was a good alternative to oak (Colour Plate 28), and so was beech, a tree which grows best on the dry soils of the chalkland. The springy hazel, which grows well in damp conditions, made excellent wattles for filling walls with a base to support mud and straw daub.

Timber supply

Even as early as the fourth millennium BC, agriculture was advancing so rapidly in England that clearances of woodland were already denuding the primeval landscape. Trees were used so extensively in manufacturing and building as well as for fuel that woodland had to be specially managed to ensure adequate supplies. This involved coppicing, a process whereby trunks were cut just above the ground, and allowed to regenerate by growing new shoots which could be harvested almost indefinitely (Orme 1982). Woodland which has been coppiced for a very long time is particularly evident in Kent, for instance on the North Downs in Blean and Lyminge Forests. Still more coppices in the heavily wooded parishes of the Weald are evidence of this ancient practice continuing into modern times.

Coppiced trees produce straight poles, ideal for light building work as well as for fencing and fuel. Heavier building timbers came from the whole trunks of standard trees, which could be grown from seed, or, equally, be the product of coppicing (Rackham 1976, 23, 76-7). Direct evidence is slight, but in the Middle Ages, as in prehistory, this timber probably came from trees in managed woodland, as well as from trees on land used for pasture, and from trees on other farmland including those in hedges. The Domesday Survey showed that England was one of the least wooded countries in Europe: woodland covered only fifteen per cent of the land and was unevenly distributed. The northern and eastern parts of Kent had been cleared for a long time to satisfy the needs of agriculture, but Domesday suggests that there was plenty of woodland in the vales. The sparsely inhabited and, of course, still densely wooded Weald was largely omitted from this record. More importantly, Kent was not greatly encumbered with extensive forests and parks reserved for royal or aristocratic use, so all kinds of builders could readily exploit its timber reserves.

Until the seventeenth century, timber was the most important of Kent's building materials. The common fallacy that building in timber declined after that because all the trees had been consumed by the furnaces of the iron industry or by the insatiable needs of ship-building is shown for what it is by the extensive ancient woodland still evident in much of Kent today. How that woodland was worked is less evident, for the ancient methods have almost entirely vanished, so far as building is concerned.

In the main, timber was commercially produced in the Middle Ages by woodmen, and its supply depended on customary methods of working which were already of great age. This meant coppicing or felling standard trees when they were comparatively young, but had grown quickly and upright among surrounding underwood trees, which were cut more frequently for other purposes. The great advantage of managed woodland was the assured supply of good straight building timber it provided. When buildings needed especially long or thick timbers, these had to be taken from mature trees in woodland which was not intensively harvested in this way. These might come from wood pasture, where the oaks grown for timber tended to be further apart than trees in managed woodland, and grew more slowly to a larger girth. The same was true for curved timber. In many eastern counties of England, intensively managed woodland met a demand for building timber so great that no other source could have fulfilled it. This probably determined the traditions of carpentry which evolved there.

Until the end of the Middle Ages, the quickly grown trunks were used whole, not halved or quartered. The construction of a modest house required seventy or eighty trunks for its framing and studding alone, and these might take from twenty-five to eighty years to grow. Kent's large yeoman houses could easily take eighty trunks for their main frames and another 250 for smaller studs, joists and rafters, not to mention a handful of wide old trunks for floorboards. Annual production probably amounted to roughly two and a half trunks per hectare or one per acre, so Wealden parishes could easily sustain their needs for house timber. The more densely populated parts of Kent were less well endowed, and probably had to bring in some of their supplies from elsewhere in the county. Transport was so difficult because roads were poor and heavy loads sank into ruts that a journey of fifty miles could double the cost of timber (Rackham 1972, 1982). It is unlikely that timber ever had to travel even a quarter of that distance in Kent, but precisely which sources were used for individual houses is obscure.

Timber framing

The oldest of Kent's surviving houses are built of stone because in the twelfth and early thirteenth centuries construction in timber was incompatible with durability, even though it had the advantage of cheapness. From then onwards, a new way of making timber buildings durable was employed, and, with the continuing advantage of lower cost, these were constructed in ever increasing numbers. This is particularly evident in Canterbury: nearly all building of any substance in the two centuries after the Conquest was in stone, but, thereafter, substantial houses were mostly built in timber

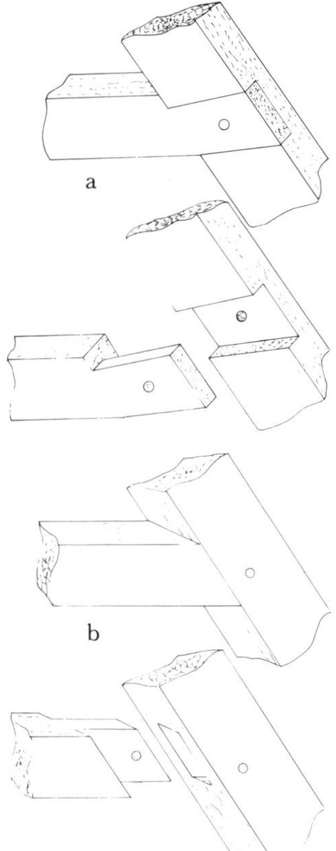

Figure 6. Joints, shown assembled and exploded. Collar and rafter: (a) with lap-joint, upper side of which is dovetailed to reduce tendency to withdraw; (b) with mortise and tenon.

and some existing stone houses were even rebuilt in timber as well. This involved a timber frame which more than satisfied the needs of stability and served the needs of decoration and status as well (Quiney 1990, 41-59).

The water-logged remains of building timber uncovered by archaeologists in the Somerset Levels and the Cambridge Fens show that sophisticated traditions of carpentry had developed by the Bronze Age, if not before, in which mortise and tenon joints were common. The Romans, who excelled as builders, brought their own sophisticated methods of carpentry to Britain, but Saxon traditions changed them beyond recognition. Simple lap-joints were commonly used because they were less dependent on accurate carpentry and easier to assemble than mortises and tenons. Saxon buildings had walls based in trenches or framed by earth-fast posts, and the latter method continued until well after the Conquest. This provided stability, but it was at the cost of eventual decay.

The solution to this problem was to frame buildings so that the posts could be set above ground on a water-proof plinth. This happened shortly before 1200. Increasing economic activity encouraged building. In rich towns like Canterbury shops and houses were often built on stone undercrofts; if they were to be of timber, their posts could not be set in the ground in the usual way, so a method of stabilising them was needed. It was just at this time that an improved knowledge of mathematics gave carpenters the means of building more skilfully. They could now set out right angles accurately, which helped them mount a frame on a timber sill with joinery that increasingly made use of efficient mortise and tenon joints rather than the simpler but weaker lap-joints (Figure 6).

By the early fourteenth century, carpenters had discovered how to build a rigid frame, and had developed various standard joints which remained in use for as long as people built houses with frames of hard wood. So effective were their methods and those of the woodmen who supplied the timber that framed buildings became far cheaper to build than stone ones, and, thanks to the fine qualities of oak, they also had a potential lifespan which compared favourably with stone. This, as it turned out, was far longer than their builders realised.

The timber frames were made up of a series of units or bays which were defined by vertical posts linked together by lengthwise and crosswise beams. Bays were usually rather wider than long, and normally measured between 12 and 20ft. (4 and 6m) each way, limits imposed by the length of readily available timber from managed woodland. This was an admirable size for a room, and particularly large rooms could be two bays long or occasionally more.

Carpenters learned much from the construction of great cathedral roofs, but the principal timber-framed buildings which promoted these developments were apparently the great barns which a number of monasteries and the quasi-monastic Knights Templar built on their estates in Essex. They made use of an old technique in which the great weight of their roofs was supported by arcades of posts running down their length and dividing their width into a central nave and side aisles. Although medieval carpenters were unsure of how the stresses produced by the heavy roofs operated, the junction between the roof and the wall was obviously critical. If the roof were too heavy and improperly supported, the joints would shear apart and the walls splay outwards under its burden. The arcade-posts carried most of the weight, not the walls, and, to keep them rigidly in place and to link them to both roof and external wall, numerous ties and triangulating braces were simply lapped across them. At first, this involved large numbers of timbers, some of extreme length, but,

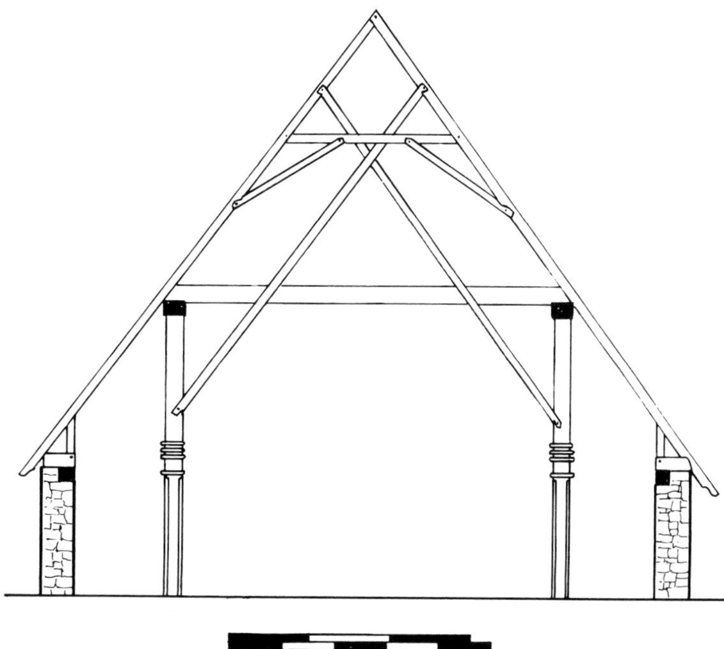

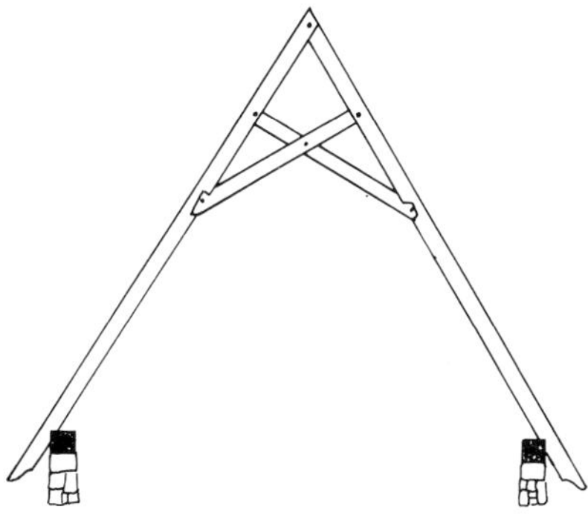

Figure 7. Cogan House, Canterbury. Cross-section of aisled frame, showing passing-braces rising from the arcade-posts (which divide the main body of the hall from its side aisles), over the tie-beam, to cross just beneath the collar before meeting a pair of roof rafters. (After Parkin 1970.)

Figure 8. Court Lodge, Mersham. Section of roof, showing scissor-braced rafters. (After Bismanis 1987.)

as more sophisticated techniques of joinery were developed during the thirteenth century, the mortise and tenon joint was increasingly used and the number and length of the timbers were greatly reduced.

Since the long timbers had to come from mature trees, there was a great advantage in doing without them. Indeed, by the fourteenth century, mature oaks had become rare enough in some places to jeopardise the supply of long, heavy timber. Consequently, short and straight timber of comparatively thin scantling, readily available from managed woodland, determined the way carpentry was to develop. Large curved timbers, by distinction, had to come from trees outside the general run of managed woodland, and, indeed, most curved timbers in Kent's houses are small and confined to secondary and decorative roles.

For a while, very long timbers called passing-braces were a hallmark of aisled framing. Their purpose was to stabilise the roof and the awkward junction of timbers at the top of the arcade-posts and wall-posts. Here, the vertical timbers met the intersecting plates that ran the length of the building and the ties that ran across it, producing points of weakness made the more precarious now that the posts were no longer set in the ground. Each passing-brace crossed over all the main transverse framing members, rising from a pegged lap-joint on a wall-post to be trenched over an arcade-post, over the tie-beam that linked it to its opposite number, finally to reach the roof and cross over the opposite passing-brace shortly before being pegged to a rafter with a second lap-joint. These timbers were developed in the twelfth century for wide church spans, and carpenters probably adapted them shortly before 1200 for the needs of large aisled buildings.

The fact that passing-braces might have to be up to 50ft. (15m) in length and could only have come from old oaks which had grown straight must have made them expensive. During the thirteenth century they were superseded by shorter timbers which did the same job, but were split into two lengths, meeting each other at the arcade-post. Each one was no more than some 20ft. (6m) long and therefore within the reach of managed woodland. The aisled hall of Cogan House, Canterbury (Figure 7), was given a simpler curtailed form of passing-brace possibly before 1230. A related

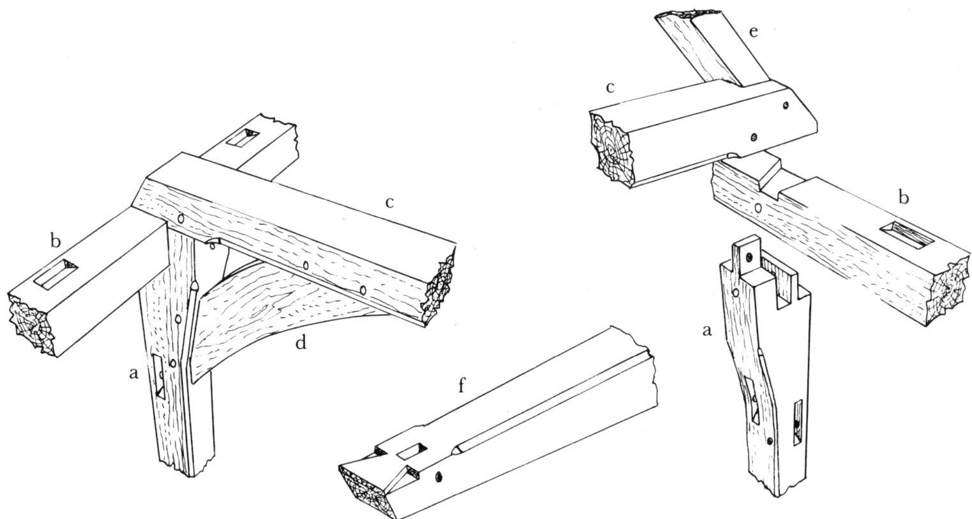

Figure 9. No. 21 High Street, Canterbury. Assembly at top of main-post, assembled (left) and exploded (right and below): (a) jowled top of main-post; (b) wall-plate with open mortises to receive bottom ends of rafters; (c) tie-beam; (d) brace; (e) lower end of rafter; (f) underside of tie-beam showing dovetail to engage wall-plate and mortise for upper tenon in main-post. (After Canterbury Archaeological Trust 1988.)

form of roof was simply triangulated by braces which again cross over each other near the apex of the roof, but rise from the rafters themselves. Alone, these so-called scissor-braces provided adequate support for the common roof rafters of Mersham Court (Figure 8), which has stone walls and no aisles, but scissor-braces were often used in conjunction with other forms of bracing in larger buildings.

The experimental nature of the carpentry employed in these aisled buildings is shown by the multiplicity of secondary braces that triangulated the main members of their frames to ensure their security against movement. Economy and stability required the development of a crucial part of the aisled frame, namely the junction of the uppermost longitudinal timbers or plates, the vertical arcade-posts and the transverse tie-beams. The purpose was to ensure that the weight of the roof rafters would not twist the frame out of position. This was achieved by a method of assembly in which the plate is tenoned on to the top of the posts and the tie-beam is placed over both of them and so helps to counter any twisting action caused by the thrust of the rafters (Figure 9). A joint was developed, apparently by carpenters working for the Knights Templar in Essex, which united post, plate and tie-beam. The aisle-post swells outwards at the top and has a staggered head, designed to accommodate two tenons at different levels. The outer, lower tenon engages a mortise in the aisle-plate, and the upstanding inner half, rising beside the inner face of the plate, has a second tenon which engages a mortise on the underside of the aisle-tie. The underside of this tie ends in a dovetail, which laps on to the top of the plate, thus securing it, firmly uniting all three timbers, and preventing any tendency to splay outwards. This neat solution was reached before 1300, and soon became universal, remaining so with hardly any change until the tradition of framing in hard wood died out some five hundred years later.

While these developments stabilised the frame laterally, a series of triangulating braces stabilised it longitudinally. At first these were simply lapped on to the main framing members, but by the fourteenth century the mortise and tenon had become universal and gave the frame rigidity without a multiplicity of timbers.

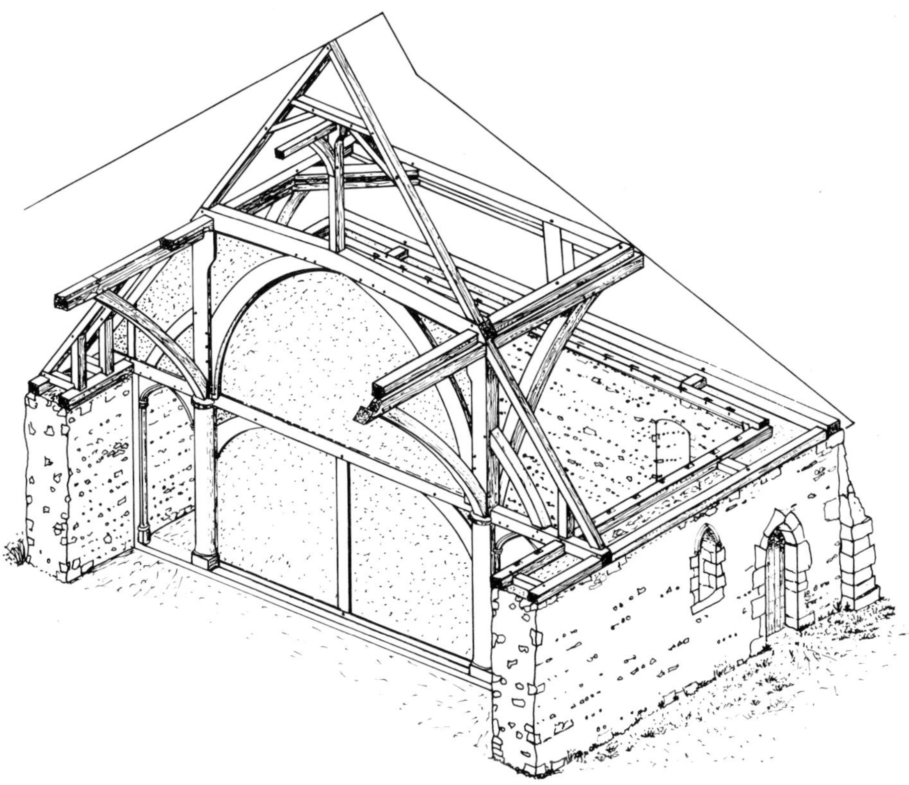

Figure 10. Nurstead Court. Conjectural perspective of surviving end of hall, showing aisled frame set within rubble walls, cantilevered arcade-plates extending to hipped end of roof, and doorway to adjacent chamber (further to right, not shown). (After Cherry 1989.)

A characteristic of aisled buildings in Kent was the way the arcades terminated, not with a pair of arcade-posts, but half way between one pair and where the next would be, leaving the ends of the arcade-plates braced and seemingly cantilevered to carry a tie-beam. This was usually clamped on to a lower beam and, in barns, also cantilevered from a post in the centre of the end wall, although there might be the additional support of posts at the corners of the wall and the studs set between them. The terminating cantilevered half bay is typical of the numerous aisled barns which filled Kent in the last two or three hundred years of the Middle Ages, and among many of the few early aisled halls as well. These include the unpretentious Dormer Cottage at Petham (Figure 34) as well as the grand Cogan House at Canterbury. Rather later, about 1314, Nurstead Court was again given cantilevered ends to its arcade-plates, although here the outer walls are of stone (Figure 10); and at least one of the aisled ends of Hamden at Smarden seems to have been cantilevered a decade or so later still.

The roof rafters also needed longitudinal stability, particularly to counter the effects of the wind. It became common practice in Kent to avoid gables, which would catch the wind. Instead, the ends of the roof were made to pitch inwards, producing so-called hips at the angles with the main slopes. A hipped roof reduced the effect of wind pressure, and the pitched ends countered any tendency for the roof to move or rack longitudinally in either direction.

Most of Kent's medieval roofs were supported by fairly thin rafters of uniform scantling, typical products of the quickly grown trees of managed woodland, and known as common-rafter roofs. Generally their pitch was about fifty-five degrees, which suited thatch or tile equally. The rafters were pegged together at their apex, and usually linked about a third of the way down by an equally thin collar. This was simply lapped on to them at first, but once again it was mortised and tenoned later. A method widely adopted in the fourteenth century to stabilise these pairs of collared rafters was to raise a longitudinal plate centrally within the roof on posts called crown-posts set on the tie-beams; the so-called crown-plate then supported the series of collars which braced every pair of rafters and, because of the friction between the plate and the

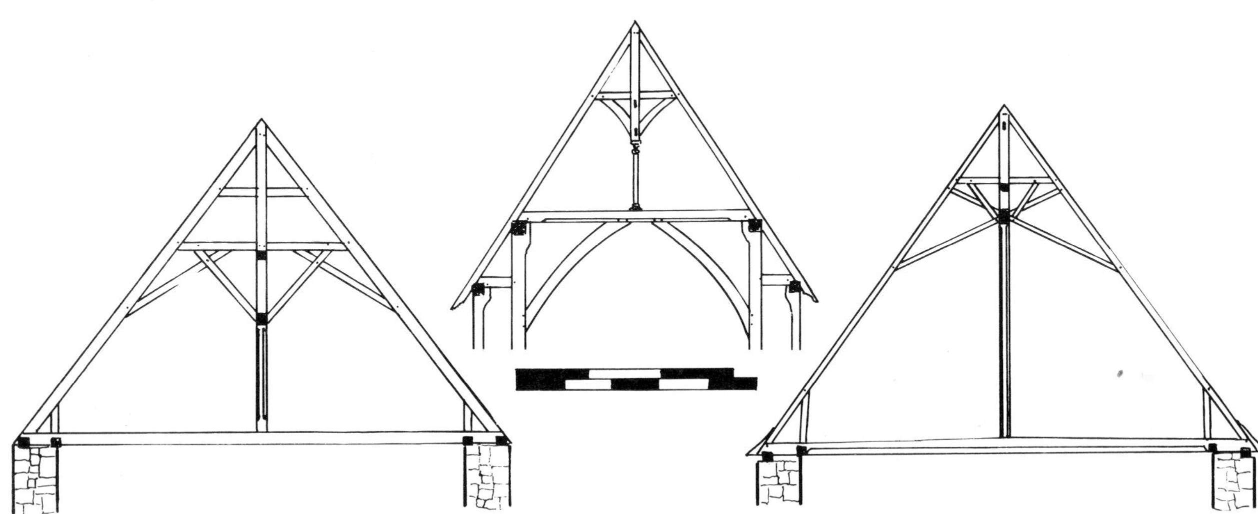

Figure 11. Cross-sections of three halls showing their king-strut roofs (from left to right): St Augustine's Guest Hall, Canterbury; the hall of Ratling Court, Aylesham; Christ Church Table Hall, Canterbury. In each case the king-strut rises from the tie-beam to the apex of the roof where it is jointed to a pair of rafters. (After Munby et al. *1983.)*

undersides of the collars, it reduced any tendency to longitudinal movement.

This so-called crown-post roof may have a French origin, but its first use in English aisled halls was in the 1260s or 1270s (Fletcher and Spokes 1964). Its first dated appearance in Kent is as late as 1313 in the stone-walled hall of Court Lodge, Great Chart, but the chamber block of Old Soar at Plaxtol already had this form of roof about 1290 (Figure 12). These crown-post roofs were possibly taken more immediately from the roofs probably erected in the 1260s or '70s over two large halls in Canterbury, namely the 'Guest Hall' of St Augustine's Abbey and the 'Table Hall' of Christ Church Priory, later known as the Choir House (Figure 11). Both have similar common-rafter roofs, but in each case these are supported at bay intervals by king-struts, that is by struts which rise from the tie-beams to the junction of the individual pairs of rafters above them. Longitudinal plates are tenoned into the king-struts, and these support collars, one for each pair of the remaining rafters; and additional braces are also attached to the king-struts to support the rafters transversely.

The carpenters of these roofs were probably adopting this new practice from France, where it had appeared, notably at Amiens Cathedral, a short while beforehand. This type of roof is rare in England, and in Kent confined to another building in the former Priory, to a couple of churches, to the halls of Ratling Court at Aylesham and the demolished All Saints' Vicarage, Maidstone, and to the chapel of Dane Chantry, Petham, all of which may predate the fourteenth century. The reduction of the king-strut's height to form a crown-post would be a simple development, and so, equally, would be the scarfing together of the lengths of plate, previously tenoned between the struts, to form a continuous crown-plate. Moreover, this would follow the general tendency of the time to reduce the number and size of individual timbers. The earliest crown-posts tend to be the tallest, again suggesting their origin in king-struts.

While the chronology of the earliest king-strut and crown-post roofs has yet to be precisely determined, by the early fourteenth century the king-strut seems to have been superseded, except in the occasional gable end of a crown-post roof, as exemplified by The Chequers at Tonbridge and the adjacent house (Munby *et al.* 1983). Although crown-post roofs were to be widely used in much of the eastern half of England and the Midlands, Kent made them its own: they were adopted to the exclusion of nearly all other forms of roof right until the end of the Middle Ages (Plate

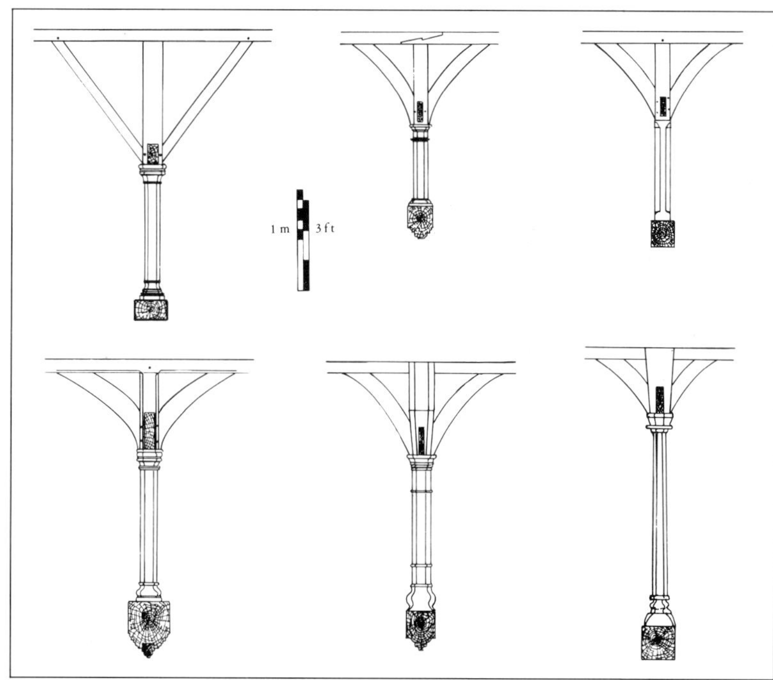

Plate 25. The crown-post roof of an upper chamber in the northern cross-wing of Cobrahamsole Farmhouse, Sheldwich.

Figure 12. Six crown-post roofs viewed from the side with cross-section of tie-beam below and crown-plate mounted above them (from left to right, top to bottom): Old Soar, Plaxtol, late 13th century (after Wood 1947); Hamden, Smarden, hall, mid-14th century (after Rigold 1967); Hamden, Smarden, cross-wing, mid-14th century (after Rigold 1967); Rooting, Pluckley, late 14th century (after Rigold 1967); Yardhurst, Great Chart, late 15th century (after Rigold 1969g); Payne Street Farm, Charing, 15th century (after Swain 1968).

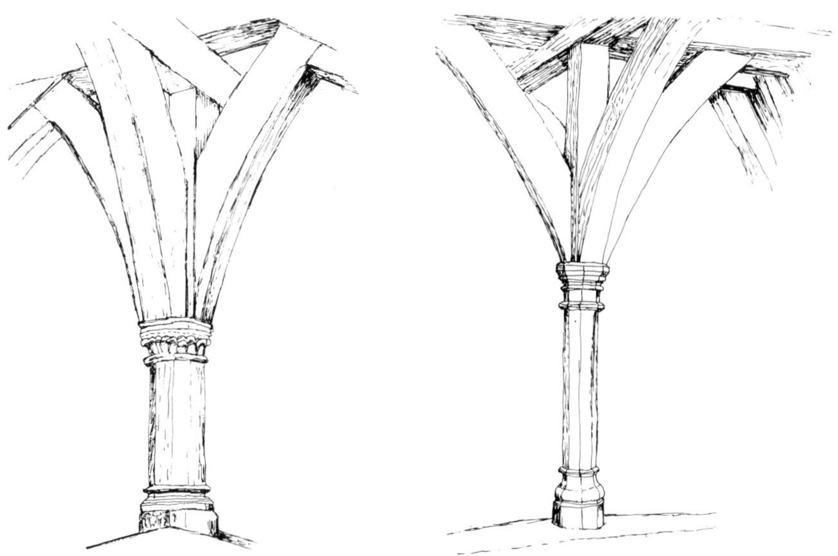

Figure 13. Two crown-posts: perspectives of Nurstead Court, early 14th century (left), and High Hall House, Larkfield, East Malling, probably late 14th century.

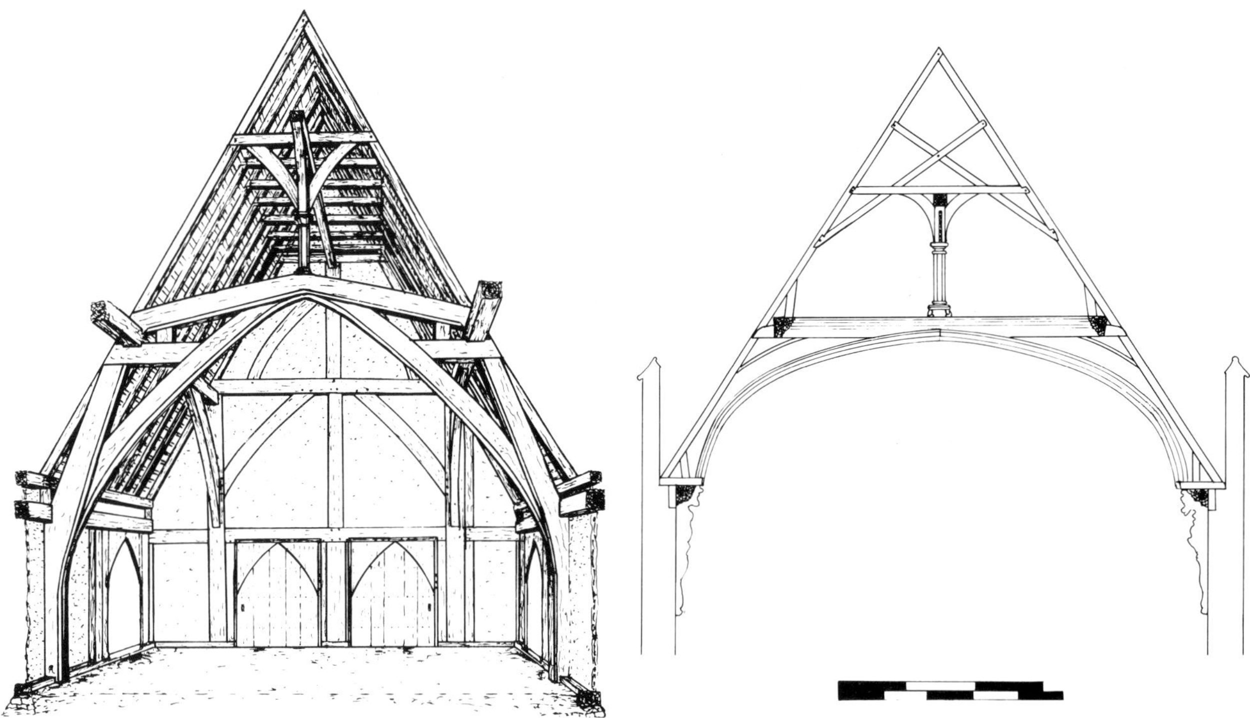

Figure 14. Hamden, Smarden. Conjectural perspective of interior of hall showing base-crucks in central open truss with arch-braced tie-beam and crown-post roof, and arcade-posts in further, closed truss with a pair of service doors set into the partitioning.

Figure 15. Penshurst Place. Section of great hall roof, possibly designed by the Master Carpenter William Hurley, showing false hammer-beam truss with arch-braced collar mounting a crown-post and scissor-braced upper section.

25 and Figures 12 and 13). They died out finally about 1550 when their decorative qualities were no longer valued and other forms of roof construction were adopted which could do the same job more efficiently and with less timber.

About thirty aisled halls survive in Kent, even though there are great numbers of similarly framed aisled barns (Sandall 1986). The greatest survivor of these halls was built about 1314 at Nurstead Court with immense round columns dividing the aisles from the centre of the hall. They are very grand, yet arcade-posts interfered with the internal spaces of a hall, and various ways of removing them were found before the end of the thirteenth century. Because aisles were associated with the status of great halls, they nevertheless remained in use long after they had been superseded constructionally, and a handful of the surviving aisled halls may have been built as late as the fifteenth century.

When it was necessary to provide a wide span, Kent turned to a method of framing developed in the thirteenth century which combined curved timbers known as base-crucks with tie-beams in such a way that these arched across what would otherwise have been the aisles of an arcaded structure. This avoided the penalties of both excessively long timbers and the intrusion of arcade-posts into the open space of a wide hall, although the timbers were still of comparatively wide scantling, and, being curved, were particularly expensive.

The hall of Hamden at Smarden was spanned in this way around the middle of the fourteenth century (Figure 14), and so were the halls of Burnt House, Yalding, and Bourne Place, Barnes Street, East Peckham. The great, curved base-crucks made

Figure 16. Ightham Mote. Conjecturally restored interior perspective of hall, showing the stone arch supporting the central truss of the roof, and a timber arch supporting the truss immediately before the end wall.

these halls unusually grand, on account of their rare form and the cost of their curved timbers.

Similar though independently developed forms of curved timber were used in a number of wide halls with stone walls where tie-beams were less important structurally. These had their roofs spanned by collars, which were again braced by great arching timbers rising from the top of the walls just below the wall-plate in a way already established for church roofs, and they often carried crown-posts to support upper collars as well. This form was employed at its most ostentatious during the 1340s to span the great hall of Penshurst Place (Figure 15). This incomparable roof is so magnificently conceived that it has been tentatively ascribed to William Hurley on the grounds that Penshurst's builder, Sir John de Pulteney, could have had access to Edward III's Master Carpenter, and that a roof spanning 39ft. (12m) would have been impossible without skills of his order (Harvey, 1984, 154-5). Here, the great arch of the roof rises from false hammer-beams, and the wall-posts are decorated with secular figures, now sadly mutilated, rather than the angels which a church roof would have had (Colour Plate 28).

The arch-braced roof was also used occasionally on a smaller scale, without a crown-post and upper collar, for instance at Ightham Mote, where the central arch, though not the end arches, is of stone rather than timber (Figure 16), and this was again the case at Battel Hall, Leeds. Timber arch-braced collars appear in one or two later framed buildings as well, notably at Hurst Farm, Chilham, and also at Shakespeare House, Headcorn, where the intention may have been to add an element of status to a cloth hall (Figure 17).

Smaller houses with a width of 20ft. (6m) or less had no need of arcade-posts and aisles, or for base-crucks, and the box frame was universally used instead. This was

Figure 17. Shakespeare House, Headcorn. Conjectural perspective of arch-braced collared roof.

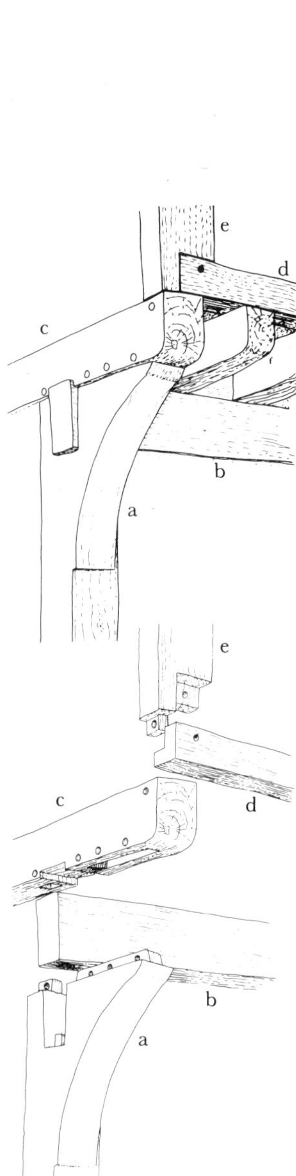

Figure 18. No. 1 High Street, Chiddingstone. Jetty: assembled (above) and exploded: (a) lower main-post, swelling into hewn bracket; (b) jetty-plate; (c) end joist (or girding-rail, or mid-rail); (d) bressummer; (e) upper main-post; (f) floor-joist.

no more than an aisled frame shorn of its aisles, and lacking internal load-bearing timbers. Most of their timbers were short, 20ft. (6m) being about the maximum length, and scantlings of 6in. (.15m) square were usual. Timbers from managed woodland suited these dimensions well, and were readily available to meet the demand for the thousands of substantial houses which were built before the end of the Middle Ages to satisfy Kent's affluent population. Timbers of more than double this scantling were exceptional, even for posts and tie-beams, simply because there was no constructional need for them, and no reason to pay for them either.

An important development in framing, made necessary when timber houses grew tall enough to accommodate upper floors, was a means of fixing both ends of the floor joists without interfering with the assembly of the main part of the frame and making this impossibly difficult. It was achieved by tenoning the inner end of the joists firmly to a bridging-piece or bressummer and simply resting the outer end on a second bressummer at the front and projecting them forward from it to produce an overhanging jetty. This avoided the difficulty of framing floor joists with mortise and tenon joints at both ends, and the projection provided a bit more floor space above. Moreover, the jetty would advertise the existence of an upper floor and, when such floors were still a rarity, they would bring a degree of ostentation as well (Figure 18).

Jetties, like other sophisticated forms of framing, were probably developed during the thirteenth century, particularly in towns where crowded circumstances made it advantageous to have upper floors. Canterbury's surviving jetties appear to date only from the 1390s and later; by the fifteenth century they had become very common, and the same is also true in other towns such as Sandwich. Kent's oldest jetty — and one of England's — may be in the much smaller town of Wingham, if the jetty of Canon Cottage, one of the houses built after 1287 for the clergy of Archbishop Peckham's prebendal college (Parkin 1979), really belongs to the late thirteenth century rather than to a later rebuild (Figure 19). At all events, within a century a combination of a box-framed hall and jettied end wings had given Kent its most characteristic forms

Figure 19. Canon Cottage, Wingham. Cross-section, showing undercroft with stone walls and stairs and external steps leading up to main, framed storey, and, above it, upper, jettied storey rising into roof space; the roof rafters are simply supported by lap-jointed collars in a primitive fashion. (After Parkin 1977.)

Plate 26. The timber framing and jettied upper storeys of some of the houses in Strand Street, Sandwich, which superseded the flint walls of the town's earliest houses.

of yeoman house, and jetties remained popular in town and country alike for as long as houses were built of timber (Plate 26).

Early jetties simply projected over the lower wall, the serrated line of joist ends being decoration enough. Sometimes plain, curving brackets supported those joists which lay above principal framing posts below. In the sixteenth century and occasionally later the brackets were adorned with grotesque figures (Plate 27); these take the form of crouching figures at 134-140 Bridge Street, Wye, and they were often used again in Canterbury (Figure 20). The jetty at Abbot's Fireside, Elham, was supported by grotesque caryatids in 1614, and these are by no means the last of them, but, by then, classical scrolled or console brackets were the latest fashion. Among the earliest of these are the brackets which support the jetty at Yew Trees, Wye, apparently as early as 1605 (Plate 28). Console brackets went from strength to strength thereafter, supporting timber porches, overhanging eaves and dripmoulds above windows as well as jetties, and soon came to be moulded in stucco and carved from stone.

A more ostentatious way of decorating a jetty was to attach a moulded fascia to the front of the joists, but fascias were less popular in Kent than in Essex and East Anglia. The carving on the fascia attached, presumably in the seventeenth century, to the upper jetty of Dragon House at Smarden is unusual enough to have prompted the name of the house (Plate 29). The classical guilloche moulding decorating the fascias of Tudor House, 28 Palace Street, Canterbury, is similarly rare, and probably belongs to the last phase of building after 1665 (Plate 30).

A similar form of decoration to the fascias attached to jetties were the verge-boards or bargeboards attached to the rafters beneath a gable. Gables came into use in towns where houses were commonly built end-on to the street and needed extra accommodation within the roof space. Gables were well established by the fifteenth

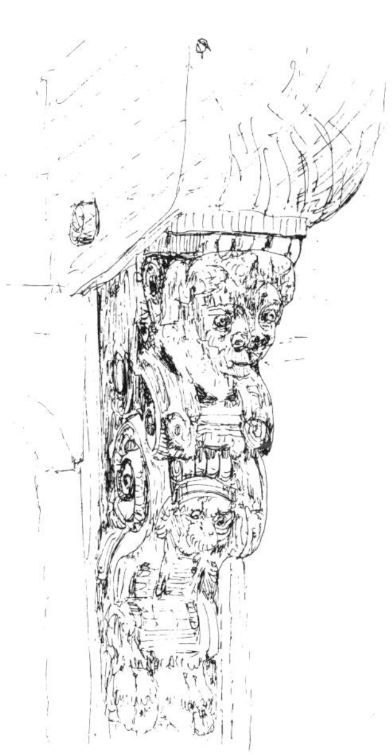

Figure 20. All Saints' Lane, St Peter's Street, Canterbury. Grotesque bracket supporting jetty.

Plate 27. One of the many grotesque brackets supporting the jetties of Canterbury's houses.

Plate 28. Yew Trees, Scotton Street, Wye, maybe of 1605, showing the brick infilling (or nogging) to the timber frame, which was both very fashionable then and uncommon in Kent always, and the console brackets supporting the jetty and also the oriel windows and eaves; the jetty is finished with a moulded fascia board, and the windows extend in the form of clerestories almost from one end of the house to the other.

Plate 29. A detail of the gable of Dragon House, Smarden, showing the fascia carved with dragons, and a carved console bracket supporting the end timber of the projecting jetty.

Plate 30. Tudor House, the former St. Alphege's Rectory, 8 Palace Street, Canterbury, showing the guilloche moulding on its fascias and the grotesquely carved brackets supporting the upper jetty.

Plate 31. Church House, Penshurst, showing the close-studding, cusped bargeboards, and iron casement windows with small pieces of glass held in lead cames, as photographed at the end of the 19th century by Galsworthy Davie and reproduced by the collotype process in Davie and Dawber (1900).

Plate 32. The right-hand wing of Lynsted Court, which is jettied on two adjacent sides, the corner being carried by a so-called dragon-post, and the jettied joists being masked by moulded fascias; both gables are fitted with ornate bargeboards.

century at Canterbury, and, as an urban fashion, slowly penetrated the countryside to become common there in the seventeenth century. Because bargeboards were exposed to the weather, indeed their purpose was to stop rainwater from blowing underneath the roof, they quickly deteriorated, and, if they were ornately carved, they deteriorated even more quickly. Even so, a number of sixteenth-century bargeboards survive, some replete with cusped and foiled carving, others with intertwining patterns of foliage (Plate 31). Lynsted Court has a splendid variety of bargeboards (Plate 32), and so has the gabled wing of The Barracks at Well Street, East Malling (Colour Plate 29). Later bargeboards were carved with geometrical patterns or simply moulded. Moulded bargeboards with pendants were common in the seventeenth century, and had already arrived by 1598 as Valence House at Sutton Valence shows. The bargeboards in the gable of Baxon Manor at Bredgar, which is dated 1617, are plain, but their apex is ornamented with a carved pendant (Colour Plates 30, 49 and 75). Similarly carved upward pointing finials occasionally survive, but their exposed position was inimical to a long life.

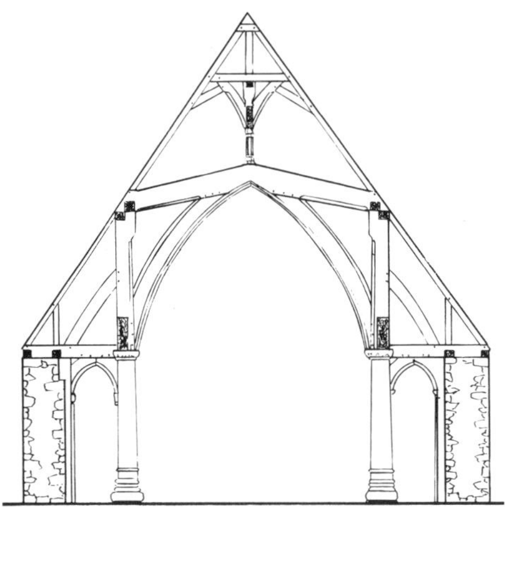

Plate 33. A hall-house at South Street, Boughton-under-Blean, showing the elbowed post framing the corner of the jettied upper storey and the gable end of the half-hipped roof.

Figure 21. Nurstead Court. Section through centre of hall, showing pointed arch formed by braces and cranked tie-beam, and also the subsidiary arches spanning the narrow aisles (compare Figure 10). (After Cherry 1989.)

Kent made only limited use of large curved timbers. A lesser form of cruck, sometimes called an upper cruck but really only a form of elbowed post, was occasionally used as a corner post above a jetty to embrace the angle of the roof by rising above the level of the wall-plate to form a short rafter reaching collar level. This arrangement was used in the upper parts of the end walls of Burnt House, Yalding, of Old Kent Cottage, Newington (near Folkestone), again at Upstreet Cottages at Lyminge, probably as late as 1500 (Mercer 1975 [222]), and in a number of other hall-houses all over the county, for instance at South Street, Boughton under Blean (Rigold 1969a) (Plate 33).

For the most part, curved timbers were almost universally confined to ostentatious braces, and in this role they are widespread. Supporting a tie-beam, they had already taken on the form of a graceful Gothic two-centred arch about 1314 in the central truss of Nurstead Court (Figure 21), and probably earlier at Ratling Court, Aylesham. This continued for at least a century, until two-centred arches dropped out of fashion in favour of flat, four-centred arches. The upper part of doorways was similarly arched by a pair of solid pieces of timber, meeting at the middle, known as derns. The fifteenth century adopted simpler lintels carved into four-centred arches (Figure 22). In the fourteenth century curved braces superseded straight braces above the capital carved on most crown-posts, and rose in all four directions to support the crown-plate and the single collar overhead, and to add an element of decoration (Figure 13).

With similar ostentation, curved braces spanned the lower angles of the large framed panels which made up a wall (Colour Plate 19). These became synonymous with Kentish framing because most other counties preferred their braces to span the upper angles instead. Very occasionally, curved braces were worked into a feature of a prominent house and embraced all the angles in a panel, thus producing the pattern of arcs and circles of the later fourteenth-century wing at Rooting Court, Pluckley, which also has double-curved, or ogee braces as well (Figure 23). This was exceptional, and Kent preferred to decorate its framed houses more soberly.

Figure 22. Door arches. Two-centred arches, of stone at 3-4 West Street, New Romney (a), of timber with derns at Canon Cottage, Wingham (b), and Hoggeshawes, Milstead (c). Three service doorways at High Hall House, Larkfield, East Malling (d). Four-centred timber arches at: Corner Farm, Langley (e); Old Bell Farm, Harrietsham (f); Cotterell Court, Petham (g); and High Street, Milton Regis (h). Base of jamb at 68 Burgate, Canterbury (i).

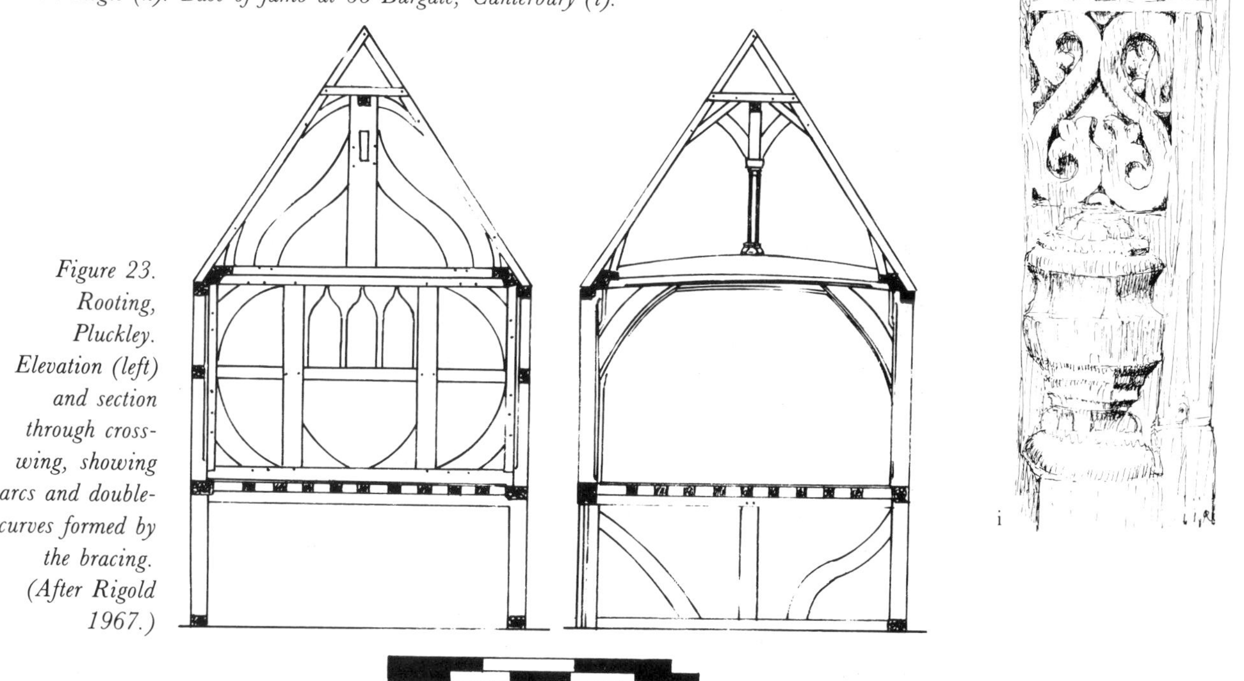

Figure 23. Rooting, Pluckley. Elevation (left) and section through cross-wing, showing arcs and double-curves formed by the bracing. (After Rigold 1967.)

Colour Plate 27. Pellicane House, High Street, Sandwich, built with knapped flint and the unusual local yellow bricks made from mud from the River Stour.

Colour Plate 28. Part of the roof of the Great Hall of Penshurst Place, showing one of the figures decorating the wall-posts and part of one of the arches carrying the roof, executed during the 1340s in chestnut rather than the usual oak.

Colour Plate 29. The Barracks, Well Street, East Malling, a mid-15th century hall-house whose windows were originally unglazed and fitted with diagonally set bars, some of which have been restored; the later gabled chamber wing to the right has fine cusped bargeboards.

Colour Plate 30. The porch of Baxon Manor, Bredgar, is replete with carved brackets, tie-beam, bargeboards and pendant, repeating on a small scale the decoration of the larger gable; even the studs are carved into the form of flat balusters (see Colour Plate 75).

Plate 34. Decorative panelling at 77 High Street, Milton Regis, echoing the pattern of the mullions and transoms of the long bands of windows.

Figure 24. Deanery Farm, Chartham. Cross-section through hall, showing doorway into chamber at high end, jetty at front only causing the centre line of the roof framing to be offset to the right of the framing below it, and how this is concealed by the avoidance of a central crown-post. (After Canterbury Archaeological Trust 1982-3.)

In Kent, as in much of the south-east, it was common to divide the walls into large panels until, taking a fashion from Normandy, they were divided with lines of studs placed so close together that the gaps between them were hardly wider than the studs themselves (Plate 32). This severe form of decoration appeared at Wye College about 1445 (Rigold 1969a), and eventually spread far beyond the confines of Kent. Stuart Rigold (1973) believed that close-studding demonstrated a 'precocious Puritan temper', and it certainly lasted long enough to be matched by the plain forms of yeomen's dress which Defoe observed in the 1720s. Long before that, close-studding had occasionally given way to the ostentatious patterns so commonly found in the far from puritan western Midlands. There, walls were divided into small panels, purely for decorative effect, and often these panels were further decorated by minute curved or cusped diagonals set across the corners to produce diamonds or a starry effect. These reached Kent in the later sixteenth century, and then mostly in towns, notably Milton Regis (Plate 34), but also occasionally in such rural houses as Standen, Biddenden, in 1578 (Colour Plate 31), Wickens at Charing (Colour Plate 32), and Waystrode at Cowden.

Another importation from outside the county was a form of roof framing which finally replaced the crown-post and common-rafter roof. The common rafters over the tie-beams were replaced by stout principal rafters, bay by bay, and these carried purlins to support the common rafters between them. The crown-post, the plate and the collars which it supported were also omitted; instead, a pair of so-called queen-struts supported a collar above the tie, and this trapped the purlins against the principal rafters. One of the first houses to be given a queen-strut roof was built about 1497 at Deanery Farm, Chartham (Figure 24), but it was fifty years before the crown-post roof was finally ousted by this innovation.

All in all, the development and adoption of timber framing in Kent was less innovative than in other parts of England, but its quality was assured. Conservatism was generally matched by a lack of ostentation, except in the use of prodigious quantities of timber for its close-studded houses. Set against these qualities is the large size of the everyday timber houses of its affluent yeomen, but even these suggest an egalitarian attitude to building because of their standardised form and because of the immense numbers of them which still survive after five hundred years of decay and destruction.

When a house solidly built of oak at last became more expensive than an equivalent brick house at the start of the eighteenth century, carpenters sought economies. These came with lighter frames employing posts made from quartered trunks rather than squared whole trunks. Carpenters also turned to other, cheaper woods, elm for instance, and eventually to soft wood such as Baltic fir, which was imported through Kent's many small ports. Frames made of soft wood were increasingly based on new types which were being disseminated through copybooks, and sophisticated joinery gave way to iron bolts, nails and clasps. Tradition quietly faded away.

It was better to conceal frames constructed from these timbers, either by hanging tiles on them or by weatherboarding them (Colour Plates 6 and 51), and this was often done to old oak frames as well (Colour Plate 13). To achieve a rather grand architectural effect, the boards could be applied in the form of imitation ashlar by rebating the upper edge, laying them flat and allowing a recessed groove to appear between them. Sometimes vertical grooves added an appearance of rustication, or blocks of masonry, particularly at the corners to suggest quoin stones (Colour Plate 47). Sometimes the boarding looks like plaster or stucco, itself applied to suggest quoins — a double deception. Some houses had this treatment applied across stretches of wall: 28 Palace Street, Canterbury, of 1617, is an early example if the rustication is an original feature. These patterns appear again in The Pantiles at Tunbridge Wells (Colour Plate 15), and were occasionally used outside town, for instance at Frognal, Teynham, which is dated 1668. Before the century was out, the full grammar of classical ornament was being carved in wood and applied to framed houses in much the same way as it would come to be executed in stucco.

Plaster and paint

Apart from alluvium, most of Kent's soils are the progeny of the geological formations beneath them. These soils provided the oldest of building materials. Mixed with a binding material of straw, bramble, or animal hair, they could easily be raised into a substantial wall, but associations of poverty seem to have caused this primitive form of construction to disappear, even from the most lowly of Kent's surviving buildings. Instead, soil was mixed with clay and a binding material to make daub, the necessary complement to a timber frame. Pressed on to the wattles or laths which filled in the panels of a framed building, daub insulates a wall well, and, with a finish of limewashed plaster, keeps out the damp as well as the cold. Being comparatively soft,

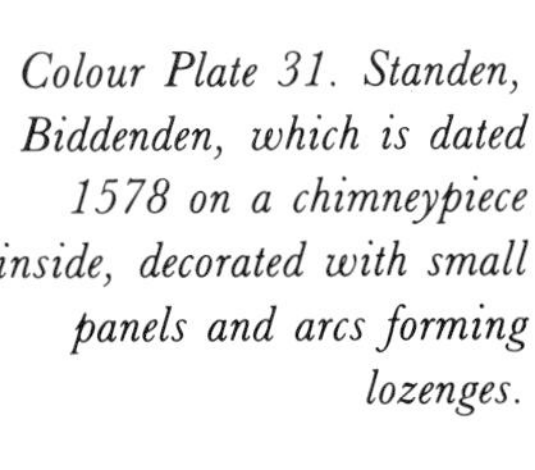

Colour Plate 31. Standen, Biddenden, which is dated 1578 on a chimneypiece inside, decorated with small panels and arcs forming lozenges.

Colour Plate 32. Wickens Manor, Charing, a medieval house, refronted to include a band of small panels enriched with diagonal arcs, and also, unusually, diagonal studs beside the doorway.

Colour Plate 33. No. 78 Bank Street, Maidstone, showing the spectacular pargeting dated 1611, vigorously painted in modern times, and the Ipswich window framed by classical columns.

Colour Plate 34. Queen Elizabeth's Guest House, High Street, Canterbury, a medieval house with two jettied storeys, modernised in the 17th century, with two oriels with Ipswich windows, and lovely pargeting setting off the later sash windows of the upper storey; above that, channelled plaster represents a few courses of ashlar blocks beneath the parapet.

Colour Plate 35. Calico House, Newnham, a close-studded house, plastered and painted in 1710.

it responds well to movement in the frame, and to small changes brought by variations in temperature.

Plaster, a waterproof mixture of lime and sand with a binding material such as cowhair, makes a good finish to the infilling of a framed wall. With the decline of framing, it came to be used in the seventeenth century to cover entire walls. This process was known as pargeting, although the word more usually describes the patterns which could be formed in the plaster before it set hard.

A small framed house close to Bredgar Church has its daubed panels finished with plaster decorated with incised dots and arcs in a way commonly seen in Essex and East Anglia, but less often in Kent. Raised patterns are also far more common north of the Thames than in Kent. The Wool House at Loose has a raised daisy coloured pale pink, perhaps by faded reddle (red ochre), and probably executed early in the seventeenth century (Plate 35). In 1697 the plastered front of 4 High Street, Chiddingstone, was decorated with circles and upturned hearts (Plate 36). The most spectacular pargeting is in Maidstone on the jettied front of 78 Bank Street, where the royal arms and the Prince of Wales' feathers flank an ornate window and shine out in splendid colour (Colour Plates 8 and 33). This dates from 1611, although the paint has been renewed, and its exuberant moulding contrasts well with

Plate 35. Pargeting, Wool House, Loose, showing two sorts of raised patterning, both currently painted pink to contrast with the overall limewash.

Plate 36. The evening sun highlighting the pargeting on the front of 4 High Street, Chiddingstone, the hearts and the date 1697 contrasting with the shadows of the diamond cames of the open casement windows.

Plate 37. Nos. 55-7 Week Street, Maidstone, showing the pargeting, dated 1680, which articulates the two upper storeys with Ionic and Corinthian pilasters and voussoirs supporting a cornice and the eaves.

the restraint and pastel tints of the pretty but rather enfeebled Ionic pilasters and swags at 55-57 Week Street, which is dated 1680 (Plate 37). The swags and scrolls of 1697 at 121 West Street, Faversham, are definitely old fashioned by comparison, but a good deal more vigorous. By the eighteenth century pargeting was dying out, soon to be replaced by classical decoration executed in stucco, a plastic material similar to plaster but with the addition of cement and therefore harder and longer lasting.

With all their decoration, it is certain that timber frames were meant to be seen. Even so, the timbers may have been limewashed to deter the effects of weathering. They were sometimes colour-washed too, although surviving evidence is slight. Ochre, reddle and other earthen colours were commonly used in the Middle Ages to brighten the framed houses of northern France, but only hints of colour come to light in Kent. The frame of a hall-house at North Cray (now Bexley, Greater London) was found to be ingrained with reddle after its demolition and removal to the Weald and Downland Open Air Museum at Singleton, but most colour of this sort has been washed entirely away or obliterated by timber preservative and the unfortunate desire for a vigorous black and white magpie appearance. The rear of the Wool House at Loose still has part of a scheme of decoration on a pink ground with squares and circles linked together into a strapwork pattern typical of the early seventeenth century. Houses entirely covered in plaster were often colour-washed, and more of this survives, but only one has the extensive remains of an elaborate decorative scheme. This is Calico House at Newnham, which was naïvely painted in 1710 with red floral patterns including vases of what look like wilting tulips (Colour Plate 35).

Colour Plate 36. The gatehouse of Lullingstone Castle, built in 1497 as one of Kent's earliest brick structures, with evidence of diaper patterns in darker brick.

Colour Plate 37. Cobham Hall, the imposing porch, dated 1594, and apparently removed here from the main hall block in the 1660s.

Colour Plate 38. Lees Court, Sheldwich, built about 1652, but probably altered above the entablature in the 18th century and given heavily overhanging eaves.

Colour Plate 39. Ford Place, Wrotham, of about 1589, showing the crow-stepped end gable to the right, and the three shaped gables which may be an addition of about 1605.

Colour Plate 40. The south front of Broome Park, Barham, built for Sir Basil Dixwell in 1635-39.

Plate 38. *Wall-painting at Calico House, Newnham, showing panels arranged independently of the timber framing, with an inscription in the frieze, reading: 'And tenderly beloved of my mother' and 'He taught me also language'.*

Figure 25. Decorative wall-painting in an upper chamber at Basing, Cowden, executed in bright red, dark red, yellow and light blue; the frieze at the top frames the text, the foliated strapwork pattern below it extends towards the floor.

The interiors of many timber houses were again painted (Colour Plate 71 and Plate 38), often with patterns representing hangings which carried over timber and plaster alike. Fragments of more ambitious schemes occasionally survive in small houses. The walls of a room at Richard and Elizabeth Knight's Basing at Cowden were painted about 1600 with a combination of strapwork and stylised foliage and a text loosely based on *Proverbs:* 'For hee that will not heare ye crye, of them that stande in neede, Shall crye himselfe and not be hard When he doth hope to spede' (Figure 25). If this implies any incipient puritanism, the interior painting at Sir John Roper's Bumpit at Lynsted, some of it dated 1605, depicts the religious symbols of his family's Roman Catholic faith as well as his and the royal arms.

Brick

A completely new building material which the Romans introduced to Britain was brick. They used it for the Pharos (or lighthouse) at Dover Castle, and for much else in Kent. The firing of blocks of clay to make bricks was a cheap process, and bricks were light enough to be more easily transported than stone. Despite these advantages, they were abandoned along with other Roman building methods and revived only

Plate 39. The ruined flint and ragstone walls of Tonford Manor, Thanington, showing the brick diaper applied to the masonry of one of the towers (centre); in the background is the rebuilt hall which still contains its chestnut hammerbeam roof.

towards the end of the Middle Ages. Then it was Continental practice and imports from the Low Countries which spurred the revival. The early brickwork at Salmestone Grange, Margate, apparently used imported bricks from Flanders. After Wat Tyler had attacked Horne's Place at Appledore in 1381 the house was rebuilt with a brick vaulted undercroft. Tonford Manor at Thanington combined red brick and flint into a chequerwork pattern about 1449 (Plate 39). The first major use of native brick in Kent came soon after 1469 when Sir Henry Heydon built Wickham Court at West Wickham (now Bromley, Greater London). He was the heir of a Norfolk magnate, and probably imported the idea from that county, where there was already an established tradition of using brick (Rigold 1973).

Sandwich had its own brickyard in the third quarter of the fifteenth century, and made use of the river mud to produce yellowish bricks for local use (Colour Plate 27). Despite this, and the construction of a number of fine brick monuments in other eastern counties towards the end of the Middle Ages, bricks only became popular in Kent through the initiative of Archbishop Morton. He supported the Lancastrians in the Wars of the Roses, and escaped arrest by fleeing to Flanders. The manufacture and use of bricks had flourished there for a long time, and this so impressed Morton that, when Henry VII recalled him in 1485 and he was appointed to the see of Canterbury in the following year, he instigated the use of brick in the construction of Bell Harry, Canterbury Cathedral's central tower, where the strength and lightness of brick were particularly advantageous.

This work required half a million bricks, and re-established the practice of brick-making in Kent for good. Possibly because Bell Harry was faced in Caen stone, it was not the best advertisement for the new material. While brick came into use at the archiepiscopal palaces, first at Charing and then, more extensively, in 1503 at Otford, the remarkable thing is that the county took to it so slowly. Yet the few prominent monuments that were built of it, notably Lullingstone Castle gateway as early as 1497 (Colour Plate 36), Smallhythe Church rebuilt at Archbishop Warham's instigation in 1516-17, the Roper Gateway in Canterbury, starting about 1524, but mostly at some time between 1530 and 1560, the earlier parts of Sissinghurst Castle (Colour Plate 10), and Shurland at Eastchurch on the Isle of Sheppey, do at least show that Kent came to excel in its manufacture as well as construction by the middle of the sixteenth century (T. P Smith 1990).

The slow progress of bricks is readily explained. The status of stone, even ragstone, counted for more, and oak was so abundant and the skill of carpenters so assured that

Colour Plate 41. Wingham Well Farmhouse, a modest house apart from this elaborate gabled façade.

Colour Plate 43. Horizontal zigzag diaper in the brickwork of the north-eastern 1550s range of Cobham Hall.

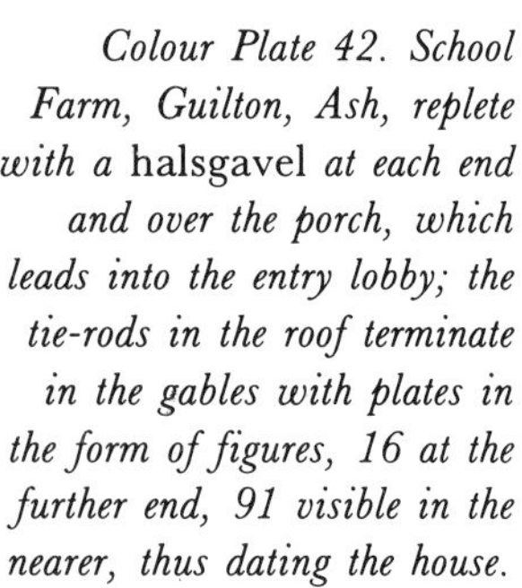

Colour Plate 42. School Farm, Guilton, Ash, replete with a halsgavel *at each end and over the porch, which leads into the entry lobby; the tie-rods in the roof terminate in the gables with plates in the form of figures, 16 at the further end, 91 visible in the nearer, thus dating the house.*

Colour Plate 44. The classical garden front of Bradbourne, East Malling, executed in four shades of red brick in 1712-15.

Colour Plate 45. Dormer Cottage, Petham; although rebuilt at the nearer end, this remarkable little house, probably of the 13th century, contains much of its original primitive framing.

Figure 26. Chimneys in the late 16th and 17th centuries were objects of esteem, and decorated accordingly. The brick stack could be treated as a cluster of shafts with oversailing courses of brick at the top, as at Wissenden Farmhouse, Bethersden (a), and Priory Farm, Tenterden (b); an unusual variant of the oversailing courses came with the inclusion of a course of bricks set edgewise to form a so-called cogging-course and the upper layers interrupted to form an embattled effect, as at Fuller House, Staplehurst (c); the clusters of shafts could be turned diagonally as at Bilting Grange, Godmersham (d); these two forms could be combined, as at Glass House, Benover, Yalding (e); a more ornate form could have octagonal shafts with oversailing courses forming eight-pointed stars, either attached to a central core, as at Marle Place, Brenchley, of 1619 (f), or with completely separate shafts, as at Great Pagehurst, Staplehurst (g); an unusual variant of this in Kent has completely circular shafts, often decorated with slightly protruding bricks to form spirals, as added to a Wealden house at Elham (h); as the 17th century wore on, forms became plainer, decoration comprising no more than a projecting fillet along the centre-line, as at Hartnup House, Smarden (i); and this might be emphasised by a symmetrical step-back at each end, as at Lydian Farm, Leeds (j); by the end of the 17th century, chimney-stacks were almost entirely unadorned, as at Hoggeshawes, Milstead, which carries a plaque dated 1700 (k).

Plate 40. The inner face of the tower of Sissinghurst Castle, with its classical frontispiece, executed in plastered brickwork, comprising Doric pilasters and an entablature framing both the entrance arch and the window above.

novelty was not enough to tempt ordinary builders. Only by the middle of Elizabeth's reign was brick becoming well established with such houses as Chillington Manor at Maidstone, of 1561, Ightham Court of 1575, Bybrook at Kennington, of 1577, and Ford Place at Wrotham, of about 1589 (Colour Plate 39). In smaller houses brick was largely confined to the construction of a chimney-stack, itself an innovation at the time. In the seventeenth century brick was used as infilling in framed buildings (Plate 28), and sometimes for end walls with chimney-stacks built into them. In east Kent brick was well established before 1700, but it took all of the eighteenth century to displace timber at the lower levels of house building in some parts of the Weald.

Although Kent comes behind Essex and East Anglia in the decoration of its brick chimney-stacks, these became prominent features of all kinds of houses for a century, starting around 1550 (Figure 26). The first stacks were plain, like those built soon after the fire of 1516 at Smallhythe (Colour Plate 65), with only a few oversailing courses of brick decorating the top, and a tendency to rely on height for the sake of effect. As stacks were designed to serve more and more hearths and therefore contained more flues, these came to be expressed by projections and recessions of various kinds, or by keeling, that is by the projection of an edge diagonally as though a shaft had been rotated through forty-five degrees and allowed to emerge along the side of the stack. Glass House at Yalding has a keeled stack of about 1600 with diagonally shaped ends comprising four shafts in all. Sometimes the stacks were made up from a series of diagonal shafts, each cutting into the next, or, like one of the stacks built in 1578 at Standen, Biddenden, just separate (Colour Plate 31). Other stacks comprised completely separate shafts, like the group of seven at Bilting Grange, Godmersham. These often emerged from a plain square base but this might be ornamented with panelling or have a beaded and chamfered top. The shafts might have the octagonal, bell-shaped lower section, which is all that remains at Honywood, Lenham, of 1621 (Colour Plate 73); they might remain separate right up to the oversailing courses at the top, as the splendid stack at Great Pagehurst, Staplehurst, does, or rejoin in the profusion of star-shaped angles at Manor Farm, Cliffe. Occasionally, the shafts were circular and decorated with mouldings or spirals, as at Cotterell Court, Petham. Like much other decoration, this exuberance faded before the advance of classical restraint and chimney-stacks became plain and purely national in character until a Victorian revival brought back the forms of old England.

Foreign influences

A different form of classical decoration, which came to England through copybooks from France and the Lowlands, was the application of columns or pilasters and entablatures to emphasise archways and windows, and, eventually, to articulate whole façades. This metropolitan fashion, which had been established by Old Somerset House in London soon after 1547, was taken up in the Tuscan pilasters and entablatures framing the inner openings of Sir Richard Baker's tower at Sissinghurst Castle a little over ten years later (Plate 40). How far the imperative need for order and proportion in classical detailing could be misunderstood is almost embarrassingly evident in the spindly columns of the frontispiece of 1575 at Ightham Court (Plate 41).

Plate 41. Ightham Court, with its widely spaced, thin Doric pilasters decorating each storey of the frontispiece, dated 1575; neither proportion nor the lack of a full entablature beneath the pediment concerned the designer.

Plate 42. A detail of the mutilated remains of the brick façade of 1625 at 16 Watling Street, Canterbury, articulated by stone quoining and a frieze of triglyphs and rosettes; the sash windows are a later insertion.

Yet by 1594, the date of the porch attached to Cobham Hall's north wing of 1591-4, a fair understanding of classical ways was at last visible in Kent (Colour Plate 37). Even so, for a century local craftsmen continued to add pilasters here and there in an often pleasingly slapdash way for clients who wanted status without understanding what they were getting.

The way pilasters slowly found their way into lesser buildings also applied to the application of rusticated stonework. The bays of 16 Watling Street, Canterbury, were articulated by rustication cut into the brickwork in 1625 (Plate 42). Cut brick pilasters also served in this way from much the same time. They were used particularly in the upper storeys of brick houses, and often rose from a band-course acting as a plinth at first-floor level, with a carved bracket beneath each one of them, to finish beneath

Plate 43. Wallets Court, West Cliffe, dated 1627, with its haphazardly placed brick pilasters, maybe not an original feature of the house, articulating the upper storey, and now grossly over-emphasised by shiny black paint.

Plate 44. The forlorn surviving wing of Bridge Place, a courtyard house raised in the 1640s or '50s, making a brave show of classical taste with its learned demonstration of how classical pilasters should be correctly used.

another band-course acting as an entablature at eaves level above.

This distant memory of Bramante's House of Raphael in Rome, transported to England by copybooks, reached fruition in Inigo Jones' Covent Garden of the 1630s, but it may have been used in Kent already by 1627 at Wallets Court, West Cliffe, where two different sizes of pilaster with two different intervals between them show a complete disregard for order and proportion (Plate 43). They could be a later addition, yet, from 1635, 66 Crooms Hill, Greenwich (in Kent until 1889), was demonstrating the comparative sophistication of a designer who could incorporate large window bays and smaller blind bays into a pilastered scheme which also embraced a gabled garret above. Even this showed little appreciation of the rules of classicism so clearly evident in the Queen's House, which Inigo Jones was then completing almost opposite it.

The surviving fragment of Bridge Place shows that his lesson had been understood by the end of the 1650s in the way that the two upper storeys are articulated by Tuscan pilasters with a full entablature between them and a cornice above (Plate 44). Yet, despite this example, Kent naïvely continued in its own sweet way to the end of the century, with Padbrook at Paramour Street, Ash, in 1675, where the lower windows have rusticated surrounds and the upper ones are flanked by pilasters on brackets, and perhaps as late as 1698 at Vicarage House, Wingham, where the alternate wide and narrow bays articulated by the finely moulded brick pilasters and band-courses of the upper floor are a deal more assured, but still not entirely regular in the spacing of the wide and narrow bays.

As long beforehand as 1652, Lees Court at Sheldwich was demonstrating to Kent a sophisticated metropolitan understanding of how giant classical pilasters should be used to embrace two storeys in a miraculously grand house executed in plastered brick, with its bases and capitals carved in stone, but its lesson was largely ignored and the house has few surviving imitators (Colour Plate 38).

Shaped gables

For all Kent's naïve classicism, a more overt sign of foreign influence came with the shaped and pedimented gables of the Low Countries (Percival 1966). These were really inspiring, and east Kent, like Norfolk, made them its own. Hipped ends to roofs rather than gables had been the established form in the Middle Ages, but they made no allowance for garret windows. A gable did, and in towns, where roof space was valuable, gables were popular. When houses were built of brick, rather than timber, the gable wall was often taken up into a parapet in front of the roof. The parapet usually had plain sloping slides (Colour Plate 10), and it might terminate at its base and apex with finials, as can be seen at Somerhill, Tonbridge, of 1611 (Colour Plate 11); but here was an opportunity for still more decoration.

The earliest way of achieving this was to step the gable (Figure 27). The intervals between each level were so small that these have come to be known as crow-step gables. They appeared in Norfolk about 1500 at Hales Court, and also may owe their origin to a fashion brought from the Low Countries and the Baltic states. In Kent, the gables of Smallhythe church were crow-stepped in 1516-17, each of the ten steps having the form of a gabled roof in line with the wall itself. The five steps on each side of the Roper Gateway's crow-step gable at Canterbury mark the start of their popularity. Hode Farm at Patrixbourne has a crow-stepped end gable dated 1566 in vitrified bricks; the end wall of Ford Place at Wrotham was completed with a crow-stepped gable about 1589, and shaped gables were possibly added about sixteen years later (Colour Plate 39). This happened at Hode Farm, where a shaped gable was added at the opposite end of the house in 1674.

This change from the crow-stepped form to the shaped form seems to be attributable to one fashion ousting another, and the development of the two forms seems to have followed the same course too. In the Low Countries, the size of the individual crow-steps was increased and their number decreased until three or four sufficed; each level was sometimes treated decoratively as an individual storey, with an applied order of pilasters and scrolls finishing the ends to conceal the roof slope, and the top of the gable was formed into a pediment. Such was the so-called Dutch gable or *halsgavel,* to use the native term of the United Provinces (later Holland). Other, plainer forms emerged with scrolled sides and a curved pediment, and these were further simplified into a series of concave and convex shapes.

In England scrolled sides and curved tops first appeared on gables about 1570, for instance in the extraordinary porch at Kirby Hall, Northamptonshire, which is dated 1572. By 1600 gables formed from concave and convex quadrants, usually with a step between them, had appeared in a handful of grand houses; they reached Kent in 1605 with the Earl of Dorset's remodelling of Knole at Sevenoaks (Colour Plate 7), and about the same year when they were added to the nearby Ford Place at Wrotham. Charlton Court at East Sutton was given more drawn-out ogee curves for its gables in 1612 (Plate 5). Shaped gables with varying degrees of complexity were taken up widely in east Kent in the later seventeenth century, presumably to please the large number of Protestant immigrants from the Low Countries who had settled here: Rushbourne Manor at Hoath was given shaped gables in 1659 and, from here, they descended to the level of small cottages like Rose Cottage at Combe, Woodnesborough, in 1723, and the even smaller Hilltop at Finglesham, Ham.

The combination of scrolled sides, pilastered centre and pedimented top made slower headway. This form was suggested in some of Inigo Jones' early designs before 1610, but, with or without the pilasters, it only came into common use in the 1630s. The Queen's (or Dutch) House at Kew Gardens in Greater London had both straight and rounded pediments over its shaped gables in the 'Dutch' form, and in Kent the scrolls and open and broken, straight and segmental pediments of Broome Park at Barham had been raised by 1640 into a confection of incomparable fantasy (Colour Plate 40). A few lesser houses tried to keep their end up in a similar way: a cottage at Goodnestone has giant pilasters supporting its scrolled 'Dutch' gable; Wingham Well Farmhouse has double pediments, the lower one broken, the upper one open (Colour Plate 41); and School Farm at Ash of 1691 has a debased form of *halsgavel* with two pilastered storeys with scrolls, and a pedimented top (Colour Plate 42). The common 'Dutch' pedimented gable was, even so, a lesser affair, sometimes with no more than a small triangle of brickwork representing a pediment sitting astride a curve or two lower down. For all their lack of definition, in their playful way they are one of east Kent's most attractive features.

Coloured brick and bonding

It was not until the later seventeenth century that brick dominated all the other materials. Then Kent's variety of clays played their full part in giving its houses many of their distinctive colours. The alluvial clays and brick-earths of the Thames estuary produced the soft red and reddish brown bricks of many downland houses in north Kent, while the river muds of the Stour gave Sandwich yellow bricks. The limestone content of the Gault clay to the south-west of the North Downs produced a distinctive light yellow brick, much favoured by neo-classical architects in the early nineteenth century, as can be seen at Soane's Ringwould House of 1813. The strong iron content of Wealden clay gave its bricks the brightest colour of all, the vermilion of Sissinghurst and countless farmhouses.

Sometimes steely blue vitrified bricks were set into a red brick wall to form lozenge patterns or diapering. A stone turret of Tonford Manor at Thanington was diapered in brick in the middle of the fifteenth century. Diapering only became well established in the 1550s, first at Cobham Hall (Colour Plate 43 and Figure 28A). The crow-stepped gable wall of Hode Farm was patterned with lozenges in 1566 (Figure 27); Acrise Place was similarly diapered during the sixteenth century, and so was Ruffin's Hill at Aldington. A century later taste turned towards a chequerwork of vitrified headers set among red bricks, as shown by 72-74 Broad Street, Canterbury, in 1693. Well before the eighteenth century, strongly coloured red bricks, often cut and rubbed to shape, were used to accentuate windows and doorways, and all the classical detailing which articulated the houses of the period (Colour Plates 82 and 83). It stood

a
b
c
d
e
f
g
h
i
j
k
l
m

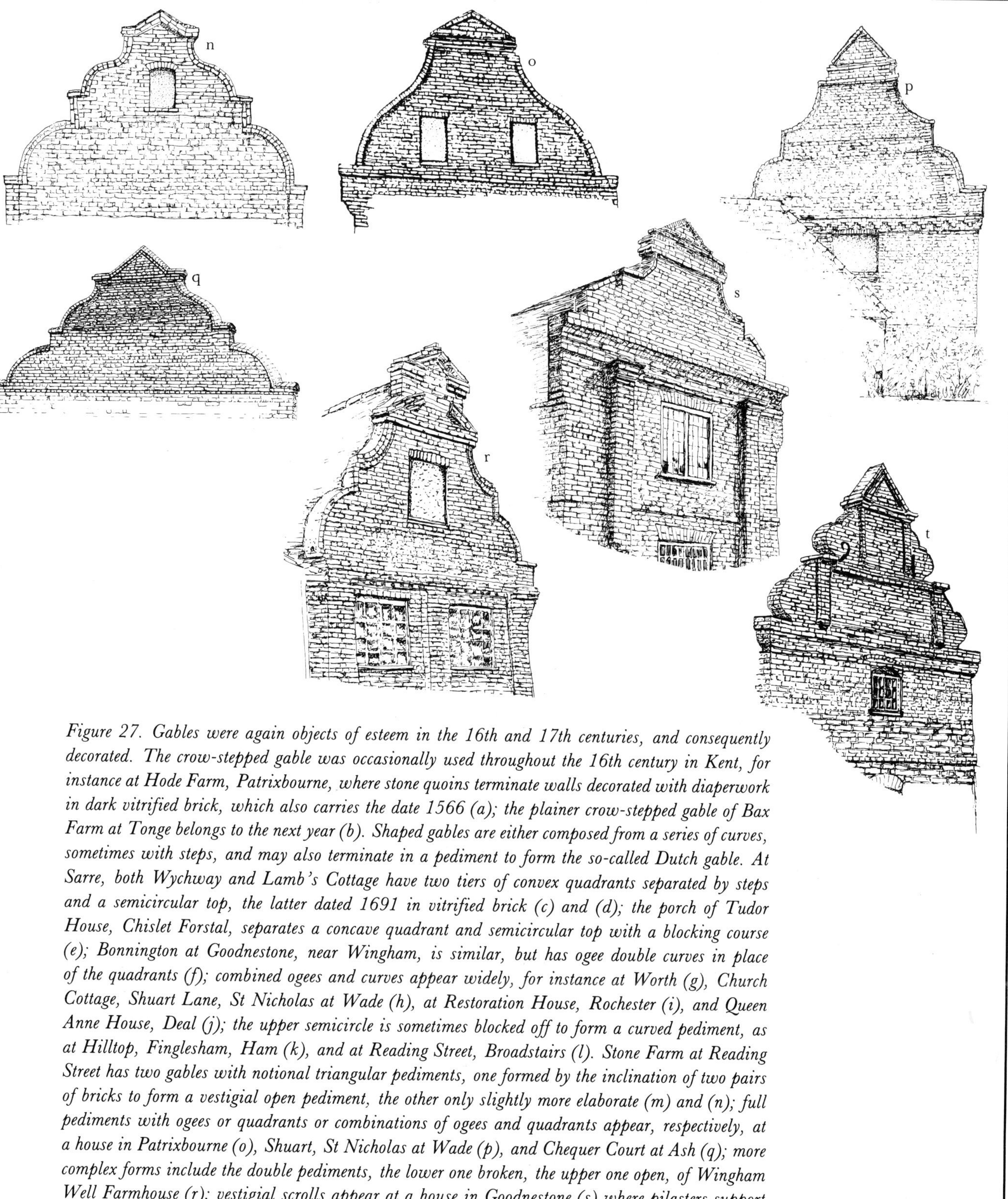

Figure 27. Gables were again objects of esteem in the 16th and 17th centuries, and consequently decorated. The crow-stepped gable was occasionally used throughout the 16th century in Kent, for instance at Hode Farm, Patrixbourne, where stone quoins terminate walls decorated with diaperwork in dark vitrified brick, which also carries the date 1566 (a); the plainer crow-stepped gable of Bax Farm at Tonge belongs to the next year (b). Shaped gables are either composed from a series of curves, sometimes with steps, and may also terminate in a pediment to form the so-called Dutch gable. At Sarre, both Wychway and Lamb's Cottage have two tiers of convex quadrants separated by steps and a semicircular top, the latter dated 1691 in vitrified brick (c) and (d); the porch of Tudor House, Chislet Forstal, separates a concave quadrant and semicircular top with a blocking course (e); Bonnington at Goodnestone, near Wingham, is similar, but has ogee double curves in place of the quadrants (f); combined ogees and curves appear widely, for instance at Worth (g), Church Cottage, Shuart Lane, St Nicholas at Wade (h), at Restoration House, Rochester (i), and Queen Anne House, Deal (j); the upper semicircle is sometimes blocked off to form a curved pediment, as at Hilltop, Finglesham, Ham (k), and at Reading Street, Broadstairs (l). Stone Farm at Reading Street has two gables with notional triangular pediments, one formed by the inclination of two pairs of bricks to form a vestigial open pediment, the other only slightly more elaborate (m) and (n); full pediments with ogees or quadrants or combinations of ogees and quadrants appear, respectively, at a house in Patrixbourne (o), Shuart, St Nicholas at Wade (p), and Chequer Court at Ash (q); more complex forms include the double pediments, the lower one broken, the upper one open, of Wingham Well Farmhouse (r); vestigial scrolls appear at a house in Goodnestone (s) where pilasters support a cornice below the gables; and there are far more pronounced scrolls in the halsgavel *of School Farm at Ash (t) of 1691.*

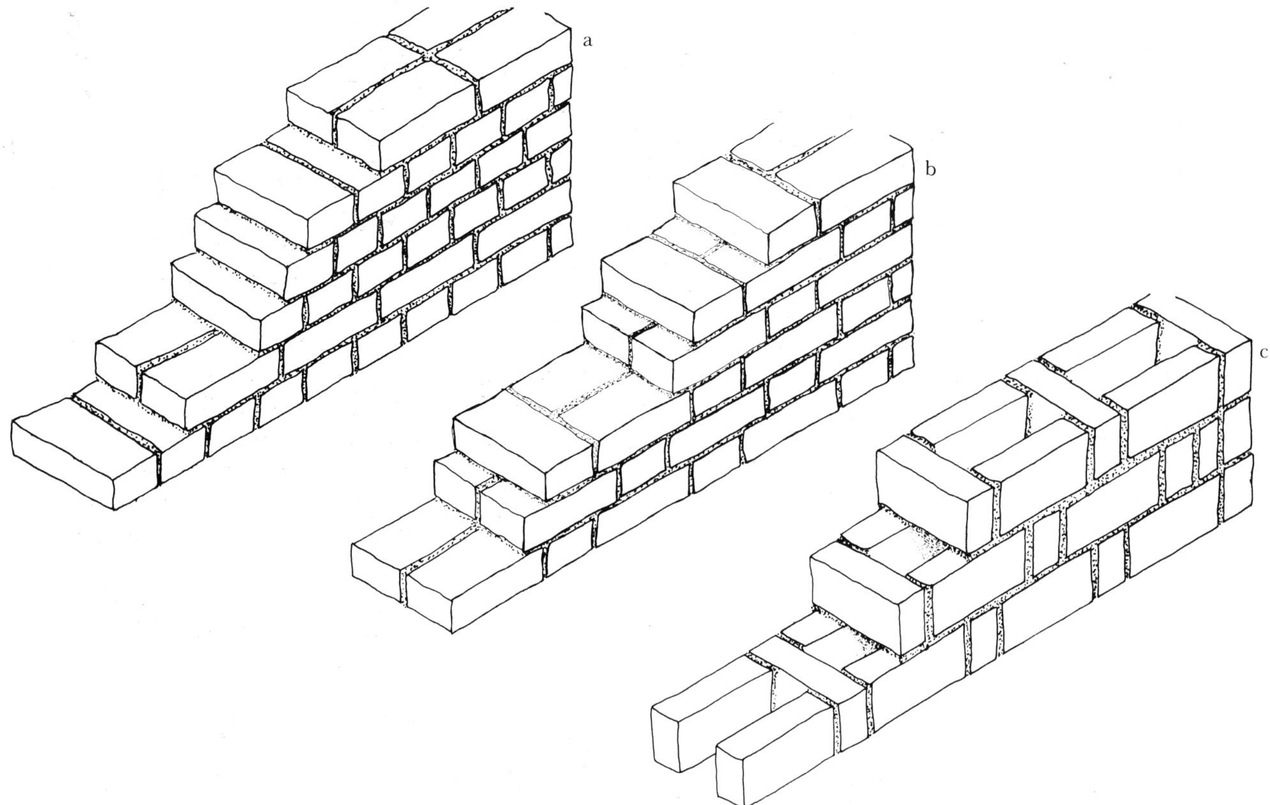

Figure 28. Brick bonds. English bond (a), showing courses (layers) of headers laid across the depth of the wall from front to back, and courses of stretchers laid along the length of the wall on the inner and outer faces, in this case with three courses of headers laid between single courses of stretchers. Flemish bond (b), showing stretchers and headers, alternating course by course, with a stretcher placed centrally over each header and vice versa. The rare rat-trap bond (c) in which bricks are laid on their sides, producing courses roughly half as high again as in ordinary brickwork, and laid in the manner of Flemish bond, thus producing a network of cavities within the wall (the rat-traps).

out well from the pinker or browner common bricks used for the rest of the façade, and was better able to survive weathering than the plastering which had been applied in the sixteenth and early seventeenth centuries in imitation of stone. No house took better advantage of the great variety of Kent's brick than Bradbourne at East Malling, where no less than four separate shades of brick were used about 1712-15 in a wonderfully ingenious application of colour applied to classical detailing (Colour Plate 44). This excellence made up for Kent's rather timid approach to the baroque style, so evident at Finchcocks, Goudhurst.

During the sixteenth century nearly all of Kent's best brickwork was laid in what is now called English bond (Figure 28). This comprises horizontal courses of bricks laid lengthwise along the wall as so-called stretchers, with further courses of bricks laid across the thickness of the wall as headers, leaving just their ends showing. In more ordinary buildings the bricks were laid randomly, headers intermingling with stretchers. English bond was still used as late as 1736 at Fordwich, although by then it had largely given way to Flemish bond, where headers and stretchers alternate regularly in each course. This came into use in England progressively after the 1630s, but Kent remained conservative, as in much else, particularly when compared with Norfolk. One of the first major uses of Flemish bond was at Groombridge Place as late

Figure 28A. Cobham Hall. Detail of brick diapering of soon after 1550 on the north face of the stair tower at the eastern end of the north-east range. Usually diapering took the form of a network of crossing diagonal lines; here the pattern of diagonally set interlocking crosses is the most sophisticated diaperwork in the county; the south face of the range, also unusually, has horizontal zigzags. (See Colour Plate 43.)

as about 1660. After the Restoration, Flemish bond was almost invariably used in Kent's greater houses, and with these brick established a superiority over stone as a status symbol, and added a local characteristic to what increasingly were national styles. A curiosity found in a row of nineteenth-century cottages at Cowden is rat-trap bond, in which the bricks are all laid on their sides, causing small cavities behind each stretcher — the rat-trap. A house south of the green at Ightham and another house at Newland Green, Egerton, are again built in this rare bond. Economy of brick rather than catching rodents was the objective, and maybe insulation too.

Tile and thatch

Tile was another material used in Roman times which, like brick, fell out of use with the collapse of Roman rule. From the earliest times, roofs had been covered with

Colour Plate 46. Belmont, Throwley, which Samuel Wyatt rebuilt with a mathematical tile facing about 1787-92 for Lord Harris, with characteristic domed corners.

thatch, but this is not prominent in Kent. The manufacture of clay tiles was revived well before the end of the Middle Ages, and rapidly displaced it. Thatch came from the reeds gathered on the coastal marshes as well as from straw, a by-product of arable farming. In each case the material was tightly bundled and bound in horizontal layers to laths. Starting at the eaves and working upwards to the ridge so that each layer overlapped the last, thatch produced a covering at once waterproof and warm.

Like clay tiles, thatch is best laid on a steeply pitched roof so that the rain will quickly run off, and this allowed an easy conversion from one material to the other. Thatch is unsatisfactory when faced with awkward angles. As, characteristically, Kent roofs were plain in the Middle Ages and generally had few projections, that was not a problem. Thatch used to be cheap too, but it has two major disadvantages: it needs to be replaced every generation or so, and it readily catches fire. It was rapidly replaced by tile, and, from the fifteenth century onward, became increasingly associated with poverty.

One or two early houses with thatched roofs nevertheless do survive: the primitive Dormer Cottage at Petham, perhaps of the thirteenth century, is as old an example as any (Colour Plate 45). Some thatched cottages still remain in villages close to the reedy coastal marshes and river estuaries, for instance at Worth, and at Preston overlooking the Little Stour, but, with so little poverty in Kent, there is correspondingly little thatch.

At the end of the eighteenth century thatch started a sporadic revival because of its

Colour Plate 47. A glowing façade of mathematical tile at 19-21 High Street, Tenterden, edged with timber quoining rather than angled corner tiles, and continued on the sides with ordinary hung tiles.

rustic charm. Such *cottages ornées* as the eponymous Thatched House at Wateringbury made a feature of it, and this also applied to toll houses like the one at Bridge (Colour Plate 18), and lodges, like the Lees Court Lodge at Selling.

Early in the fourteenth century, both the Benedictines and Cistercians were promoting the manufacture of tiles, for instance at Boxley and Wye (Clifton-Taylor 1983), and these soon found their way on to the roofs of monastic barns and yeomen's houses alike. With wooden pegs to hold them in place, they lasted far longer than the lifespan of thatch, unless they were caught in a tearing gale. Kent produced tiles of fine quality, just as it was to produce excellent bricks, and apart from a gentle convex curve from side to side, they were seldom decorated in any other way. Sometimes, tiles with a more pronounced curve were used to cover the central part of open halls, for instance at the demolished Durlock Grange, Minster-in-Thanet, where they allowed smoke to escape from inside through the small gaps which they bridged (Parkin 1962).

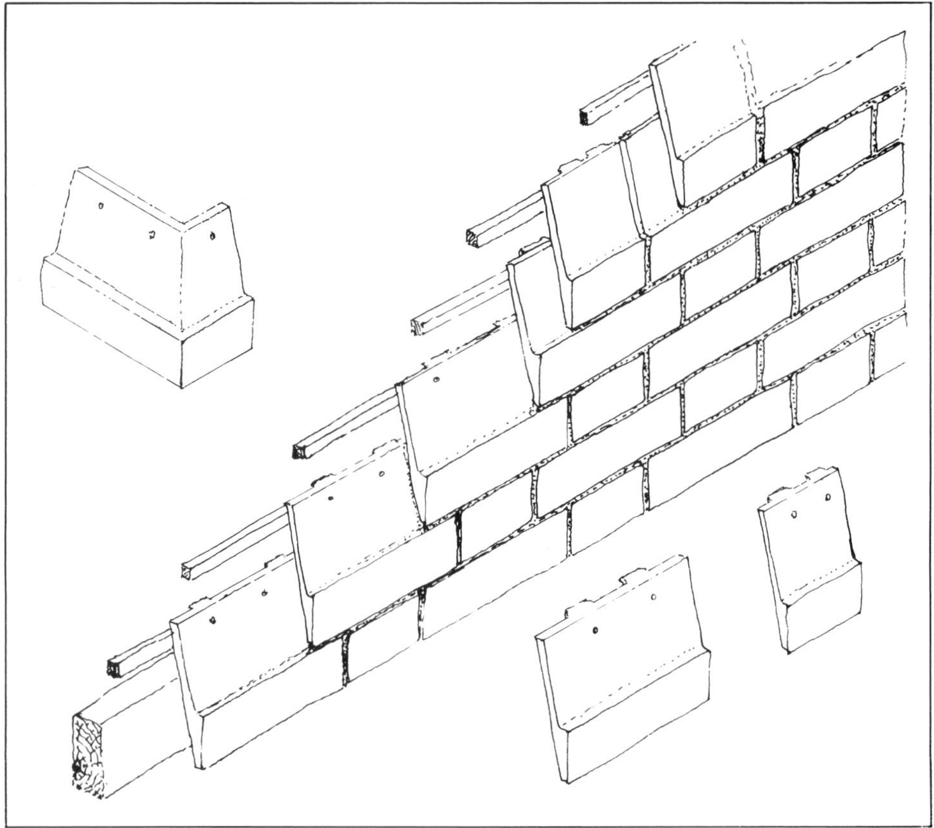

Figure 29. Mathematical tiling, showing alternating wide and narrow tiles laid on battens in emulation of Flemish bond, and (bottom right) a wide and narrow tile, and (top left) a corner tile.

Tiles had a further use beyond replacing thatch as a roof covering. Towards the end of the seventeenth century, just as timber-framing was dropping out of fashion in favour of brick, the practice of hanging tiles on the walls of framed buildings gave them a new, durable weather-tight and fire-proof skin, and, at the same time, the semblance of an up-to-date appearance which accorded with fashion. Ideas of fashion are different today, but a rippling tile-hung wall makes the best of matches with a mossy tiled roof, and this traditional appearance is one of Kent's most loved features (Colour Plate 13). From the archaeological point of view, there are almost too many medieval and sixteenth-century houses in Kent where tile-hanging covers the evidence which a visible timber frame would offer of their structure, age and arrangements.

A less usual deception came with the introduction of so-called mathematical tiles, which were shaped with a stepped flange to hide the overlap when hung on a wall (Arschavir 1956). If they are skilfully laid and mortared between their joints, mathematical tiles have all the appearance of bricks, and only framed walls which are not completely true quickly give the game away. Mathematical tiles come in as many colours as brick — red, orange, yellow, brown — and they remained in current building practice for a long period. Eventually, they were made to represent bricks laid as headers as well as stretchers, and were even angled so that they could neatly turn corners (Figure 29).

Their first documented use was in 1715 to cover the flint transept wall of Bekesbourne church, where the intention seems to have been to imitate brick. This intention remained their purpose well into the nineteenth century. Some surprisingly

Plate 45. The opulent tracery of the Great Hall at Penshurst Place, maybe the design of William de Ramsey III, and reproduced in the later staircase tower projecting to the left.

monumental houses employed this deception, notably Chevening Park, which the architect James Wyatt refaced in dun-grey mathematical tiles in 1786-96, and Belmont, Throwley, which his brother Samuel Wyatt rebuilt at exactly the same time using fashionably pale yellow mathematical tiles (Colour Plate 46).

Mathematical tiles were not cheap, and actually cost more than bricks. Their use is therefore probably due to the continuing skills of carpenters with soft wood in the eighteenth and nineteenth centuries; these encouraged the use of mathematical tile to satisfy the needs of fashion and to provide a durable, fire-proof skin. Their real province is less in grand mansions than in the more everyday houses of fashion-conscious towns. Canterbury has as many as 138 buildings faced with these tiles, and in Tenterden they came in all colours and continued to be used until well into the nineteenth century (Colour Plate 47). They allowed an old framed building to be fashionably reclad, and did so without projecting as far as a brick skin would do, especially where jettied upper storeys could cause a new brick front to curtail the width of narrow lanes by as much as 3ft. (1m) (T.P. Smith 1979, Exwood 1981).

Windows

Glass is another ancient product manufactured from raw material taken from the ground. Sand, which was abundant in Kent, and soda, which came from ash, were put in a furnace and melted together. The chartland of Kent was a good source of sand and established a glass-making industry on the back of it: this 'fine white sand for the glass-houses, esteemed the best in England for melting into flint-glass, and looking glass-plates', was exported in the eighteenth century to London from Maidstone, as Defoe recalled (Rogers 1971, 131). Glass was manufactured around Sevenoaks, notably on the Knole estate, and had found a ready market among yeoman houses by the end of the sixteenth century.

Before the end of the Middle Ages, only the windows of great houses were glazed, and their windows in general followed the forms of Gothic tracery established by great churches. The cusped tracery of the great hall of Penshurst Place could be to the design of William Ramsey III (Plate 45), who, John Harvey (1984, 242-5) says, may have provided a general design or given advice; as Edward III's Master Mason he was an

Colour Plate 48. Chessenden, Smarden, a Wealden hall-house, modernised by the insertion of a floor across the hall and the addition of a tall canted bay with windows to light the ground floor hall, the room in the new floor above, and also a garret in the gabled roof.

Colour Plate 50. Boughton Place, Boughton Malherbe. The mullioned and transomed arched windows of the left-hand side are part of Sir Edward Wotton's building of the 1520s, still in the medieval tradition; the right-hand side, which has classically proportioned cross-barred windows, was added in the 1550s.

Colour Plate 49. Norman Cottages, Benover, Yalding, glazed from end to end on both floors, and decorated with a full complement of brackets, moulded fascias, carved bargeboards and pendants and finials in the gables.

obvious man for Pulteney to approach. The tracery at the smaller Court Lodge at Mersham is much plainer, but again clearly belongs to the earlier thirteenth century (Colour Plate 59). The timber-framed houses of most yeomen had unglazed openings which were simply barred, but occasionally they were glazed and had tracery showing a similar attention to fashion (Figure 30). The cusped tracery of a blocked window of the former High Hall House at Larkfield, East Malling, is similar to the Decorated tracery of the later fourteenth century. The repetitive foiled heads of the windows of Duke's Place at West Peckham and Yardhurst at Great Chart are typical of the later Perpendicular style, as is Headcorn Manor's tracery which is said to date from after 1516 (Colour Plates 60 and 61).

Plainer windows in framed houses were unglazed and simply protected by diagonally set bars, which often exist in replaced form (Colour Plate 29). Grander windows, particularly those of the hall, might have thicker bars with hollowed concavities cut down the full length of their angles. In the later fifteenth century, these bars were grooved to take lead window frames or cames. A century later, instead of concave hollow mouldings, the corners were given recessed convex or ovolo mouldings instead. Where a service room needed ventilation but not light, the window was filled with horizontally slatted louvers, as can still be seen at Westhoy, Smarden.

The arrival of tolerably cheap glass at the end of the sixteenth century gave builders the occasion to show off its presence with deep windows, often cantilevered and bayed outwards at an angle to form oriels (Plate 28), or, when a hall was being modernised,

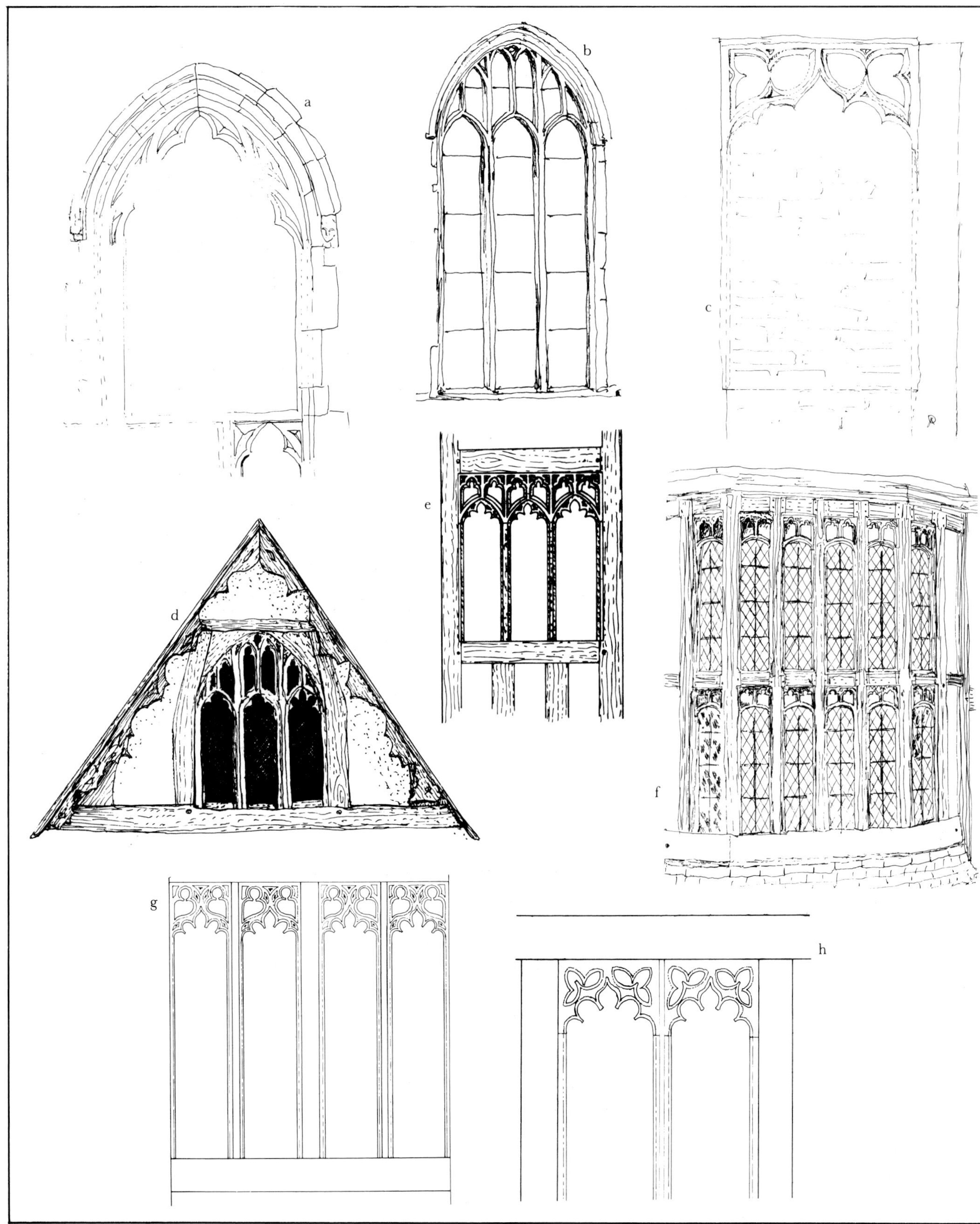
a
b
c
d
e
f
g
h

Figure 30. Window tracery generally followed the stylistic forms used in stone churches. Nurstead Court (a) consequently has cusped Decorated tracery executed in stone typical of the early 14th century; Starkey Castle Farm, Wouldham (b), has the repetitive forms of 15th century Perpendicular tracery, as restored early in the 19th century. The same forms could be carved in timber: High Hall House, Larkfield, East Malling (c), has cusped Decorated tracery, probably cut late in the 14th century. Perpendicular tracery appears in an elaborately cusped form at Goodnestone Court (near Faversham) (d), at Yardhurst, Great Chart (e), and Duke's Place, West Peckham (f), and, maybe after 1516, at Headcorn Manor, where curved daggers (mouchettes) *fill the gaps over the main lights in the hall windows (g) in place of the rather plainer trefoils used for the other windows (h); Corner Farm, Langley (i), meanwhile has restored Perpendicular tracery of the simplest sort, probably dating from the later 15th century. The windows of framed houses were far more usually simply barred, the timber bars being turned diagonally edge-on, or given a hollow chamfer, as at Cotterell Court, Petham (j). The arrival of relatively cheap glass at the end of the 16th century allowed windows of great size to be inserted into houses, often with sideways extensions in the form of clerestories, as at the gable end of Bassett's Farm, Cowden (k).*

to form tall bays with canted sides, which might rise all of two storeys and then on into a gabled garret (Colour Plate 48). The upper half of the main windows was often extended on each side by shallower windows which were called clerestories. These could join up and even stretch along the entire length of a façade, as they do at Norman Cottages, Yalding (Colour Plate 49), and in the great gabled fronts of dozens of town houses.

The larger windows were divided by timber mullions into a series of vertical lights, and deep windows were similarly divided by timber transoms into two or three levels. A few windows comprising multiple groups of lights had their centre light arched to form what has come to be known as an Ipswich window, after their appearance in Sparrow's House at Ipswich. A window of this type fills the upper storey of the frontispiece of Charlton House (since 1889 in Greenwich, London), which was built about 1607. Its origin may lie in an illiterate interpretation of the so-called Venetian or Serlian window illustrated in the first published books devoted to Italian architecture. Kent's first Ipswich windows may be at Valence House, Sutton Valence, which is dated 1598, but these look like additions. That would leave the ostentatious Ipswich window at 78 Bank Street, Maidstone, apparently of 1611, as the earliest example (Colour Plate 33).

Such large windows, replete with bands of clerestories, did not readily fit into a stone or brick mass-walled house, although many such houses have them. The classical taste of the seventeenth century required smaller and more precisely proportioned windows anyway. A single mullion dividing a single transom, sometimes executed in wood, sometimes in brick or stone, to form a cross, became a model of classical taste, already visible at Boughton Place, Boughton Malherbe, as early as 1553 (Colour Plate 50). Their heyday came a century later, as a few of these windows which survived a campaign of replacement at Groombridge Place still show. An opening casement with vertically set hinges like a door's completed the arrangements. By then, ostentation was no longer served by a display of vast areas of glass because it had become so cheap that anyone could afford it. Moreover, bright light quickly faded the coloured interiors, so smaller windows had some practical advantages.

Vertically sliding sash windows reached Kent from London around the start of the eighteenth century, and remained standard thereafter. They were fitted into the canted bays which had been used to modernise hall-houses in the seventeenth century, and these bays began to appear regularly on new framed houses as well. Glazed with pairs of sash windows, the bays added yet another local feature to the classical façades of the eighteenth and nineteenth centuries (Colour Plate 51). Regularly placed, one each side of a copybook doorcase, and rising even to the full height of a house, they did much to mitigate the typical flat front of the Georgian house and provided a panoramic view as well. They fitted well into the lightly framed houses of towns like Tenterden, and give a special seaside quality to coastal towns even though their use was ubiquitous in Kent.

The nineteenth century

By 1800 the Industrial Revolution was in full swing. The old traditional art of building faded before it. Many people regretted its passing, and, as though to halt the passage of time, a number of architects attempted to revive its appearance. This began with a self-conscious rusticity, at once romantic and faintly absurd. By the middle of the century serious-minded Gothic had displaced it. Only then did architects find inspiration in the singular appearance of Kent's rural houses. By the 1860s they had

Colour Plate 51. Symmetrical façades with canted bays are typical of Kent's lightly framed houses of the later 18th and 19th centuries, such as this one in High Street, Cranbrook.

invented the Old English style. It was essentially a superficial amalgam of the timber studding, tile-hanging and brickwork which gave most surviving yeomen's houses their appearance, but applied as clothing rather than as structure (Colour Plate 103). Appearances may not be everything, but the style suited the countryside. It suited the taste of new rich magnates who wanted large country establishments, and it suited the morally inclined who believed that a villagy appearance would benefit the inhabitants of the estates built through their benevolence (Colour Plate 106). Despite the different moral ideology promoted by the architects of Modernism, the Old English style, nowadays called neo-vernacular, still keeps its lead in public affection.

Chapter 3

HOUSES

Halls and chambers

Long before Kent's first surviving houses came to be built, the hall had become synonymous with the house at all but the lowest levels of society. In essence, the hall was simply a large room, open right up to the roof, with a hearth near the middle and a place for its occupants to sit with a degree of formality. It originated in Germany, where tribal chieftains made it the architectural centrepiece of their governmental and domestic buildings. Here they conferred with their thegns; here they dispensed justice; here they feasted and lived in proper style. The hall came to symbolise political power itself.

A hall with all these attributes is described in the Old English saga *Beowulf,* and just such a hall belonging to the seventh-century Bernician King Edwin has been excavated at Yeavering in Northumberland. The hall reached Kent with the new settlers, following the collapse of Romano-British rule, but there is only tangible evidence of these halls from the start of the thirteenth century.

By then, the hall had come to dominate ideas of domestic planning far below the level of rulers. The tortuous processes of manorial administration — the resolution of legal and financial problems, the computation of rents and fines and their quarterly payment, the everyday dealing with tenants and the settlement of disputes and transgressions of the manor's customary laws — all these needed a building in which the parties could be brought together, where judgements could be made and records kept. This was the manorial hall. Because it acted as a court, like the king's but on a small scale, it was appropriate to build it in emulation of the grandest domestic buildings in the land. This suited its lord's need for a residence, which, at the same time, would confer a degree of status on its owner.

The manorial hall became one of the most characteristic buildings of the countryside. This was even true of Kent, where manorial power was never strong and had faded well before many of its surviving manor houses came to be built. In recognition of their manorial pedigree rather than their power, these halls bear such names as 'Manor', 'Hall', 'Court' and 'Place'. Because of this prestige, several pretenders took these names as well, in the hope that the ignorant would associate them with ancient traditions.

By the thirteenth century, the hall had already descended much further in society. Free ceorls were probably building halls on a modest scale from the first. This is dimly perceptible before the Norman Conquest; again, by the thirteenth century, halls had reached the level of Kent's yeomen, and, while not universal, had become attainable objects of desire for many people.

A rather later process, although once again dimly perceptible long beforehand, was the inclusion of secondary rooms within the hall's overall fabric. A royal hall was a public place, and kings and queens retired to their bowers for privacy. Similarly, entertainment required service rooms and kitchens for the preparation of feasts. Both kinds of rooms began as separate structures, but, for the sake of convenience, they were eventually brought under the same roof.

Ultimately, the whole history of medieval domestic planning is concerned with how the hall descended from royalty to the peasantry, and how it embraced private rooms and service rooms within its walls. In Kent, with its well-spread wealth, this process is more readily visible than in any other English county.

Figure 31. The Archbishop's Palace, Canterbury. Conjectural perspective based on archaeological evidence: the entrance is in the projecting porch on the right, the body of the hall to its left with an undercroft and chamber built against the gable end; at the other end is a detached kitchen with a tall chimney-stack. (After Canterbury Archaeological Trust 1982-3.)

The king owned six castles in Kent at one time or another. These contained halls of various kinds, but the only surviving royal hall is in that part of Kent now within the boundaries of Greater London. The great hall at Eltham Palace shows how lavishly the Crown could build. Edward III's demolished hall at Gravesend was a smaller affair. Greater than all these was the aisled hall at the centre of the Archbishop's Palace at Canterbury (Figure 31). Appropriate to his status and wealth, this was second only to William Rufus's Westminster Hall. It was built by Archbishops Hubert Walter and Stephen Langton in about 1200-1220 as an imposing aisled building of eight bays, measuring 60 by 165ft. (18 by 50m), and had great buttressed stone walls with pairs of two-light lancet windows with foils over them rising into gables which broke the roof line, because this swept so low. Running along the full width of the hall beyond its high end was an undercroft with, above it, a bower — or chamber, to use the French rather than the Saxon term. A large projecting arched porch with another chamber over it provided the main entrance and close by it lay a detached kitchen (Canterbury Archaeological Trust 1982).

This great monument to the medieval archbishops was finally demolished in the 1650s, long after their power had declined, and is known today only through documentary and archaeological investigation. That is enough to indicate its great size and opulent decoration, and also the existence of the chamber into which the archbishop could retire, with the undercroft perhaps accommodating his personal servants.

This was no innovation, but the use of a chamber for private dining was a source of criticism. In characteristically moral tones, the fourteenth-century poet William Langland complained:

Now hath vche riche a reule . to eten bi hym-selue
In a pryue parloure . for pore mennes sake,
Or in a chambre with a chymneye . and leue the chief halle,
That was made for meles . men to eten inne...

(*Piers Ploughman,* Script B, c.1377-9, Book 10)

Colour Plate 52. Old Soar, Plaxtol. The brick wall to the left shows where the adjacent open hall has been replaced by an 18th century house; then comes the late 13th century solar built of ragstone over undercrofts, with Y-tracery in its gable end window, and, projecting on the right, the chapel wing with a similar window.

Colour Plate 53. Walmer Court, the ruined flint wall of the 12th century house framing a view of its successor built some seven centuries later.

Colour Plate 54. Old Rectory, Southfleet, a winged hall-house built of stone; the rearward section of the right-hand wing (with three dormers in its roof) may comprise an earlier chamber block.

Colour Plate 55. The mid-13th century undercroft of Nettlestead Place.

Colour Plate 56. Fairfield, Eastry. Here only the upper part of each end bay projects, the ground storey continuing the line of the front aisle wall.

Although the chamber block was attached to the hall, architecturally it was still distinct, and the kitchen and service rooms were completely detached. In many large establishments kitchens remained detached for the rest of the Middle Ages as a precaution against fire. On the other hand, both private chambers and service rooms were soon incorporated into the structure of halls at all levels of society. At lower levels, the hall fire served for cooking since there was no other kitchen at all.

By the late fourteenth century, the ancient combination of hall and bower in a single building had even entered the realm of poor smallholders, and, if Chaucer can be trusted, was common:

A poore widwe, somdel stape in age,
Was whylom dwelling in a narwe cotage,
Bisyde a grove, stonding in a dale...
Ful sooty was hir bour, and eek hir halle,
In which she eet ful many a sclendre meel.

(The Canterbury Tales c.1386-7; *The nonnes preestes tale)*

Dormer Cottage at Petham would fill this description well, right down to a bower, open to the roof, beside the hall (Colour Plate 45 and Figure 34).

For peasants, unlike archbishops and aristocrats, a hall was not necessarily of much consequence, but it still had to be high enough to allow the smoke from its open hearth to dissipate, and height became a source of status as well as a necessity. The traditional view that the hall was a filthy, smoky hole is quite wrong. Langland implied as much when he said that three things made a man flee his house, a wife with a wicked tongue, a leaky roof, and

... whan smoke and smolder . smyt in his eyen,
Til he be blere-nyed or blynde . and hors in the throte,
Cougheth and curseth . that Cryst gyf hem sorwe
That sholde brynge in better wode . or blowe it til it brende.

(Piers Ploughman, Script B, Book 17)

These complaints could be avoided. Dry wood burning slowly on a heap of hot embers in the centre of a hall will produce much heat and little smoke, even though the smoke of generations eventually made hall roofs as sooty as the poor widow's. Moreover, a slowly burning wood fire will not cause great draughts that dissipate the warmth.

The poor widow's bower, like the chambers of the yeomanry, was simply a bedroom and store, not a private dining-room, and that is how these rooms remained at least until the seventeenth century; the master and mistress of the household ate communally with their family and servants in their hall.

Many of their chambers eventually took the form of a solar, that is to say an upper room built over an undercroft or full ground-floor room. This was because money often limited space, particularly in towns, and the only private room had to be over the service rooms or shops. In the countryside it was normal to have a chamber at one end of the hall, and service rooms at the other, expressing a clear divide between communal work and private rest. Until the seventeenth century, yeomen normally slept in these downstairs chambers, even though their children and servants might sleep in an upper room.

Aisled halls

Many of Kent's earliest surviving halls followed the Archbishop's Palace in their aisled

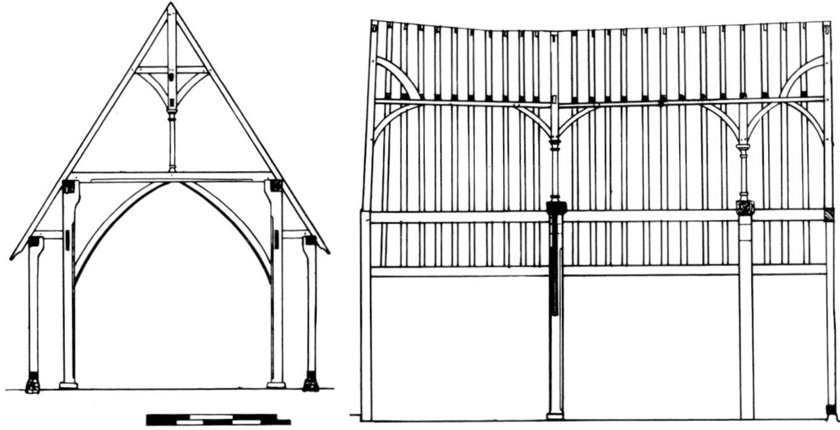

Figure 32. Ratling Court, Aylesham. Conjecturally restored transverse and longitudinal sections of timber frame of aisled hall, showing narrow aisles and full-height king-strut in centre of open hall, and crown-post over the less ornate frame dividing the two bays of the hall from the cross passage between the front and back entrances. (After Parkin 1976.)

Figure 33. Nurstead Court. Interior view, looking towards the entrance and the triple doorways into the service end, as recorded about 1837 before partial destruction. (After Parker 1853.)

form. The closest in both time and location is the hall of Cogan House in St Peter's Street, Canterbury (Figure 7); its width of 35ft. (11m) was far less than the palace's, but more than enough to confer status on its occupants, who appear to have been members of the Cokyn family and, later, other families who included a mayor of Canterbury among their number (Parkin 1970). The late thirteenth-century aisled hall of Christ Church's Eastry Court was similar, but has been greatly remodelled. The same is true of the aisled hall of Ratling Court at Aylesham (Figure 32); it spanned less than 23ft. (7m), and at 3ft. (1m) its aisles are so narrow that they already show an incipient desire to remove them for all but the sake of status. Its roof framing also shows a phase of development from Cogan House, so far as the latter's scissor-braces and braced collars had now given way to king-struts and braced collars (Parkin 1977).

If Ratling Court points towards the demise of aisles, the greatest of Kent's surviving aisled halls was yet to come. This is Nurstead Court, which the de Gravesends built about 1314 with typically low flint walls and an immense overall hipped roof, which was to become characteristic of Kent's hall-houses (Figures 10, 21 and 33). The eaves were broken by tall cusped windows which were carried up into small dormers to light the hall, an arrangement which may have been prompted by the great windows of the Archbishop's Palace. The overwhelming grandeur of the house was inside. Huge circular timber arcade-posts with foliated capitals divided the hall from its aisles. The central pair of posts were spanned by a pointed arch formed from two braces which rose up to a heavily cambered tie-beam. This supported a king-strut, which was joined by crown-plates to crown-posts mounted on the other two trusses. The crown-plates supported the collared rafters in what was to become the standard Kent fashion. Yet there was nothing standard about the quality of this monumental work, as the mutilated surviving half shows, even though the overall width of 28ft. (8.5m) with 5ft. (1.5m) for each aisle is far short of the palace's dimensions (Cherry 1989).

Well before the Black Death reached England, the profits from the high agricultural prices of the thirteenth century enabled a few yeomen to build substantial aisled halls

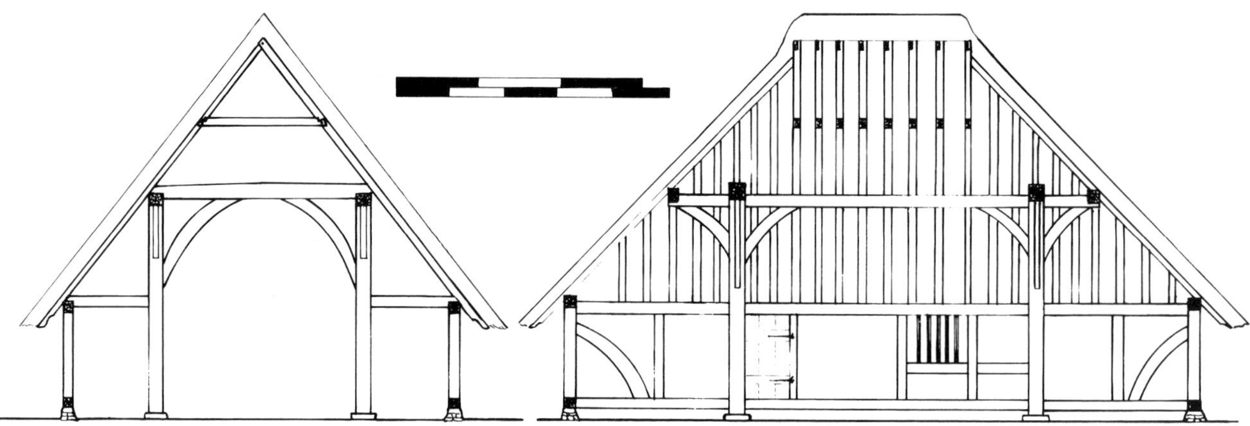

Figure 34. Dormer Cottage, Petham. Conjecturally restored transverse and longitudinal sections, showing primitive framing, comparatively wide aisles in relation to centre span, and cantilevered continuation of arcade-plates beyond central hall into end bays to accommodate service room (left) and chamber (right). (After Parkin 1981.)

too. In doing so, they had to engage the professional skills of the carpenter to provide a ready-made frame, and of other tradesmen to complete the house by filling in the panels with wattle and daub, by thatching or tiling the roof, flooring the upper rooms, and fitting doors and shutters. No longer was ordinary house-building a matter of self-help.

Attitudes therefore had to change. While this process was only complete by the sixteenth century, it had clearly started by the time Dormer Cottage at Petham was built. Its archaic framing suggests a building date in the thirteenth or early fourteenth century (Parkin 1981), although old-fashioned methods may have persisted to a later date for cheap and small houses like this. Its width of about 20ft. (6.5m), divided almost equally between the central span and the aisles, has at least a hint of Cogan House and other greater halls which must have been its model (Figure 34).

Plate 46. Nos. 3-4 West Street, New Romney, raised into a full upper storey and largely rebuilt, but still with its original arched entrance.

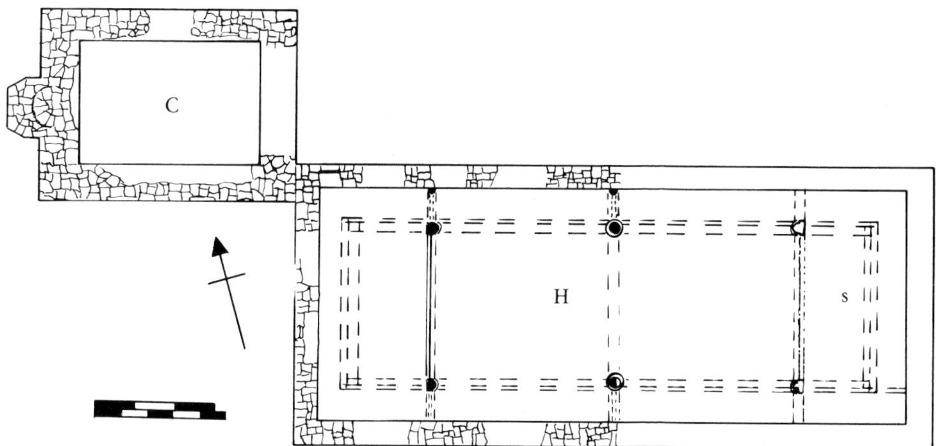

Figure 35. Nurstead Court. Plan, showing the surviving end to the left, together with the base of the attached chamber block, and the destroyed end on the right. (After Cherry 1989.)

A few other aisled halls in Kent are comparable with these early ones, for instance at Eastling Manor and at Newbury Farmhouse, Tonge. The remainder of Kent's aisled halls were built in the second half of the fourteenth century or later still, and belong to houses with a more developed plan as well. One notable exception is the small merchant's house built before the storm of 1287 at 3-4 West Street, New Romney (Plate 46 and Figure 61), which was aligned with the street and dispensed with the front aisle altogether, because this would have been too low to face directly on to the urban street (Parkin 1973).

Chambers and upper halls

For all their grandeur, these early aisled hall-houses had little more accommodation under their roofs than the open hall itself. The undercroft and solar adjoining the Archbishop's Palace were probably original features, but they were separately expressed architecturally. So was the stone block containing a chamber over a shop which was built in front of the aisled hall of Cogan House.

Rural halls were similarly extended step by step. Ratling Court may originally have comprised no more than its open hall, but the extensions added at each end have obscured the original form. On the other hand, Nurstead Court was clearly built with rooms flanking each end of the hall as an integral part of the design (Figure 35). So, by about 1314, the three-part arrangement of the majority of Kent's later hall-houses was already established, with a bay adjacent to the front and back doorways at the low end of the hall containing a pair of service rooms, and a balancing bay at the high end of the hall containing a further room. Always the front and back of the hall remained unobstructed by further building so that large windows would provide adequate light, even when wind and rain required them to be shuttered on one side.

One archaic feature nevertheless remained at Nurstead Court: neither of the end bays had upper floors, but remained open to the roof, just as they did at Dormer Cottage, Petham. Indeed, the bay at the high end of the hall was probably not a proper chamber either, but an antechamber leading to an earlier bower attached at this end of the house.

The remarkable thing about Dormer Cottage at Petham is that it seems to have followed the same arrangements very closely. The single bay between the arcade posts served as the open hall, while the cantilevered half bay at one end served as a flanking room. It is likely that a similar cantilevered bay at the other end had much the same function, the two end rooms serving respectively as a service room and a chamber, again without upper rooms beneath the roof.

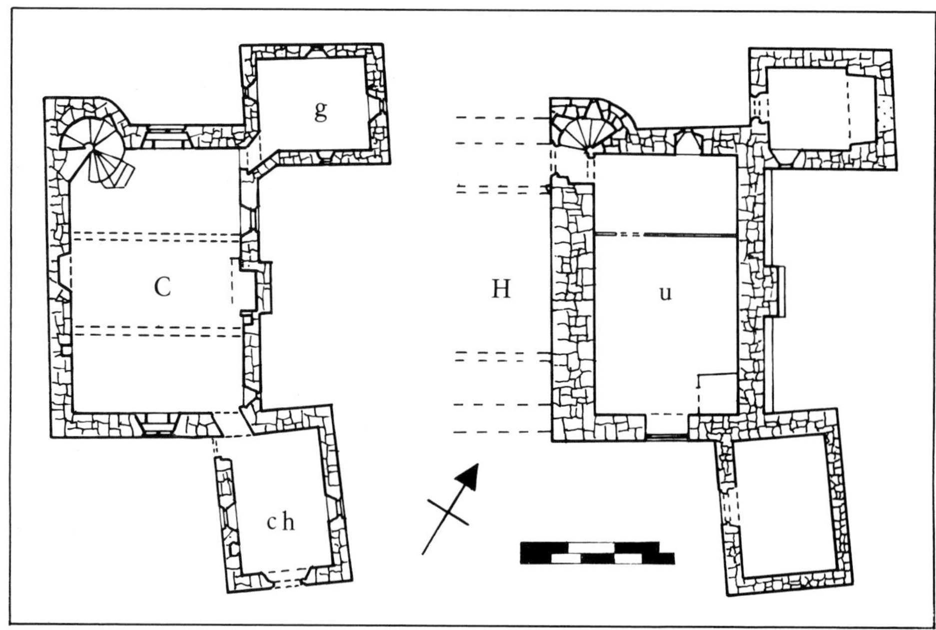

Figure 36. Old Soar, Plaxtol. Plans of ground storey (right), showing position of destroyed aisled hall, and upper storey (left), showing heated chamber with chapel (towards the bottom) and garderobe (towards the top). (After Wood 1947.)

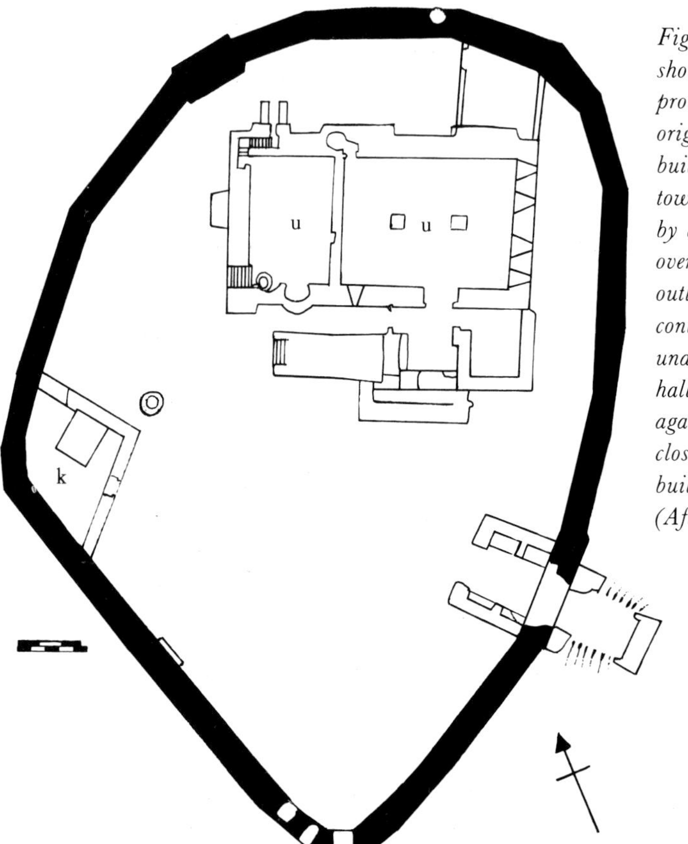

Figure 37. Eynsford Castle. Plan, showing curtain wall of motte (solid), probably built by or about 1100, originally with timber domestic buildings against it; these and a central tower were replaced after a few decades by a free-standing hall and solar built over undercrofts, shown here (in outline) together with a forebuilding containing a porch to the main undercroft and stairway to the upper hall; a detached kitchen was built against the curtain wall conveniently close to a well, and a later kitchen was built between the hall and the curtain. (After Rigold 1986.)

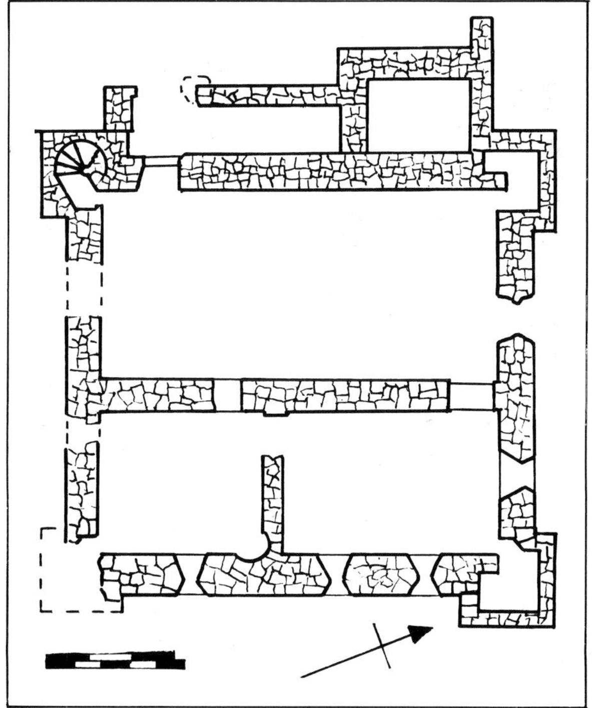

Figure 38. Walmer Court. Plan of ground storey, showing how a spine wall divides the building into two ranges to form an early double pile with the hall over the top half, a chamber over the part below. (After Rigold 1969b.)

The surviving stone chamber block of about 1280 at Old Soar, Plaxtol, shows how far Nurstead Court was behind the times in one respect (Figure 36). This block served an attached aisled hall, now demolished, in the manner of the Archbishop's Palace, with, again, two storeys comprising a lower room and solar chamber. Its amenities were augmented by the inclusion of a chapel and a garderobe in two small wings attached to its corners (Colour Plate 52).

Upper halls and chamber blocks

This stone chamber block is very similar to a whole group of domestic buildings, again built of stone, which are called upper halls. Upper halls embrace both rural and urban houses in which a room of evident status was built over a lower room. The earliest examples date from the twelfth century, and the type itself may be a Norman importation, though a few upper halls, such as King Harold's at Bosham, West Sussex, were built as part of royal palaces before the Conquest.

After the Conquest, halls were often built in the upper storeys of castle keeps such as the tallest of all at Rochester, and they were also built within castle walls as happened at Eynsford (Figure 37). Towards the end of the twelfth century a similar form of hall was appearing more widely, apparently by itself (Wood 1965, 16). By then several builders could afford masonry, and building up to two storeys visibly showed off its use. These storeyed houses are fairly uniform. The so-called upper hall and usually a secondary room stand over a similar pair below. The hall has no high or low end, and the entrance is sometimes at the top of an outside stair on a long wall with the hearth nearly opposite, and the adjacent room is reached by a doorway in a transverse wall. The lower rooms, a reflection of those above, seem to bear the same relationship to each other, but are less grand. They may have accommodated a servant or retainer (Faulkner 1958).

An alternative view is that these upper halls were no such thing, the grand upper room being no more than the principal chamber in a block designed to serve a separate hall, which in many cases has subsequently been demolished (Blair 1984). This may be true of the upper hall at Temple Manor, Strood, which was probably a lodging

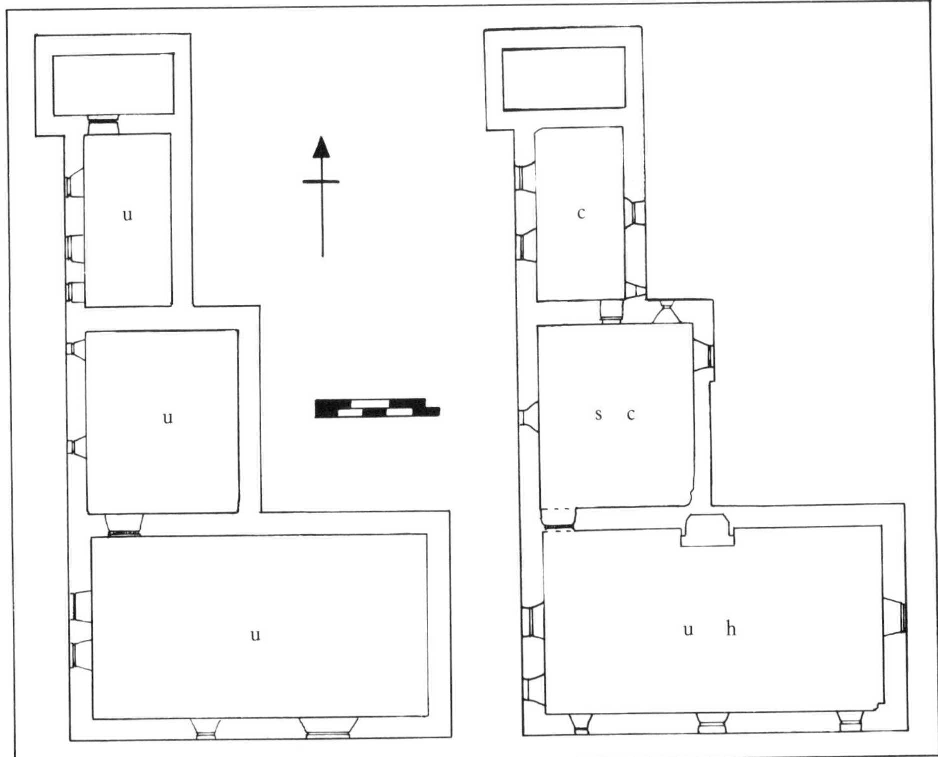

Figure 39. Luddesdown Court. Conjectural plans of medieval house; ground floor to left, with range of undercrofts and dovecot at rear; upper floor to right, with upper hall with fireplace, two chambers to its rear and upper part of dovecot. (After Peake 1920.)

Plate 47. Lake House, Eastwell, an upper hall built of flint in the late 13th century, its walls much patched and repaired in brick, its windows entirely renewed.

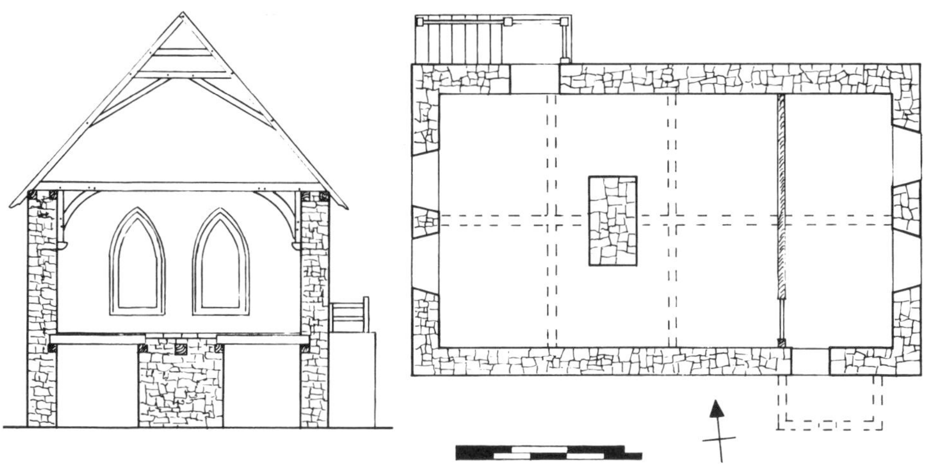

Figure 40. Lake House, Eastwell. Plan and section showing upper hall built over undercroft with pedestal to support hearth. (After Parkin 1968.)

Plate 48. The Master's House, Maidstone College, built at the end of the 14th century with an upper hall; only the cusped windows in the ground storey and the gable are original.

belonging to the Knights Templar (Rigold 1962). Possibly many other upper halls were again not really halls at all, that is with a semi-public function, but blocks of chambers.

There are several of these upper halls in rural Kent. Among the earliest is the ruined Walmer Court (Colour Plate 53), which was built early in the twelfth century to be partly fortified (Figure 38). A century later came the upper hall of Luddesdown Court (Figure 39), and possibly a century later still Lake House at Eastwell (Plate 47 and Figure 40). Finally, the Master's House at Maidstone College was built with an upper hall in 1396-8, and this was probably the grandest (Plate 48). In none of these cases is there any evidence of a normal open hall to which they were subservient.

Other similar buildings such as the chamber block of about 1300 at the Archbishop's

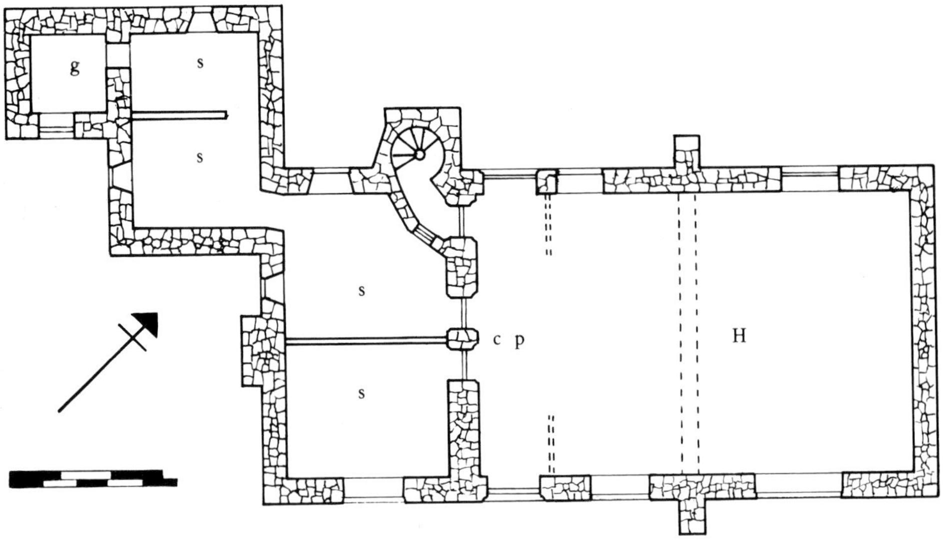

Figure 41. Starkey Castle Farm, Wouldham. Ground plan, showing (right to left) two-bay hall, front and back entrances with screens passage, doorways to newel staircase, and twin service rooms, beyond which are further service rooms and garderobe in projecting block; the demolished chamber block, not shown but for which there is archaeological evidence, lay to the right of the hall. (After Swain 1966.)

Palace at Charing (Plate 4) were definitely not upper halls and were clearly subservient to a hall but remained detached from it. Yet others were definitely attached to halls and were used as chamber blocks in the form of Old Soar. Starkey Castle Farm at Wouldham (Colour Plate 26) was built in the late fourteenth century with a wing serving as a service and solar chamber block, but recent archaeological investigation has shown that there was also a chamber block at the high end of the hall (Figure 41).

In many other cases the evidence has been obscured by later building works. The southern wing of Old Rectory, Southfleet, might have been built before the rest of the present house as a chamber block, even a detached one, for an adjacent hall which has now been replaced (Colour Plate 54). The front range of Old Rectory at Ickham was built about 1280 in the form of an upper hall, though on a small scale, but may again have been a chamber block serving a hall which has now been replaced. A similarly small thirteenth-century two-storeyed block survives at Hoad Farm, Acrise (Plate 49).

In towns, crowded circumstances produced similar buildings. Sometimes they were free-standing as at 3 Kings Yard behind Strand Street, Sandwich (Plate 50), and probably comprised an upper hall and private chamber built over a service room or shop. The Prebendal House at West Malling again took the form of an upper hall which may have had a semi-public use, although it could have served a priest's particular need for seclusion. Other blocks were definitely attached to an open hall placed at the rear, as happens at Cogan House (Figure 64). What remains there shows that the front range served the hall by providing service rooms or shops on the ground storey, and chambers above.

The one certain thing about these blocks, whether containing an upper hall or chambers alone, is that, like so much else in the medieval building world, one type of building could serve a wide number of uses, and only its fittings and decoration would differentiate that use.

Undercrofts

The ground storey of some of these buildings was in the form of an undercroft, partly sunken below ground level like a semi-basement. The Anglo-Saxons had introduced a type of building from the Continent characterised by a sunken floor, the so-called *Grubenhaus* or sunken-featured building, whose archaeological remains have been found in some numbers in Canterbury. Possibly developed from it are the larger, deeper sunken buildings which were apparently first built in the tenth and eleventh centuries.

Plate 49. The rear wing, with its surviving lancet window, of Hoad Farm, Acrise, which has the form of a 13th century upper hall.

Plate 50. No. 3 King's Yard, Sandwich, the ruins of an upper hall built over an undercroft in the usual urban way, with single and paired lancet windows.

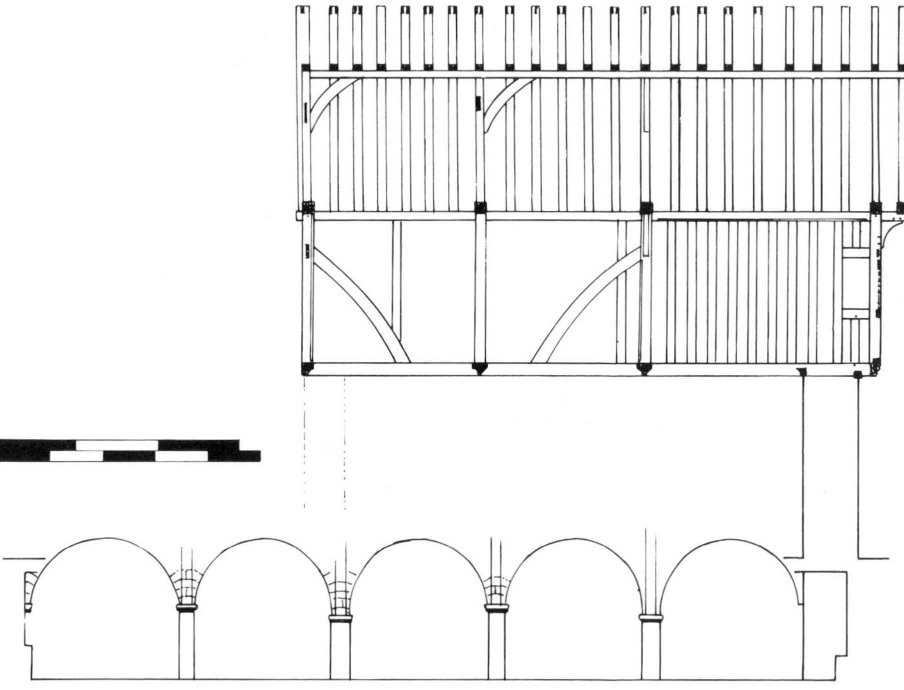

Figure 42. No. 21 High Street, Canterbury. Section, showing five bays of undercroft, the rebuilt ground storey in outline, jettied upper storey, and roof supported by crown-posts, plate and collars. (After Canterbury Archaeological Trust 1988.)

These could measure 50 by 20ft. (15 by 6m) and were dug up to 7ft. (2m) into the ground.

Substantial undercrofts appeared soon afterwards, and many of these still exist in Canterbury and Sandwich, where the earliest survivors date from the later twelfth century (Figure 42). They were all designed to carry buildings at a higher level than the street, and these were approached up a short flight of steps. Most undercrofts were

Figure 43. Nettlestead Place. Perspective of undercroft.

self-contained and had a separate entrance from the street with a wide doorway and a flight of steps leading down into them; only in special cases was there access from the buildings above. The individual use of these undercrofts varied. Their lack of direct communication with the buildings they carried shows that they were often in separate occupation and probably let out to tenants for all kinds of manufacturing and commercial use (Faulkner 1966).

Undercrofts were particularly suited to the storage of precious goods, where security from fire and theft were paramount. The undercroft at 36 High Street, Canterbury, is traditionally said to have been the city's mint, and other undercrofts could have suited its jewellers and silk merchants. Again, the cool, even temperature and shade of the interior were advantageous to the storage of wine, and many undercrofts served as taverns. By contrast, several individual undercrofts owe their origin to the wealth of the outcasts of the Middle Ages, the Jews. Jacob's House, on the site of the present County Hotel in High Street, had the form of an upper hall built over an undercroft, which probably served as a shop. Lambin Frese built his house in 1175-80 on an undercroft which still survives at the Poor Priests' Hospital in Stour Street.

The vaulted undercroft of Nettlestead Place is the only surviving part of an elaborate house of the mid-thirteenth century, all the rarer for being built on a rural manor. A central arcade of three round piers with moulded bases and capitals divides the undercroft into two four-bay aisles in the grandest way (Colour Plate 55 and Figure 43).

The demise of aisles, the winged plan and courtyards

Before the middle of the fourteenth century a number of open halls had been built with base-crucks to support their central trusses, thus removing the encumbrance of arcade-posts and full aisles, however narrow these had become. Hamden at Smarden is the grandest survivor (Figure 14), although a few other halls might have equalled it, notably Old Soar at Plaxtol and Rooting Manor at Pluckley.

The intrusion of arcade-posts was not the only disadvantage of aisled halls. Their roofs swept so low over the aisles that, when the end bays rose into upper storeys, the

Plate 51. Lower Newlands, Teynham, a hall-house of about 1385 with its service and chamber blocks contained in projecting wings.

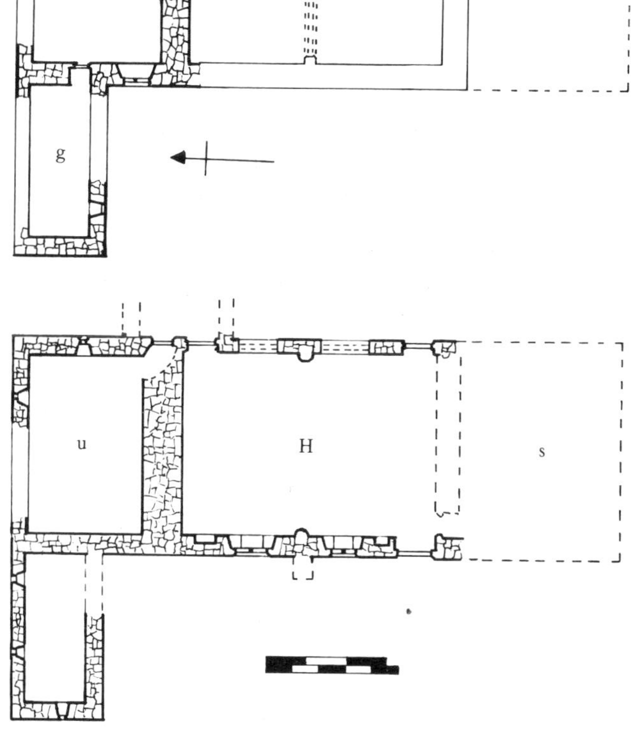

Figure 44. Battel Hall, Leeds. Plans of ground (lower) and upper storeys, showing arched, two-bay open hall, surviving chamber end, with vaulted undercroft, heated great chamber and garderobe, and (in outline) position of destroyed service end. (After Rigold 1969d.)

Figure 45. Ightham Mote. Aerial view, showing moated site, 14th century entrance in gatehouse tower, with contemporary hall on further side of courtyard, with, to its left, the timber-framed gables of Sir Richard Clement's apartments, and the framed upper storey of the north range which contains his new chapel.

roofs impinged on them, or they had to be treated as separate wings. At Hamden, the chamber was probably accommodated within a cantilevered continuation of the hall framing, and was also open to the roof. The storeyed service end, meanwhile, was accommodated in a separate, projecting wing, forming a T. Lower Newlands at Teynham (Plate 51) was built about 1385 with jettied, two-storeyed wings at each end of its aisled hall, to form an H, one wing containing a chamber, the other the services. Fairfield, Christ Church Priory's timber-framed secondary manor house at Eastry, was similarly built with an aisled hall and three-part plan (Colour Plate 56). It does not have projecting wings, and the low ground-floor end rooms rise only as high as the aisle walls. To overcome the problem of the low-sweeping roof, the jettied upper rooms in the end bays have separate roofs in the form of large hipped dormers that embraced the end of the main roof and reached its ridge. This unusual compromise was distinctly old fashioned by the end of the fourteenth century, since aisled halls had been superseded by a standard form of hall-house with higher walls all round. Even so, the rather later Hogbrook at Alkham, a farmhouse rather than a manor, had a low aisled form (Colour Plate 57), and so did a few other late medieval houses in Kent.

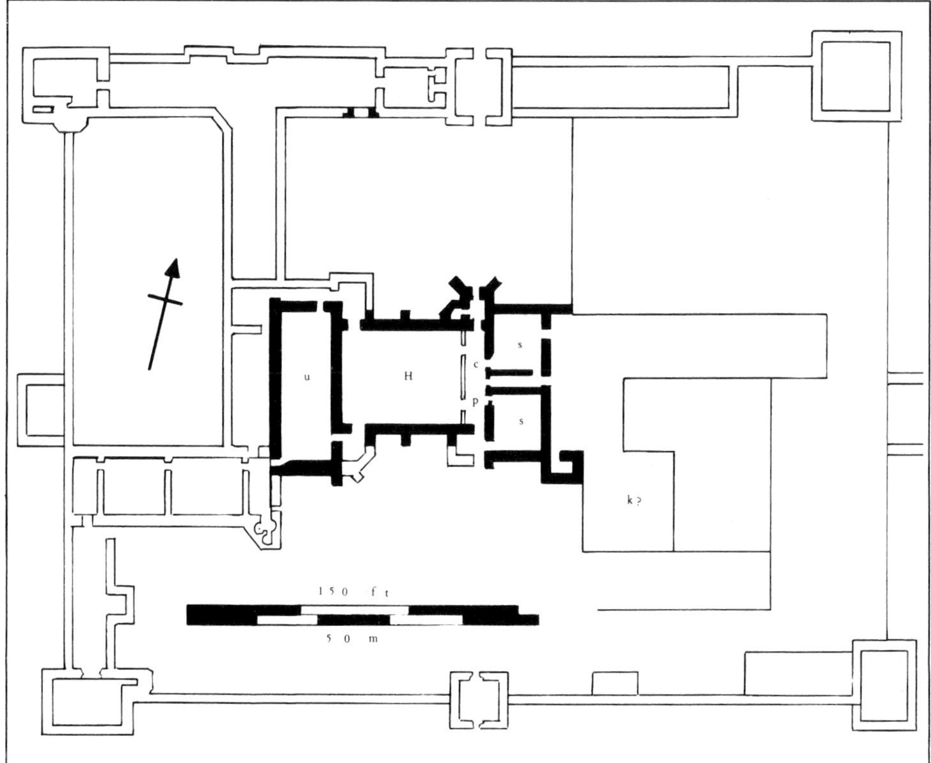

Figure 46. Penshurst Place. Conjectural plan as in c.1580, showing (in solid) Pulteney's great hall flanked by an undercroft and chamber on the left, and twin service rooms on the right, and (in outline) the Bedford building to the south-west of the hall, and other buildings forming an outer ward. (After Binney and Emery 1975.)

Several stone halls were similarly flanked by blocks of chambers and service rooms arranged as projecting wings. Among them are Old Rectory at Southfleet (Colour Plate 54), which was probably built by Thomas of Alkham, rector from 1323, and Battel Hall at Leeds (Figure 44), built shortly afterwards (Rigold 1969d). The mid-fourteenth-century hall of Ightham Mote had winged ends which were eventually extended to form a fully enclosed courtyard (Colour Plate 4 and Figure 45), and the greatest of all surviving halls which Sir John de Pulteney built on a princely scale at Penshurst Place in the 1340s was continued with wings at each end in a similar way through several building campaigns (Colour Plate 58 and Figure 46).

Before the fourteenth century was out, Sir John de Cobham had taken up the idea of the enclosed courtyard together with the imagery of the castle, which he had used in earnest at Cooling, for his toylike Hever Castle, licensed in 1384 (Colour Plate 23). Here, the buildings lining the four walls were framed to match the tiny scale. In the middle of the next century, the courtyard plan was comprehensively exploited for the largest of establishments when Archbishop Bourchier built a new palace at Knole, Sevenoaks (Colour Plate 7 and Figures 47 and 74). Between about 1456 and 1464, this rose around two courtyards, with the hall set between them; at one end a suite of private rooms ended in a chapel in one corner of the back court, and at the other end came the service rooms with a vast kitchen occupying a whole range of the court; meanwhile, the front court contains a fine gatehouse and flanking chambers. If this were not a great enough display of the archbishop's secular power, Archbishop Warham built a similarly vast palace fifty years later, only a stone's throw away at Otford.

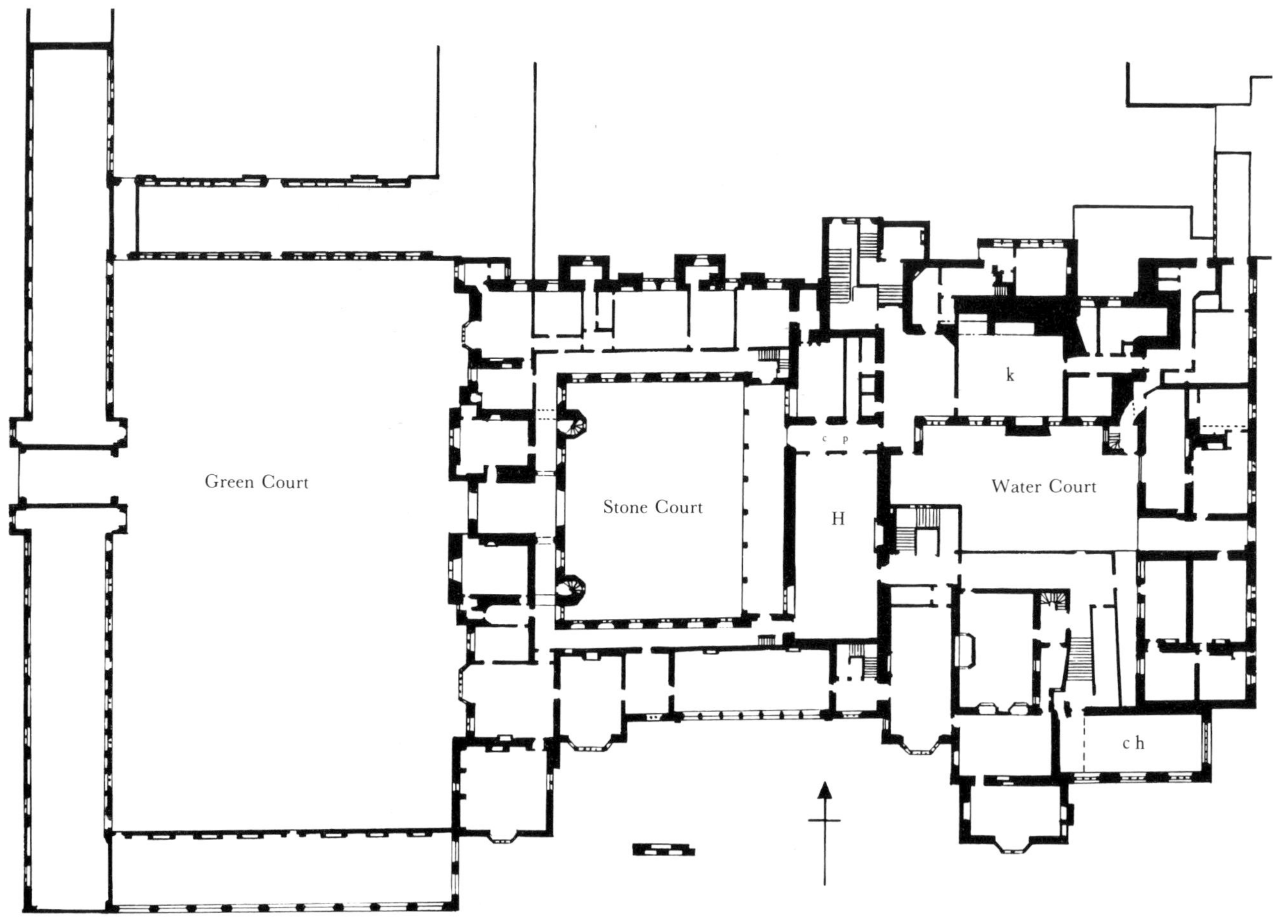

Figure 47. Knole, Sevenoaks. Plan of ground floor: on the west side is Sackville's Gatehouse opening into Green Court; opposite is Bourchier's tower and gatehouse opening into Stone Court, which has a corridor running around it; on its east side are the Great Hall, with service rooms and kitchen in the northern range flanking Water Court; the southerly range contains private apartments and a chapel. (After Faulkner 1970.)

Halls without aisles

The way the aisled hall descended from archbishop to yeoman might have continued to a greater extent if the development of box frames had not made arcade-posts redundant in spans of less than 20-23ft. (6-7m), and this embraced the width of most yeomen's houses. Similarly, the upper hall might have been developed further if stone had not been superseded by timber. As it turned out, the timber box frame dominated the planning of Kent's hall-houses during the later fourteenth century and all the fifteenth century, just when house building was at its height; and even a significant number of its stone hall-houses were built with a similar overall shape.

The earliest of these stone halls to be securely dated is Court Lodge at Great Chart (Plate 52), which was built in 1313 with a hall lacking aisles and a typical overall hipped roof carried on crown-posts, but the precise arrangement of its chambers and service rooms is unclear. Another Court Lodge, this one Christ Church Priory's manor house at Mersham, again has a tall overall hipped roof and lacks aisles (Colour Plate 59). Built of stone in the middle of the fourteenth century when the demesne was probably already let out to farm, it was only given a two-part plan with a high open hall and a storeyed bay at one end combining services and a solar. The main part of

Plate 52. Court Lodge, Great Chart, built in 1313 with an open hall and subsidiary rooms set under a typical overall roof supported by crown-posts and common rafters.

Hoad Farm at Acrise must have been built at much the same time, but with a full three-part plan and a storeyed bay at both ends.

By the middle of the fourteenth century, halls of any size were usually screened from the entrances front and back by short partitions known as speres. These formed a cross-passage at the low end of the hall of Hamden at Smarden, and similarly screened cross-passages became a standard feature of later hall-houses. The screen is commonly said to have prevented the draught from the front and rear doors from penetrating the hall. As most yeomen's halls lacked glazed windows, they must have been draughty anyway; but, even at higher levels of society, the main purpose of the screen seems to have been to block the view from the entrance doors for the sake of privacy, and to provide a clear-cut division between the formality of the hall and the workaday usage of the service rooms.

Status was what mattered, not convenience. Although the social implications may have been important for a manorial lord, as he had to keep up appearances, little divided master and servant in a yeoman's household; so, while the planning of his house implies the status conferred by this division, his daily life would have belied it. Everyone worked together for the common good and dined together at the high table.

Subsidiary rooms

The medieval three-part hall-house was complete in itself and could serve most domestic needs. Even so, many houses were soon surrounded by a number of accretions, impermanent additions which served all kinds of temporary uses. Most of these were swept away during the processes of modernisation and extension that assimilated many of their functions into the house itself. Among these subsidiary buildings none was so important as a free-standing kitchen.

It was a safety precaution. Animal fat could turn lazily glowing embers into a rush of flame and sparks that might ignite a soot-encrusted roof. Separate kitchens were favoured architectural features of grand establishments like the Archbishop's Palace. Often the only evidence for a kitchen is no more than a third service door at the low end of the hall, which once opened into a passage between the two service rooms. This led to an exterior door in the end wall, with the kitchen placed conveniently nearby. There was possibly a passage like this at Nurstead Court (Figure 33), and High Hall House at Larkfield, East Malling, still has three service doors (Figure 22).

Plate 53. Little Winkhurst, Chiddingstone, as re-erected at the Weald and Downland Open Air Museum, Singleton, West Sussex, showing its timber frame limewashed as a means of weatherproofing it, and the large vent beneath the gable to allow smoke to escape.

Plate 53A. Little Winkhurst, Chiddingstone, as re-erected to show the hearth set within the open bay of the building, and the storeyed second bay beyond it, open at ground level, with a chamber above.

Most kitchens were far from substantial, and the few survivors have been altered almost beyond recognition. The remaining part of Winkhurst Farm, formerly at Chiddingstone and now re-erected at the Weald and Downland Open Air Museum at Singleton, has only two bays, with the hall filling the open bay and extending into the other bay under the floor of a solar (Plates 53 and 53A) (Mason and Wood 1968). Its floor area of no more than 290sq. ft. (27sq. m) is hardly enough for a house, and it was possibly built as a large kitchen, before becoming part of the later farmhouse (R. Harris 1987). Around 1600, hearths enclosed by safe chimney-stacks and the added convenience of an internal kitchen were bringing external kitchens to an end, although some soldiered on converted to other uses.

Inventories of the sixteenth and seventeenth centuries list all kinds of other ancillary service rooms which were built as more or less temporary structures, either attached to the house or standing free. Brewhouses and bakehouses were synonymous with kitchens in all but their fittings. The square framed building behind 28 Wincheap, Canterbury, may have been a brewhouse, but was not originally built on this site and could have served a number of uses. Its two bays form a square, roughly 8ft 6in. (2.5m) each way at ground level; its upper floor is jettied on all four sides, and there is a typical crown-post roof.

Weaving sheds were widespread, particularly in the Weald: inventories sometimes include looms in a special room set aside for weaving. William Kidder kept looms and other weaving tackle in two of the ground-floor rooms of his hall-house at Cranbrook in 1576; one room, perhaps a chamber, was called the 'Olde Shoppe', while another, simply called the 'Shopp', may have been an outhouse (Melling 1965, 23-4). An upper chamber at The Cloth Hall, Smarden, was probably used for weaving, and the evidence of a 'taking-in' door here and in the garret, together with a hoist, suggest that bales of wool and cloth were stored there too.

Another impermanent room was seldom mentioned for decency's sake. Privies, sometimes known by their French euphemism as garderobes, are often found in stone

Plate 54. The privy at Old Soar, Plaxtol, with an outsize vent serving what originally must have been a long, public row of seats (rather than the more usual chutes which served individual seats) set in the upper chamber and lit by the cross-shaped slit window.

Plate 55. A corner of the chamber end of Noah's Ark, East Sutton, showing empty mortises in the framing, which may have carried a projecting privy, the way into which has been blocked by the closely set studs.

buildings, for instance Old Soar at Plaxtol (Plate 54 and Figure 36), but seldom in timber ones. External privies were built everywhere as flimsy structures with a seat placed over a pit, but medieval ones do not survive. Occasionally a small garderobe was jettied out from a chamber to drain into a cess-pit or a stream (Plate 55). Bayleaf has evidence for this, and a hypothetical reconstruction was included when the house was re-erected at The Weald and Downland Open Air Museum. Attached privies or closets were probably more typical of towns which lacked space for separate, outside privies. In the sixteenth century chamber pots and closed stools came into fashion, and with them came internal closets, often little more than cupboards, where they could be kept and used in privacy. Meanwhile, outside privies remained standard in the countryside until the twentieth century.

Yeoman halls

About a generation after the Black Death, the more affluent of Kent's yeomen started to build on as magnificent a scale as the manorial lord had been building beforehand. Often their houses had a hall with solar and services combined in an end bay, but these houses were usually extended to have a full, storeyed chamber bay at the other end of the hall as well. Not quite so many houses were built with this three-part form from

Plate 56. Old Kent Cottage, Newington, the smallest sort of hall-house and, consequently, an unlikely survivor; the left-hand, chamber end has a jettied upper storey; the right-hand, service end has been rebuilt.

the start, but always the aim seems to have been to have four or five rooms as well as a hall. Poorer yeomen sometimes built similar houses, but on the smallest scale. Old Kent Cottage at Newington (Plate 56) and 91 High Street, Tenterden, are both three-part hall-houses which are half the normal size. Palm Tree Farm at Upper Hardres was another (Parkin 1966), but its small size counted against it. Unlike their larger brethren, many of these small hall-houses were demolished because a later age could not adapt them conveniently, so they are not common.

Most yeomen preferred to build in stages rather than on this small scale. Crofton Farm, Orpington (now 161 Crofton Lane, Bromley, Greater London), is an extreme case (Figure 48). It was built as a simple open hall of two bays, box-framed in the Kent manner. To this were added, first, a storeyed service and solar bay and, later, a chamber bay with a jettied upper room. Filborough Farm at Chalk was first built as a hall with combined services and solar, perhaps during the time of John Martyn 'of Fylbarowth' in the 1480s, and to these a jettied chamber range was added in the form of a cross-wing (Arnold 1895). The characteristic medieval three-part form, with an open hall at the centre, was always in mind but not always achieved.

By the fifteenth century, Kent led the country in the great number of its fine new yeoman houses. However grandly this trend had been established in the second quarter of the fourteenth century with halls like Hamden at Smarden, the succeeding generations built so much after 1370, particularly in the second half of the fifteenth century, that they transformed the landscape of the whole county.

It is impossible to be specific about numbers, but in the century and a half between about 1370 and 1520 the yeomen of Kent built so many large hall houses that 3,000 of them may be standing today, and probably more. Possibly these survivors represent somewhere between a half and a quarter of the medieval houses originally built there, implying that between 6,000 and 15,000 hall-houses were built in Kent. Each one would have accommodated between five and seven people, so, at a conservative estimate, somewhere between a third and three-quarters of Kent's late medieval population of around 100,000 were living in one of these fine new houses.

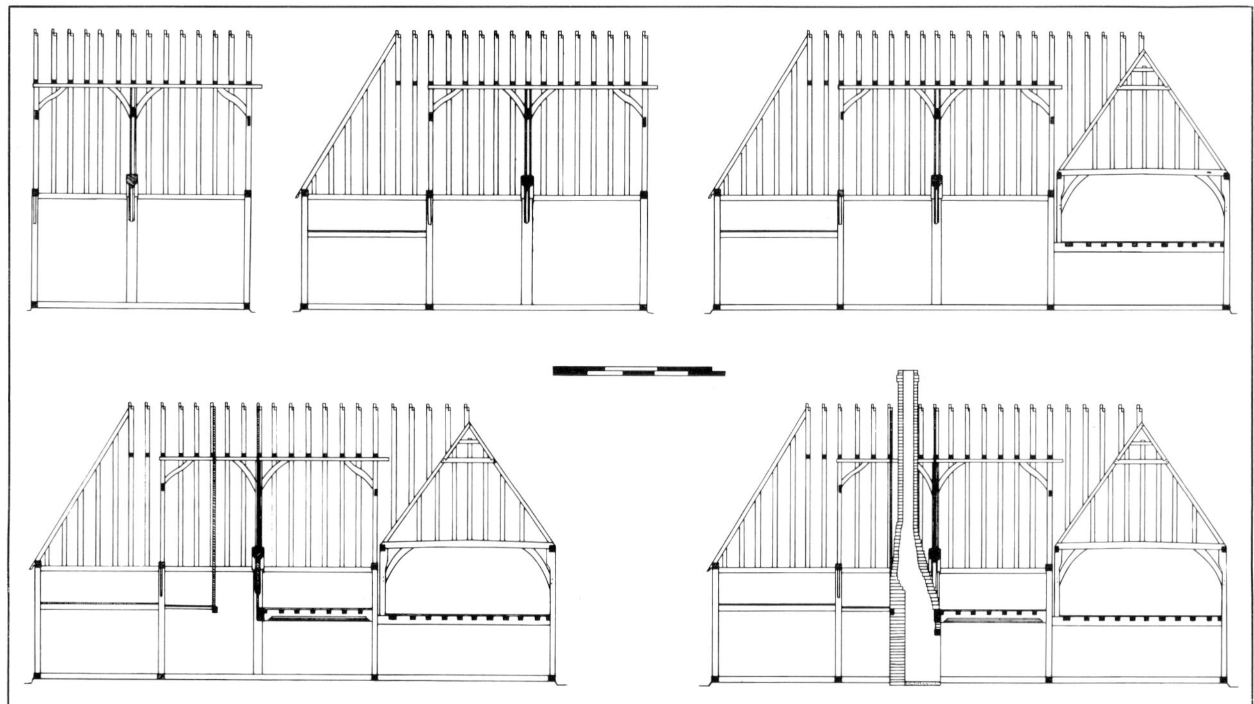

Figure 48. Crofton Farm, Orpington (now Bromley, Greater London). Sections showing five phases of construction and adaptation (from left to right, top to bottom): first there was a two-bay hall with a moulded central tie-beam and octagonal crown-post for decoration (possibly with ancillary buildings to serve for services and solar); secondly, a pair of service rooms with a chamber over were added to the left of the hall; thirdly, a large, jettied chamber block was added at the high end of the hall; modernisation began when the hall was partly floored over with a heavily moulded beam to support the joists and, perhaps a short while later, the cross-passage was also floored over, thus forming a smoke bay; later still, a chimney-stack was built into the smoke bay, and the hearth-beam was carved with the date 1671 (later still, the external framing was largely replaced by brick). (After Quiney 1990, 81.)

Though imprecise, these figures reflect the proverbial wealth of Kent's yeomanry at the end of the Middle Ages, a fact which so impressed Celia Fiennes two centuries later. Evidently, most people had satisfied their need for good, substantial houses a long time before she travelled through the county and recorded how old the houses looked. Each of the four hundred or so ancient parishes in the county may once have boasted anything from ten to thirty hall-houses. East Sutton still has a dozen, and scores of other parishes such as Benenden, Chilham, Pluckley and Smarden contain a handful of large, easily recognisable hall-houses, not to mention smaller ones, and ones so altered as to escape immediate notice.

If the number of these houses is remarkable, so is their size. The larger ones measure about 20 by 50ft. (6 by 15m) and, including the upper floors at each end, have a total floor area of 1,100 to 1,400sq. ft. (100 to 130sq.m); even floor areas of about 2,200sq.ft. (200sq.m) are not beyond the largest of these yeoman houses. Many contemporary manor houses were no larger, and today's average three-bedroomed house with its 715 to 770sq.ft. (65 to 70sq.m) of floor space packs in a slightly smaller family much more tightly.

While wealth was a prerequisite for these hall-houses, inordinate wealth was not, nor could be. Seventy-five acres (thirty hectares) divided into little fields for pasture and arable was more than enough to produce an adequate income to make one of these

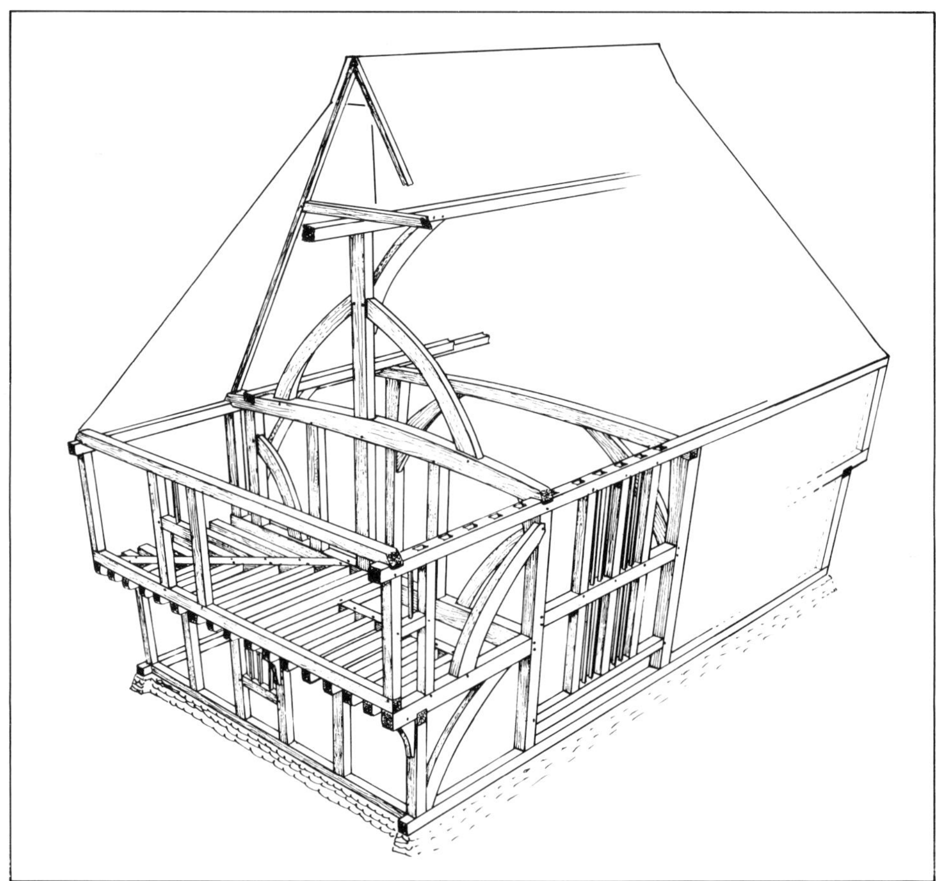

Figure 49. Burstead Manor, Pett Bottom, Bishopsbourne. Perspective of framing of storeyed bay at high end of hall, showing jetty projecting beyond end of house; there is also a jetty along the further elevation, thus requiring a diagonal (dragon) beam to support the ends of the joists at the corner. In this case, the hall is set back along the further elevation behind the line of the projecting jetty in the form of a Wealden house, and has a correspondingly set-back wall-plate. (After Canterbury Archaeological Trust 1988.)

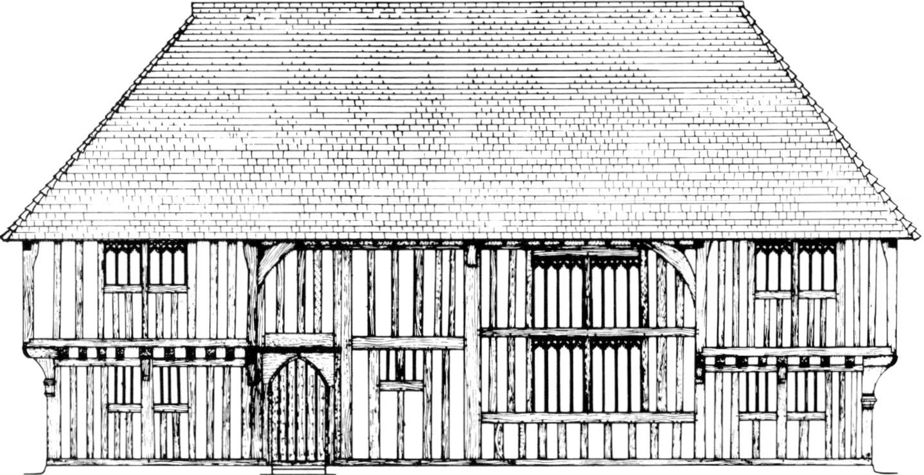

Figure 50. Wealden house. Front elevation of a Wealden house with side jetties as well as front jetties, based on Yardhurst, Great Chart. (After Rigold 1969g.)

Plate 57. Pattenden, Goudhurst, showing the side jetties as well as the front jetties, which are themselves echoed by two more jetties (underbuilt in brick) at the rear of the house.

houses affordable, and had the further advantages of attracting only nominal manorial dues and of being small enough to be worked by the household without hired labour (Rigold 1969b).

Jetties and the Wealden hall

The majority of these large hall-houses have jetties. Jetties have practical advantages and were an obvious sign of status. About a fifth of the hall-houses included in the Gazetteer follow the example of Lower Newlands at Teynham and have jettied cross-wings. A similar proportion have a jetty along the end, usually the service end, extending the house sideways, and occasionally have jetties along both ends, as Dowle Cottage at Pluckley does (Colour Plate 19).

A more distinctive group of hall-houses have both ends jettied, but along the front where the jetties can be most easily seen, thus accentuating the open hall between the jetties. The form of these hall-houses is so distinctive, and there are so many of them — nearly a half of the hall-houses included in the Gazetteer — that they have come to be known as 'Wealden' houses. Once they were called 'Yeoman' halls, as though only yeomen built them and nothing else. The current term is better, although these houses are found all over Kent, not just in the Weald itself.

Many Wealden hall-houses are jettied along one end as well (Figure 49), and occasionally at both ends like Chessenden in the centre of Smarden (Colour Plate 48), and Yardhurst at Great Chart (Rigold 1969g) (Figure 50). Some of the biggest Wealdens have more jetties at the back, so that apart from the hall in the centre, they are jettied all round. Pattenden at Goudhurst, probably built about 1470 by the Pattenden family, is one of these (Cowper 1911) (Plate 57 and Figure 51), and even more spectacular is Headcorn Manor, said to have been built after 1516 as a parsonage house (Colour Plates 60 and 61).

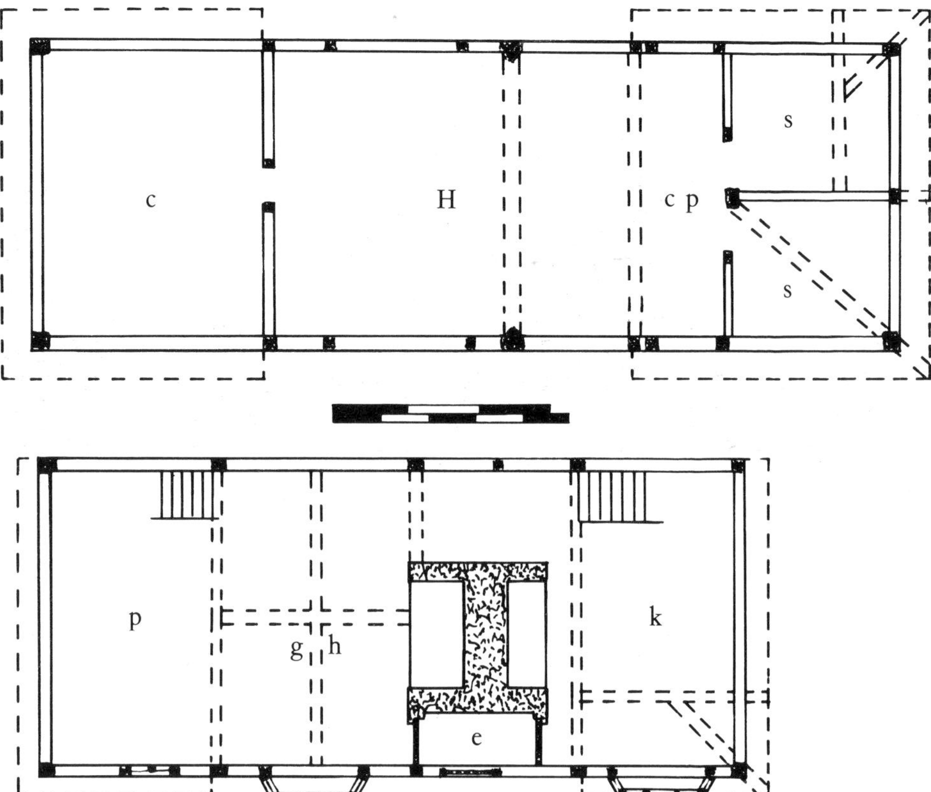

Figure 51. Plans of two Wealdens. Pattenden, Goudhurst (above), has jetties (shown dashed) at both ends and at the rear as well, causing the hall to be recessed back and front. Chessenden, Smarden (below), has extra jetties at the two ends only; the house is shown here after modernisation with oriel windows, an inserted chimney-stack and floored-over hall; the lower chamber would now be called a parlour, and the service room has become a kitchen. (After Cowper 1911.)

The principal effect of the front jetties is to leave the hall recessed between them, and, because the characteristic overall hipped roof extends forward to cover the jettied ends, the hall is recessed beneath the eaves as well. This produces a remarkably successful elevation which differentiates the hall from its flanking rooms, while the overall roof integrates them together. The elevation is well balanced, the jetties and the hips of the roof at each end giving a strong feeling of symmetry, the more unusual since symmetry was an architectural ideal only realised in England in a few castles and not at all in far grander houses until the sixteenth century.

About one hundred and fifty Wealdens are included in the Gazetteer, and at least one hundred more had already been identified twenty years ago (Rigold 1973). A close scrutiny of Kent's numerous altered medieval houses would substantially increase this number: many Wealdens are obscured by an inserted floor in the hall, filling the characteristic recess; and many more are totally hidden by brick underbuilding and tile-hanging, like Divers Farm at East Sutton and Furnace Farm at Lamberhurst. Because of their great size and, even more, the full two-storeyed height of their halls, they were easily converted by the insertion of upper floors right up to garret level, so many of them survive.

Although Wealdens are widely scattered across south-east England, their densest concentration is in the vale south-east of Maidstone, and this, combined with the variety as well as the number of early examples, suggests that they may have originated there (Rigold 1963). The numerous small, productive agricultural freeholdings on which they were built and the good market for local produce provided the wealth to make their numbers possible, but origin is another matter. The Wealden is the rational product of combining the frontal jetties of the storeyed ends with an overall roof, and simultaneously raising the hall to match. The result is a house of remarkable architectural status: it must be the product of conscious design rather than haphazard development.

Plate 58. Chart Hall Farmhouse, Chart Sutton, now recognised by the Royal Commission for Historical Monuments (England) as the oldest Wealden hall-house yet discovered and dated to about 1379; it lacks a balancing chamber end.

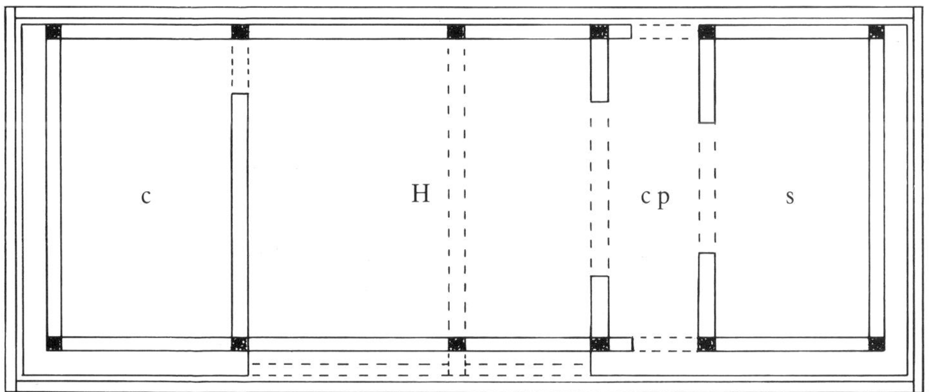

Figure 52. Brishing Court, Boughton Monchelsea. Block plan, showing projecting front and end jetties at the chamber and service ends of the hall, and also the further all-round projection of the overhanging eaves. (After Swain 1968.)

The oldest surviving Wealdens belong to the later fourteenth century. In several of these the end bay lies under the continuous roof, but it is tied longitudinally to the rest of the house as though part of a cross-wing, rather than transversely, which would be normal. This suggests that the design originated from the cross-winged house by a simple process of suppressing the wings at ground level, expressing them in the jetties and then covering them with Kent's characteristic overall hipped roof. At the same time the hall had to be raised so that its eaves were the same height as the eaves of the storeyed ends and recessed by the extent of their jetties.

The recessed hall and jettied service wing of Chart Hall (formerly Chart Bottom) Farmhouse at Chart Sutton were built with the characteristic Wealden pattern from timber felled in 1379/80 (Howard *et al.* 1991) (Plate 58). Several other Wealdens have been tentatively dated to the last quarter of the fourteenth century, for instance Wardes at Otham, and the fully developed Brishing Court at Boughton Monchelsea, whose lavish frame includes jetties at both ends as well as the front, and eaves bracketed out all round (Swain 1968) (Figure 52). No Wealdens have yet been ascribed

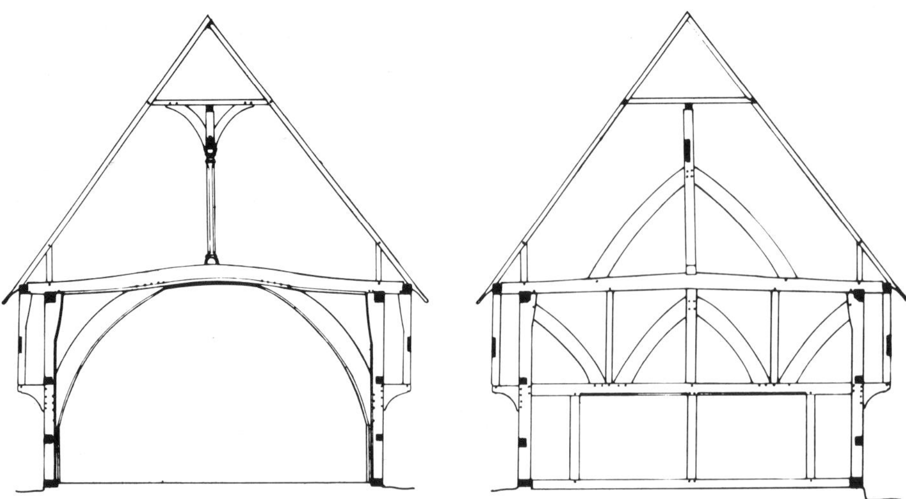

Figure 53. Vane Court, Biddenden. Sections through centre and end of hall, conjecturally restored as built c.1424, showing how the tie-beam extends to both front and back to be supported at its extremities by bracketed posts, maybe demonstrating vestiges of the Wealden's origin in the form of the aisled hall; Boyke Manor at Elham has a similarly bracketed post supporting the overhanging eaves and the projecting tie-beam spanning the centre of the hall. (After RCHM.)

to before 1370. Aisled halls were then on the wane, but there are echoes of the narrowest aisles in the Wealden design in the conjunction of the main-posts framing the hall and the corner-posts rising above the jetties, as though the hall had simply been shorn of its aisles, leaving it slightly recessed beneath the overhanging roof. The unusual way in which the tie-beams of the central truss in the hall of Vane Court at Biddenden extend beyond the main-posts to be supported on external free-standing posts rising from brackets at first-floor level may be another echo of the old forms of aisling, although this house was built after 1417 (Howard *et al.* 1990) (Figure 53).

Stuart Rigold (1963) wondered whether the recessed hall was an import from the Pays d'Auge of Normandy, but timber-framed Norman manor houses do not seem to have this form. At all events, the Wealden is Kent's major contribution to the design of England's small houses. It is at once practical and lavish, and a fitting architectural design to demonstrate the uniquely favoured role of the county's yeomanry in the last two centuries of the Middle Ages.

A feature of early Wealdens is the graceful, two-centred arch formed by the large curved braces supporting the central tie-beam of the hall. Wardes has an arched tie-beam like this (Figure 54), and so does Bayleaf, which was built about 1410 at Boughbeech, Chiddingstone, and has now been re-erected at Singleton. Although they both ultimately had the typical Wealden form with a hall flanked by jettied service and chamber bays, they were first built with the two-part form of a hall with services and solar combined in a single bay to form a 'two-thirds' Wealden (Figure 55). A few of these two-thirds Wealdens survive at Canterbury and Maidstone, and Rigold (1969a) thought that they might have originated in Maidstone with this typically urban form. The evidence is unclear, but the architectural unity of the complete design is a strong counter-argument, and so is the common practice of building rural houses in stages.

The Wealden design may have originated as a consequence of an ecclesiastical household wanting separate quarters for a priest and his guest or a female servant, such as has been proposed for The Clergy House, an early Wealden at Alfriston, East Sussex (Gravett 1981). Later Wealdens built by the Church in Kent, notably Durlock Grange at Minster-in-Thanet, apparently of 1413-14 (Parkin 1962), and Headcorn

Figure 54. Wardes, Otham. Perspective of interior of hall, looking towards the chamber end, showing the large curved braces forming an arch beneath the tie-beam spanning the hall, and the prominent, tall crown-post above.

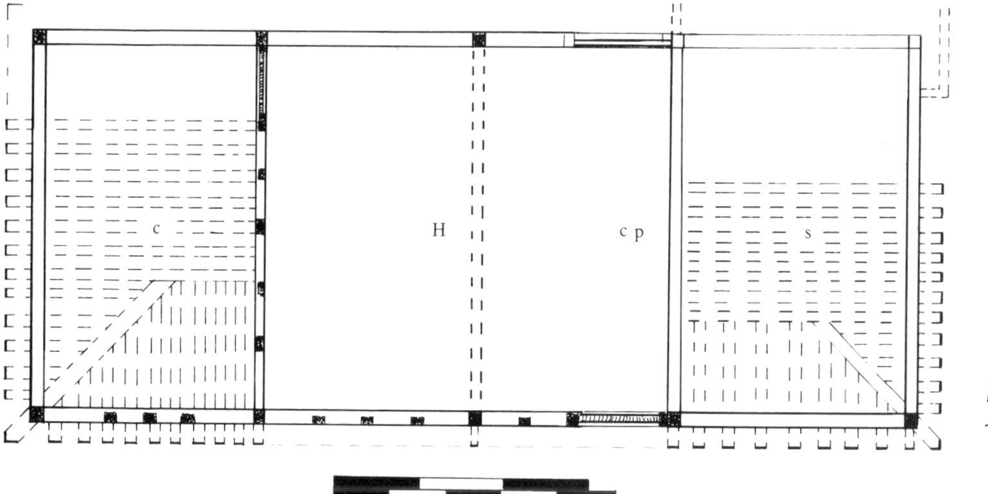

Figure 55. Wardes, Otham. Plan, showing the front and end jetties of the original eastern wing (at right), and the balancing jetties of the later wing (at left). (After Oswald 1933.)

Manor, were designed for multiple occupancy, and with status in mind.

Indeed the Wealden responds well to the needs of two separate households living under the same roof. This might arise as a consequence of the propriety which kept a parson and his servant apart or of partible inheritance physically dividing a house among heirs. When Robert Whithide of Lullingstone died in 1585 his sons split his house. The elder son agreed to have the lower end of the house, 'that is to saye, the parlor, two upper chambers, the kitchen, and the stable adjoyninge unto the said parte

Colour Plate 57. Hogbrook, Alkham, an aisled hall with a single jettied end.

Colour Plate 58. Penshurst Place, the embattled parapet of the Great Hall and the later projecting staircase tower serving the Great Chamber, seen from the parapet of the south porch; the gabled end of the Buckingham or Bedford building lies beyond.

Colour Plate 59. Court Lodge, Mersham. The blocked main entrance is just to the left of the white French doors, the two-light solar window is further to the left in the upper storey, the large hall window on the right.

Colour Plate 61. The garden front of Headcorn Manor, photographed in a different month, showing similar details except for the unjettied end of the chamber block, which, on this account and because of its Kentish framing as opposed to close-studding, is likely to belong to an earlier build than the rest of the house.

Colour Plate 60. The entrance front of Headcorn Manor, with its grand hall window (see Figure 30 (g) and (h)) flanked by the jettied chamber and service ends, all finished in fashionable close-studding.

Colour Plate 62. Hendon Place, Woodchurch, a Wealden hall-house which has probably never had a chamber block at its right-hand end since the hipped roof seems to be designed only to extend far enough to cover the hall and no further.

Plate 59. Harts Heath Farmhouse, Staplehurst, a Wealden hall-house built where the Wealden hills rise out of the vale of the River Beult, with a thinly framed lean-to in the place of its service block.

or half'; meanwhile the younger son was to have the rest 'from the lower wale of the entrie upwardes, viz. the said entrie, the hawle, the lower chamber and tooe upper chambers...' (Melling 1965, 10-11). Similarly, two heirs could share the expense of building a grand hall, but want a design in which their solar chambers were obviously separate and individually expressed. Any hall-house with storeyed ends could be adapted for occupation in this way; but the Wealden form, with its prominent jetties accentuating the importance of the solars rather than differentiating the high and low ends, demonstrated an architectural equality between them appropriate to these circumstances.

The Wealden design was particularly suited to building in stages, with the prominent jettying clearly differentiating the solar from the service rooms before the storeyed bay at the opposite end had been added. Bayleaf shows this well. Its hall was built about 1410 by Henry Bayly together with a solar over a pair of service rooms, clearly defined by the jetties to both front and side. These rooms satisfied the everyday needs of a small household, as well as any desire for status. The concept of the Wealden design was nevertheless so strong that when Edward Wellys and another generation of carpenters came to complete Bayly's house a century later they did so as faithfully to the original as though they were the first builders.

Probably a majority of Wealdens lacked one end at first and were completed only after some generations had elapsed or when new people came into occupation. Some, more obvious to the eye, were never completed at all. Rose Farm at Broomfield, Harts Heath Farm at Staplehurst (Plate 59), Luckhurst at East Sutton and Hendon Place at Woodchurch (Colour Plate 62) all lack one end, although this may be the result of destruction in one or two cases (Swain 1968).

The Wealden hall could be very grand indeed, and gabled upper storeys like those

Plate 60. Old Willesley, Cranbrook, a fine Wealden with gabled end blocks finished with cusped bargeboards and modernised windows, and, inserted at the high end of the hall when it was floored over, a canted bay window, as photographed at the end of the 19th century by Galsworthy Davie and reproduced by the collotype process in Davie and Dawber (1900).

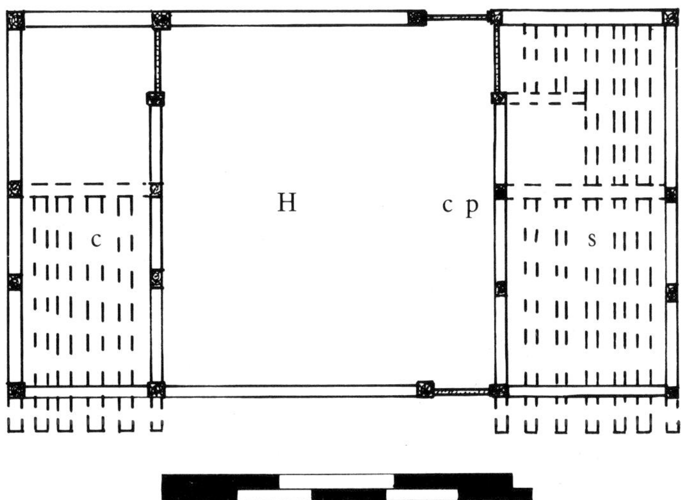

Figure 56. Wealden hall-house, Newington. Plan, showing the Wealden arrangements on the smallest scale, with a single bay for the hall and very narrow bays for the storeyed ends. (After Parkin 1986.)

of Old Willesley at Cranbrook occasionally add to the effect (Plate 60). Despite its evident grandeur, the Wealden could also be very small indeed, like any other hall-house. If it lacked one end, its normal floor area of 1,320sq. ft. (120sq. m) might be reduced by a third. The smallest complete Wealdens only had a single bay for the hall, instead of the normal two. Littlecroft at Chilham, for instance, has a total floor area of only 1,100sq. ft. (100sq. m), while a tiny Wealden at Newington had a floor area of only 615sq. ft. (57sq. m), but even this is only marginally lower than acceptable standards for family houses today (Figure 56).

Most Wealdens are nevertheless large. Lesser houses usually had end jetties,

Colour Plate 63. Corner Farm, Langley, a late Wealden hall-house with two tiers of narrow lancets making up the hall window.

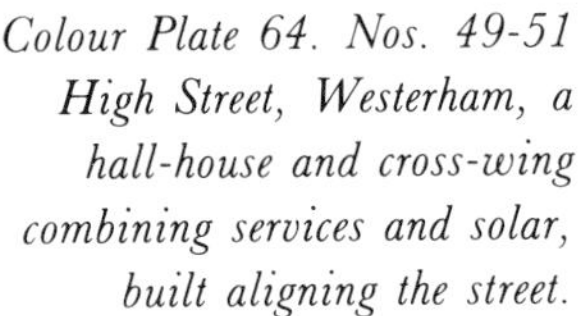

Colour Plate 64. Nos. 49-51 High Street, Westerham, a hall-house and cross-wing combining services and solar, built aligning the street.

Colour Plate 65. The so-called Priest's House, Smallhythe, built after the fire of 1516; only the right-hand entrance door is original.

generally at the service end, the oldest of these dating from about 1420. Spoute House at Plaxtol, for instance, has a jettied service end which dates from about 1429 (Howard *et al.* 1988) (Plate 61). Probably because these houses are smaller, fewer survive, maybe one for every two Wealdens. Still smaller houses usually had no jetties at all; it is probably again their survival rate, rather than total numbers built, which has limited them to an even smaller proportion of Kent's extant hall-houses.

The characteristic recessed hall of the Wealden design caused two problems. The timber plate, which carried the eaves in front of the hall, was usually supported by a pair of curved braces which rose from the jettied bays each side, and sometimes by a bracket rising from the central wall-post of the hall as well. Carpenters were never decided whether to put the plate above the central tie-beam of the hall (Figure 57), so gaining support where it was most needed, or to put the plate beneath the tie and rely on the bracket alone for support. The first method is less frequent, but Yardhurst used it (Figure 58) and so did a grand Wealden called Romden at Smarden, which was possibly built soon after 1421 when the Guldefords came into ownership of the surrounding land (Wade 1983, 4-10).

The second problem was less tractible. About 2ft. (0.6m) behind the eaves-plate, a second plate terminates the framing of the hall's front wall, and marks the extent of the recess. Because there is usually no balancing recess at the back, the centres of the transverse framing of the hall beneath the tie-beam and of the roof frame which it supports do not align (Figure 57). This looks decidedly odd at Bayleaf, where the central stud in the closed frame at the low end of the hall does not align with the

Plate 61. Spoute House, Plaxtol, a hall-house built in two stages, the nearer, jettied service end about 1429, the hall and further, chamber end some thirty years later.

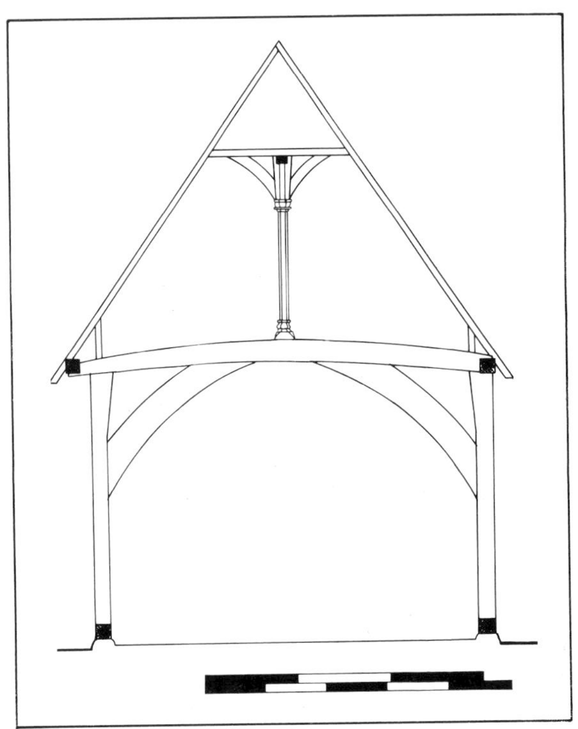

Figure 57. Payne Street Farm, Charing. Section through hall, showing asymmetrical arrangement of framing with front wall-plate above tie-beam, rear wall-plate in normal position below tie-beam. (After Swain 1968.)

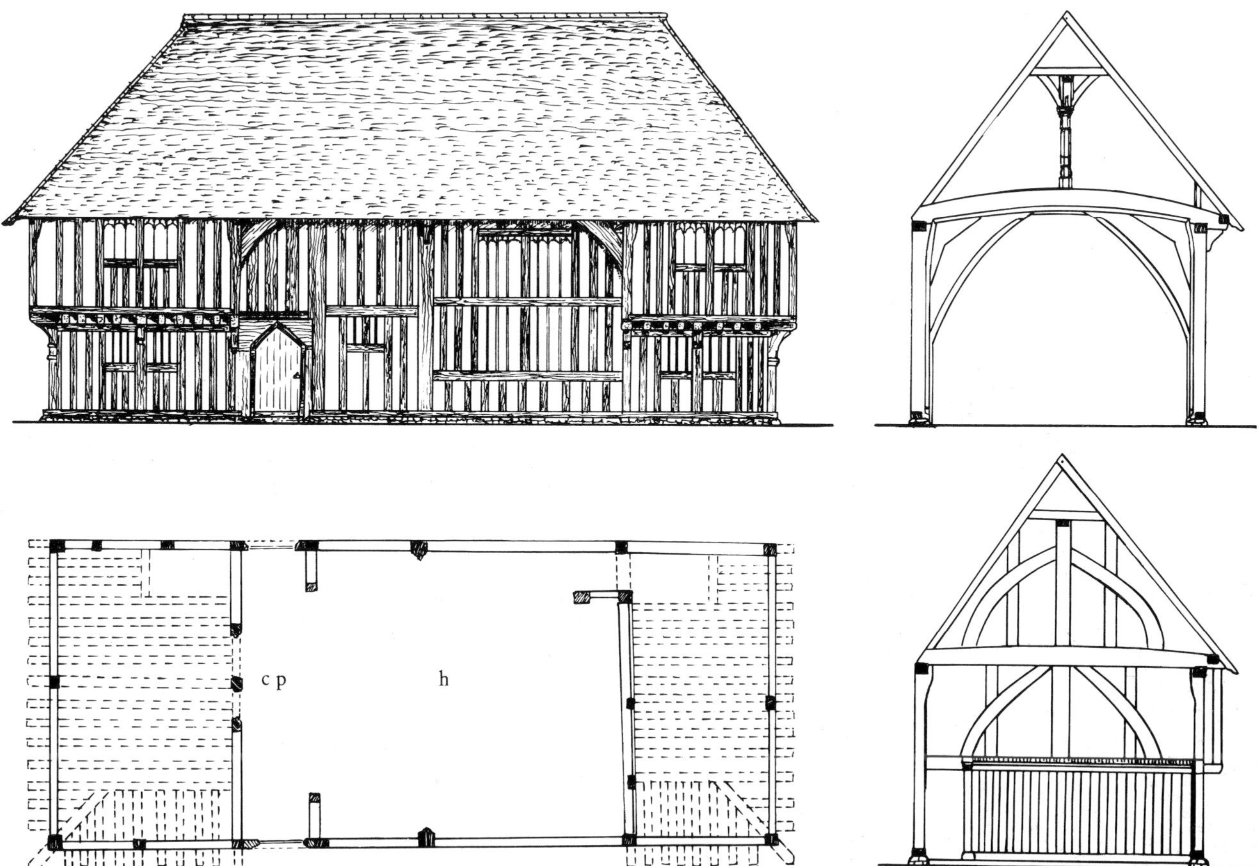

Figure 58. Yardhurst, Great Chart. Plan, front elevation, cross-section through centre of hall and at high end of hall, the latter two showing mounting of front wall-plate above the tie-beam and the asymmetrical framing of the roof with flatter pitch at the front. (After Rigold 1969g.)

crown-post above. Some carpenters eradicated this oddity by aligning the crown-post centrally to the hall, and decreasing the pitch of the front slope of the roof slightly so that the roof would extend further out to make up the difference. This occurs at Yardhurst, where the front pitch is about fifty degrees compared with fifty-two and a half degrees at the back (Figure 58). Other solutions involved eccentrically curved braces for the crown-posts or asymmetrical framing beneath the tie-beam. When the central crown-post gave way to queen-struts at the end of the Middle Ages, as happened at Deanery Farm, Chartham (Figure 24), the centre was less emphasised, allowing the discrepancy to be more easily concealed.

If the front and rear entrances and the cross-passage between them were placed in the lower end bay of the hall, as they are at Yardhurst, the hall might have two equal bays and usually a short partition or spere screened the doors from the body of the hall. Sometimes, as in Old Bell Farm at Harrietsham, the bay at the lower end of the hall is decidedly the shorter (Plate 62). This difference is even more marked in the more usual arrangement where the entrances and cross-passage are set adjacent to the hall within the service bay, with a spere framed between the cross-passage and the hall along the line of the dividing truss. Then the short bay might be only two thirds the length of the bay at the high end. The reason for this may be to give prominence to the high end of the hall and to provide enough space for a large window here.

In general, few of Kent's timber-framed hall-houses are highly decorated. Their

Colour Plate 66. Sir Richard Baker's tower at Sissinghurst Castle.

Colour Plate 68. Knole, Sevenoaks, Sackville's recast inner courtyard with its shaped gables.

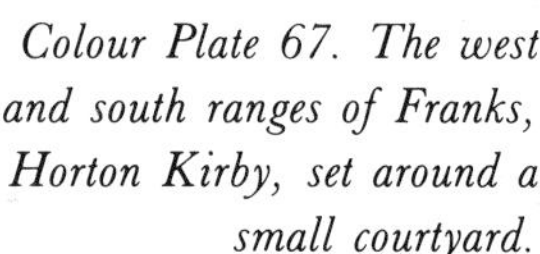

Colour Plate 67. The west and south ranges of Franks, Horton Kirby, set around a small courtyard.

Colour Plate 69. The crow-stepped gabled end of the surviving wing dated 1567 of Bax Farm, Tonge.

Colour Plate 70. Cobham Hall, showing the tenth Lord Cobham's west-facing open courtyard, and the older central range, which the sixth Duke of Lennox remodelled to the designs of Peter Mills in the 1660s.

Plate 62. Old Bell Farm, Harrietsham, an unusually finely decorated Wealden hall-house, replete with close-studding, coved eaves above the recessed hall and embattling above the entrance and within.

central crown-posts were sometimes finely carved with bases and capitals, as Yardhurst's is, and the tie-beams and braces might be moulded (Figure 59). A few houses, notably the early High Hall House at Larkfield, East Malling, and the much later Yardhurst, have traceried heads to their windows; the restored hall window of Corner Farm at Langley has two superimposed doubled rows of four lights, each with a tiny arched head (Colour Plate 63), and all the windows of Headcorn Manor are cusped. Old Bell Farm at Harrietsham and Yardhurst have conspicuously embattled hoodmoulds over their front doors, perhaps as symbols of a chivalrous age and tokens of the yeomanly rank of their builders, though this had long since ceased to imply military service. Yardhurst has a rare surviving spere extending into the high end of the hall from the chamber doorway, and it too has an embattled parapet, which also extends the length of the dais beam across the high end of the hall (Figure 60). This was no more than a horizontal timber, at head height or a little above, spanning the closed frame behind the high table or dais. A number of hall-houses have an embattled or brattished dais beam (Plate 63). Bayleaf has a moulded dais beam even though there is little other decorative carving. All in all, the puritan character of the external close-studding was carried inside with a minimum of ostentatious carving.

Urban halls

The amazing size and quality of these rural hall-houses are unmatched in Kent's few small towns. Urban renewal has taken a heavy toll and made it harder to determine how far prosperity nourished everyday building there too. The surviving houses of Canterbury, Sandwich and the other old towns nevertheless suggest that, by national standards, these places were not especially well endowed in the way that the Kent countryside was.

Towns imposed two major restrictions on building. First, because of demand, land was comparatively expensive, so it had to be used with economy. Open space was already a luxury in the sixteenth century and sparingly provided. Secondly, expense put a heavy premium on frontage since shops were best placed facing the street, and profits depended on this. Houses, therefore, were often aligned backwards along narrow sites to the disadvantage of both lighting and circulation.

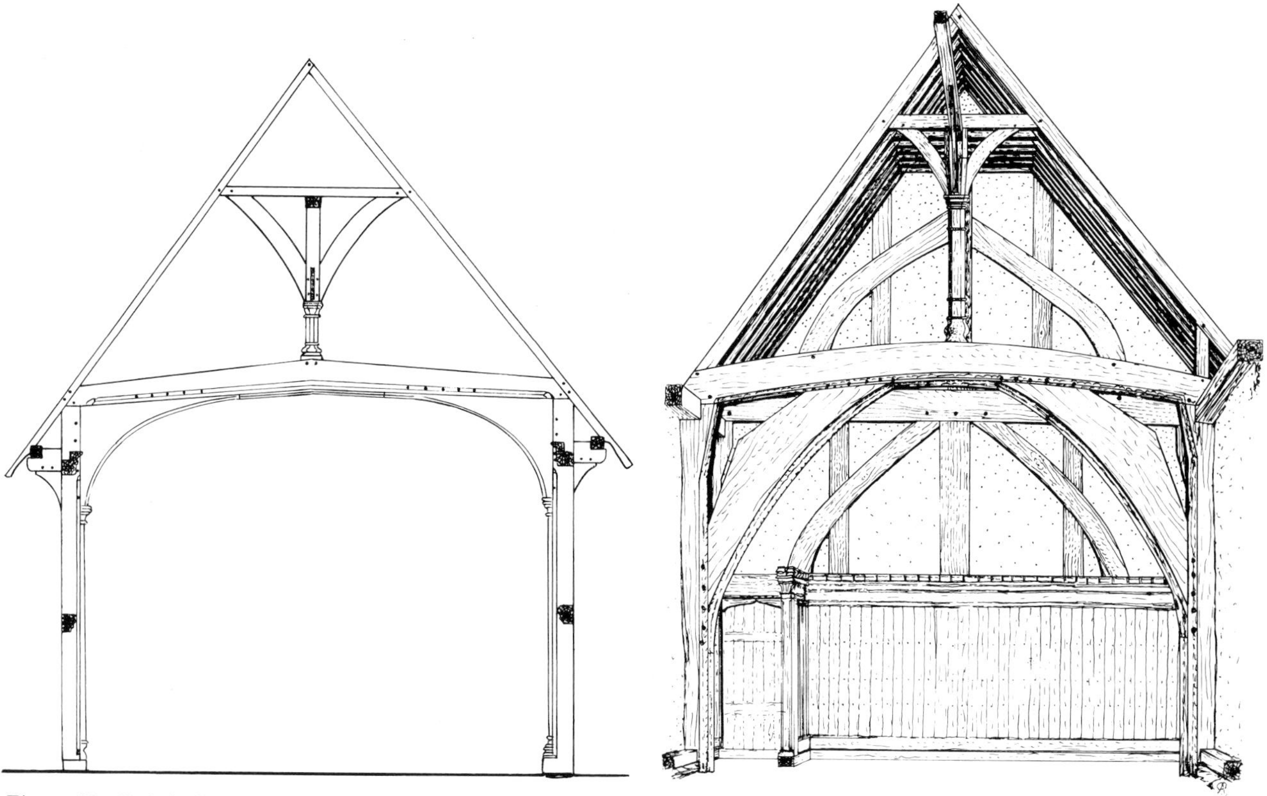

Figure 59. Duke's Place, West Peckham. Section through centre of hall, as rebuilt about 1500, showing symmetrical framing with overhanging eaves to both front and back, bracketed outer wall-plates well below the level of the tie-beam, and the inner wall-plates unusually tenoned into the main-posts below their heads, solid arch-braces entirely filling angle between posts and tie-beam, and very short carved lower section of crown-post. (After RCHM.)

Figure 60. Yardhurst, Great Chart. Conjectural perspective of open hall, looking towards the high end, showing asymmetrical framing above and below tie-beam, and also decorative embattled panelling and its continuation as a screen or spere to shield the chamber door.

Plate 63. The unusually ornate dais beam at Pickersdane Farm, Brook, which has a syncopated arrangement of castellations (more properly brattishing) embellished with roundels.

Colour Plate 71. One of the hearths at Cobb's Hall, Aldington. The restored openings in the back of the hearth may be original and designed to keep salt and spices dry; the hearth-beam is carved with an Aragonese pomegranate on the left, a Tudor rose on the right, helping to date the house to the period following Henry VIII's first marriage in 1509; the painting over the hearth-beam is a rare survival. The entry lobby was originally to the right, the staircase to the left.

Colour Plate 72. Briton House, St. Michael's, Tenterden, a close-studded lobby-entry house.

Colour Plate 73. Honywood House, Lenham, which is inscribed with Anthony Honywood's initials and the date 1621.

Colour Plate 74. Old Harrow Farm, Egerton, an ornate lobby-entry house of the early 17th century.

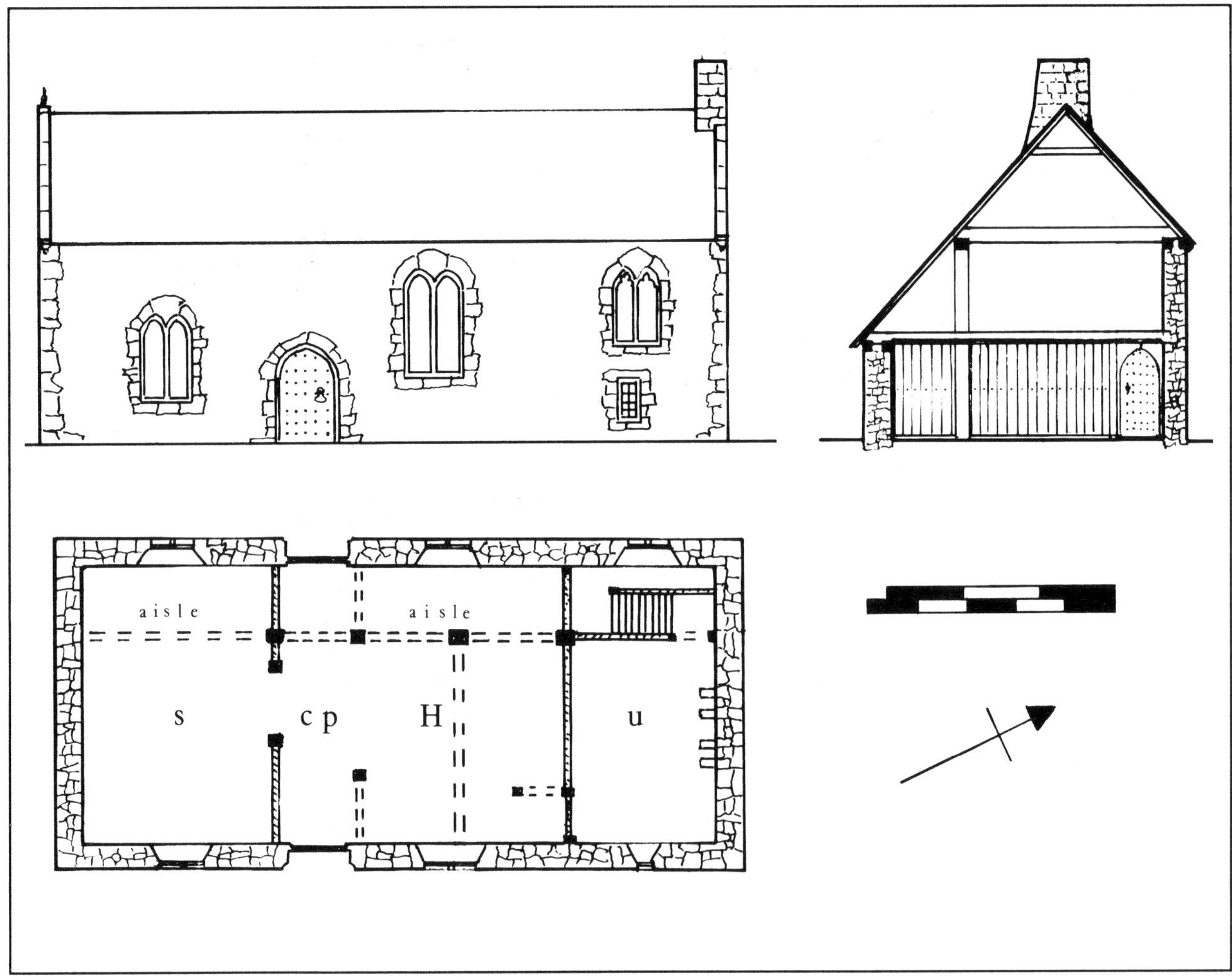

Figure 61. Nos. 3-4 West Street, New Romney. Conjectural ground plan, front elevation and cross-section, showing service room to left, central open hall and heated solar chamber over undercroft to right with single aisle running along the rear. (After Parkin 1973.)

In the countryside houses usually had a long frontage and were not constricted by their neighbours. The first buildings in Canterbury and the new and refounded towns of the eighth and ninth centuries followed suit, and, indeed, many were hardly distinguishable from rural buildings. As these towns filled up with people in the later Middle Ages, this changed: the luxury of the detached, linear form of a rural house became the preserve of ever fewer wealthy town dwellers. While the archbishops could build their palaces in extensive grounds, nearly everyone else had to concede to the limits of space. Awkward sites easily twisted a hall and its attendant chamber and service blocks out of their rural alignment into tortuous patterns.

Another important distinction between town and country was that urban populations were more shifting than rural ones. This created a demand for lodgings and rented property, and opened the way for the speculator. Typically, this was the Church. Well-lit shops at the front and stores at the back with chambers to one side or above were the aim, but it was hard to achieve this within the confines of many sites. The most frequent solutions to these difficulties accepted the hazards of building upwards and rearwards, and these produced a number of characteristic patterns (Pantin 1962-3).

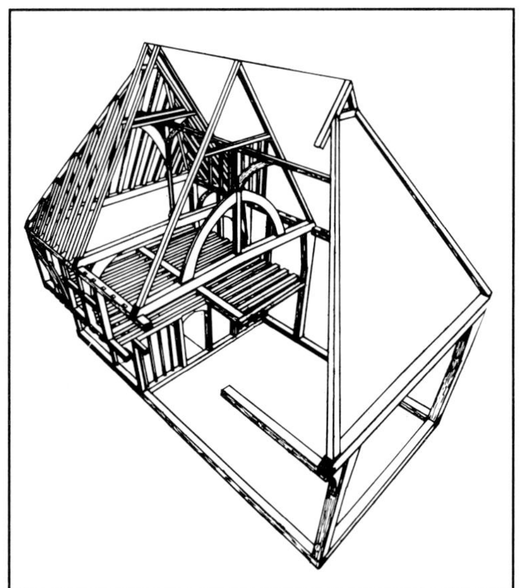

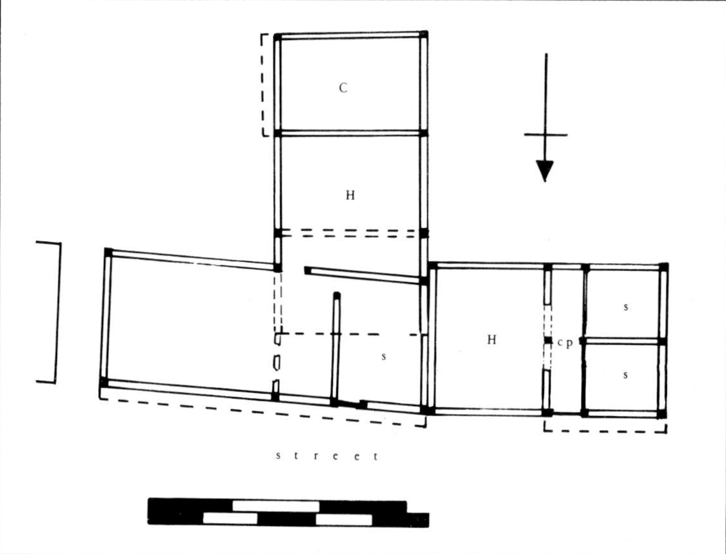

Figure 62. No. 81 St Dunstan's Street, Canterbury. Restored perspective of timber frame, showing (upper left) twin service rooms on ground floor with, above them and screens passage, a jettied chamber decorated by an ornate crown-post, and (lower right) recessed open hall contained in a single bay, forming the typically urban two-thirds Wealden pattern. (After Canterbury Archaeological Trust 1982-3.)

Figure 63. Houses in St Radigund's Street, Canterbury. Plan, showing first house with Wealden plan aligned perpendicularly to street, facing eastward (its northern jetty shown dashed), and later houses incorporating its northern end, aligned with street on east-west axis, the right-hand house with hall and jettied end forming two-thirds of a Wealden; the remainder with a jetty along entire length of street. (After Pantin 1962-3.)

In Kent there are four basic types of layout. Three of these were fully established by the time the earliest surviving town houses came to use them. The first type was built with its main range of buildings lying parallel to the street in the ancient rural way, but it was often extended by a parallel range added to the rear to make what came to be known as a double pile; alternatively, it might be extended rearwards along a perpendicular axis to form an L-plan. The second type recognised the premium on frontage and was built perpendicular to the street from the start, although it might again terminate in a short range fronting the street. A third type combined the first two arrangements into an open courtyard behind the street. The fourth and last type to be developed combined a number of individual dwellings in one building to produce a regular terrace.

The rural way of building parallel with the street was popular where frontage was not at a premium, notably where towns were too small for the cost to be significant. Nos. 3-4 West Street, New Romney (Figure 61), The Studio at Cranbrook (Plate 64) and the Tudor Rose Tea Rooms at Tenterden exemplify this well, and so do most of the numerous hall-houses at Wingham. The same conditions are found in the suburbs of larger towns, for instance at 28 Wincheap and 81 St Dunstan's Street, Canterbury (Figure 62), which are both outside the city walls. The Long House and 27 and 39 Strand Street are among Sandwich's medieval houses aligned with the street, and these have probably survived simply because the town's decline halted mounting pressures on space (Plate 26).

Sometimes the frontage of a house was reduced by contracting its plan, for instance

Colour Plate 75. Baxon Manor, Bredgar, the gabled centre dated 1617, and still using the age-old three-part medieval plan with a central hall, albeit confined to the ground floor, despite a century of symmetrically arranged yeomen's houses; the left-hand service block may be earlier than the rest.

Colour Plate 76. Brunger Farm, Tenterden, a brick lobby-entry house built no later than the middle of the 17th century.

Colour Plate 77. Coldred Manor Farm, a plainer version of Brunger Farm.

Colour Plate 78. *Chilham Castle, showing the canted wings embracing the open polygonal courtyard of the house built for Sir Dudley Digges in 1616.*

Colour Plate 79. *Mid-17th century classical restraint at Yotes Court, Mereworth.*

Colour Plate 80. *Marle Place, Brenchley, a timber-framed double-pile, dated 1619 over the entrance, and now extensively clad in Victorian tiles.*

Plate 64. The Studio, Cranbrook, a Wealden hall-house, built in two stages parallel to the southern end of the High Street, where there was plenty of space for this generous frontage; it has an enlarged, gabled service end and a wagon entrance unceremoniously punched through its once open hall; as photographed at the end of the 19th century by Galsworthy Davie and reproduced by the collotype process in Davie and Dawber (1900).

at 2-3 St Radigund's Street, Canterbury (Figure 63), and Tudor Cottage, Maidstone; both of these have the form of two-thirds Wealden halls with solar chambers built over service rooms in the usual way, but lacking a chamber bay at the high ends of their halls. Nos. 2-3 St Radigund's Street were the last phase of development on a site which, beforehand, contained a full Wealden hall built perpendicular to the street and reached by a side passage. Nos. 28-30 High Street, New Romney, is another typically contracted hall-house with combined services and solar, and Westerham also has a single-ended hall-house, aligned with the street, at 49-51 High Street (Colour Plate 64), with services and solar in a cross wing. These contracted hall-houses do not use their frontage in the most economical way, but they avoided problems with lighting since all their rooms could be lit from front and back. Consequently they are almost ubiquitous in Kent's prosperous medieval towns.

The oldest surviving house to be more economically built with its hall lying perpendicular to the street is Cogan House at Canterbury (Figure 64); its front range is parallel to the frontage but no wider than the aisled hall behind it. By the later fourteenth century, this arrangement had become the norm in Canterbury, notably in the three separate dwellings of The Weavers, St Peter's Street (Plate 65), and again at Tudor House, 8 High Street, and all along Palace Street. The same use of a long thin site running back from the street was exploited early in Sandwich's development at 3 King's Yard, behind 11 Strand Street, and was widespread in the town's later medieval timber-framed houses too. Old Canonry took the arrangement to Wingham, where it was hardly needed and not copied by most of the later hall-houses.

Courtyards were either a rare feature of Kent's towns, or comprehensively obliterated after the Middle Ages. Large hospitals and inns often comprised ranges of lodgings set round a courtyard, notably at the immense Chequers of Hope built in

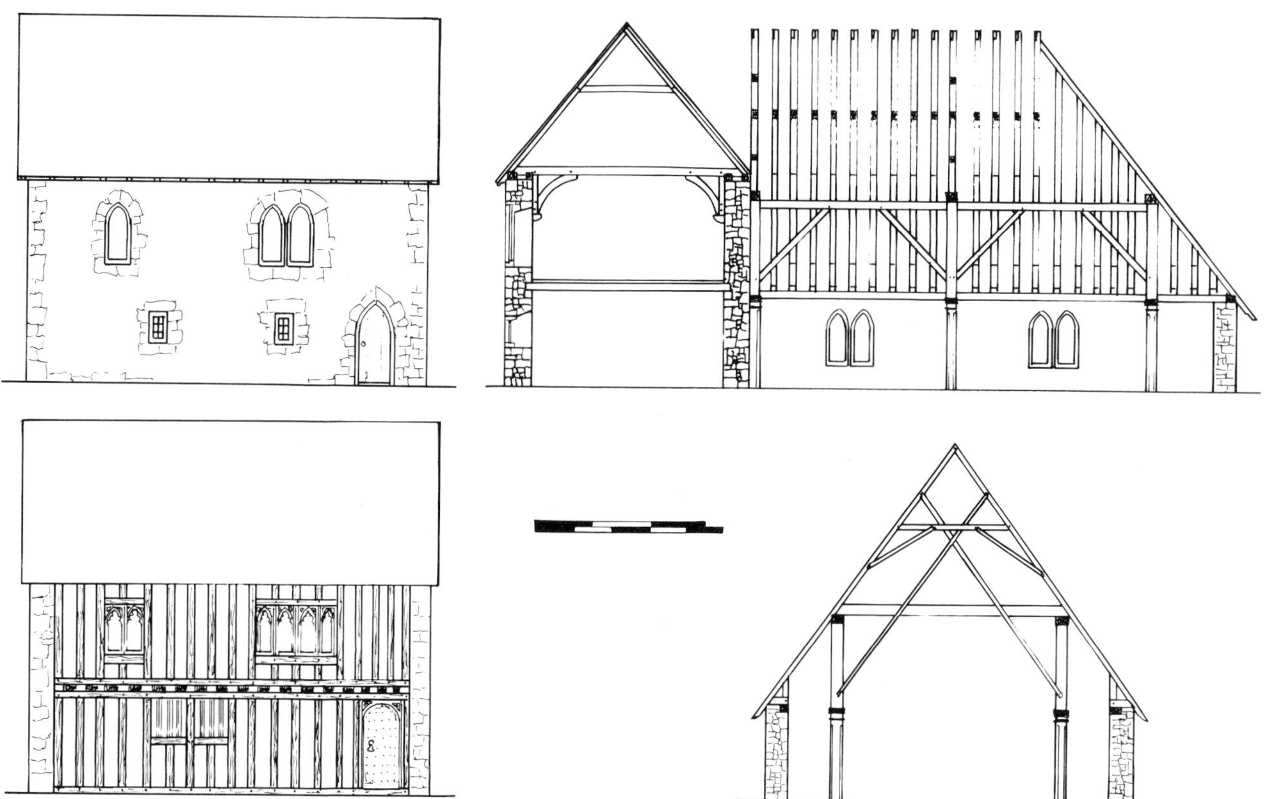

Figure 64. Cogan House, Canterbury. Conjecturally restored elevations (left) of front building as first built in stone (top) and as rebuilt in timber (bottom), and (upper right) section through original front building and aisled hall at rear, and (lower right) cross-section through aisled hall. (After Parkin 1970.)

Plate 65. The Weavers, St. Peter's Street, Canterbury, as photographed at the end of the 19th century by Galsworthy Davie and reproduced by the collotype process in Davie and Dawber (1900). The left-hand gabled shop and another gabled shop further to the left form a pair, each originally with an open hall at the rear reached by a passage; the gables of the nearer house (the laundry) similarly cover a shop with a chamber and garret over it, but the range along the side, which overlooks the River Stour, was divided up into chambers.

Colour Plate 81. Leacon Hall, Warehorne, a solid, plain, but judiciously detailed double-pile dated 1708.

Colour Plate 83. Matfield House, built in 1728 in a modest baroque style, with contemporary stables to the right.

Colour Plate 82. Westwell, Tenterden, an ostentatious double-pile dated 1711.

Colour Plate 84. Swanton Street Farm, Bredgar, Kent's most extraordinary baroque house.

Colour Plate 86. Combe Bank, Sundridge, built to Roger Morris' designs in the late 1720s.

Colour Plate 85. Mereworth Castle, Colen Campbell's house, roofed in 1723, and one of the two pavilions added a dozen or so years later, set in a landscape a far cry from Palladio's Veneto.

Plate 66. Nos. 5-6 Market Square, Faversham, the three shops with gabled chambers over them and the arched entrance to the hall and rear courtyard.

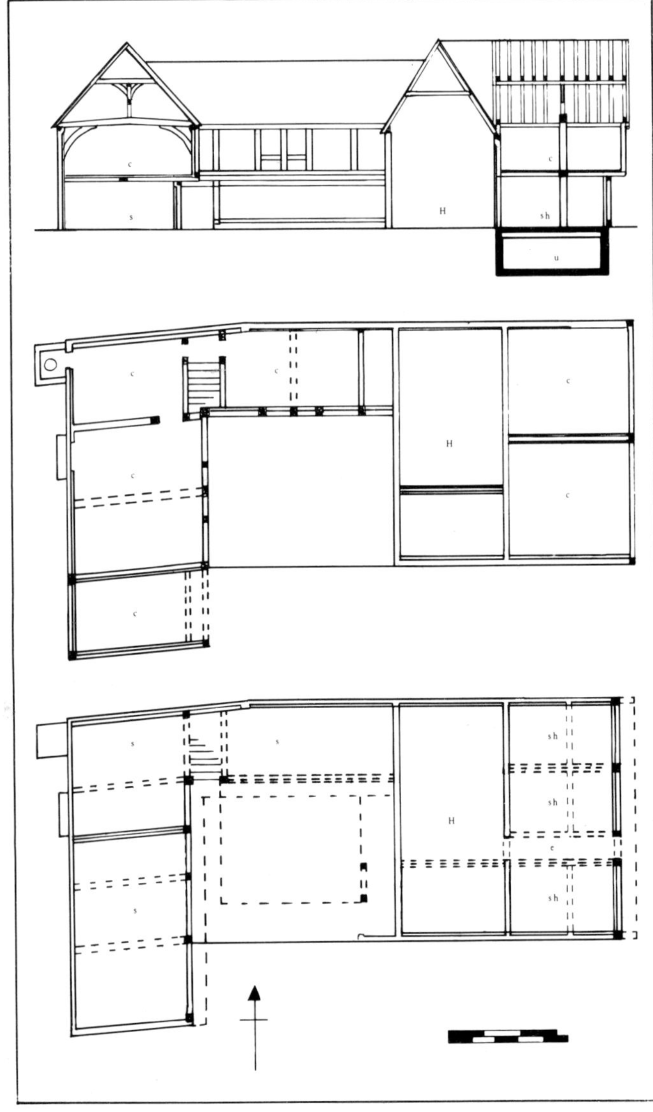

Plate 67. Turnagain Lane, Canterbury, a late medieval terrace of identical houses, each one originally with a single jettied upper chamber set above a shop, probably with an open hall at the rear, and later raised to accommodate weaving rooms, visible externally in their continuous band of windows.

Figure 65. Nos. 5-6 Market Place, Faversham. Plans of ground and upper floors, and section from east to west, showing (on right) open hall fronted by shops and entrance passage built over undercrofts, with jettied chambers over them, and open courtyard (centre and left), flanked by two-storeyed ranges of service rooms and chambers. (After Faulkner 1969.)

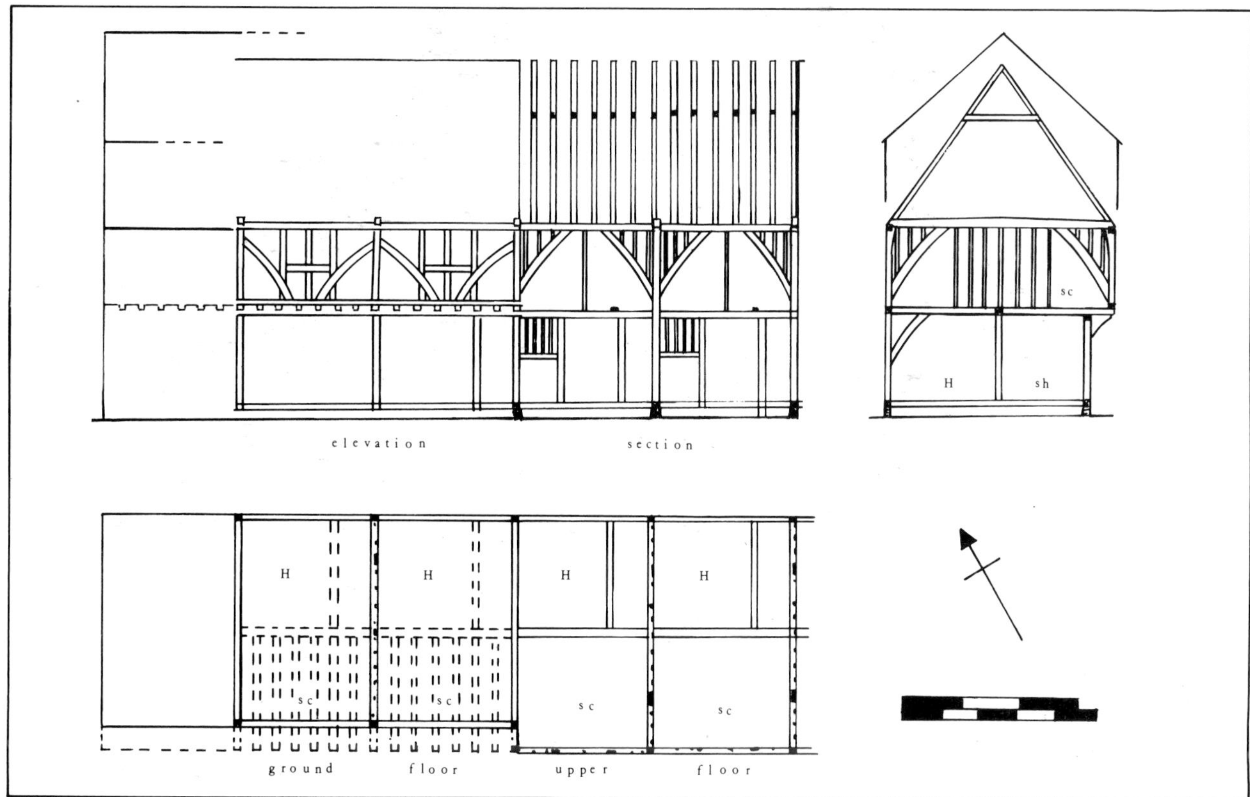

Figure 66. Nos. 5-8 Turnagain Lane, Canterbury. Conjectural plan of ground and upper floors, front elevation and longitudinal section, and cross-section, showing jettied two-storeyed front half forming notional services or shop with solar chamber over them and open rear half forming hall; the position of the present raised roofline, apparently to accommodate silk weaving, is shown in outline on the left side and over the cross-section. (After Canterbury Archaeological Trust 1983-4.)

1392-5 in Mercery Lane, Canterbury. A more ordinary survivor, though rare enough, is 5-6 Market Place, Faversham (Figure 65). This was progressively built up over the years, first with an open hall parallel to the street, then with three shops and an archway and a pair of chambers over them fronting it to form a double pile (Plate 66), and lastly with a courtyard behind the hall, lined by chambers set over service rooms (Faulkner 1969).

Terraces

Rows of individual medieval houses are commonplace. Terraces of uniform houses are much rarer. They were built all of a piece by speculators willing to invest in an extensive building, standing alone and divided up into individual units. The Church was among the earliest speculators to build terraces, and probably the most influential. It may have developed them from the lodgings which it built for pilgrims and other travellers. Terraces were being built in London and York early in the fourteenth century, and possibly in Canterbury too, but the oldest surviving terraces here apparently belong to the fifteenth century. These are in Turnagain Lane, All Saints Lane, on the corners formed by 8-9 The Parade and 25-26 St Margaret's Street, and by 41-44 Burgate and 1-3 Butchery Lane.

Nos. 5-8 Turnagain Lane (Plate 67 and Figure 66) are the remains of perhaps seven or eight houses, arranged bay by bay as a terrace near the corner with Palace Street. They backed St Alphege's Church, which probably built them for the sake of the

Plate 68. The corner of Butchery Lane and Burgate, Canterbury, built by Christ Church Priory as part of a range of lodgings.

enhanced income which would accrue from their rents. Each house comprised a ground-floor room, partitioned into a shop and a rear room, and an upper chamber, jettied at the front, but otherwise modestly treated. This would have suited traders and craftsmen who were well enough established to want the comforts of substantial quarters, however small, but who had yet to strike gold and move into fully-fledged hall-houses. The rear room, nevertheless, probably extended upwards to the roof forming a narrow hall. If it was floored over, winter braziers must have warmed their inhabitants, since a fire in an open hearth was then out of the question, and food would have been taken to local bakeries to be cooked, just as it was among the urban poor until this century.

The terrace which turns the corner of Burgate and Butchery Lane (Plate 68) was altogether more substantially built by Christ Church about 1449-68 during Prior Goldstone's time, with two jettied upper storeys, and, originally, a complement of paired and tripled four-centred windows. There were undercrofts below and shops on the ground storey, and possibly as many as thirty-eight single-roomed lodgings on the two floors above (Figures 67 and 68).

The terrace on the corner of St Margaret's Street and The Parade similarly has two jettied storeys, and, unusually for Kent, once had roofs prominently terminating in gables facing each way at the corner instead of the usual hipped angle. The gables apart, the eight bays of shops and lodgings are framed with simple and rather archaic joinery, and therefore might have originated well before the fifteenth century. The jettied terrace in All Saints Lane, on the other hand, may only date from the sixteenth century.

Chimney-stacks and new plans

Archbishop Morton's encouragement of brick had far-reaching consequences for the development of house plans, principally because a brick chimney-stack made the open

Figure 67. Nos. 1-3 Butchery Lane and 41-44 Burgate, Canterbury. Conjecturally restored perspective, showing stone plinth with windows to undercrofts, ground storey with entrances and shop windows, and two jettied upper storeys with ranges of windows lighting the lodging chambers. (After Canterbury Archaeological Trust 1983-4.)

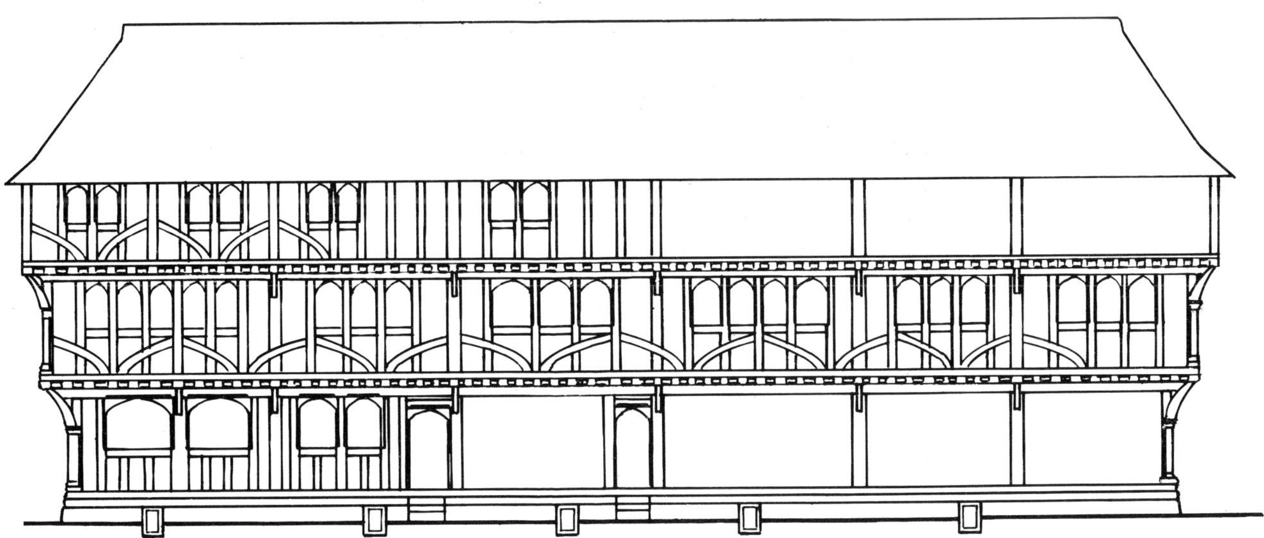

Figure 68. Nos. 41-44 Burgate, Canterbury. Conjecturally restored front elevation. (After Canterbury Archaeological Trust 1983-4.)

Plate 69. The Museum, King Street, Margate, a fully two-storeyed house with a continuous jetty all round and close-studding.

hall redundant and allowed a complete upper storey to run the full length of a house. These changes were easily introduced into the numerous hall-houses of the yeomanry, and the common three-part arrangement of rooms could similarly be easily adapted when new houses came to be built. Yet, however well the old arrangements were adapted, it eventually became clear that a radical re-appraisal of the arrangement of rooms could lead to their greater convenience.

So, in the first decades of the sixteenth century builders began the process of devising new house plans which rationalised the introduction of the enclosed hearth and chimney-stack and the full-length upper storey. Within a century this process was complete so far as the countryside was concerned, but the special difficulties of fitting chimney-stacks into town houses took longer to resolve. House builders worked within a tradition, and, since it was easier to adapt to tradition than to cast it aside and start afresh, novelties were accepted slowly. Even so, before 1550 Kent had produced a new form of house plan which eventually spread to most of England and was even exported to Ireland, where it rapidly withered, and to New England, where it flourished as never before.

The first new houses with chimney-stacks continued to use the medieval three-part plan of hall flanked by services and chambers. The hall, though obsolescent, remained in progressively attenuated form. By taking the smoke from the hearth, the chimney-stack allowed the hall to be floored over to make a continuous upper storey which linked the first-floor rooms at the high and low ends, formerly separated by the open hall between them. The linear arrangement of rooms continued, partly because it was easier to comprehend in terms of layout and circulation, since it maintained the idea of the high and low ends of the house, and partly because it was easier to construct the roof. Moreover, windows were not generally glazed until about 1600, so the need for lighting on both sides of the house remained for a while. In addition, yeomen were unready to adapt their lives and their uses for rooms all at once just because they could afford new standards.

Nevertheless the hall was progressively demoted as the main communal room about which the few subsidiary rooms revolved, and simultaneously a number of smaller rooms were promoted, each one increasingly designed for a particular role. These changes brought problems, and they may account for the slow progress of modification. The first problem was cost; the second was the chimney itself, the feature that made it all possible; finally there were difficulties with space and circulation. Bricks for a chimney-stack were relatively expensive before the seventeenth century and took up a lot of space and impeded circulation. Because of this, smaller houses at first had only one stack, and, while the earlier ones usually served only a single hearth, much effort went into placing the stack in such a position that there could be back-to-back hearths, two per storey. This brought obvious economies, though it was difficult to achieve.

There had been chimney-stacks in castles and a few other domestic establishments since the twelfth century, but their first appearance in yeoman houses was shortly before 1500. In 1490 John Grangeman bequeathed to his wife Alice the use of 'the Chimney Chambyre within my tenement and place at Wode in the paryshe of Borden...', a peculiar reference to a room so novel that it had no established name yet. A contract of 1500 specified the erection at Cranbrook of 'a newe house... to be lofted over with 3 particions beneth and 3 above... and a chymney with 2 fyres...' (Melling 1965, 7, 9-10).

At Smallhythe, where the church was rebuilt entirely in brick after a disastrous fire in the village in 1516, the so-called Priest's House (Colour Plate 65) and Smallhythe Place were also built shortly after the fire, each with a timber frame and a three-part arrangement of rooms with the hall in the centre in the traditional way. A continuously jettied floor spanned the hall of each house, a novelty made possible at the Priest's House because a brick chimney-stack took the smoke from the hall fire. At Smallhythe Place, the smoke was confined to a narrow bay at first, but this was soon replaced by a brick chimney-stack in the new way. These innovations were due not to Church and manor, as their modern names suggest (Whinifrith 1980), but probably to men connected with trade through Smallhythe's now silted-up harbour.

Three-part hall-houses with chimney-stacks and jetties to advertise their full upper floor began to appear in some numbers. The real limit was the already generous housing stock. The Museum at Margate (Plate 69) and Coggers Hall at Lamberhurst show these houses at their grandest. Both were eventually given more than one chimney-stack, but, while bricks were expensive, much effort went into using a single stack as efficiently as possible. There were difficulties with its placing. If it was at the high end of the hall, and served for cooking as well as warmth, this immediately played havoc with the medieval arrangements (Figures 69 and 70). The room at the low end of the hall would be a service room, following ancient usage, so both servants and prepared food would have to go back and forth to the hearth past the high table. This table could no longer be at the high end of the hall, but would have to be in the middle or at the low end near the screened entrance, an uncomfortable position which upset medieval ideas of propriety.

One way of solving this problem was to break with tradition and put the service room beyond the high end of the hall, in the traditional place of the private chamber. This would ease the problems of cooking and serving food without the high table being in the centre of the bustle, but it still placed the table uncomfortably between the hearth and the entrance, and the chamber to which the head of the house would retire would now have to be inconveniently placed at the low end of the hall beyond the entrance.

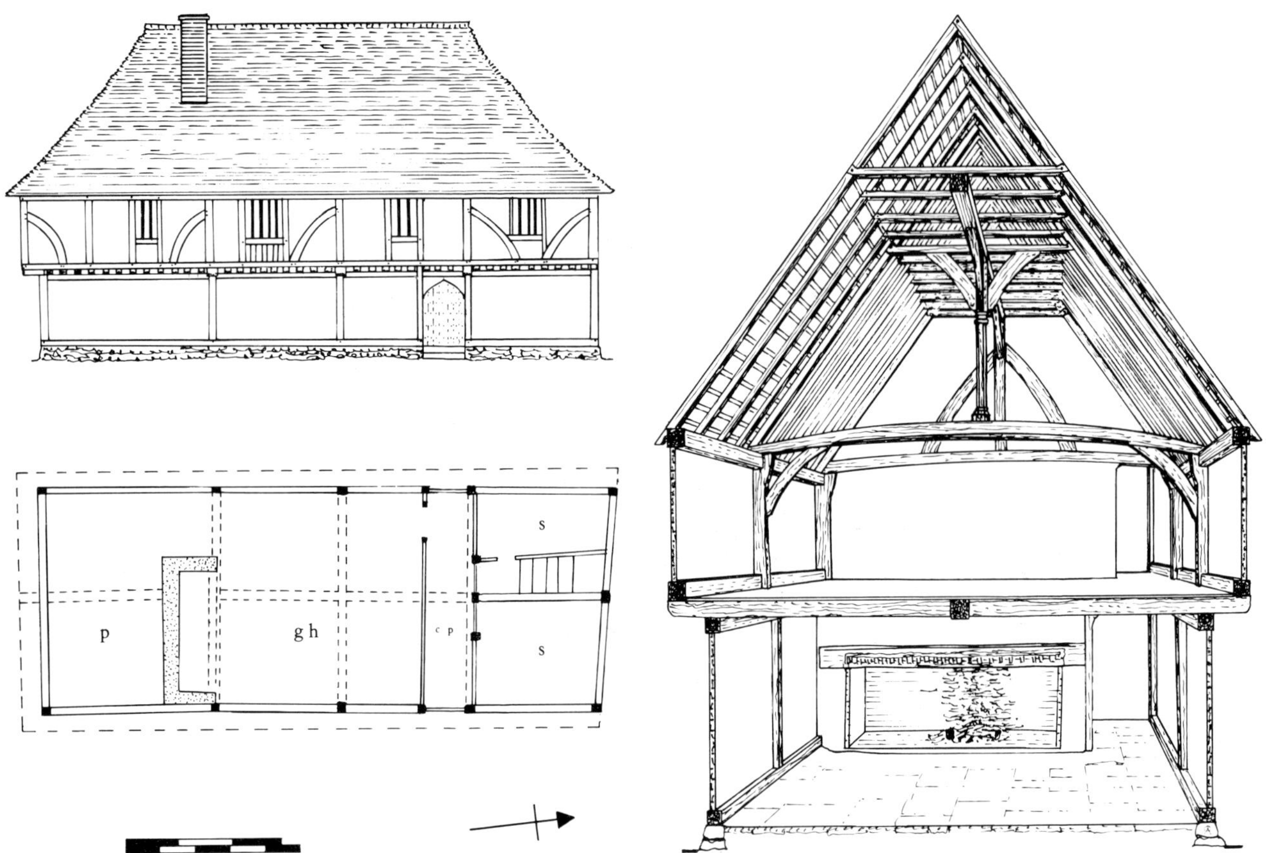

Figure 69. Forstal Farm, Brook. Ground plan and front elevation, conjecturally restored, showing a traditional medieval plan modified by the incorporation of a chimney-stack with single hearth to heat the hall contained in the centre two bays, with the chamber or parlour (left) and screens passage and service rooms (right) laid out in the usual way, but now all floored over from end to end with a continuous jetty, which extends along one end and the rear as well. (After Wade 1986.)

Figure 70. Forstal Farm, Brook. Conjectural interior perspective, showing hall confined to ground storey, with enclosed hearth and passage beside it leading to chamber or parlour, front and back jetties supporting principal upper chamber, which is decorated with an ornate crown-post in the open frame spanning the room. (After Wade 1986.)

All of this would have been awkward if the old-established hierarchy of rooms mattered. Presumably it did not, or, at least, it did not matter as much as having the new status symbol of a hearth enclosed by a chimney-stack, and a full upper floor, end to end, with jetties to show it to the outside world.

A second position for the chimney-stack, almost as widely adopted, was at the low end of the hall, backing the cross-passage. This did not upset the medieval arrangements based on the high and low ends of the hall, and the stack could continue the screen or spere, making the division between the hall and passage greater than before and so adding to the sense of privacy; but there were still two disadvantages. Because the stack backed against the cross-passage, it could not contain a second hearth in this position and that was an inefficient use of bricks; and there was no question of providing warmth for the parlour. Nevertheless the chimney-stack was placed in this way at Sunderland, Lynsted (Plate 70), and in nearly half the open hall-houses that were converted, Upper Bush at Cuxton being typical of hundreds.

Plate 70. Sunderland, Lynsted, a 16th century house with a continuous jetty and upper floor with a chimney-stack heating the ground-floor hall and two of the chambers above; the blanks in the close-studding show where there originally were clerestory windows.

The great advantage of cooking over an enclosed fire, however far from the service rooms or with whatever disruption of the old medieval arrangements, cannot have been lost on those who previously had had to make do with an open fire in the hall; and those who had formerly used a detached kitchen preferred to cook their food near where it would be eaten. Beside the fire and its andirons was space for a battery of pans, posnets and skillets as well as the gridirons and trivets that supported them. Above, inside the stack, were hooks for hanging kettles and cauldrons, cobirons to support a spit, and sometimes the mechanism for turning it. There might be a separate oven set into the chimney-stack, and other recesses within the brickwork were used to keep salt, dried fruit and spices dry (Colour Plate 71). All these as well as large size differentiate a fireplace used for cooking. The chamber's fireplace was usually better decorated with carving or a moulded brick arch instead of a plain timber bressummer.

A majority of the houses in Kent which have this adapted plan are medieval houses which have been brought up to the new standards. Biddenden is unusual for its many houses built from scratch with chimney-stacks and continuous jetties as original features. The village did well from cloth in the sixteenth century and, even though several yeomen already occupied large hall-houses there, this prompted the building of several new houses like Castweazel, The Cott and Standen. The Cott (Plate 71 and Figure 71) was probably built about 1535 from the profits of weaving, though its recent name, Weaver's Court, falsely assumes manorial status. Its long, jettied frontage of nearly 63ft. 6in. (20m) and extended cross-wing for service rooms recall Loddenden Manor at Staplehurst (Plate 72). This again was not a manor house, but owes its grandeur to Thomas Usborne (1520-88), whose wealthy family farmed locally on a big scale and were also tanners. Its single chimney-stack was economically planned with back-to-back hearths for the hall, where cooking was originally done, for the parlour on the opposite side, and for the two chambers above (Cowper 1911). Another of Biddenden's new houses, Standen, is a bit later and has a chimney-piece dated 1578 (Colour Plate 31).

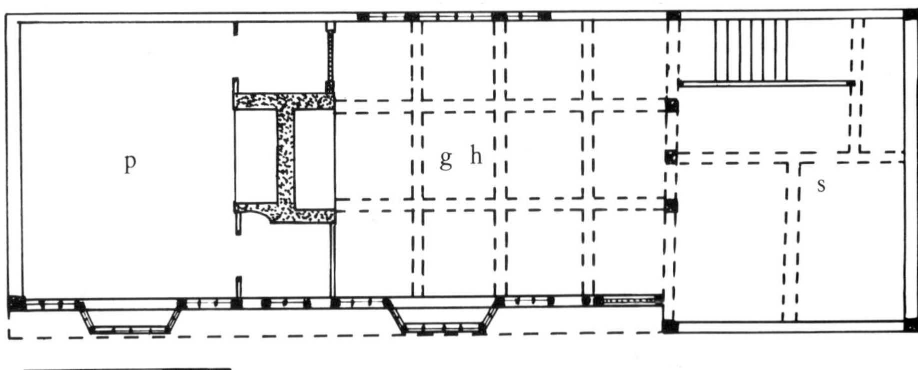

Figure 71. The Cott, Biddenden. Ground plan, showing a traditional medieval plan modified by the incorporation of a chimney-stack, with back-to-back hearths, dividing the chamber or parlour (left) from the ground-floor hall with panelled ceiling (centre); the service rooms lie beyond it (right) in the usual way. (After Cowper 1911.)

Plate 71. The Cott, Biddenden, an early 16th century house, built with a continuous upper storey, jettied along the front (now partly underbuilt in brick), and later extended into a rear wing and given new oriel windows.

Plate 72. Loddenden Manor, Staplehurst, built by the Usbornes, probably about 1566.

Smoke bays

By Usborne's time the building of new houses was a small business among Kent's yeomen compared with a century beforehand. Their money went into adding chimney-stacks and an upper chamber over their halls. They did not always undertake this process at one go, simply by inserting a chimney-stack wherever it would serve the hall. Instead, many yeomen covered over half of the hall with an inserted floor, thereby reducing the open portion through which the smoke could still escape, and providing a reasonably large upper room that might receive some warmth from the open fire below. This did not upset the traditional arrangement of rooms at the high and low ends of the hall, nor did it cause the increased draughts which an enclosed hearth and chimney-stack brought. It was a relatively simple matter to floor over the bay at the high end, leaving the low end open for the smoke. Sometimes smaller parts of the hall were left open, perhaps only half a bay, and sometimes one side of the open bay was confined by a gallery. When the opening was confined all round it became

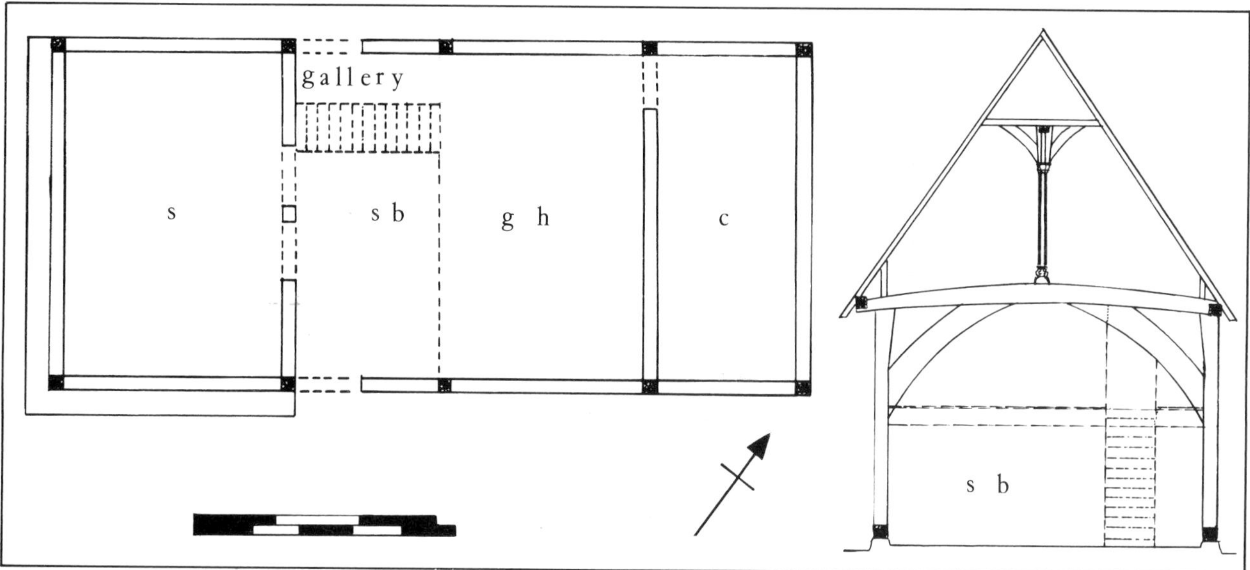

Figure 72. Payne Street Farm, Charing. Plan and section, showing how one bay of the formerly open hall of a Wealden house has been floored over, leaving a smoke bay at the other end with a staircase rising within it and a gallery spanning it to link the storeyed ends. (After Swain 1968.)

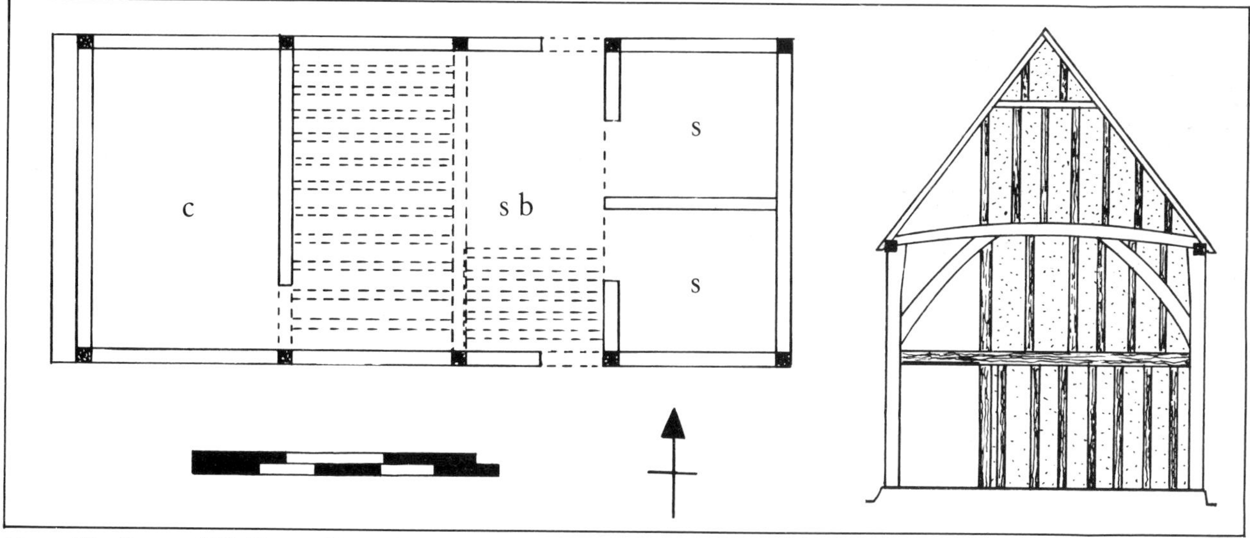

Figure 73. Barrow Hill House, Upper Bush, Cuxton. A hall-house with an end jetty, modified by the insertion of a new floor across half of the hall, leaving the other half to serve as a smoke bay. Plan (left), showing position of floor (its new joists shown dashed) inserted into open hall, thus providing space in one bay for a new upper room and, in the other bay, for a gallery to join it to the upper storey in the service end; and section (right), showing new partition dividing the new upper room from the smoke bay and the position of the gallery (on left). (After Swain 1968.)

little more than a timber chimney, made fireproof by a thorough application of plaster to its inner surfaces. There was not the status of a visible chimney-stack or jetty, nor was a smoke bay as safe as a chimney, but it was a significantly better place to smoke meat. If a gallery bridged one side of the smoke bay to link the upper floors of both ends of the hall, much that a chimney achieved was done at far less cost.

Plate 73. Spong Farm, Elmstead, built with a continuous jetty along the front, but this extends inside only to form a gallery across the front of the hall, linking the upper chambers at each end.

Smoke bays served for many generations even though they were really only a half-way stage towards a brick chimney-stack and a complete upper floor. The first smoke bays appeared at the end of the fifteenth century, although houses were still being built with fully open halls for another generation. Possibly a third of Kent's halls were progressively modernised by the provision of a smoke bay before a brick chimney-stack was inserted into them. Payne Street Farm at Charing (Figure 72), Barrow Hill House, Upper Bush, Cuxton (Figure 73), and The Old Farm House at Dean Bottom, Fawkham, all additionally had galleries to link the new floors over the high ends of their halls with the original upper floors at their low ends. Tonge Corner at Sittingbourne was unusual in having galleries across both sides of the smoke bay, and in all these houses there was a partition fitted into the formerly open truss to keep the smoke from penetrating the new upper room.

Between the late fifteenth century and the end of the sixteenth or later both Tonge Corner and Brishing Court at Boughton Monchelsea were partly floored to form smoke bays, that is long after they had first been built as fully open halls. On the other hand, Swallows in Church Street, Boughton Monchelsea, was probably built with an open hall late in the fifteenth century, then partly floored to form a smoke bay in the sixteenth century, and finally was fully floored and given a chimney-stack in 1616, all in the relatively short period of 150 years or less (Swain 1968).

This division of large halls with the insertion of a new floor and perhaps a gallery was also achieved in smaller ones. The small open hall of 49-51 High Street, Westerham, was divided to form a smoke bay which typically extended over the cross-passage. A very narrow smoke bay was created at Crofton Farm, Orpington (Figure 48). Both the upper bay of the hall and the lower half of the lower bay which contains the cross-passage were ceiled, thus leaving only half a bay for the smoke. This remained in use until 1671 when a single-flued stack was inserted into it with the date emblazoned on its bressummer together with a fleur-de-lis and some very old-fashioned carving. The whole process from the first build to the insertion of this chimney-stack could have taken three hundred years at the least. It was not the last of Kent's halls to be converted. Hoggeshawes, a fine Wealden hall at Milstead, did not get its chimney-stack until 1700, and it may not be the last (Figure 26k).

Some houses were built from scratch with smoke bays and a gallery, usually across the front, to connect the two floored ends. The occasional half-way house was built with an open hall and jettied ends, as though in the form of a Wealden, but with the jetty continuing across the front of the hall and extending inside only far enough to support a gallery linking the two floored ends. Spong Farm at Elmstead (Plate 73), one of the few houses in Kent with this arrangement, was built with timber felled about 1520, and so is a contemporary of the first generation of fully floored timber houses with brick chimney-stacks (Howard *et al.* 1991).

A few houses were given timber smoke hoods instead of smoke bays. These were really little more than funnel-shaped chimney-stacks, plastered inside to make them fireproof. They were really only poor men's versions of brick stacks, and eventually they were nearly all replaced because they were both flimsy and rather unsafe. Dormer Cottage at Petham was given a plastered smoke hood when it came to be modernised, and it is one of the few in Kent which still survives.

Use of rooms

The rooms of these houses were used much as they had been in the later Middle Ages, even though the hall slowly declined as an all-purpose room. The chamber beyond was now increasingly called the parlour, but was still often the principal bedroom and also served as a store as well as a private room. The upper chambers were used as bedrooms for junior members of the family, for servants and guests, but for a long time were not the preferred place to sleep. They continued as stores for produce and for light items of farm and domestic equipment, at least until the eighteenth century and often for longer.

Inventories bring these rooms to life. In 1566/7 an upper room of John Austen's house at Chillenden contained 'one linen whele, a woolen wheale, a payer a sock cardes [a pair of stock cards, used in weaving]', and an oast cloth, on which malt or hops were dried over a kiln, and 'bruing tubs, tryes, milk bolles, dishes, trenchers, spoones, certyen barlets [perhaps baskets for barley], a charne, 2 boteles, one oryn pot and a breadgrat'. In the 1570s John Sharppye occupied a large house at Cranbrook which had two full storeys and a garret in the roof space. Its hall was probably used for cooking since the kitchen was furnished with a table, a bench, a chair, a cradle, a desk and 'one Byble and other servyce books'; and a bakehouse and larder were furnished with all the necessary items for cooking and storing food. The parlour was furnished with some finely joined tables, benches and stools, and there were fourteen cushions, and a cupboard for silver. The great chamber over the hall contained a bedstead, a table, benches, stools, a chest and a cupboard, and a painted hanging for decoration. 'The Gesson chamber' was similarly furnished, and there were more chambers — one over the kitchen, a 'Maydes chamber', a 'Folkes chamber', and a 'Boyes chamber'. The garret was filled with malt and oats, and there was more produce in a wheat chamber, a quern room, a cheese house, an apple chamber and a cellar, that is to say a bottle store rather than a basement room.

Sharppye's household was a full one, and unusual because everyone slept upstairs. William Cullinge of Barham typically slept downstairs. He died in 1585 in a featherbed in his parlour. 'An olde Bible, a Book of Common Praier and a Cronacle' gave him spiritual solace, and his worldly comfort derived from plenty of bedclothes, sheets, tablecloths, towels and napkins as well as '11 platters, 4 pewter disshes, 2 saltes, 4 saucers and 13 pewter spoones...' His hall contained the usual table and bench, with two chairs for places of honour. However, the hall was also becoming a general store as well as the main communal room and a kitchen (Melling 1965, 17, 27-30).

Tudor gentry houses

Tradition and innovation were similarly mixed in the houses of the gentry and Kent's few aristocrats. As early as the 1470s, Sir Henry Heydon was building Wickham Court around a courtyard in the old way, but this was of the smallest size and there was no gatehouse as Hever Castle had had a century beforehand. As well as the innovatory use of brick, several rooms in the house had enclosed hearths served by

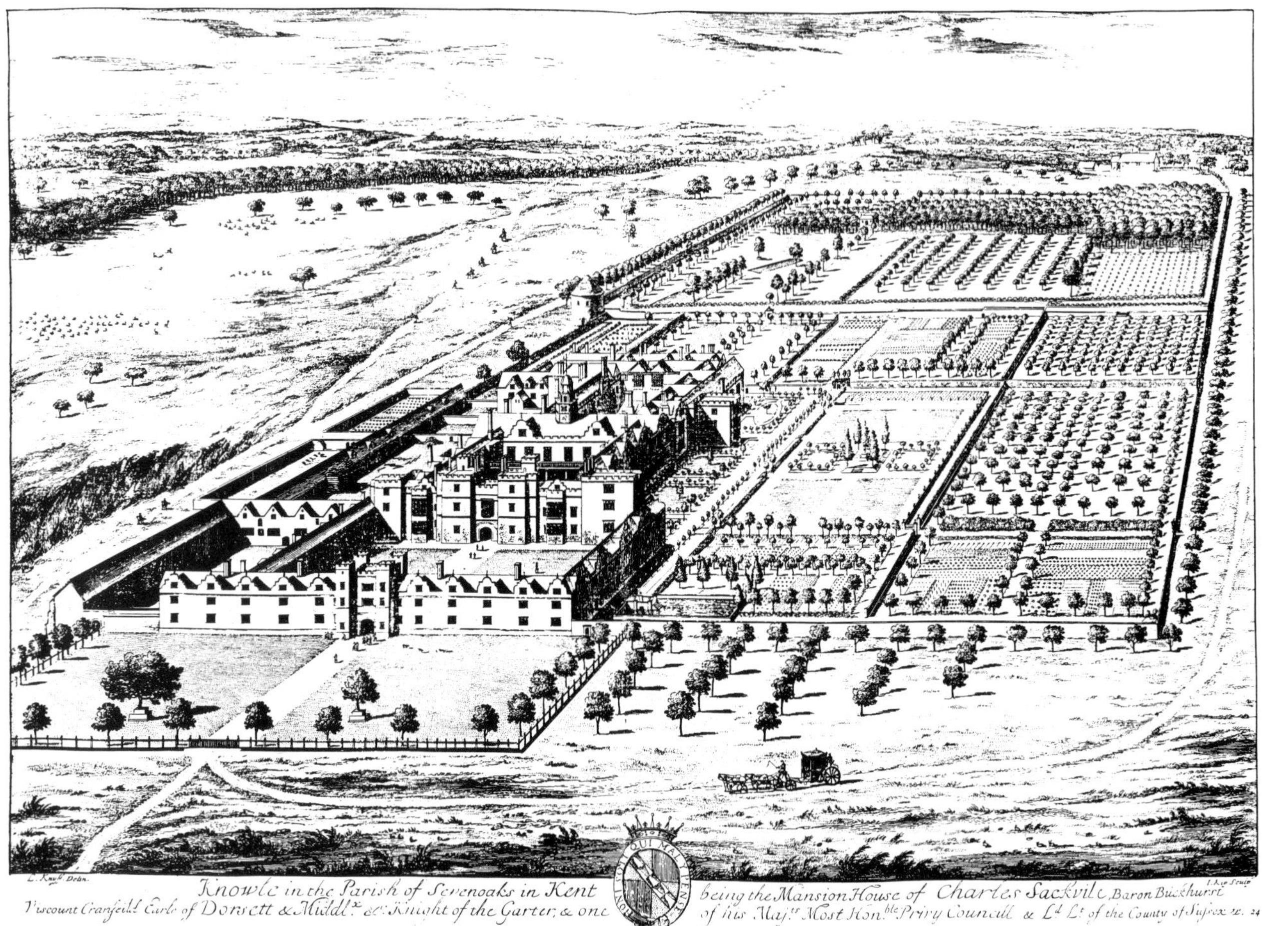

Figure 74. Knole, Sevenoaks. Kip's view, showing Sackville's outer courtyard at the front, decorated with shaped gables, and, towards the rear, the two original courtyards separated by the Archbishop's hall (with the lantern).

chimney-stacks, and these included the hall which could therefore be confined to the ground storey. Courtyards with prominent gate towers continued to symbolise ancient chivalry in the largest houses until well after the end of the sixteenth century. Sir Thomas Cheyney's Shurland at Eastchurch had been built in this form by 1532, and Sir Richard Baker took it up again after 1558 with the prodigious tower and courtyard at Sissinghurst (Colour Plate 66). A London alderman built Franks at Horton Kirby with a gatehouse and a small courtyard as late as 1591 (Colour Plate 67). Even in the first decade of the seventeenth century Sir Thomas Sackville was extending Knole in the way it had begun with an outer courtyard with a memorable turreted gatehouse (Figure 74); otherwise, these works were fairly plain despite the innovatory use of shaped gables (Colour Plate 68). The courtyard plan soldiered on until the middle of the seventeenth century, when, finally, its now archaic form was combined with a correct usage of classical pilasters to articulate the ranges of Bridge Place (Plate 44). These houses, typically, show Kent's gentry maintaining a conservative stance in the face of change.

The typical large Elizabethan house was again conservative, being simply an extension of the three-part medieval hall-house plan with symmetrical cross-wings forming an open courtyard, or an H-plan, or with a projecting entrance porch to make an E-plan. The surviving wing of Boughton Place at Boughton Malherbe was built

Plate 74. Hollingbourne Manor, showing the central range and the south wing which was to have been balanced by a northern wing on the right.

in stages about 1520 and 1553 with an open courtyard in mind (Colour Plate 50). Before partial demolition, Bax Farm at Tonge, which is dated 1567, showed how the H-plan worked on a fairly small scale (Colour Plate 69).

Symmetry was now important, and that meant contorting the essentially different needs of private apartments and perhaps a chapel at the high end of the hall and service rooms at the low end into similar blocks. Few such houses were ever completed, evidence that Kent remained beyond the grasp of much aristocratic wealth, even after the Dissolution. The 9th Lord Cobham, who had been granted the estates of Rochester Abbey, apparently began Cobham Hall in this way about 1550, probably as part of an intended courtyard arrangement. The 10th Lord continued the house along a different tack to form a grand open courtyard on the other side of the hall, evidently with houses of the aristocratic Cecils as a model; he was also hoping for a visit from Queen Elizabeth, vainly as it turned out (Colour Plate 70). His south range has a notably symmetrical south elevation terminating in octagonal towers, which are balanced by a second pair terminating the north range. Meanwhile, Otterden Place and Ford Place, Wrotham (Colour Plate 39), got no further than a single wing, and Christopher Roper's Lynsted Lodge, which was completed, has now largely gone.

More compact gentry houses fared only a little better. The lawyer and MP for Maidstone Nicholas Barham bought Chillington Manor in 1561 and proceeded to build a new house, now Maidstone Museum. Its hall lies to the right of a projecting central entrance porch, still with its screens passage, balancing service rooms to the

Plate 75. The symmetrical front of Groombridge Place, belying its asymmetrically placed entrance to the central hall.

other side, and projecting wings at each end. This set the pattern for the Astley's refronting of the Archbishop's Palace at Maidstone, and also for a few other houses such as Hollingbourne Manor (Plate 74), East Sutton Park and Bybrook at Kennington, but none of these was completed.

This plan was still in use in the third quarter of the seventeenth century. However old fashioned it had now become, it was convenient. The poet, dramatist and writer on country matters Gervase Markham had published an example in a revised edition of *The English Husbandman* in 1635 and described its benefits. The plan could be executed in any materials, it could be fully embellished with towers and bay windows, and be easily enlarged. Its north wing provided plenty of space for a kitchen and a full complement of service rooms; meanwhile, its south wing accommodated a dining parlour for guests, a guests' lodging and a closet for the lady of the house. Sir Basil Dixwell's Broome Park (Colour Plate 40) followed these arrangements in the 1630s, possibly in response to Markham's publicity, and Philip Packer used them for Groombridge Place as late as the 1660s (Plate 75). Here, modernity was introduced by hiding the asymmetrical layout of the hall by a central porch and a loggia running between the projecting wings (Figure 75) (Maguire 1989).

The lack of symmetry in the plan was resolved in Kent as early as about 1603-13 with the Earl of Clanricarde's Somerhill at Tonbridge (Colour Plate 11), where the hall is placed centrally, end-on to the entrance (Figure 76). The surveyor John Thorpe devised this arrangement, and it foreshadows the decline of the hall into no more than a grand entrance vestibule. This arrangement exactly reflects the contemporary Charlton House, built for the royal tutor Sir Adam Newton in the metropolitan fringe of Kent.

Symmetrical planning

Tradition, understandably, ruled the yeoman's house during the sixteenth century, so the old three-part plan with a central hall remained and, indeed, continued into the seventeenth century. Nevertheless, a desire for symmetry and a rational re-ordering

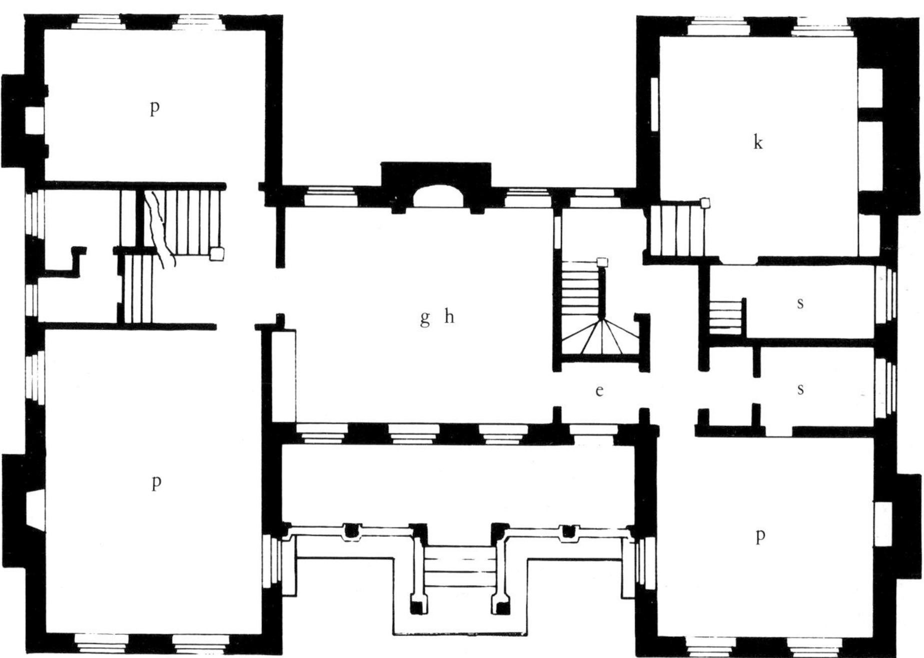

Figure 75. Groombridge Place. Ground plan: still reflecting the old medieval arrangements, the ground floor hall is in the centre, entered from one corner, disguised by the symmetrical arcaded porch; the kitchen and two service rooms are beyond the entrance in the right-hand wing, together with a little parlour acting as the master's office where he could oversee the housekeeping; in the opposite wing are two family parlours. (After Maguire 1989.)

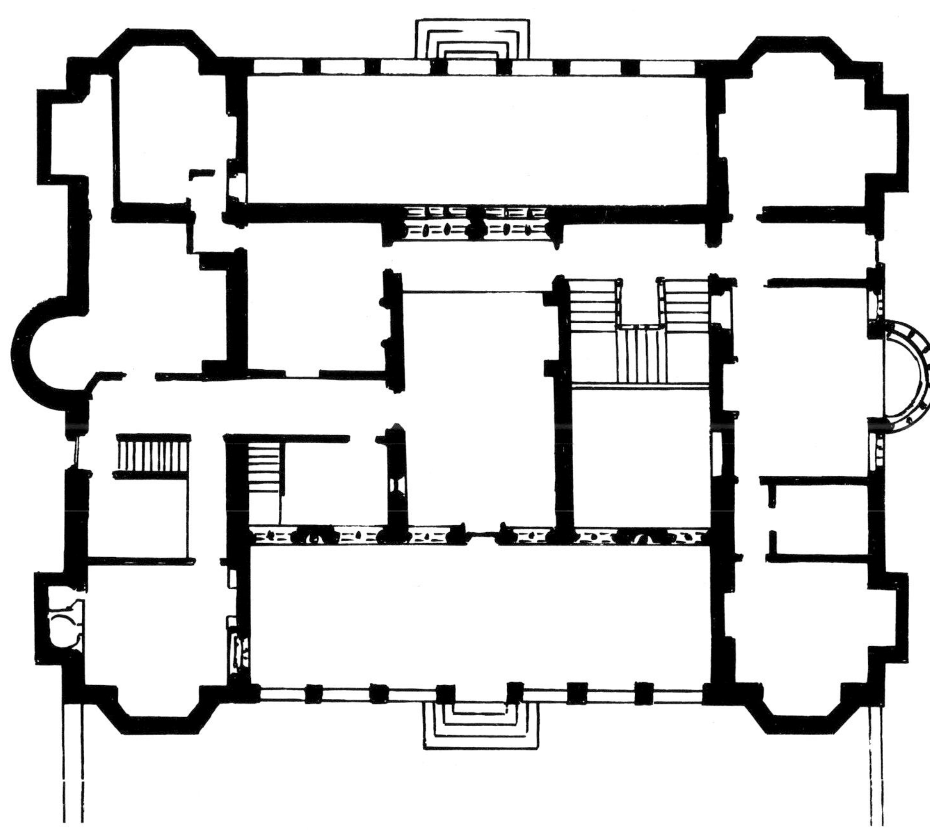

Figure 76. Somerhill, Tonbridge. Plan, based on original in the Soane Museum by the 17th century surveyor John Thorpe; the hall is in the centre with an entrance at one end and a form of screens passage across the other, leading to the main staircase and formal rooms to the right, and to service rooms to the left. (After Oswald 1933, 128.)

Plate 76. Cobb's Hall, Aldington, probably built as the Court House of the Archbishop of Canterbury's steward at Aldington, between 1509 and 1526, with a nearly symmetrical lobby-entry plan.

of the plan brought quick rewards to a few of their houses early in the sixteenth century and put Kent in the vanguard of design, just as it had been when it devised the Wealden design of hall-house some hundred and fifty years beforehand. This time, though, it exploited the innovations with little urgency.

When medieval houses were modernised, a chimney-stack was sometimes extended from the low end of the hall so that it blocked the cross-passage and provided a second hearth in the room beyond it. This reduced the passage to no more than an entrance lobby, seldom more than 6ft. (2m) square, but it provided separate access to each of the flanking rooms and screened them from draughts. A tight newel staircase might be fitted into the remaining space at the rear of the stack, though it could be placed at the front to rise from the lobby itself.

The main advantage of this new arrangement was that both the principal ground-floor rooms opening off the lobby could have fireplaces built into the centrally placed chimney-stack, and corresponding upper rooms could be similarly heated, requiring the stack characteristically to have four flues. Above the lobby, a cupboard or closet could open off one or both of the upper rooms, and it might extend over an open porch to make a fair-sized third room. In many houses the roof space was used as a loft or garret, and it might be tall enough for fully fledged rooms with dormer windows and even fireplaces of their own.

The origins of this so-called lobby-entry plan lie in lodgings and inns, such as the demolished Fleur-de-Lys at Canterbury, which was built about 1500 with a high standard of accommodation and comfort provided by enclosed hearths in several rooms on at least two floors, each with its own access. The first known use of the lobby-entry plan did not result from a process of adaptation, but was designed for a new house, Cobb's Hall at Aldington, so the plan seems to have been an invention.

Cobb's Hall was apparently built at some time between 1509 and 1526 as the combined lodging and court-house of Thomas Cobbe, the steward of the Archbishop

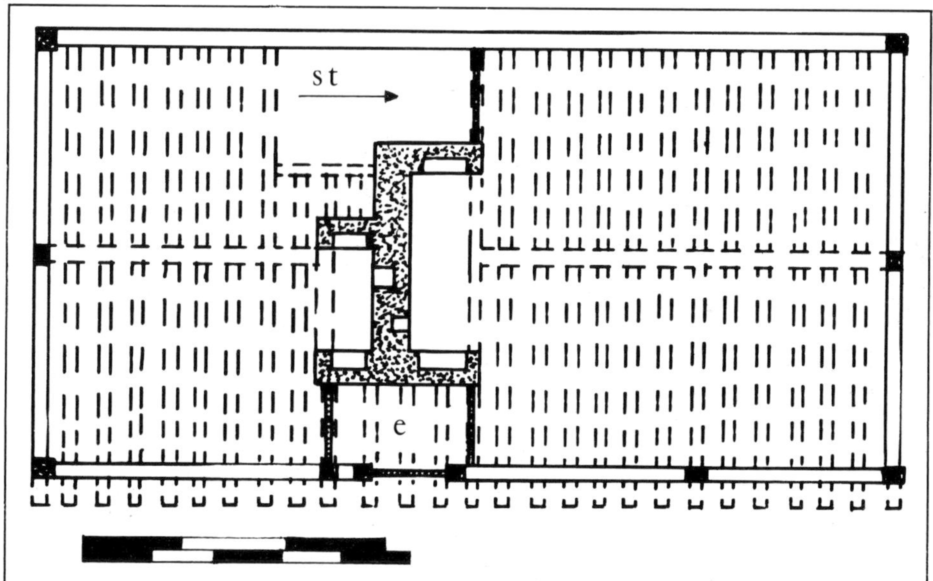

Figure 77. Cobb's Hall, Aldington. Restored plan, showing entrance lobby, chimney-stack with back-to-back hearths and position of staircase, running from front to back across centre of house, with single, heated room each side. (After Quiney 1984.)

of Canterbury's Aldington estate. It had a single heated room on each side of the entry lobby and chimney-stack (Colour Plate 71 and Plate 76), perhaps a court hall and service room, originally with a staircase behind the stack leading to a pair of heated chambers in the upper storey (Figure 77). This arrangement of rooms is reflected in the nearly symmetrical front, which is jettied along its full length.

This attention to fashion might have had greater consequences if the shadow of the Reformation had not been hanging over Canterbury and the carpenters who served the archbishop's and prior's needs. The Dissolution wrought such havoc that the Church ceased to build. Cobb's Hall and its plan remained for a generation or two as a local curiosity and little more (Quiney 1984).

Among the few but undated lobby-entry houses which appear to have followed Cobb's Hall closely are Jordans at Plaxtol (Plate 77), Briton House at St Michael's, Tenterden (Colour Plate 72), and, perhaps, Lashenden at Biddenden, which could be a house called Horcheyard Podsole in a will of 1531-2.

The compact plan of the lobby-entry house is well suited to box-framed construction. The stack, entry lobby and staircase neatly fit into a narrrow bay, framed by two trusses, and give each other mutual support. With the adoption of trussed roofs with side purlins instead of the medieval crown-plate and collared rafters of the south-east, the axial stack does not interrupt the roof framing. Apart from giving a house a fashionably symmetrical appearance, the great advantage of the plan is that no space is wasted: individual access to each room required no passages. Further rooms in a third storey brought no problems, but when, more commonly, they were added to one end or at the rear, they needed their own chimney-stack or remained cold, and could only be approached through one of the other rooms with a consequent loss of privacy. This hardly mattered so long as the upper rooms were used by children and servants. If the master and his wife slept upstairs, they could at least resort to the seclusion of a four-poster with its curtains and hangings; but a later, more fastidious age had to erect partitions and form passageways.

Nevertheless, successful yeomen like the Usbornes of Staplehurst ignored the lobby-entry plan when they were building in the 1560s. Symmetry slowly became

Plate 77. Jordans, Plaxtol, an early 16th century lobby-entry house which seems to have had a central smoke hood before the present stack was built.

fashionable, but often did without the lobby-entry plan: Ludgate at Lynsted lacks a central entry, and Standen at Biddenden, of 1578, lacks a central stack (Colour Plate 31). By then the lobby-entry plan had come into common use in Essex and Suffolk, but was still rare in Kent, thanks to the small need for new houses.

Kent's oldest dated lobby-entry house is Godfrey House at Hollingbourne, whose inscription bearing the date 1587 unfortunately belongs to a restoration of 1859. It continues the old three-part arrangement of rooms, so it cannot be symmetrically designed around the entrance, but it does have up-to-date decorative framing with ogee bracing, a fine open porch with a room in the gabled and jettied upper storey and dormered garrets. Manor Farm at Cliffe has the same asymmetrical arrangement of rooms, and its close-studding and full-length jetty could be evidence of an earlier date. Both houses have very ornate chimneys. When the Knights built Basing at Cowden in the 1590s, they could give it a symmetrical lobby-entry plan because they put its kitchen in a rear wing (Colour Plate 13).

This was not a necessity. Often the third room was omitted from lobby-entry houses, leaving the remaining two to share the functions of the three in what became a perfectly symmetrical arrangement. This is the way of Valence House at Sutton Valence, which is dated 1598; here, an open porch supports a full upper room, and this and the flanking bays are surmounted by gables, a new fashion taken from the towns.

A necessity of its two-part plan was that the hall took on some of the attributes of a service room as well as being used for cooking and eating. It gradually came to be

Plate 78. Hilders Farm, Chiddingstone, a hall-house converted into a lobby-entry house and given a nearly symmetrical front.

known as the kitchen. Smaller service rooms for special purposes like brewing or cheese-making were often partitioned from it or housed in complete bays of their own. The chamber on the further side of the lobby, increasingly called the parlour, took on some of the functions of the high end of the hall as a formal place where a yeoman could conduct his business or eat in private; otherwise it was a sitting-room, bedroom and general storage place for household goods, clothing and linen, and again might have an inner room partitioned from it. The upper rooms served as before, and, when a house had a garret, as Godfrey House does, it too was used for storage; no one slept there, not even servants, who commonly slept in garrets in towns.

Valence House established a pattern repeated several times in the lobby-entry houses of the next generation, for instance Bishop's Farm, Boughton Monchelsea. Honywood House at Lenham of 1621 exemplifies them all with its fine decorative carving and prominent front and side gables (Colour Plate 73); only the chimney-stack shorn of its four shafts and caps detracts from its lavish finish. Equally lavish, although lacking gables, is Yew Trees at Wye, which is dated 1605 (Plate 28), and again exemplifies a widespread variation of the type which includes Old Harrow Farm at Egerton (Colour Plate 74) and the rebuilding of Dane Chantry at Petham, dated 1638.

Hilders Farm at Chiddingstone (Plate 78) and Eastling Manor, an aisled hall rebuilt in 1616, show how this fashionable pattern was impressed on old houses at the start of the seventeenth century. The comfort, privacy and economy of the lobby-entry plan were at last bringing it success and would give it a remarkably long life span of over four hundred years. Soon the first emigrants were taking its plan to New England,

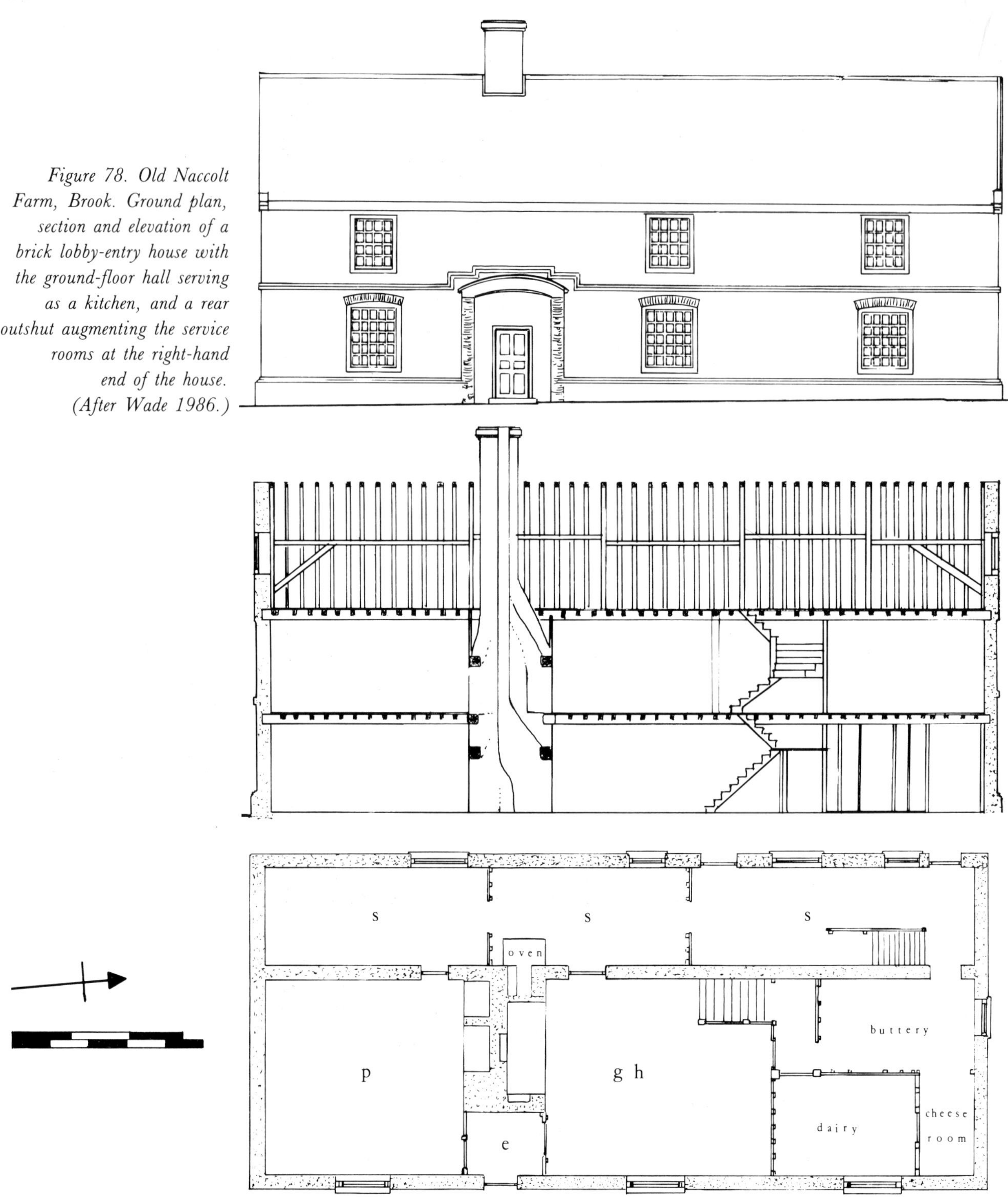

Figure 78. Old Naccolt Farm, Brook. Ground plan, section and elevation of a brick lobby-entry house with the ground-floor hall serving as a kitchen, and a rear outshut augmenting the service rooms at the right-hand end of the house. (After Wade 1986.)

where it was used for thousands of houses. Still the old three-part plan continued in Kent, sometimes with the lavish grandeur of Baxon Manor at Bredgar, which is dated as late as 1617 (Colour Plate 75). Nevertheless, chimney-stacks blocked numerous cross-passages to form lobbies in old houses, and new lobby-entry houses eventually became standard form.

The lobby-entry plan was particularly suited to the needs of a workhouse since the

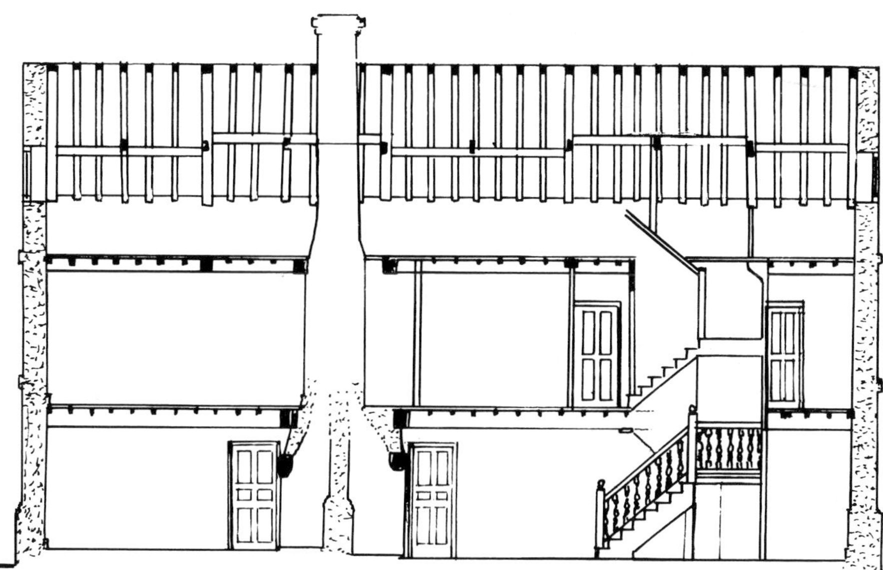

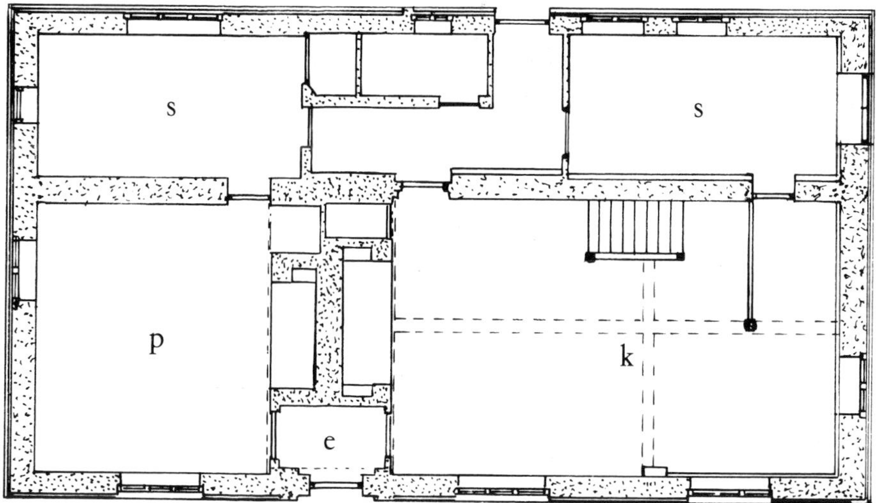

Figure 79. Troy Town House, Brook. Ground-plan and section of another brick lobby-entry house with a rear outshut augmenting the kitchen on the right-hand side of the chimney-stack. (After Wade 1986.)

chimney-stack effectively divided it into two sections, one range for men, the other for women. This is how Chiddingstone Workhouse came to be built in the seventeenth century, though probably rather later than the date of the Elizabethan Poor Law, 1601, inscribed on it (Colour Plate 14). It is nevertheless a rarity, probably because most parishes in need of a workhouse preferred to adapt a cheap old house than to build from scratch.

The change from timber to brick should have caused the plan to fall out of favour, since the central chimney-stack made a good marriage with a narrow bay framed in timber, but was an unnecessary intrusion into a brick house since stacks were more easily attached to the external walls. Nevertheless, conservatism allowed brick houses to adopt the plan with a fair degree of style. The loveliest is Brunger Farm, Tenterden (Colour Plate 76), where crow-stepped gables, even for its porch, lift it well beyond the ordinary. Old Naccolt Farm and Troy Town House at Brook (Figures 78 and 79) and Coldred Manor Farm (Colour Plate 77) gain from the seventeenth century's high quality of brickwork, but none of them matches School Farm at Ash, which was built in 1691 with a fairly symmetrical lobby-entry plan, and scrolled end gables of the *halsgavel* type (Colour Plate 42).

Plate 79. Bogle, Lynsted, built with brick end walls and chimney-stacks, but framed front and back and nogged with brick, and bearing the date 1643.

Symmetrical brick and stone houses

While the central stack of a lobby-entry house wasted no radiant heat, it consumed space and materials, and restricted circulation. Hearths built into the external walls of a brick house immediately freed its centre so that the lobby could extend rearwards to become a fully fledged vestibule giving individual access to all the rooms, to a wide staircase and to one or two service rooms within the main body of the house or in a rear outshut or a separate wing. The cost might be the loss of some heat from the exposed backs of the chimney-stacks, but the gain in convenience was more than recompense. Stylishly turned balusters, a moulded rail and carved tread ends could make the prominent staircase an effective decorative feature of the new vestibule, and the front of the house could be designed symmetrically.

While the principal room was at first still called the hall, it eventually became known as the kitchen or dining-room depending on its function; meanwhile the vestibule became known as the entrance hall or staircase hall and in the end simply as the hall. Its only connection with the medieval hall is that, by lying in the centre of the house with all the rooms opening off it, it reflected changes in great houses where the medieval hall had been demoted to the role of a ceremonial place of welcome providing access between the entrance and the reception rooms.

This plan had come into existence before the end of the Middle Ages, but its introduction to Kent only occurred when brick had become the accepted norm. In 1643 William Hugesson built Bogle at Lynsted in this way with a brick-nogged timber-framed front, and gable walls entirely of brick with chimney-stacks built into them (Plate 79). The heyday of this plan arrived in the eighteenth century with such rural houses as Sevenscore at Minster-in-Thanet, Chilton Farm, Ramsgate of c.1700 (Plate 80) and later on at Eastry for Heronden of 1766.

The linear arrangement of rooms continued throughout the seventeenth and eighteenth centuries in numerous houses, large and small. Winged houses forming courtyards, front or rear, started the seventeenth century at a low but lavish level with

Plate 80. Chilton Farm, Ramsgate, a house of c.1700, with a central entrance vestibule, chimney-stacks built into the end walls, and the shaped and pedimented gables typical of this date in east Kent.

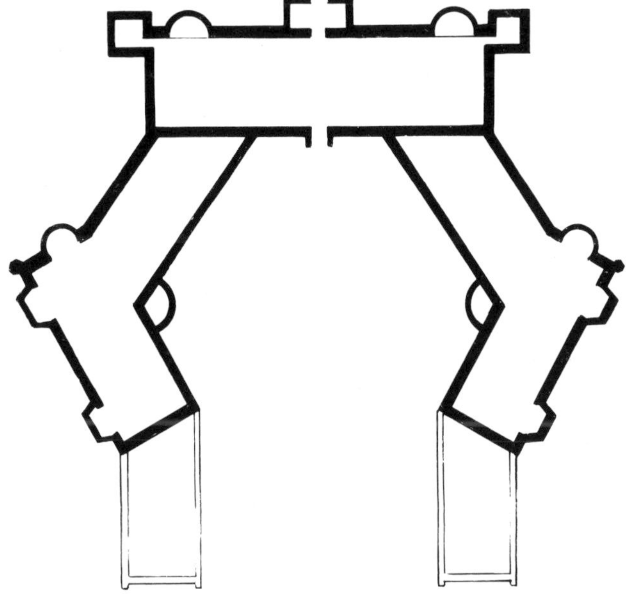

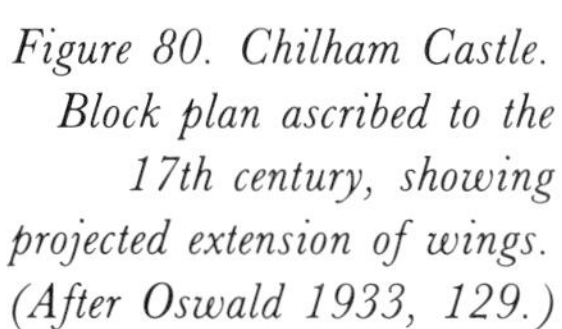

Figure 80. Chilham Castle. Block plan ascribed to the 17th century, showing projected extension of wings. (After Oswald 1933, 129.)

the timber-framed Norman Cottages at Benover, Yalding (Colour Plate 49), and continued into the eighteenth century with the bravura display of brickwork in the remodelling of Bradbourne at East Malling in 1712-16 (Colour Plate 44); Milgate at Bearstead followed it closely. The canted wings forming an open hexagon at Chilham Castle (Colour Plate 78) in 1616 were an unequalled Jacobean conceit (Figure 80), and most large houses of the century preferred ordinary cross-wings forming an H-plan.

Plate 81. Marle Place, Brenchley. The entrance front.

Plate 82. No. 45 Earl Street, Maidstone, a timber-framed urban double-pile, based on the lobby-entry plan with gabled bays each side of the central entrance, and a cross-gabled rear pile.

Broome Park made a special show of the plan in the middle of the century with its extravagant gables (Colour Plate 40), just as Yotes Court at Mereworth was exemplifying the new classical restraint inaugurated by Inigo Jones (Colour Plate 79). Groombridge Place (Plate 75) is restrained too, but its hall, placed to one side of the entrance passage in the old medieval way, however convenient, is a remarkable archaism when compared with its up-to-date brickwork in Flemish bond (Figure 75).

Double piles

All these plans were only one room deep, in conception at least. They were easy to construct and served usage. The disadvantages were not felt at first. The lack of privacy resulting from one chamber opening into the next offended few. The meandering wings of a large house hardly mattered at all; space never constrained countrymen as it constrained merchants and traders in towns. Nevertheless there was an alternative plan, at once compact and convenient. Its adoption was the last step in the development of the traditional rural house.

The semi-fortified Walmer Court, built before 1200 in emulation of a castle keep, with parallel ranges of flanking hall and chamber built over an undercroft (Figure 38), was echoed in towns where narrow house plots put frontage at a premium, while depth was less restricted. This method of building two blocks together to make a 'double pile', as the architect Sir Roger Pratt called it in the seventeenth century, had been used in towns, notably Southampton and Lincoln, again by 1200. Some of Canterbury's later shops fronting halls were in essence double piles too, and so was the front section of the courtyard house at 5-6 Market Place, Faversham (Figure 65). Apart from solving a particularly urban problem, a hierarchy of rooms was established, with the front pile as a shop, the rear pile as a residence, or, in a purely domestic building, with formal rooms at the front, service rooms at the back. This suited the changing social attitudes which began to appear after the Restoration.

Until the advent of bricks for chimneys and glass for windows, heating and lighting

Plate 83. Quebec House, Westerham, an early 17th century double-pile, so-named because James Wolfe, victor of Quebec, spent his childhood here.

these double piles had been problems, and so was the roof. When the need to build bay by bay that dominated the timber frame had been superseded by construction in brick, the compact double-pile plan could be more easily built. The widespread use of chimney-stacks and glazed windows, common after 1600, solved further problems, and a variety of roof patterns to cover the double span was devised to facilitate drainage.

Many late medieval houses in Canterbury and Kent's other towns became double piles through a process of extension, but this hardly affected the countryside. The first rural double piles which were designed and built as such in any numbers were, not surprisingly, adaptations of the timber-framed lobby-entry house. Marle Place at Brenchley, which is dated 1619, has a pair of front rooms flanking the lobby and a second pair at the rear, reached through an archway in the chimney-stack (Colour Plate 80 and Plate 81); otherwise it is similar to Valence House, which had been built a generation beforehand. Bilting Grange at Godmersham appears to have been much the same, despite alteration, and is dominated by a tall chimney-stack comprising no fewer than seven diagonally set shafts to serve most of the rooms (Figure 26d). These double-pile houses stand out because they are timber framed, early in date, and, exceptionally, do follow the local tradition of house building. So there must be some common link between them and the similar single-pile lobby-entry houses such as Valence House on which they appear to be based. Just as remarkable is 45 Earl Street, Maidstone (Plate 82), which is again timber-framed and possibly not much later in date; its front range with a lobby-entry and flanking rooms with two-storeyed canted bays and front gables, and rear range with gables to the sides, is clearly an urban adaptation of the same form.

Before the Civil War the double pile was appearing in occasional brick houses, to which it was more suited, notably at Ash Manor (in west Kent) of 1637, and Quebec House at Westerham (Plate 83), which are both traditional in style. Simultaneously the double-pile arrangement was used for Chevening Park, which had been started for

Colour Plate 87. Robert Adam's splendidly Roman garden front of Brasted Place.

Colour Plate 89. Eastgate House, High Street, Rochester, Sir Peter Buck's house of 1590, with a pedimented entrance, but more traditional decoration elsewhere.

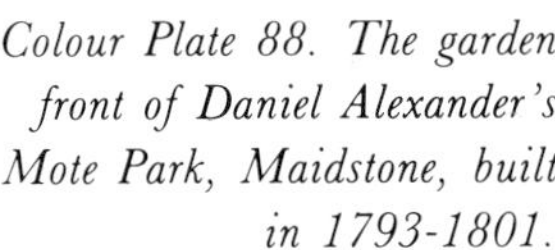

Colour Plate 88. The garden front of Daniel Alexander's Mote Park, Maidstone, built in 1793-1801.

Colour Plate 90. No. 7 Cumberland Walk, Tunbridge Wells, of about 1830, its stucco channelled to look like rusticated ashlar, and its fluted pilasters rising into exotic ammonite capitals.

Colour Plate 91. No. 8 Cumberland Walk, Tunbridge Wells, brick and regularly laid flint cobbles set off by sparkling cast iron.

Colour Plate 92. Crown Cottages, Staplehurst, a close-studded terrace of houses, each with two rooms per floor.

Plate 84. Chevening Park, heavily restored in recent years to become an official residence of HM Foreign Secretary, photographed on a public open day.

the 13th Baron Dacre by 1630 (Plate 84). Its plain symmetrical lines exemplified a national taste so advanced that the house has been associated with Inigo Jones, just as Lees Court at Sheldwich was to be. This probably gave rise to the design of another double pile, Sir John Sedley's St Clere at Kemsing, which was seemingly finished in 1633. National styles soon flooded into Kent, but the older linear winged plans continued, fully demonstrating Kent's conservatism. The remarkable thing, none the less, was that, typically, Kent had first adopted the double pile at the lower social level of its rich yeomanry, not the higher level of newcomers from the gentry and aristocracy.

After the Restoration the advantages of this compact plan were appreciated, as, about 1675, Pratt noted: 'we have there much room in a little compass... and there may be a great spare of walling, and of other material for the roof.' In fact a large double-pile house might use only half the material for its walling that would be needed by a linear house of the same floor area (Barley 1979). Convenience was well served too. A vestibule could link the front door with four ground-floor rooms and the staircase, and similarly a small landing could serve four chambers upstairs and a further flight to the garret: easy access and privacy went hand in hand. In larger double-pile houses there was space for a servants' staircase, greatly increasing both the privacy and the social divisions within the house, although this was uncommon at the social level of most yeomen for a long time.

The house was easy to heat and less draughty. A pair of internal chimney-stacks between the front and back rooms could help to support a spine wall as well as to provide hearths in all the four main rooms of each storey; nor would they cramp circulation as happened in a lobby-entry house where only a narrow bay was devoted both to this and to containing the chimney-stack. With glazing, no room had to be lit from opposing sides, though most important rooms could have windows on two adjacent sides.

Where fashion was concerned, the plan offered all the potential symmetry of the lobby-entry and central vestibule plans, nor was this jeopardised if further rooms were needed. The plan already provided for a hall and parlour at the front, later known as a front kitchen or dining-room and living-room, while there was space for a back kitchen and a service room or two at the rear. Still more rooms could be fitted in at

Plate 85. The garden front of Squerries Court, Westerham, built for Sir Nicholas Crisp in the 1680s.

the back without affecting the design as seen from the front. That mattered most: to be seen was often the main objective of the builders of these houses, because status was as important as convenience and any constructional advantage.

The double pile rapidly asserted its ascendency in the planning of all but the smallest houses after the Restoration. A corridor was inserted between the front and rear piles of the larger houses, greatly improving circulation. Two great rooms could then flank an imposing central vestibule. This might lead to both a formal staircase and a servants' stair fitted into opposite sides of the central space, and three more grand rooms could be fitted across the back if the service rooms were confined to the basement. The architect Hugh May designed Eltham Lodge (now in Greenwich, Greater London) with this arrangement in the 1660s, and numerous expensive houses like Squerries Court at Westerham, built after 1680, followed it (Plate 85).

Meanwhile the smaller but hardly less gorgeous Red House at Sevenoaks was built as a double pile in 1686, and Bradbourne Farm followed it a decade or so later with a fashionable front and a disorganised back where brickwork and timber framing make a patchwork good enough for the servants but not the visitors (Figure 81). Leacon Hall at Warehorne (Colour Plate 81) and Westwell at Tenterden (Colour Plate 82) took the plan into the eighteenth century with all the confidence of the Queen Anne style, and it went on and on to reach the twentieth century in the three great houses which Lutyens gave to the county, Wittersham House, The Salutation at Sandwich (Plate 86 and Figure 82) and Great Maythem at Rolvenden (Colour Plate 20), itself a reworking of a double-pile house first built in the eighteenth century.

Demand for new houses was only enough to scatter double-piles around, with most of them going up wherever prosperous new men wanted to demonstrate their taste and their wealth. Their standards were conspicuously metropolitan; so, after three hundred years of marked individuality, Kent's rural houses came ever closer to the common stream of building in England.

Architects and style

Increasingly fashion fell into the hands of men who had learnt their vocabulary of design from pattern books rather than from practice alone, that is to say architects as

Colour Plate 93. Battel Hall Cottages, Leeds, a terrace unusual for its site on the fringe of a village, and for the jettied and gabled garrets.

Colour Plate 94. Star Hill, Rochester, a first-rate terrace built to the best metropolitan standards of the 1790s in fashionable yellow brick.

Colour Plate 95. Bay windows and balconies adding a whiff of seaside air to Spencer Square, Ramsgate.

Colour Plate 96. Waterloo Crescent, Dover, built in 1834-38 in three sections to Philip Hardwick's designs.

Colour Plate 97. By 1911-12 Kent's two railway companies had merged as the South Eastern and Chatham Railway, so, with its engineering works concentrated at Ashford, new terraces were built in the New Town for its workers in a simple but 'improving' Arts and Crafts style.

Colour Plate 98. Balconies and bay windows in Ramsgate.

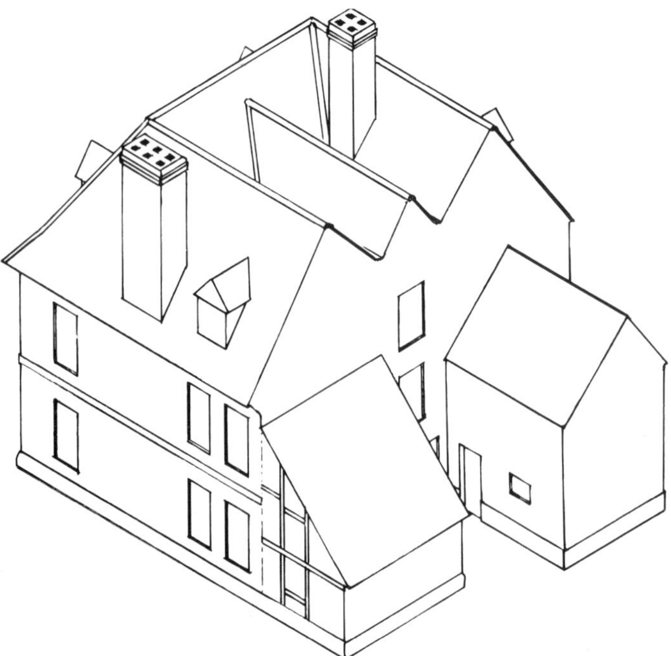

Figure 81. Bradbourne Farmhouse, Sevenoaks. Isometric from rear quarter of a double-pile house of about 1700, showing the symmetrical, formal front pile (upper left), with long, hipped roof stretching from end to end, and the informal rear pile, with three gabled roofs stretching backwards with valleys between them, and two extensions, one of them thinly framed in timber. (After Barley 1979.)

Plate 86. The Salutation, Sandwich, designed by Lutyens in 1911.

opposed to craftsmen. This affected style as well as planning. The baroque style adorned Finchcocks at Goudhurst in 1718-25 (Plate 87). No known architect is associated with its design, but shared characteristics suggest that the same man also designed Matfield House in 1728 (Colour Plate 83). Kent's superlative brickwork was still fully expressed in these houses, so traditional elements were not entirely subdued. Neither match the extraordinary façade of Swanton Street Farm at Bredgar, which the London goldsmith Edward Holliday introduced in 1719 (Colour Plate 84).

None the less, displays of this kind were now under immediate threat. When Colen Campbell designed Mereworth Castle (Colour Plate 85 and Figure 83) and Roger Morris designed Combe Bank at Sundridge (Colour Plate 86) in the 1720s, the

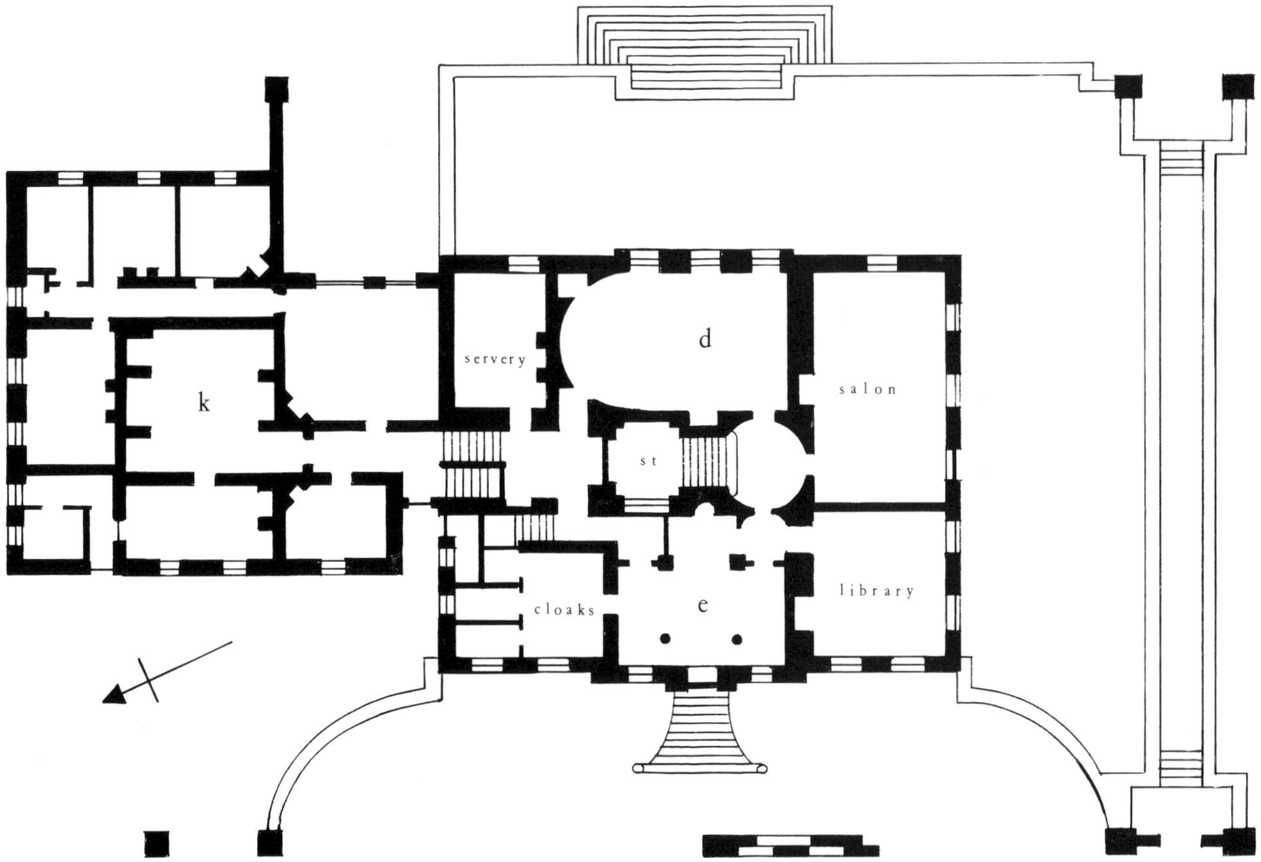

Figure 82. The Salutation, Sandwich. Plan, showing double-pile arrangement with formal entrance hall in centre, flanked by cloakrooms and library, in front part, with main staircase and, to its left, servants' stairs and a passageway leading to the servants' quarters in separate block, and, in rear part, a library, dining-room with an apsidal end and a servery.

Plate 87. Finchcocks, Goudhurst, Edward Bathurst's sumptuous house of the 1720s, a splendid pile despite the timidity of its baroque detail.

Colour Plate 99. One of Decimus Burton's characteristic villas at Calverley Park, Tunbridge Wells.

Colour Plate 100. The Grange, Ramsgate, with the tower from which Pugin kept a look-out over the Channel, and his church beyond, still without its intended spire.

Colour Plate 101. The Old Rectory, Brasted, asymmetrical and Gothic in detail, yet lacking the ins and outs beloved by many revivalists.

Colour Plate 102. No. 275 Dover Road, Walmer.

Colour Plate 103. Hillside, Groombridge, Norman Shaw's 1870s version of Old Kent.

Colour Plate 104. The garden front of How Green House, Hever, Mowbray Charrington's house of 1904-5, designed by Robert Weir Schultz.

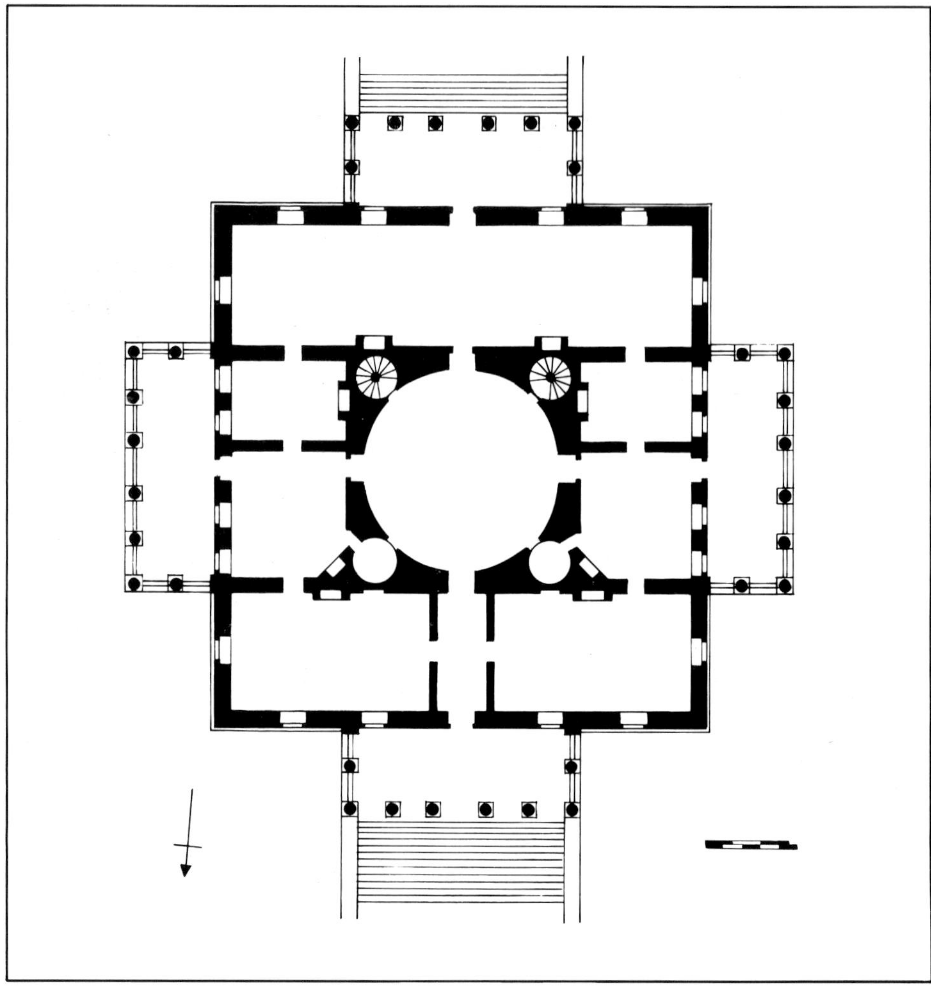

Figure 83. Mereworth Castle. Plan, showing symmetrical arrangement with central rotunda and four porticoes, based on Palladio's Villa Rotonda at Vicenza, but with a progression of rooms (instead of Palladio's four individual suites), starting with an entrance vestibule, passing through a salon under the rotunda, and ending with a gallery on the opposite side; the service rooms were in the basement, bedrooms and servants' rooms in the mezzanine and attic — an Italian arrangement, but also an urban English one; the fireplaces grouped around the rotunda are served by flues which rise up the curve of the dome to chimneys built into the central lantern. (After Vitruvius Britannicus.)

italianate taste inaugurated by Inigo Jones a century beforehand now arrived with a vengeance. True Palladianism had no place for fine brickwork. Chaste masonry or the pretence of stucco killed off its exuberance as the new style banished baroque's licentiousness.

Kent's few great houses still to come are in Kent, but not of Kent. They now belonged to the correct styles of architects: Robert Adam, young and Palladian at Mersham-le-Hatch in the 1760s (Plate 88), grandly Roman at Brasted Place in the 1780s (Colour Plate 87); Samuel Wyatt and Daniel Asher Alexander, both of them sharp and geometrical in the neo-classical way at Belmont, Throwley (Colour Plate 46), and Mote Park, Maidstone (Colour Plate 88 and Figure 84), in the 1790s; Sir John Soane, diffident even for him, at Ringwould House in 1813 (Plate 89), demonstrate it all.

Plate 88. Mersham-le-Hatch, Robert Adam's early essay in neo-classicism, built for the Knatchbulls in the 1760s.

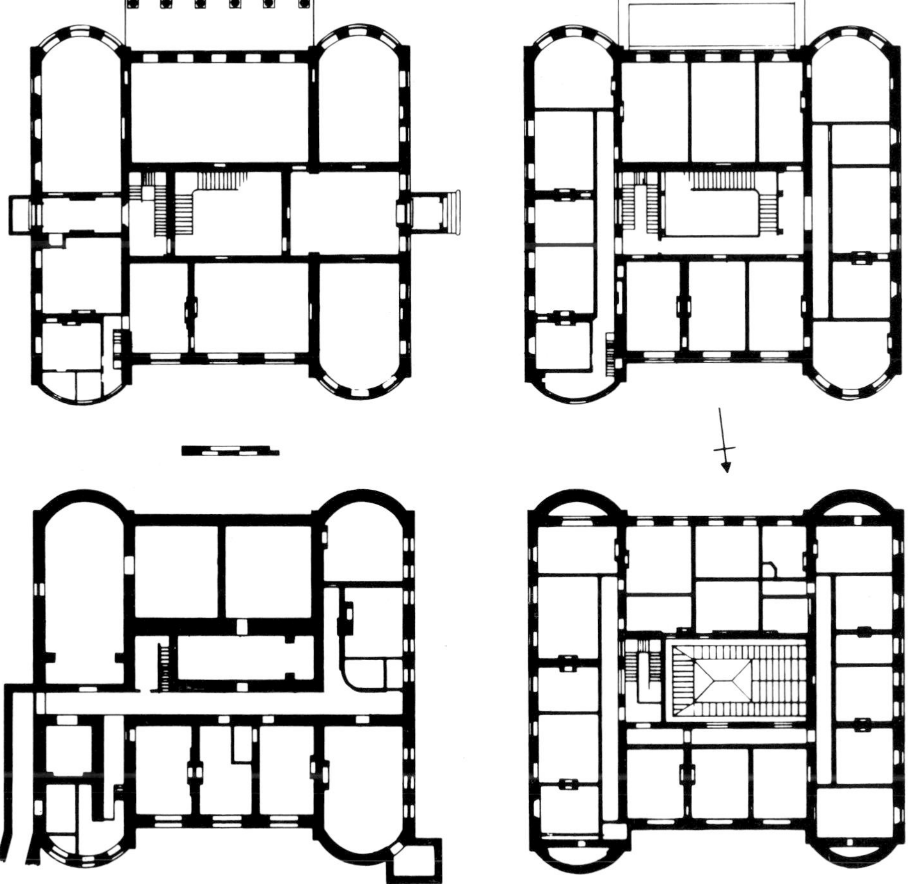

Figure 84. Mote Park, Maidstone. Plans, in clockwise order from bottom left, of basement, ground, first and attic storeys: the south side of the basement was devoted to wine and beer cellars, the north side to a furnace room, housekeeper's room, stores and kitchen, with a tunnel leading to a detached service block; the ground floor comprised a main entrance hall, main staircase hall, servants' stairs and service entrance across the middle of the plan, from east to west, with a billiard room, drawing-room and master's study and gun room to the north, a second drawing-room, library with loggia, and dining-room to the south; the first floor contained the main bedrooms, dressing-rooms and a boudoir and sitting room; the attic the bachelors' rooms, nurseries and servants' rooms. (After a sale catalogue of 1911.)

Colour Plate 105. Lime Tree Walk, Sevenoaks, a terrace spiced here and there with traditional features including oriels and a shaped gable.

Colour Plate 106. Estate cottages designed by Ernest George at Leigh in an exuberant Old English style owing more to the West Midlands than to Kent.

Colour Plate 107. Denge Beach, Lydd, Kent's least characteristic landscape.

Colour Plate 108. The Hopfield, Platt, which, despite its name, is an ideological declaration of allegiance to the International Modern style of the 1930s.

Colour Plate 109. Wood House, Shipbourne, an early reaction against internationalism from one of its first devotees, the German architect Walter Gropius, who designed it in 1937.

Colour Plate 110. Oak House, Biddenden, a remarkably happy marriage of tradition and modernism, created in the 1980s by Michael Coombes.

Colour Plate 111. Oasts at Penshurst, converted by the Quirks.

Plate 89. Ringwould House, Soane's plain yet quirky neo-classical design of 1813, built for the Reverend John Monins.

Modernised urban plans

In Kent's towns the wholesale introduction of chimney-stacks and continuous upper floors with the consequent reduction of the hall to no more than one heated room among several others took much the same course as it had in the countryside. The need for change was all the more pressing because the concomitant savings in space were so valuable. They remained harder to achieve because of problems with lighting and circulation, and their progress is harder to evaluate because, ultimately, the changes were so much more extensive in town than in the countryside that they obliterated more of the past.

All this took time. For a century or two after the Middle Ages, tradition adapted rather than tradition overturned was the rule. Piecemeal change was more easily assimilated, and left people well satisfied. Large inns, in the widest sense of grand town houses and lodging houses for academics and lawyers as well as public lodgings for travellers, were in the vanguard here, particularly in the use of multi-flued chimney-stacks to heat many rooms. The best chambers in the comparatively modest Fleur-de-Lys at Canterbury had fireplaces set back-to-back in a single stack by about 1500 (Pantin 1961 [6]).

Canterbury's numerous medieval houses were modernised in the same way. A stack with back-to-back hearths was built into 8 Palace Street to heat the front and rear chambers on the first floor, and a jettied upper storey was added later (Figure 85). The remodelling of 17 Palace Street eventually gave it a stack with back-to-back hearths heating the shop at the front and the hall at the rear as well as hearths for the front chambers on the two floors above (Figure 86). No. 39 Strand Street, Sandwich, was modernised by having a floor inserted across its open hall and a two-storeyed rear wing added in 1606, with the hall and the new chambers being heated by back-to-back hearths on both floors. Some houses, for instance 13-13a St Peter's Street, Canterbury, may only have had a timber and plaster firehood, despite such status symbols as jettied upper floors and gables and long bands of clerestory windows (Canterbury Archaeological Trust 1983-4).

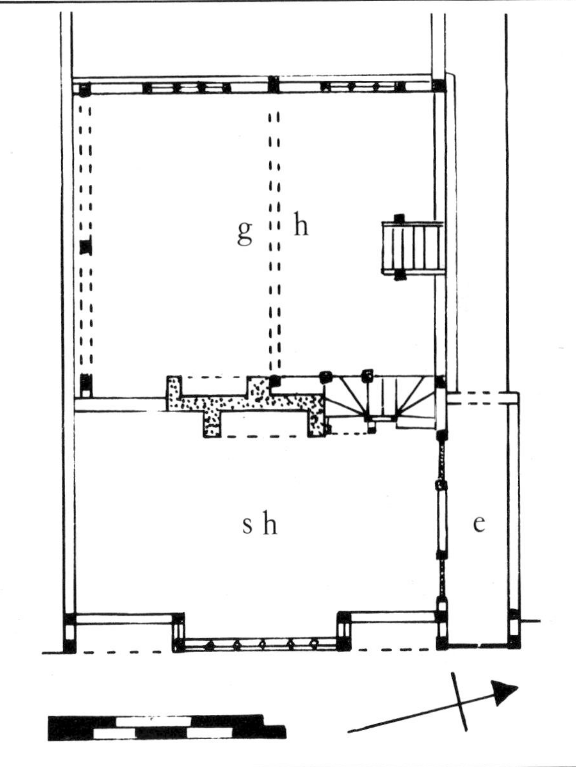

Figure 85. Former Rectory of St Alphege, 8 Palace Street, Canterbury. Section, showing remains of stone ground floor with jettied upper floors, the lower of which is heated by a chimney-stack with back-to-back hearths. (After Parkin 1969b.)

Figure 86. No. 17 Palace Street, Canterbury. Plan, showing inserted chimney-stack with back-to-back hearths serving front and back rooms, and entry by way of side passage. (After Parkin 1972.)

Plate 90. No. 28 Palace Street, Canterbury, its prominent jetties turning the corner site, with prominent clerestory windows and plasterwork in imitation of rusticated ashlar.

Plate 91. No. 25 Court Street, Faversham, probably built soon after 1608 for the shipmaster John Trowtes.

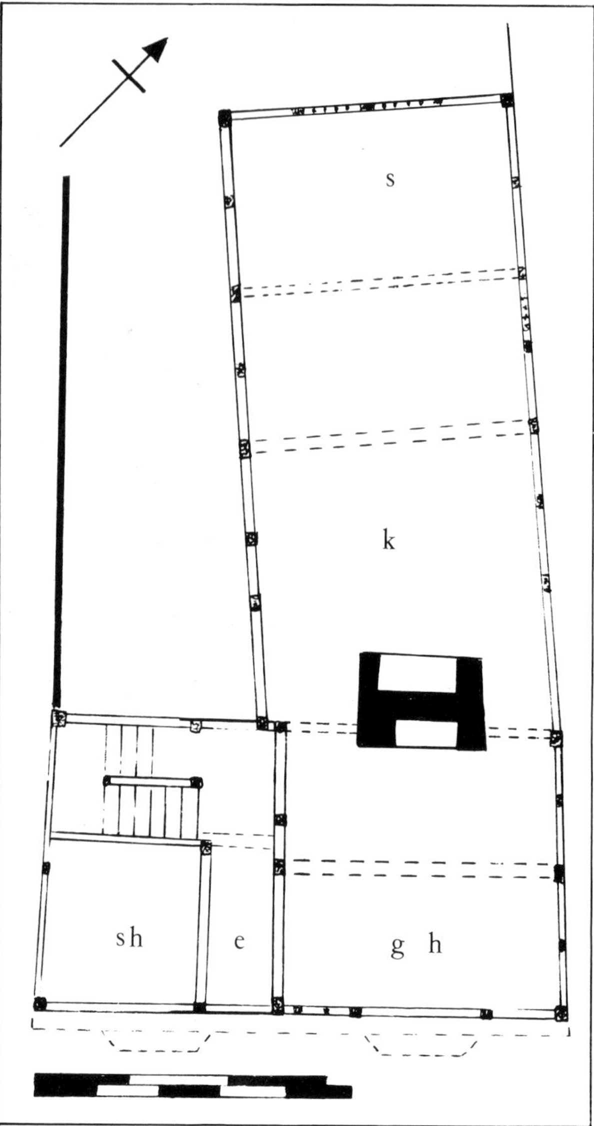

Figure 87. No. 25 Court Street, Faversham. Conjectural plan showing shop and ground-floor hall flanking the entry at the front, and kitchen and services at rear facing yard; the front jetty and oriel windows are shown dashed. (After Laithwaite 1968.)

New houses similarly relied on chimney-stacks built between their front and back rooms, floor by floor, often in association with a staircase. Alternatively, the stacks could rise against the party wall, as at 28 Palace Street, which was built in 1617 with the advantage of a corner site and therefore windows on two adjacent sides, and prominent jetties to its two storeys and gabled garret (Plate 90).

Where plots were wide enough to allow the retention of a fully open passage running between the main street and a back lane, the rooms again had the advantage of side lighting for part of the house. A pattern already in use by 1576 at Rye, East Sussex, allowed for a double front with a main entrance, placed between an office or shop and a ground-floor hall; this led by way of a passage to a back yard. The hall was divided by a chimney-stack with back-to-back hearths from a rear wing containing a parlour, facing the yard, and the pair of chambers over the hall and parlour were heated by further back-to-back hearths in the same stack. This arrangement was possibly widespread: it was used at 25 Court Street, Faversham, which the ship-master John Trowtes probably built soon after 1608; it has a kitchen and buttery in place of the rear parlour (Plate 91 and Figure 87), but these are differences in nomenclature rather than in planning (Laithwaite 1968).

Plate 92. One of the long row of gabled houses in St. Dunstan's Street, Canterbury, as photographed at the end of the 19th century by Galsworthy Davie and reproduced by the collotype process in Davie and Dawber (1900).

Plate 93. The oriels, jetties and gables of 150-54 High Street, Rochester.

Even wider plots, particularly those outside the medieval walls, allowed full double-fronted houses, like those in St Dunstan's Street, Canterbury, whose jetties and gables make such a fine show (Plate 92). They were designed with entrance passages providing access to single-storeyed halls and parlours or shops at the front. Nos. 150-154 High Street, Rochester, was similarly built just outside the town's medieval walls where building plots were less cramped (Plate 93). When Sir Peter Buck's Eastgate House was built across the road in 1590, the problem of space was solved by siting it end-on to the street, thus allowing room for the rural E-plan and a courtyard in front of it (Colour Plate 89). This plan appeared again at much the same date in Restoration House, which, being further still from the centre of Rochester, could have a wider plot allowing it to face the street. A short while later, Andrew Broughton built 31-33 Earl Street, Maidstone, with a similar winged plan forming a small courtyard facing the street. No. 38 Earl Street shows how the same plan was used for a later seventeenth-century house built of brick, and so does The Chantry at Sevenoaks.

The double-pile, which had, significantly, been the first major incursion into the countryside of a plan evolved in town, was now widely adopted for all but the largest of individual urban houses, and given a full complement of heated rooms, front and back. No. 45 Earl Street, Maidstone, is a rare seventeenth-century timber-framed example, but it was brick and the new nation-wide classical taste then being

Plate 94. The Red House, built in 1686 for John Couchman in the centre of Sevenoaks.

introduced which gave this plan its chance. Progressive styles are well shown by The Red House at Sevenoaks of 1686 (Plate 94), 22 North Street, Bridge House and Brook Place in East Hill, Ashford, Westgate House, St Dunstan's Street, Canterbury, of 1760, Cooksditch, Faversham, of the 1780s, and 6 and 7 Cumberland Walk, Tunbridge Wells, of the 1830s, and 8 Cumberland Walk later still (Colour Plates 90 and 91).

The linear arrangement of rooms perpendicular to the street held greater promise for crowded streets, and ultimately led to the widespread adoption of the terrace. London's building traditions began to crumble when Inigo Jones brought back classical ideas and a copy of Palladio's *I Quattro Libri del'Architettura* from Italy and used them on a grand scale for the fourth Earl of Bedford's speculative development of Covent Garden with terraces in the 1630s. Following the Great Fire of London in 1666, the Rebuilding Act of 1667 killed off traditional building in timber in the City at a stroke, and the Building Acts of 1707, 1709 and particularly 1774, hand in hand with fashions expressed in a growing flood of books, eventually established new standards of construction for terraced houses throughout London.

The standardised terrace

Speculators simultaneously improved the plan of London's terrace houses, and by the 1680s had developed what became the definitive arrangement. An entrance passage running along one side provided access to a front and back room, heated by fireplaces built against the opposite side wall, and to rear staircases leading to the basement and the upper storeys, which again had two principal rooms each (Kelsall 1974). The plan was readily adaptable to houses large and small, as the London Building Acts recognised. The major feature they had in common was that the ground and first floors contained the principal rooms, and the basement was where the servants worked and the attic where they lived.

Kent slowly adopted this plan of terrace. Such early seventeenth-century timber-framed terraces as Crown Cottages at Staplehurst (Colour Plate 92) and Battel Hall

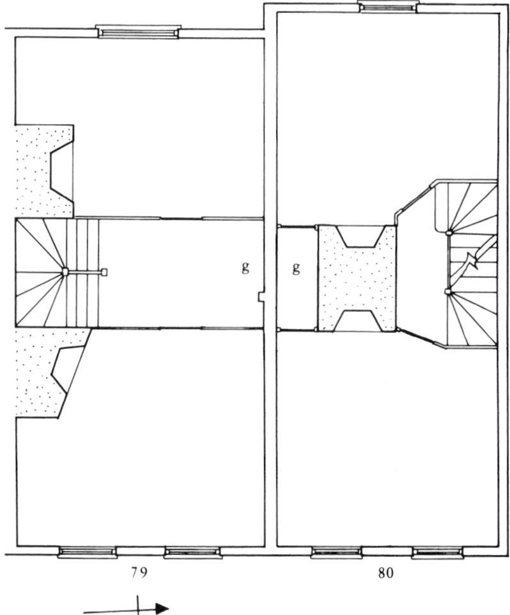

Figure 88. Nos. 79 and 80 High Street, Gravesend. Plan of first floors, showing chimney-stacks built against party wall of No. 79 in the usual 18th century way, although the staircase rises between them and has no direct lighting from windows, and the far more archaic arrangements of No. 80, where the chimney-stack is built across the centre of the house, distantly (and inconveniently) echoing the old rural lobby-entry plan; each pair of front and back rooms and the closet between them could be used as a small suite, or the rooms could be used individually. (After Newman 1988.)

Plate 95. Officers Terrace, Chatham, of 1727-9, one of Kent's earliest terraces to follow metropolitan fashions, but distinguished by its embattled parapet signifying military use.

Cottages at Leeds (Colour Plate 93) may have been the starting point for brick terraces such as 19-33 Old Dover Road at Canterbury; meanwhile medieval terraces like 5-8 Turnagain Lane were modernised, and in this case were raised by a storey to provide accommodation for silk weavers (Plate 67 and Figure 66). After a disastrous fire in 1727, the lower end of the High Street at Gravesend was rebuilt; the surviving Nos. 78-80 show the still hesitant local builders adopting an internal chimney-stack for No. 80, but placing the stacks for the front and back rooms of No. 79 against the party wall (Figure 88); even then, the staircase rose between the stacks in a way which was forty years behind London practice (Newman *et al.* 1988).

These houses were cheaply built with a light timber frame, and that accounts for the old-fashioned planning. London standards of the most lavish kind had reached Kent by 1732 with the Officers' Terrace in the Royal Naval Dockyard at Chatham, which, significantly, was a government work (Plate 95). The terrace of seven brick houses forming Minor Canon Row at Rochester shows metropolitan standards more modestly applied to Kent in the 1730s. London standards were taken up with alacrity in the second half of the eighteenth century, giving Margate the terraces of Cecil Square in 1769. Star Hill was laid out at Rochester in the 1790s with large terrace houses, indistinguishable from anything in London (Colour Plate 94), to be immediately followed by Gibraltar Place at Chatham, and the seaside terraces at Ramsgate from 1798 (Colour Plate 95), Herne Bay from 1830, Dover from 1834 (Colour Plate 96), and Folkestone from 1848. Most of these were at least three storeys

Plate 96. The triple entrances of one of Edenbridge's terraces (in The Row, Main Street) of artisan houses, the centre one giving access to back yards and their privies.

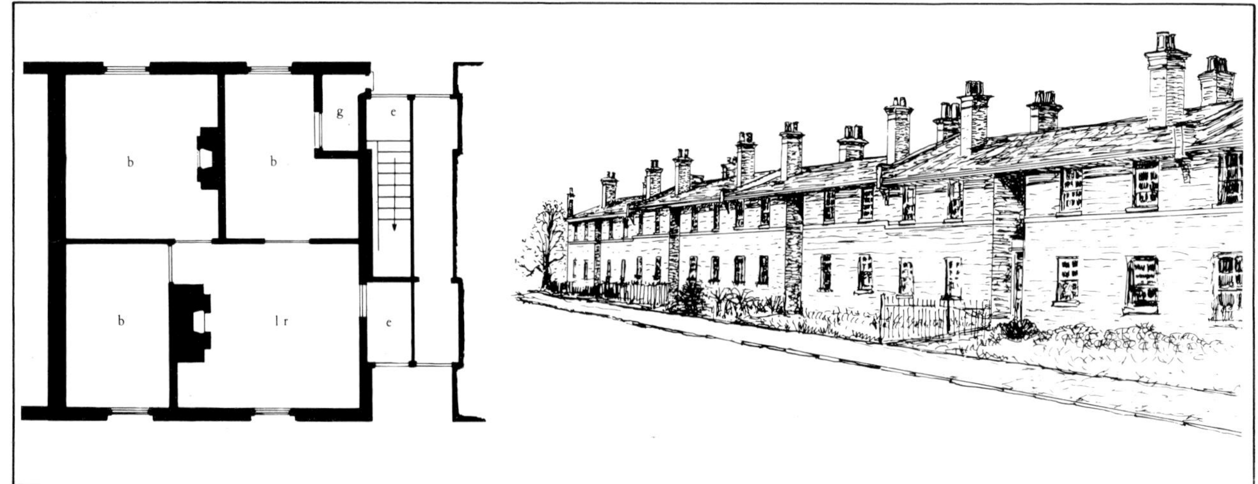

Figure 89. Ashford New Town. Plan of one of the ground-floor flats, built to Samuel Beazley's design in 1847-8 for the South Eastern Railway Company, showing the living-room and three further rooms, notionally bedrooms, reached from it, one with a closet; in the bay between the flat and the next block are its entrance, opening from the front, and the staircase, reached from the back, leading to the upper flat, which has an identical arrangement of rooms.

Figure 90. Ashford New Town. Perspective of one of the two rows of flats built in 1847-8; only the mutilated remains of one block survives in recognisable form today.

high over basements, providing numerous adaptable rooms which could house large families and their servants in comfort and privacy.

Most houses for artisans were also laid out as terraces, but with only a small living room and a scullery on the ground floor and two equally small bedrooms above. The Row in Main Street, Edenbridge, is typical of these, and follows northern English practice with passages inserted between some of the adjacent front doors to provide access to the privies at the back, which had to be dug out from time to time (Plate 96). Samuel Beazley's two-storeyed terraces of flats built for the South Eastern Railway at Ashford in 1847-8 also provided four small rooms, but arranged in a way unique in Kent (Figures 89 and 90). He soon turned to the more conventional two-up

Figure 91. Ashford New Town. Perspective of one of the terraces of houses built in 1851 to Samuel Beazley's design with shaped gables marking each end.

Plate 97. The terraces of Wellington Crescent, Ramsgate, rising towards the central opening where The Plains of Waterloo lead inland towards La Belle Alliance Square.

two-down arrangement of terraces, but dressed this up with shaped gables (Figure 91). Only in 1911-12 were the railway workers given terraces with a rear extension allowing a full kitchen and scullery as well as a front parlour, and also a third bedroom (Colour Plate 97). By then, this had become standard among speculative terraces because propriety required parents and male and female children to sleep separately.

Some of the terraces built in seaside towns were picturesquely curved (Plate 97), following fashions long established, for instance, in Bath, and more recently with Michael Searles' Paragon at Blackheath and Gloucester Circus at Greenwich in Kent's suburban fringe. A more obviously local response was the provision of bow windows and balconies (Colour Plates 95 and 98), which made the best of a desire to enjoy a maritime view. This feeling for the picturesque imbued style inland as well, leading to Decimus Burton's planning of Calverley Park at Tunbridge Wells in 1828 with its arcaded crescent (Plate 98) and arc of italianate villas set among trees and lawns in an ideal marriage of art and nature (Colour Plates 25 and 99).

Plate 98. Calverley Park Crescent, Tunbridge Wells, Decimus Burton's introduction to the arc of villas in Calverley Park; the arcades originally sheltered shops, but these were soon put to domestic use.

Nineteenth-century revivalism

Despite the continuing fashion for classicism in one form or another, the old national styles were coming back into vogue by the nineteenth century. Mock castles had enjoyed a fitful popularity ever since Vanbrugh had built himself what is now called Vanbrugh Castle facing Greenwich Park in 1718-26. The Officers' Terrace at Chatham was given battlemented ends and centre a decade later to accord with its martial connection. Soon after 1800, High Street House at Chiddingstone was refronted in stone with a full complement of embattled towers and renamed Chiddingstone Castle (Plate 99).

No style was so picturesque or sublime as Gothic. This prompted the construction of Lee Priory at Littlebourne, long since demolished, but Hadlow Castle showed what the style might achieve before it became serious and moralistic. Walter Barton May designed it for his own use in the 1820s, as William Cobbett recorded in 1823:

> At a village called Hadlow, there is a house belonging to a Mr. May, the most singular looking thing I ever saw. An immense house stuck all over with a parcel of chimneys, or things like chimneys; little brick columns, with a sort of caps on them, looking like carnation sticks, with caps at the top to catch the earwigs. The building is all of brick, and has the oddest appearance of anything I ever saw *(Rural Rides,* 1912, 254).

It became even more singular fifteen years later when George Ledwell Taylor made a landmark of it by adding a Gothic tower 170ft. (52m) high (Plate 100).

Pugin imposed the full moral weight of Englishness and Christianity on Gothic with The Grange, which he built for himself in 1843-4 at Ramsgate as the first part of a projected monastery (Colour Plate 100). Yet his fervent rendering of the style was even better expressed in Kent by his follower Richard Cromwell Carpenter with the Gothic windows of Old Rectory at Brasted (Colour Plate 101) and the irregular outline of Kilndown Parsonage.

All this was rather hectic for ordinary domestic use. More appropriately, Kent was the first place to see the revival of the traditional forms of its medieval yeomen's houses. Self-consciously rustic *cottages ornées* such as Thatched House at Wateringbury

Plate 99. High Street House, refronted and renamed Chiddingtone Castle about 1805.

Plate 100. Hadlow Castle, May's weird Gothic confection and weirder tower, still standing up to the elements, despite damage in the great gale of 1987.

Plate 101. Leicester Square, Penshurst, where in 1850 George Devey invented the Old English style.

and 275 Dover Road, Walmer (Colour Plate 102), had been built since the start of the nineteenth century. Then, in 1850 George Devey took a less fanciful approach at Penshurst when he built Leicester Square by extending the timber-framed Tudor houses fronting the churchyard in their own style (Plate 101). Thus was the Old English style born.

He built The Cottage in Rogue's Hill with the recessed centre of a Wealden hall in 1867, but by then he had already passed on his inspiration to Norman Shaw. Shaw

Plate 102. Betteshanger House, Devey's neo-Jacobean pile which began its rambling career about 1856 for Lord Northbourne.

Plate 103. East Court, Ramsgate, Ernest George's version of the Old English style built in 1889 with greeny grey tiles and deep red chimney-stacks, both of them notable strangers in Old Kent.

Plate 104. Sir Philip Sassoon's Port Lympne, built about 1912 to Sir Herbert Baker's design, with his favourite shaped gables taken not from Kent's traditional houses but from the South African Dutch style.

travelled widely in the Weald in 1862 to study its framed and tile-hung houses, and was soon using their forms and materials, particularly the happy mixture of half-timbering, brick and tile-hanging which so many houses displayed as a result of centuries of accretion. He was less concerned with the clear-cut form of medieval houses in which the planning of central hall and flanking chamber and service ends

Plate 105. The front of Salvin's new house at Scotney Castle, Lamberhurst, built in 1837-44 for Edward Hussey.

was visibly expressed outside. The Wealden was not for him; instead, he piled gable on gable, and articulated them with applied timberwork and tile-hanging, as well as soaring chimney-stacks.

His best houses are just across the border in East Sussex, but he built the strenuously gabled Hillside at Groombridge, replete with black and white timbering and tall chimney-stacks, in 1871 (Colour Plate 103), and the softer, tile-hung Old Forge at Hawkhurst three years later. He established the Old English style, apparently for good: it recaptured the image of sterling values and past affluence so firmly in people's minds that it has remained the most popular style for small houses ever since. Yet, even in Kent, this style is only a dress of fancy clothes, having none of the combination of integrated form, structure and decoration which gave Kent's medieval houses their special architectural qualities.

Devey's later work, the overbearing Hall Place at Leigh, the rambling neo-Jacobean Betteshanger House (Plate 102) and St Alban's, Nonington, were less influential, and it was left to Norman Shaw's followers to inspire the Old English style with imagination in the way Sir Ernest George did at East Court, Ramsgate, in 1889 (Plate 103). C. F. A. Voysey's Spade House (Colour Plate 24), which he designed at the turn of the century for H.G. Wells at Sandgate, turned its back on local tradition with its rendered walls, and later houses such as Robert Weir Schultz's How Green House at Hever (Colour Plate 104), Baillie Scott's Havisham House at Harbledown, Herbert Baker's Port Lympne (Plate 104), and, of course, Lutyens' three houses at Rolvenden (Colour Plate 20), Sandwich (Plate 86) and Wittersham made only partial use of local traditions with their variations on the styles of the later seventeenth and early eighteenth centuries.

Complex planning in the gentleman's home

Devey's St Alban's was, nevertheless, a *tour de force* in its planning. This demonstrates to the full the way large houses had become increasingly complicated since the Middle Ages as they attempted to accommodate the multifarious requirements of rich people, here Devey's friend William Hammond. Already Anthony Salvin had designed Scotney Castle in 1835 as an irregular double pile with one side of the entrance hall given over to a drawing-room and library, the other to a dining-room and a conveniently close butler's pantry leading by way of a corridor to a servants' wing

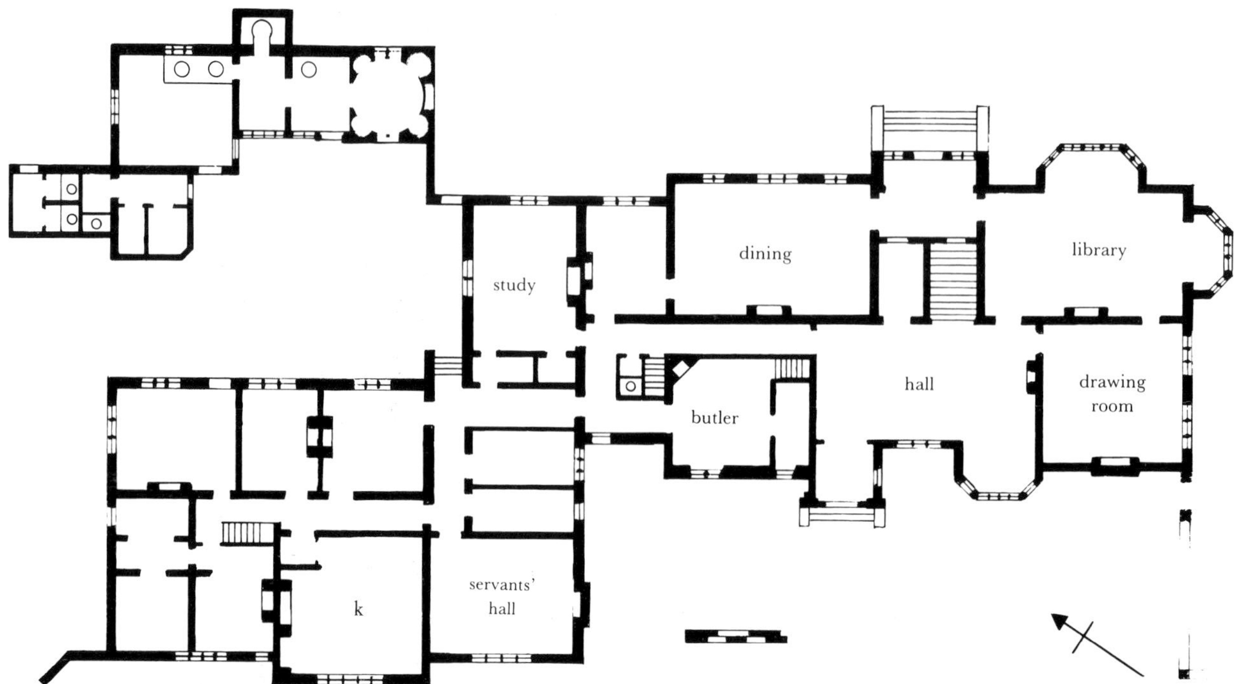

Figure 92. Scotney Castle, Lamberhurst. Ground plan, showing asymmetrical arrangement with the combined entrance hall and billiard room leading to the main staircase with a drawing-room and library to the right, the dining-room and butler's pantry to the left; beyond these are the servants' stairs and the master's study and then the separate servants' quarters, which include a brewhouse, bakehouse and dairy in the upper range, larders, wash-house, still-room, scullery and housekeeper's room in the lower range; the stabling lay to the west beyond the lower left-hand corner. (After Allibone 1987, 25.)

(Plate 105 and Figure 92). This was in essence only the three-part medieval plan taken to an extreme. Salvin established a hierarchy of rooms, as in the past, with full privacy on one side of the entrance hall and the servants kept where they were needed on the other. Forty years later Devey took these ideas to their furthest extent when he designed St Alban's on a much larger scale with three irregular ranges laid out around a courtyard (Figure 93).

The principal entrance in the middle opened into a small hall which could be reached by the butler coming from the servants' quarters on the left. The entrance provided access to a reception hall on the right where a corridor led to the principal rooms in the west range, a drawing-room, library and personal room as well as a gun room and W.C., to the dining-room in the south range, and, via the main staircase, to the bedrooms above. Next to the dining-room in the south range came the butler's living-room and bedroom, conveniently beside it and near the entrance. Beyond this, in the east range, were the servants' quarters, starting with the housekeeper's room placed so as to guard the servants' hall and the stairs to their bedrooms so that she could stop them from engaging in anti-social pranks; then came the service rooms, a kitchen, a bakehouse, a scullery, a still room, three larders, and separate rooms for cutlery, brushes, and coal, as well as two small W.C.s. All of these were fully expressed by the ins and outs of the Old English style, their relative importance in the social hierarchy of the house being demonstrated by imposing bay windows for the drawing-room and reception hall, large mullioned and transomed windows for the dining-room and library, small ones for the housekeeper's room and the servants' quarters (Girouard 1971, 103-7; Franklin 1981, 158 and 194).

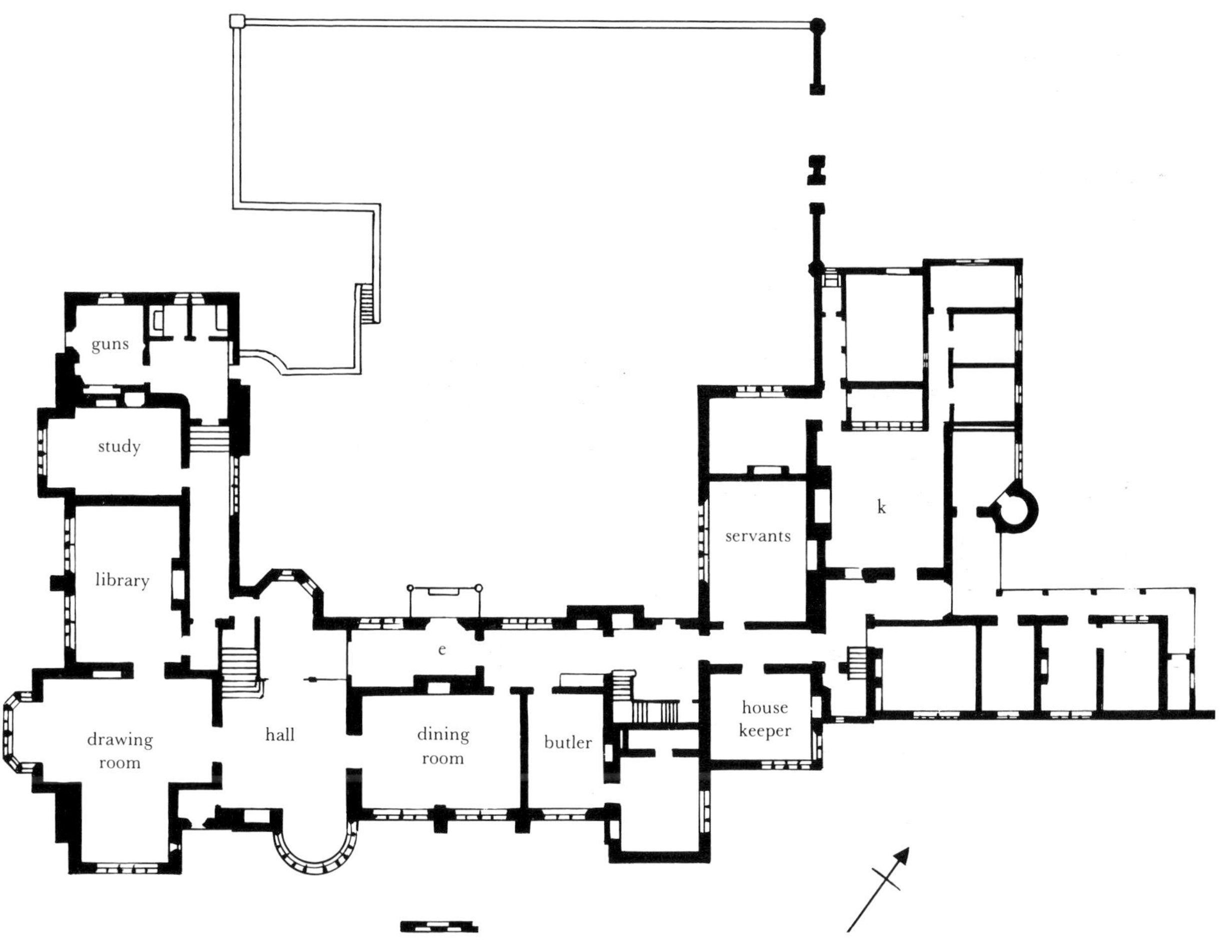

Figure 93. St Alban's, Nonington. Ground plan, showing entrance hall and main staircase, with, to the left, the drawing-room, library, master's room and gun room, and, to the right, the dining-room, butler's pantry, and the housekeeper's room acting as a guardroom for the service rooms. (After Allibone 1991, 77.)

The real problem with such tightly fitting arrangements was that when Hammond's needs died with him, and, more particularly, when the next century learned to live more modestly without servants, this and indeed most large houses found themselves full of unwanted rooms, designed for lives which no one could lead.

Style in the small house

The Old English style and the revived traditions of the seventeenth century were put under less strain in small houses, such as Sir T. G. Jackson's Lime Tree Walk at Sevenoaks (Colour Plate 105), George's estate cottages at Leigh (Colour Plate 106), and Frank Pearson's village attached to Hever Castle for Lord Astor (Plate 106). After the Great War, simpler forms were preferred because they were cheaper, and plain Georgian made headway at The Durlocks and The Stade at Folkestone (Plate 107), at the mining villages at Aylesham (Plate 108) and Hersden, and the mill village at Kemsley.

Style ultimately depended on money, and, so far as bungalows were concerned, it was usually at a premium. Nevertheless J. P. Seddon's pioneering Tower Bungalows of 1886 at Birchington took the verandas and overhanging eaves of Indian houses as a starting point for a seaside style (Plate 109). It was partially successful, but, in

Plate 106. Hever Castle village, Astor's toy 'medieval' village designed as lodgings for his guests so as to maintain the privacy of his castle.

Plate 107. The Durlocks, Folkestone, built at Sassoon's instigation in 1919, again with shaped gables, but designed here by Culpin and Bowers.

Plate 108. Pairs of miners' houses at Aylesham, linked by arches giving access to the back gardens.

general, most bungalow builders preferred to add a dash of Old English mixed with a cheap version of the rendered and pebble-dashed walls favoured by Voysey if their budgets ran that far. This gave them just enough style to sell their houses at prices tailored to suit people retiring on a shoestring as well as the more affluent looking for second, seaside homes.

Homes for heroes were more modest. The bungalows of Preston Hall Colony at Aylesford are minimal, apart from their verandas (Plate 20), and the bungalows which smallholders built at Biddenden, Charing and elsewhere do not stretch that far (Plate 110). Not even these are so redolent of the pioneer as the converted railway carriages and the other shacks scattered along Denge Beach at Lydd (Colour Plate 107).

Plate 109. The frieze on the upper storey of one of Seddon's Tower Bungalows at Birchington.

Plate 110. A smallholder's bungalow, sporting a pair of gabled bay windows, built at Biddenden beside the Benenden Road.

Style was also anathema to the architects of the Modern Movement, so they said, but that was because it represented the dim past, not the bright future. They wanted the integrated form, structure and decoration which had given Kent's medieval houses their special character, but they did not want the style that went with it. 'Truth to materials', particularly to modern materials, was what counted, and the shape of a house had to express the utility of its planning. The first criterion could gain nothing from tradition where untried concrete was concerned, and steel and plate glass fell into the same category. So the 'truth to materials', namely cement, which Colin Lucas expressed in his weekend cottage, The Hopfield at Platt, of 1933 (Colour Plate 108), clearly belongs to the International Modern style and owes nothing to Kent. Glass and steel with reinforced concrete for the roof make Capel Manor House at Horsmonden the most ideologically sound International Modern design of all, its architects Michael Manser Associates taking up the theme which the German architect Mies van der Rohe had started in Chicago in the 1940s and doing it suavely, albeit thirty years later.

Already Britain had shown little patience with the ideology of Modernism, and it has never been widely adopted for individual houses. However International Modern in concept, Brian O'Rourke's Sea Breezes at Kingsgate of about 1939 is at least weatherboarded, a happy recognition of its maritime site. Walter Gropius, another German architect like Mies who fled Nazi Germany, was again modifying the purity, some would say the harshness, of Modernism, when he designed Wood House at Shipbourne with timber cladding in 1937, but this is Scandinavian in character, not Kentish (Colour Plate 109). Eric Lyons took this precedent one stage further with his post-war Span development at New Ash Green, despite turning to tile-hanging as well as weatherboarding; his houses wonderfully compress all the needs of modern households into a small compass (Plate 111). Only Michael Coombes's Oak House, which he built for himself in the 1980s at Biddenden, is true to oak in the old way (Colour Plate 110); without any antiquarianism, it alone recaptures the spirit of Kent's medieval aisled halls, a great tiled roof adding its splash of red to countless others in the Weald, an open centre leading to numerous peripheral rooms built into the side aisles and the two ends.

Planning in the twentieth century

Picturesque principles increasingly imbued the planning of progressive housing estates

Plate 111. The vertical weatherboarding and picture windows of Span's houses at New Ash Green.

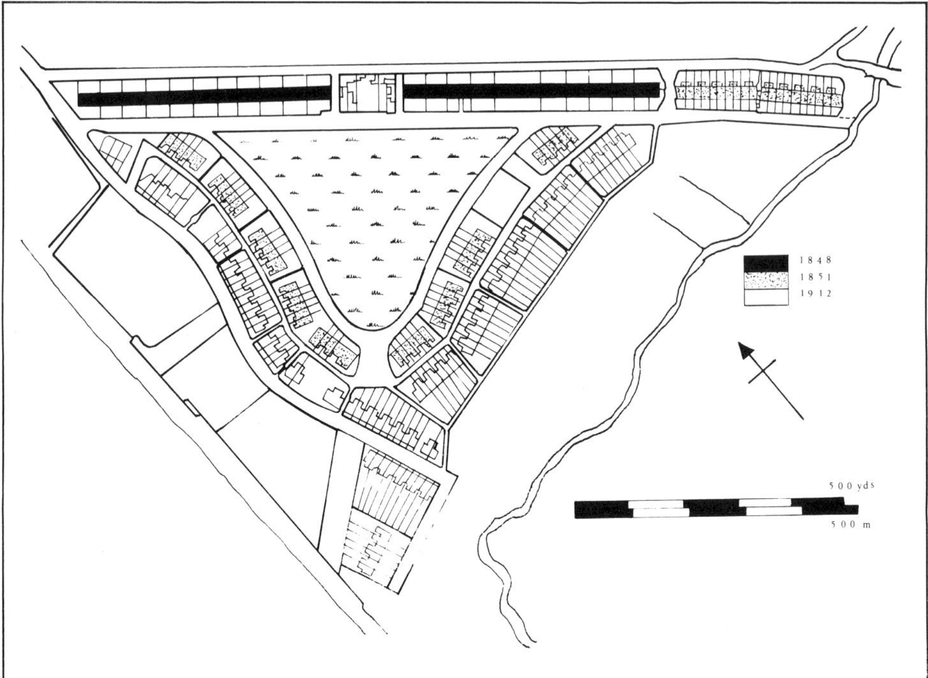

Figure 94. Ashford. Plan of the New Town, showing the two rows of flats of 1847-8, with the bath-house between them (shown solid), and the houses with shaped gables of 1851 (shown dotted), surrounding the green, and the larger, surviving houses of 1912 (shown in outline).

in the later nineteenth century. Apart from being attractive to the eye, they emulated rural values at a time when urban overcrowding weighed heavily as a national problem. Beazley's New Town at Ashford, which combined curving streets with a symmetrical layout based on a green, went far beyond the typical speculative housing of the day (Figure 94), which was usually laid out on a grid of streets. By the twentieth century, picturesque planning of a perfunctory sort had become commonplace among

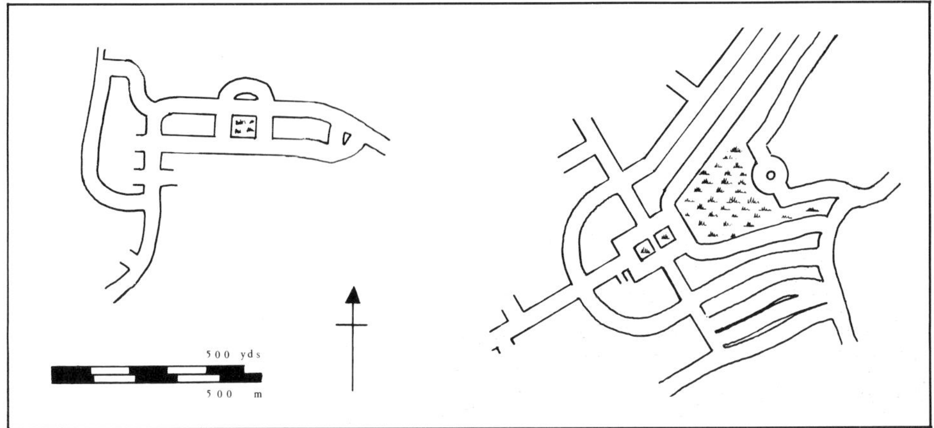

Figure 95. Kemsley (left) and Aylesham (right). Formal village planning in the 1920s.

speculative housing estates, such as those surrounding Maidstone, although their sheer endlessness weakened any sensible comparison with the irregularity of traditional village plans. It remained for Eric Lyons and Span to reassert these values at their most potent in the 1960s with the first neighbourhoods of New Ash Green, where small groups of terraced houses nestle among mature trees and screens of shrubs.

New Ash Green was expensive, a quality already associated with picturesque planning by the time of the Great War. Regularity in planning and a plain style of architecture brought economies which became particularly attractive in the lean years for public housing which followed. Adams, Thomson and Fry laid out Kemsley for the workers at the Bowater paper mill in 1925-6 with a square green at its centre and a crescent and two parallel streets of widely spaced terraces of houses in a plain Georgian style (Figure 95). The mining village of Aylesham followed the next year with Archibald, Martindale and Abercrombie's more ambitious symmetrical layout, based on a green, hopefully called the Market Place, and a crescent and a common. Neither of them has ever reached the completion envisaged by their planners, and too much open space leaves them uncomfortably wind-swept. The most ambitious of these symmetrical estates, Shepway in the south-eastern suburbs of Maidstone, has a large green, used for sports, surrounded by rings of crescents all named after the counties of England. Unfortunately, these names cannot give the estate the architectural character which the formal planning needs.

Adaptation and modern usage

A very different form of architectural development came about with the need to adapt old houses to modern uses. Many large houses like St Alban's have dropped out of domestic use; others like How Green House have been divided up into several units. For smaller houses, modernisation was a simple process until architects began to understand the reality of medieval planning. Endeavouring to recapture the essence of the hall-house, a number of conversions removed the inserted floor across the hall, in an attempt to re-establish the medieval form and, with it, the communal life once lived there.

Lately, a more pressing problem has been the plight of unwanted farm buildings. Kent's most picturesque farm building, the oast-house, has suffered all kinds of conversion, with excessively large windows punched through the roundels, and so breaking up their shape in a way that ruins their original character (Plate 112). The architects Martin and Mitzi Quirk have been more successful than most here in their

Plate 112. Oasts at Watersmeet Farm, Whetstead, Tudeley, converted for domestic use with obtrusive windows set into the roundels.

conversions at Chiddingstone and Penshurst, simply by keeping their inserted windows as unobtrusive as possible (Colour Plate 111).

The sophistication of a few architect-designed houses ought to be hope for the future. Nevertheless, the design of houses in Kent today is largely dominated by a sentimental attachment to misunderstood architectural values. These are the guiding light of every other prestige estate being run up to catch the eye of today's affluent consumer society. Surely Kent deserves something better. The setting of Oak House in the heart of the Weald carries the story of Kent houses full circle back to the fourteenth century, and it carries it forward in a spirit of progress attuned to its surroundings. It might point a way to the future if its scale and cost could be matched to more ordinary needs.

Gazetteer

ACRISE (4½ miles NNW of Folkestone): a wooded chalkland parish with scattered farmhouses on ancient enclosures. By the church, **Acrise Place** has a sixteenth-century red brick front with diapering, but it was altered and given a block cornice during the eighteenth century when the house was remodelled and extended; a large hall window in a canted bay rising through both storeys is balanced on the further side of the two-storeyed porch by a smaller square bay. The oldest part of **Hoad Farm**, a seemingly unprepossessing house of flint, was built early in the thirteenth century as an upper hall or storeyed chamber block with lancet windows, back and front (Plate 49); this projects from the rear of the main range, which was built a century later as a three-part hall-house, and contains the remains of its screens passage.

ADISHAM (5¼ miles ESE of Canterbury): a chalkland village with most of its houses strung out along a street beyond the parish church. **Adisham Court**, a large seventeenth-century brick house beside the church, is notable for shaped end gables with chimney-stacks rising through them, and five prominent dormer windows matching those in the two storeys below. **Dane Court** and **Little Bossington Farm** are both typical three-part hall-houses with single end jetties.

ALDINGTON (5¼ miles W of Hythe): formerly one of the Archbishop of Canterbury's richest manors, the parish comprises several clusters of farmhouses on the ridge of fertile Wealden clay based on sandstone and limestone overlooking Romney Marsh. **Court Lodge**, originally the Archbishop's manor house, has largely been rebuilt, but an agricultural building contains the remains of a medieval stone wing and a second stone wing, at the back of the present house, has the remains of Decorated tracery in a blocked window, suggesting that it may have been a private chapel (*see* Horne's Place, Appledore). **Symnel**, Stone Street, is a hall-house with an end jetty built with timber felled about 1450-1485 (Howard *et al.* 1989), **Frith Farm** is another, and there are more medieval houses near the church. Not the oldest framed house, but the most significant is **Cobb's Hall** (Plate 76), which may well be the Court House of Thomas Cobbe (d.1528), the Archbishop of Canterbury's steward; the carving of a Tudor rose and an Aragonese pomegranate on three of its four hearth-beams (Colour Plate 71) suggests that it was built after 1509 as the earliest lobby-entry house to be recognised in England (Quiney 1984); it survives remarkably unchanged, although the entrance has been moved and the original staircase has gone; there are moulded floor joists, contemporary wall-paintings and, upstairs, a plaster frieze depicting Adam and Eve; the rear, south wall was rebuilt in brick during the Napoleonic invasion scare to provide a defensive position for gunners overlooking the Marsh. **Goldwell**, Cobbe's own house, now has a rambling brick exterior, a result of eighteenth-century rebuilding, but some of its medieval timber frame remains. **Ruffin's Hill**, built in the sixteenth century with a single-storeyed hall, is notable for its early use of brick with diaper patterns of blue on red in its prominent two-storeyed porch which has an arched opening and a mullioned and transomed window with a hoodmould above.

ALKHAM (3¾ miles WNW of Dover): a village astride a long, tight valley in the North Downs. The timber-framed **Hogbrook** (Colour Plate 57) was probably built by St Radegund's Abbey: like Fairfield at Eastry, it comprises a fifteenth-century aisled hall, with a jettied dormer at only one end; the entrance, now in the centre of the hall, used to be at the right-hand end, but that may not have been the original position either. The **Old Rectory** is an early eighteenth-century two-storeyed double pile, with bright red bricks for the window surrounds and a wooden dentil cornice beneath the M-roof.

APPLEDORE (5¼ miles SE of Tenterden): a delightful village built on a Greensand promontory overlooking the Royal Military Canal and the Rother Levels. The main street runs southwards from Appledore Heath to the parish church and here dips suddenly to a bridge over the canal. The late medieval timber-framed **Swan House** is jettied and has close-studding in the upper storey, and a doorway and grouped windows with four-centred arched heads. There are several brick-fronted lobby-entry houses in the street (notably opposite Swan House) and symmetrical eighteenth-century houses with entrances flanked by pairs of typical canted bays, fully glazed on two or three storeys, as at **Poplar Hall** at the north end of the street. **Horne's Place**, on the road to Kennardington, was rebuilt after Wat Tyler's attack during the Peasant's Revolt of 1381; it conceals a vaulted undercroft, remarkably

Appledore. Horne's Place, with the chapel to the right.

for this date built of brick, and a timber frame beneath tile hanging; extending from the rear is a domestic chapel, built of ragstone by William Horne and licensed for worship in 1366.

ASH (2¾ miles W of Sandwich): a parish lying on a sandy gravel ridge S of the River Stour; the village itself is strung out along the Canterbury-Sandwich road, and there are many individual brick houses lying to its north. Typically of this part of Kent, at least a dozen of these have shaped gables: **Chequer Court**, set within a moated site, has convex and ogee curves beneath a triangle (Figure 27q); **Poplar Farm**, Lower Goldstone, a symmetrical, three-bay house, has convex and then concave curves beneath a pediment; but the prize goes to **School Farm**, Guilton (Colour Plate 42), a lobby-entry house whose gables of *halsgavel* type bear the date 1695 and are shaped with two tiers of scrolls carrying pediments (Figure 27t), and whose porch also has a shaped gable with convex curves, scrolls and a pediment. The upper windows of **Padbrook**, Paramour Street, are flanked by pilasters, a naïve version of the sophisticated fashion popularised by Inigo Jones at Covent Garden in the 1630s.

ASH (6½ miles SSW of Gravesend): church and **Ash Manor** lie on wooded chalkland, secluded from the encroaching suburbanisation of north-west Kent; the house, of brick and dated 1637, is an early symmetrical, two-storeyed double pile with a gabled attic and dominating porch; chimney-stacks with

Ash (near Gravesend). South Ash Manor.

triple diagonally set shafts rise up each side. **South Ash Manor** has a long, timber-framed north front with jettied ends and a two-storeyed porch.

New Ash Green has achieved deserved fame, and some infamy as well. In the 1960s the development company Span proposed to build a new garden suburb for 6,000 people in London's green belt. The chosen site on the wooded downland north of Ash church aroused controversy, although it was to be built on the principles the company had already established in London's suburbs at Blackheath and Twickenham. The high standards of design achieved there by their architect Eric Lyons would continue, notably with traditional materials — weatherboarding, tile-hanging and brick — used in an uncompromisingly modern way, though with a Scandinavian flavour rather than a Kentish one, and with strong overtones of Aarne Ervi's Tapiola, begun in 1953 to the west of Helsinki. Large plate-glass windows and split-pitch roofs would demonstrate the modernity of the scheme, and help to achieve remarkable utilitarian qualities within a small but attractive compass. Landscaping was important too: large communal areas and semi-private spaces devoted to groups of houses would bring a sense of enclosure and allow existing trees to be retained. Despite opposition, planning permission came in 1965, and construction started in partnership with the newly formed Greater London Council, which wanted 450 houses for its overspill population. The first neighbourhood, **Punch Croft**, was completed in 1968, and within five years three more were started, **Knight's Croft**, **Lambardes** and **Over Minnis**; but financial problems with houses whose design had already proved to be expensive to build, and the withdrawal of the GLC from the project pushed Span into bankruptcy and the development into the hands of builders who preferred profit and humdrum standards. This left the early neighbourhoods with their secluded groups of linked houses, complete with sensitively planted communal gardens, separately routed approach roads and discreetly sited garage blocks as an exemplar of the best domestic planning in England of the 1960s, but also as a hard lesson in the economics of such ideal schemes (Plates 23 and 111).

ASHFORD. Lying at the southern end of the route cut by the River Stour through the North Downs on its way to Canterbury, Ashford is still recognisably a thriving market town, centred on a substantial medieval parish church and wide High Street. In 1842 the South Eastern Railway opened its line from London via Tonbridge, and extended it to Folkestone and then Dover within little more than a year. When the connecting line to Canterbury was opened in 1846 and to Hastings in 1851, Ashford became the fulcrum of Kent's railway system, and here the SER established its chief engineering works, turning out its first coaches in 1851 and first locomotives in 1853 (Kidner 1963). To provide for its staff, the railway built the New Town to the design of their architect Samuel Beazley (*see* Tonbridge Castle), to the south of the old town; Beazley's layout, a block of his flats, a bath-house and public house survive, but the rest of the houses belong to later phases (Figure 94).

Ashford's oldest house is **The Vicarage**, built in the mid or later fifteenth century facing a courtyard on the east side of the churchyard, with close-studding on two storeys. Prosperous brick houses line the north side of the churchyard and the way out to **Middle Row's** timber-framed, gabled seventeenth-century houses, notably **No. 4** dated 1659. **No. 54 High Street** has a plastered upper storey, grooved to look like rusticated masonry, and deep eaves supported on carved brackets. East Hill still contains a few large but plain Georgian houses, notably the yellow brick **Brooke Place** at the top and the red brick **Bridge House** just before the River Stour; both are symmetrically arranged double piles with five bays and three storeys. **North Street** contains a happy mixture of timber-framed and close-studded houses, one gabled and dated 1671, others tile-hung, and brick Georgian houses, particularly **No. 22**, which is more ornately treated than those in East Hill, with a Doric doorcase, bright red brick quoining and a wooden modillion eaves cornice. The **New Town** began in 1847 with two long rows of flats centred on the bath-house; the flats were grouped into blocks of four with set-back entrances between the blocks, the doors to the ground-floor flats opening toward a curving green on the south side, the doors to the upper floors opening toward the road on the north; otherwise the flats were identical, comprising four rooms and closet. Just one block survives in relatively unaltered state (Figures 89 and 90). All the terraces of four-room houses with shaped gables which Beazley built in 1851 have been demolished (Figure 91). The next phase of building came in 1911-12 when the old London Chatham and Dover Railway works at Battersea were closed and amalgamated with the SER works here, causing a need for more houses (Colour Plate 97); these are in the form of short rows, built of brick, partly roughcast, with tile-hung gables at the ends; these had the advantage of three bedrooms and sculleries and so have survived. Recently the older houses with shaped gables have been replaced by the sharper outlines of houses built of hard brick.

ASHURST (3¼ miles W of Tunbridge Wells): a parish towards the western end of the Kentish Weald. The Elizabethan **Chafford Park** was pulled down in 1743; in its place there is a symmetrical, five-bay, double-pile house of red brick with an M-roof, adorned with large plaques depicting antique busts named Sara and Iekretia, possibly removed from the old house.

AYLESFORD (2¾ miles NW of Maidstone): the centre of the village lies on the north side of the Medway, where old tiled roofs and Victorian gables crowded above the river are an admirable foil to the arches of the medieval bridge. On the south side of the bridge are a number of nineteenth-century Tudor style houses, before the scene is dominated by a paper mill and attendant speculative housing. Further south is the M20 motorway and then **Preston Hall** (now a hospital), rebuilt in an unenterprising Jacobean style for the railway contractor Edward Ladd Betts in 1850 to the designs of John Thomas (Colour Plate 21). Around it are a few groups of plain semi-detached houses, the remnants of the original **British Legion Village**, built for veteran soldiers shortly after the Great War, now mostly replaced by modern groups of houses. At the junction of the A20 and the road to Barming is **Preston Hall Colony** (Plate 20), a spread-out group of bungalows rather than a village, laid out in 1923, again by the British Legion for veterans of the First World War; each bungalow is four-square, with a low-pitched slate roof extending over a veranda at the front, and a centrally placed doorway flanked by a single window for the living-room on the south side and another window for the bedroom on the north.

AYLESHAM (6½ miles SE of Canterbury): a downland parish with a formally planned village, laid out in 1926-7 to serve Snowdon Colliery by J. Archibald, C.T.F. Martindale and Patrick Abercrombie with a 'Market Place' at its centre. The roads radiate symmetrically, and were to have extended into a town for 15,000, but this was a gross over-estimate of the colliery's needs (Figure 95). There are a few streets of plain semi-detached houses built of red or yellow brick with hipped tiled roofs; some of the shorter groups of houses are linked by arches (Plate 108); the formal centre of the town is incomplete and scruffy, exactly echoing the depressed state of coal mining in Kent. The most important house in the parish lies outside this unkempt scene: behind the picturesque façade of **Ratling Court** are the remains of an aisled hall of about 1300 with a king-strut roof (Figures 11 and 32), the forerunner of the common crown-post roof (Munby *et al.* 1983); a cross-wing was added to the low end about a century and a half later, and in 1637 the high end was rebuilt by William Cowper, ancestor of the poet (Parkin 1976).

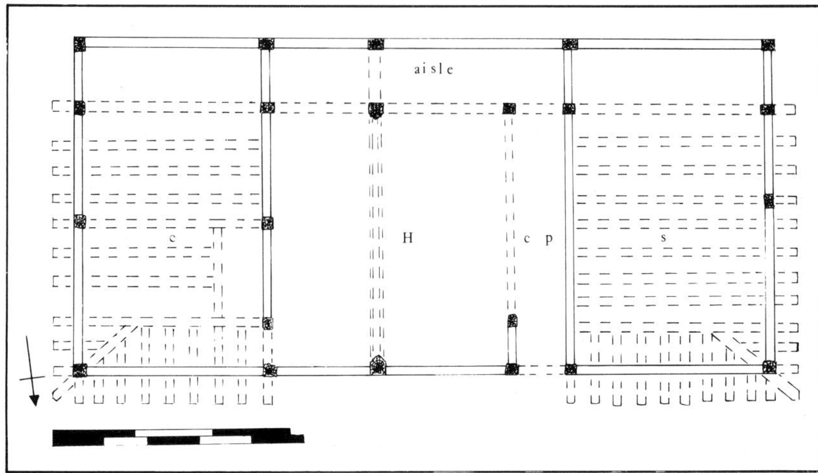

Nos. 1 and 2 Church Hill, Barham. Plan of aisled hall-house converted to Wealden form. (After Parkin 1989).

Benenden. Hemsted House (Benenden School).

BARHAM (6¼ miles SSE of Canterbury): a memorable downland village built along Church Hill, which tumbles down from the old Dover Road towards the valley of the Nail Bourne. At the top of the hill is **Barham Court**, its magnificent pedimented early eighteenth-century front appearing over the churchyard wall, and dramatically approached by way of an entrance added in 1912 by Lutyens with a curved wall and end pavilions framing a flight of steps which lead to a doorway opening into the side of the house, thus leaving the main façades of the house free. **Nos. 1 and 2 Church Hill** comprise an aisled hall-house converted to a Wealden configuration with a good deal of duplication in its timber framing, and now weather-boarded (Parkin 1989). Down the hill is a stuccoed house with shallow, full-height curved bays to its symmetrical front. A short way outside the village, almost beside the Nail Bourne, are the three brick gables fronting **Lower Digges Place**. Further away on the downland in the other direction are the fantastic gables of **Broome Park**, an invention of scrolls, curves and broken pediments, half Dutch, half baroque, and owing no allegiance to the strict classicism of Inigo Jones who was just beginning to affect architectural design at the time. The house was built in 1635-9 for Sir Basil Dixwell, a newcomer to the county, with an H-plan (Maguire 1989, 308), but was modified when a central bay was added to the south front in 1778 and again when a balancing porch was added to the north front and the ground-floor windows were raised for Lord Kitchener early this century by the architects Detmar Blow and Fernand Billerey (Colour Plate 40).

BEARSTED (2½ miles E of Maidstone): an attractive village with numerous timber-framed and tile-hung houses set round a green. **Olde Manor Cottages**, on the north side, was built as a hall-house to which were added cross-wings, the close-studded one in the sixteenth century. **The Limes**, next door, has a continuous jetty. On the south side of The Green is another house with a continuous jetty and Kentish framing, and a gabled cross-wing with a crown-post roof. An early Wealden at **Ware Street** has large down-braces and a restored hall window with diagonally set mullions and an entrance and two windows, all with four-centered heads, under the service end jetty. **Milgate**, set in its own park to the south-east, is a splendid though smaller version of Bradbourne at Larkfield (*see* under East Malling), and perhaps by the same hand. A house here was improved in the sixteenth century, but the present house, seemingly of the second decade of the eighteenth century, has a pedimented front flanked by slightly recessed bays, with tall sash windows and sunken panels between the two storeys and in the parapet above a wooden block cornice. The unusual doorcase has Corinthian pilasters with a panel of foliage and a flat hood above.

BENENDEN (4¾ miles W of Tenterden): a Wealden parish of scattered farms and a tidy village laid out around a green for Lord Cranbrook in the 1860s. Several late Wealden hall-houses in the parish have four-centred arches over their doorways and some of their windows. Most are close-studded. The largest of them is **Pympne Manor**, where a jettied floor has been inserted across the hall; **The Paper Mill** has a jetty at the right-hand end as well as at the front, and **Watermill House** has jetties at both ends and a restored hall open to the roof in the upper storey; two more Wealdens, the large, early and ornate **Manor House**, at the village cross-roads, and **The Moat**, hide behind bright red tile-hanging. Among a row of tile-hung cottages on the north side of the green is one inscribed '1609 Edmund Gibbon Founder of this School'. At the centre of *the* school, synonymous with the village, is the former **Hemsted House**, built in 1859-62 to David Brandon's neo-Elizabethan design with money made from a Staffordshire ironworks for Gathorne Gathorne-Hardy, later first Earl of Cranbrook. George Devey designed Staplehurst Lodge, Cranbrook Lodge, the Gardener's Cottage and Church Cottage for Hemsted Park between 1868 and 1881; and he also designed Ash Lawn for the Misses Neave, and refronted the Rectory for the Rev. E. D. Cree (Allibone 1991, 159, 173).

BETHERSDEN (5¼ miles WSW of Ashford): an attractive village with a winding street on the clays of the Wealden vale with numerous medieval farmhouses encased in brick scattered about the rest of this large woody parish. A small thatched hall-house with Kentish framing and an end jetty set among trees off Mill Road remarkably conjures up the original appearance of these once lonely settlements. **Wissenden Farm House** is an early Wealden with a two-centred arched main doorway and, again, Kentish framing (Figure 26a). **Wissenden House**, also timber-framed, has a plastered Georgian front with sash windows and an off-centre entrance beneath an overall hipped roof, all reflecting the medieval arrangement of a hall-house; a framed wing projects from the back.

BETTESHANGER (4 miles W of Deal): a secluded downland parish, dominated by **Betteshanger House** (now a school), built for Sir Walter James, a friend of Gladstone, who gave him his peerage as Baron Northbourne. James was devout, rebuilding the parish church and teaching in the Sunday School, and artistic as well, studying for a while under James Duffield Harding, the landscape painter who also taught the architect George Devey. So it was Devey who between about 1856 and 1886 remodelled and greatly extended a small existing villa on the large estate which James had purchased in 1850, giving it its complicated outline of towers, shaped and crow-stepped gables, and triple-shafted chimney-stacks, which pile up into a studied patchwork of east Kent's late seventeenth-century styles (Plate 102). Devey also laid out the garden terraces, and added a double cottage and another cottage in his Old English style, **The Cloisters**. These works gave Devey an entrée to Gladstone's circle and the foundation of his practice, thus leading him to build St Alban's Court at

Nonington for James' friend William Hammond (Girouard 1971, 103-7; Allibone 1991, 41-6 *et passim*).

BICKNOR (4 miles SW of Sittingbourne): a downland parish of scattered farms among woods and orchards. Intriguingly, **Bicknor Court** is of at least two builds, with a timber frame partly encased in brick. The east range, with its large panels and curved down-braces and overall hipped roof, has all the appearance of a hall-house; extending westward from this is a second, later range, encased in brick, which has two prominent gables on its south side, and the date 1628 scratched on a plaster partition in the roof; the mullioned windows are of plastered brickwork and have prominent hoodmoulds over them.

BIDDENDEN (4 miles NW of Tenterden): a rich parish on the edge of the Weald whose prosperity grew with cloth. This shows in the centre of the village in the long range of timber houses sweeping round the south-west corner of the High Street (Plate 3), which is characterised by numerous oriel windows carried on console brackets, added in the seventeenth century. Behind the street,

Biddenden. The Old Cloth Hall, photographed a hundred years ago.

The Old Cloth Hall is a jettied and gabled building containing weaving rooms, which was continually extended until the eastern gable was added in 1672, long after the Wealden cloth industry was in decline. No less remarkable are the numerous scattered farms. One of the oldest is **Vane Court**, built with timber felled between 1417 and 1444 (Howard *et al.* 1990) as a Wealden, with upward-curving braces for the lower panels and down-braces for the upper ones; the centres of the flying plates spanning the recessed hall, front and back, are supported unusually by posts bracketed out at first-floor level (Figure 53). **The Cott** or **Weavers Court**, a large two-storeyed, early or mid-sixteenth-century house (*see* Loddenden, Staplehurst, Plate 72), is jettied along the front of the hall and parlour, and down the side of the service wing, which extends to the rear (Figure 71). The front is close-studded with canted oriel windows added under the jetty, one for the hall, one for the parlour; above these are the remains of four original windows extended by clerestories (Plate 71). The main entrance is into the hall at the service end in the traditional way; and a large chimney-stack with back-to-back hearths separates the hall and parlour; part of the upper storey and the long rear wing, which contains the staircase, was probably used for weaving (Cowper 1911). Picturesquely sited by a pond, **Castweazel Manor** is similarly close-studded and jettied. **Lashenden**, which has a close-studded ground storey and a jetty supporting large panels and down-braces above, now has the form of a lobby-entry house, but asymmetrically arranged with an oriel beneath a gable on the right, and a longer range on the left containing a service room. It looks significantly older than **Worsenden**, another lobby-entry house, whose frame is hidden by later brickwork but is immediately apparent in the delightfully sagging jetty, and also **Standen**, a curious jettied house apparently dated 1578 on a fireplace; here the stacks are placed on the outside walls, as though as an afterthought, and the framing of the jettied upper storey is unusually decorated with small panels, braced across the corners to form curved lozenges (Colour Plate 31).

Built opposite each other at the southern end of the village in Tenterden Road are two houses faced in glowing red brick and characterised by windows divided by wooden mullions and transoms into four lights; **Biddenden Place**, which is not quite symmetrical and has a hipped roof with dormers, carries a plaque inscribed '1624 EH', but the older body of the house probably gained its present appearance early in the eighteenth century, at about the same time that **Hendon Hall** gained its present appearance, with diapering of vitrified headers, six windows on each storey and an open pediment on brackets over the doorcase. The twentieth century is represented in contrasting ways: first by a series of minimal bungalows (Plate 19), one with gabled bay windows (Plate 110), built along Benenden Road after the Great War as homes for smallholding heroes; then by a few recent houses in North Street designed to look like converted barns, one with an oast cowl for decoration; and, finally, by **The Oak House** in Sandpit Wood, which has an oak frame, albeit bolted rather than joined, and the form of an immense archaic aisled hall, with panelled and weather-boarded rooms tucked into the aisled spaces in the most imaginative combination of modernism and tradition in all Kent; it was designed and built during the 1980s by the architect Michael Coombes for himself (Colour Plate 110).

BIRCHINGTON (3½ miles WSW of Margate): at the west end of Thanet's built-up northern coastline, and notable for **Quex Park**, a large, dour, rendered Italianate house built in extensive grounds inland as early as 1813, but altered and given wings seventy years later. One of the earliest of seaside estates of bungalows was started by J.P. Seddon on his own land in the late 1860s; the large individual houses, which were designed by John Taylor, have now all gone, but soon afterwards Seddon himself designed **Tower**

Birchington. Quex Park.

Bungalows in Spencer Road, and these survive, though altered. They are in an appropriately Indian style (the word bungalow originally referred to the houses of Bengal and did not imply a single-storeyed house as it now does), so they have verandas, over-hanging tiled roofs and low towers; the panelled upper storeys are pargeted with rustic figures, swags and other patterns (Plate 109), and bear the inscriptions 'YE TOWER BUNGALOWS 1882' and 'J P SEDDON YE ARCH.' **Nos. 1 and 2 Beach Road** may also be his: they have applied timber panelling and verandas in the upper storey set between projecting bays with prominent dormers over them. Elsewhere along the front, the bungalows are of the usual sort, their Indian origins lost for ever.

BISHOPSBOURNE (4 miles SE of Canterbury): a downland village beside the Nail Bourne with one notable mansion, **Bourne Park**. This is a double pile built in 1701 by Dame Elizabeth Aucher for her son in red brick with timber cornices and a pediment, but is still planned internally with the hall entered at one end in the medieval way. **Court House** is a Wealden, **Burstead Manor** at Pett Bottom is another (Figure 49), and **Old Cottage** is yet another late medieval hall-house, but with jetties at both ends, not the front.

BOBBING (2 miles WNW of Sittingbourne): a parish of small farmhouses set among orchards on the north side of the Dover Road. **Sole Place**, a small, symmetrical, brick house, has two terracotta plaques with open pediments inscribed TM, CM, and the date 1709 (*see* Mill Farmhouse, Cobham).

BORDEN (1½ miles SW of Sittingbourne): a parish dotted with orchards and individual farmhouses. At least six of these are Wealden halls, including one on the road to **Harmans Corner**, another one there, two more on the road to Sittingbourne, **Hook's Hole** at Chestnut Street, and the close-studded **Sutton Baron**, which was extended by the naturalist and antiquarian Robert Plot after 1690. **Old Stede** at Chestnut Street has a prominent twice-jettied gable fronting the street, close-studded below and inscribed 'ITA 1613' on the tie-beam. Another close-studded house at **Oad Street** has a very shallow jetty across its front and retains the medieval three-part arrangement of rooms, although its hall is completely floored over; the house opposite, now encased in brick, originally had an open hall and still retains its medieval crown-post roof; the brick front of **Yew Tree Cottage** hides a fourteenth-century hall-house with an aisle at the rear.

BOROUGH GREEN (5 miles ENE of Sevenoaks): a built-up parish on the Sevenoaks-Maidstone road beneath the scarp of the North Downs. A few timber-framed houses survive among the later brick ones, including a medieval hall-house with Kentish framing and jetties at both ends on the road to Wrotham.

BOUGHTON MALHERBE (8 miles ESE of Maidstone): a chartland village of scattered farms. **Boughton Place**, on the edge of the scarp overlooking the Weald, is a fragment of one of Kent's few but memorable aristocratic houses, and owes its existence to the Wottons, first the courtier Sir Edward Wotton, who served Henry VIII at Calais, then his son Thomas Wotton, both of them Sheriffs of Kent in their time; grandson Sir Henry Wotton, diplomat, poet and author of *Elements of Architecture*, lived here too. The surviving ragstone wing comprises a two-storeyed range facing west (Colour Plate 50), the earlier, northern part of the 1520s characterised by mullioned and transomed windows with pointed arches to the individual lights, particularly a full-height canted bay with these windows on both storeys; the later, southern part, dated on a fireplace to 1553, is characterised by the singularly early use of classically proportioned windows divided each way by a mullion and transom; the range ends at the north with a brick crow-step gable bearing a chimneybreast. **Sandway Place**, formerly Chilston Park, down the chartland dip-slope to the north, is a much Georgianised courtyard house, with a pedimented north front dated 1728 set between projecting wings. Below the chartland scarp to the south-west, **Mansion House Farmhouse** has a plain eighteenth-century front with giant pilasters, a bracketed porch in the centre and keystones to the symmetrical windows.

BOUGHTON MONCHELSEA (3½ miles SSE of Maidstone): a chartland parish of scattered farms with its church perched on the scarp overlooking the Weald. Beside it is **Boughton Monchelsea Place**, built of ragstone about 1567-75 by Robert Rudston as a courtyard house, but of the surviving south and east ranges only the east range is substantially intact; it contains a projecting entrance porch and gabled dormers rise from the parapet, which was embattled about 1819 when the south front was rebuilt and given some of the original mullioned and transomed windows of the east front. Two timber-framed hall-houses with end jetties face each other across Cock Street, **Martin's Farm** and **Swallows**, the latter with a hall floored over in two stages, first to produce a smoke bay perhaps with a gallery linking the two floors, and completed probably in 1616 when the ragstone chimney was inserted. There are at least three Wealden hall-houses as well. **Brishing Court** (Figure 52) has jetties to both ends as well as the front, and projecting eaves supported by brackets all round; heavy framing and mouldings in the hall suggest a building date about 1380-1400, making this an early example of the type in its fully developed form; the house was modernised long afterwards in two stages with a narrow smoke bay eventually giving way to a brick chimney-stack (Swain 1968).

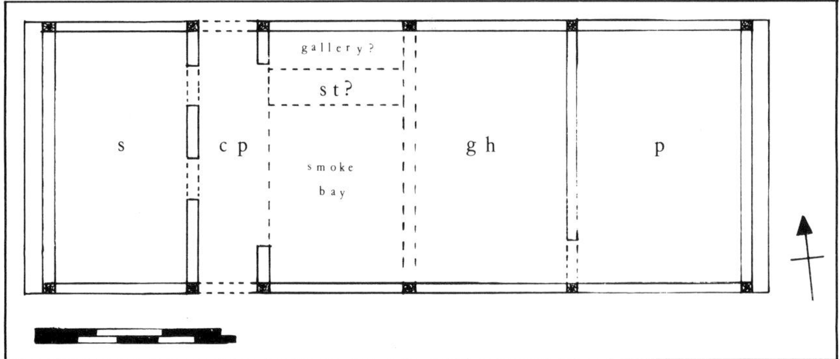

Swallows, Boughton Monchelsea. Plan of end-jetty hall-house, showing the position of added smoke bay and possible gallery. (After Swain 1968.)

Boughton Monchelsea. Lewis Court, Boughton Green.

The other two Wealdens are **Lewis Court** at Boughton Green, now limewashed as many of these houses originally may have been, and **Rabbits Cross Farm**, below the Greensand scarp near the River Beult; both are comparatively late, with close-studding and four-centred arches to their doorways. **Bishop's Farm**, again below the scarp, is a good example of the more ornate sort of lobby-entry house built about 1600 *(see* Honywood House, Lenham) with close-studding and symmetrically placed canted bays rising into large gables. Little more than a hundred years separate it from the ornate and splendidly finished brick front of an otherwise insignificant house at **Boughton Green**, which is finished with corner pilasters and five sash windows on each storey set within rubbed brick architraves, with projecting heads and keystones and recessed aprons.

BOUGHTON UNDER BLEAN (2¼ miles SE of Faversham): a parish of scattered farms on the fertile dip-slope of the North Downs with two street villages, Boughton Street, built along the old Dover road, and South Street, running in a little valley down from the parish church. Their characters are utterly different. Several of **South Street's** houses are evidently medieval, two being fairly late Wealdens with four-centred arches to their doorways, though not close-studded, a third with an end jetty instead (Plate 33). Jetties prevail at the north end of the busy **Boughton Street**, but here they are full length and of the sixteenth or seventeenth century; close-studding and ogee-curved down-braces are the order of the day, and one house, built over high cellars, has bracketed oriels in the upper storey joined by continuous clerestories from end to end.

Boughton under Blean. Boughton Street.

Further down the street, among weatherboarded houses are the Georgian fronts of two small double piles, **Apsley House**, where the boarding is grooved to look like stucco pretending to be masonry, a conceit found again at Tenterden and Tunbridge Wells, and **Oak Lodge**, where the front is of brick — and looks it. Out in the countryside to the west is **Colkins**, another double pile, earlier and of red brick, but, with its three storeys, still decidedly urban in character.

BRASTED (4 miles WNW of Sevenoaks): a street village on the Sevenoaks-Westerham road, notable for an attractive variety of houses ranging from a small Wealden hall-house to the blue bricks of **Rectory Lodge**, which has red brick window surrounds and white-painted sashes with Gothic intersecting tracery on the ground floor. The houses set back facing the green have a happy mixture of golden sandstone, red brick and tile-hanging with bands of scalloped tiles. Behind the street, **Brasted Place**, a villa which Robert Adam built for George III's physician Dr John Turton in 1784-5, is his finest work in Kent; the garden front is articulated by a giant Ionic order in the form of closely paired pilasters at each end and similarly paired columns carrying a pediment in the centre (Colour Plate 87). The **Old Rectory** is a serious Gothic essay by R. C. Carpenter *(see* his picturesque Kilndown Parsonage) of 1843-53, with a plain two-storeyed range of stone, enlivened only by a projecting bay with a crenellated parapet and groups of pointed windows set beneath hoodmoulds (Colour Plate 101).

BREDGAR (2½ miles SW of Sittingbourne): a prosperous parish of scattered farms and orchards on the fertile dip-slope of the North Downs, with a pretty centre by a pond. **Chantry Cottages** only show themselves as the college which Robert de Bradagare founded for a chaplain and two clerks about 1392 by their crown-post roof and a pair of cinquefoiled lights on the north wall; in its original form there was a central open hall flanked by a kitchen and vaulted service rooms, both with chambers in the upper floors (Parkin 1975). A small framed house beyond the church has its daub pargeted with dots and arcs. **Baxon Farm** is a late Wealden hall, close studded and converted with a jettied floor thrown across the hall, its new wall again close-studded to match the rest, and given large windows with clerestories on both storeys at the high end. The similar but far grander early seventeenth-century **Baxon Manor** again has the medieval three-part arrangement of services and entrance passage, hall and chamber, although now with a full upper floor as an original feature (Colour Plate 75); the close-studding extends to the gabled porch, where the studs are shaped like balusters (Colour Plate 30), and to the tall central gable over the hall and chamber above, which is dated 1617 over the garret window; beneath and at the chamber end are grand oriel windows on both floors, extended sideways by clerestories; the long rear wing in the same style is in fact modern and makes use of material taken from demolished houses in Ashford. **Downings**, Silver Street, is again timber-framed, but recased in lovely brickwork, diapered in red and grey, with bright red window surrounds, and an upper window with a fanlight over the central light to give it a naïve Venetian form.

The finest brickwork is at **Swanton Street Farm**, built in 1719 for Edward Holiday, a London goldsmith. Its architecture is all façade, as imposing as the house behind is inconsequential (Colour Plate 84). The excellence of its brickwork is true to Kent, but its façade comes from the likes of such architects as James Gibbs and Thomas Archer. The front stretches to five bays with a round-arched entrance and windows above it in the centre bay, which projects and swells outwards below the cornice of the parapet; its first-floor window has a Gibbs surround whose keystone carries a projecting plinth, as do all the keystones of the flat-arched windows to each side and below; the three garret windows have round heads too, the outer ones echoing the parapet, which curves downwards over them, steps sideways, and finally curves outwards to meet the cornice over the pilasters which flank the elevation. All these details are picked out in orange bricks, but, were the façade colour-washed in gentle pastel shades, it would not be out of place in the Roman Catholic south of Germany or northern Italy. The plinths would need to carry gesticulating statues; indeed pastoral gods would suit the house well. The clue to its design lies in its builder who retired to the Kentish downland here in 1719; he must have had the knowledge and artistry to make the façade possible if he did not design it himself. In complete contrast, a sixteenth-century framed house nearly opposite has a full-length jetty and a lobby entry.

BRENCHLEY (6½ miles ENE of Tunbridge Wells): a Wealden village built along a short street with numerous farmhouses scattered about the heavily wooded parish. The white-painted, tile-hung **Old Vicarage** with a long jetty on two sides overlooks the churchyard, and more white-painted, weatherboarded houses face the tiny adjacent green. The ancient appearance of **Old Palace** is a modern dress, but it does contain the remains of a large Wealden whose timbers were felled about 1485 (Howard *et al.* 1991); further up the street, **The Old Workhouse** is a late example of close-studding, with a two-storeyed porch and dormers in the roof (Plate 7), and, opposite, **Portobello**, dated 1739, looks a hundred years later still; to the north-west of these is the impressive **Brenchley Manor**, timber-framed with small panels for the ground storey and close-studding for the jettied upper storey — panelling inside is dated 1573. The most significant house in the parish is **Marle Place**, away to the south: though hung with Victorian tiles, it is that rare thing, a timber-framed double pile, and dated 1619 on the projecting two-storeyed porch (Colour Plate 80 and Plate 81); this leads by way of a lobby to a pair of rooms each side, and the central chimney-stack (Figure 26f) splits to form a passage to the pair of rear rooms *(see* Bilting Grange, Godmersham).

BRIDGE (3 miles SE of Canterbury): an attractive village where the Roman road to Dover crosses the Nail Bourne. **Bridge Place** is a fragment of a large brick courtyard house, built between 1638 and 1659 for Sir Arnold Braems in a correct classical style with Tuscan pilasters, a first-floor entablature and eaves cornice articulating the elevations (Plate 44). **Golf Cottage**, on the A2 about 1 mile south-east of the village, is a typically picturesque toll cottage, octagonal, with its thatched roof rising up to a central, castellated chimney-stack; a Gothic bay window provided a look-out (Colour Plate 18).

BROADSTAIRS (1¾ miles NNE of Ramsgate): the girdle of houses overlooking a curved harbour on Thanet's east coast (Colour Plate 17) are inseparable from Charles Dickens; he spent his holidays here, and here he wrote five of his novels as well as completing *David Copperfield.* A plaque marks one of his houses, now the Royal Albion Hotel, and several others connected with him and his characters. Stucco and cast-iron balconies predominate, but without the formality of Ramsgate and Folkestone. Broadstairs has two further centres inland, both marked by brick and flint houses with shaped gables: at St Peter's there is **Old Farm House**, dated 1686 and 1710, and at Reading Street there are more including **Stone Farm**, Lanthorne Road, dated 1710 (Figure 27, l, m and n).

BROOK (3½ miles ENE of Ashford): a superficially unremarkable village set along a street in the valley of the Great Stour, but full of good things (Wade 1986). Brick and tile-hung fronts hide a number of houses built by Christ Church's carpenters in the heyday of building before the Reformation. **Court Lodge** was the centre of the estate, and had a massively framed open hall. **Brook House** was first built possibly with an aisled hall, to which were added a services and solar block forming a cross-wing, jettied at the front and down the side; at a later stage the hall was rebuilt and also jettied along the front before being underbuilt in brick and tile-hung above. **Amage Farmhouse** also had an open hall, again possibly aisled, but only on one side. **Elm Cottage** had yet another open hall, though of a single bay, and two further storeyed bays at each end for services and a chamber in the usual way. **Pickersdane Farm** was built with a jetty at the chamber end (Plate 63), and so was **Garden Cottage,** but on a much smaller scale, in the small enclave called Troy Town. Early jettied houses of the sixteenth century include **Forstal Farm** which has a hearth-beam perhaps dated 1518, and is jettied front and back and at one end (Figures 69 and 70). **Yew Tree House** was built about 1600 as a lobby-entry house with jetties front and back, while **Troy Town House** and the larger **Old Naccolt Farm** were both built of brick in the first instance with lobby-entry plans, which continue beyond their hall-kitchens to accommodate service rooms and into rear outshuts for yet more work rooms (Figures 78 and 79).

BROOMFIELD (5¼ miles ESE of Maidstone): a chartland parish of scattered farms, which include **Rose Farm**, two-thirds of a Wealden hall.

CANTERBURY. Lying astride the ancient road from London to Dover and strategically sited where the River Stour cuts through the North Downs, the decaying Roman town of

Durovernum had much to recommend it as the capital of the new Kingdom of Kent. Its revival made Canterbury the centre of English Christianity, and it continued to grow in importance after Kent was absorbed into Wessex. It became Kent's only town of national importance. Pilgrims flocked here after the murder of Archbishop Thomas à Becket in 1170, and required an unusual number of hostels and inns to accommodate them. Many of these survive in recognisable form, particularly **The Chequers** of Hope, Mercery Lane, a courtyard inn built for £868 in 1392-5 with a dormitory for a hundred beds. The Church's interests extended further than religion and pilgrimage, so Canterbury maintained its role as an important market, even though it did not become the county town. Its status as the county's principal centre of trade and industry continued long after the Reformation had cut the Church down to size. In 1697 Celia Fiennes recorded its wealth in glowing terms: 'its a flourishing town, good tradeing in the Weaving of Silks: I saw 20 Loomes in one house with several fine flower'd silks...' This craft had its ups and downs; nevertheless a little over a generation later Defoe found three thousand French Protestants employed in broad silk weaving here, and some evidence of this remains today. Oddly, Celia Fiennes spoke of a modern town: 'the streetes are most of them large and long and the buildings handsome, very neat but not very lofty, most are of brickwork.' On this point, Defoe sounds more accurate: 'its antiquity seems to be its greatest beauty. The houses are truly ancient...' (Morris 1984, 119; Rogers 1971, 134). The roles of the Church and trade are still evident and so are those of tourism, education and light industry; so Canterbury continues today in a traditional way with differences from the past mainly in detail.

In 1200 there were around thirty stone houses in Canterbury of the type still evident in Sandwich, that is with chambers or an 'upper hall' built over an undercroft. One of these belonged to Jacob, a Jewish financier, but it was demolished when the County Hotel was built. Rather more survives of the house which the notorious usurer Lambin Frese built in 1175-80 on the site of the present Poor Priests' Hospital in Stour Street. Many more of these houses belonged to merchants, but only their undercrofts which were used as shops survive in any number. It was the rebuilding in timber which followed that gave the place the antiquity recorded by Defoe. These early timber buildings are hidden by later timber façades, themselves often hidden by more recent plaster and brickwork (Figure 42). Much of the southern part of the town was devastated by bombing in the Second World War. Nevertheless Canterbury still has the greatest variety of medieval houses in Kent, many of them the result of the typically urban process of continual adaptation.

This progression of building and rebuilding is epitomised by **Cogan House**, 53 St Peter's Street. Today, a shop front obscures its antiquity; nevertheless building began on the site in the late twelfth century with a two-storeyed stone house belonging to Luke the Moneyer which comprised chambers or a hall built over an undercroft in the standard way; this came into the hands of William Cokyn, who lived next door, and he granted it to the hospital which he had founded shortly before 1203. A large aisled hall with stone walls and a roof supported by scissor-braces was built at the rear, and this reduced the status of the front to a services and solar block (Figures 7 and 64). The hospital was not a success; about 1230 it was united with the adjoining Eastbridge Hospital, but by then Cogan House had already been leased out and returned to ordinary domestic and commercial uses. Later in the Middle Ages, the stone front was rebuilt in timber with an upper storey jettied over shops and a new block was added at the rear; very much later still came the present shop front (Parkin 1970; Canterbury Archaeological Trust 1979).

A few other medieval houses are less obscured than this. The so-called **Tudor House**, 8 Palace Street, is one example, although its name and appearance of antiquity is less than the reality. It was probably built about 1250 as the priest's house of St Alphege, with an upper hall or chamber built over an undercroft; at the end of the fifteenth century it was given a new timber-framed front with a jettied upper chamber and this is part of what can be seen today. Within the next hundred years a chimney-stack with back-to-back hearths was built into the upper storey supported by a pedestal; then, in 1665, a new priest's house was built (since demolished), and the old house was let out and extended with a second jettied storey built into the roof over the first (Figure 85). The fascias with guilloche mouldings attached to both jetties belong to this last phase, but the grotesquely carved brackets (Plate 30) probably belong to about 1495 and served to carry the eaves (Parkin 1969b).

The front of **17 Palace Street** (Figure 86) tells yet another ambiguous story: its front was rebuilt early in this century with some of its original timbers and others brought from elsewhere as a remarkable but not reliable version of its seventeenth-century form; it then comprised a shop and two storeys of chambers fronting an open hall built in the fourteenth century over yet another undercroft of about 1200 (Parkin 1972; Canterbury Archaeological Trust 1984). **No. 8 High Street** is yet another medieval house, its three bays lying end-on to the street in a typically urban way with jetties to advertise the upper storeys in the front bay. There are further fifteenth-century houses with shops and jetties at the front at **12-13 High Street, 1 Palace Street, 20 Orange Street, 70-71 Castle Street** and **26 St Peter's Street.**

At **5-8 Turnagain Lane** are the remains of a medieval terrace of identical houses, probably built early in the fifteenth century (Plate 67 and Figure 66). The terrace is framed parallel to the lane and appears to have been divided into individual units, bay

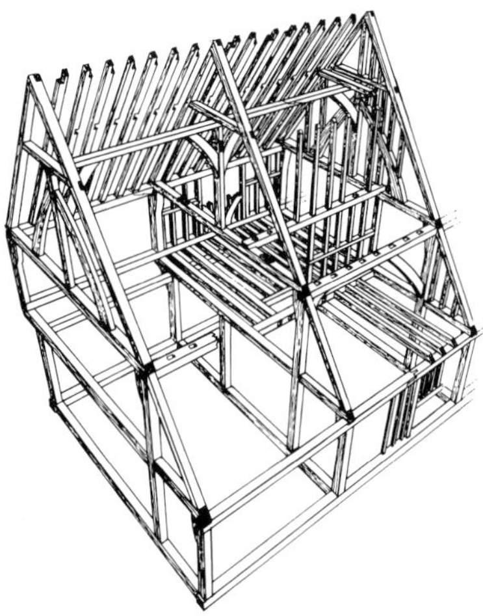

Nos. 70-71 Castle Street, Canterbury. Perspective of frame from rear quarter of two bays of, originally, four, forming a terrace of four houses, probably built in the later 15th century, each jettied at the front with a solar over a shop, and an open hall at the rear, extending into a rear aisle or outshut, later floored over as partly shown in further house. (After Canterbury Archaeological Trust 1988.)

by bay, each with a shop and jettied chamber above occupying the front half of each bay, and an open hall occupying the rear half. This form of terrace appears elsewhere in England, notably backing Tewkesbury Abbey, and here, significantly, the terrace backs St Alphege's churchyard, once again strongly suggesting that the Church was involved in speculative building for the sake of enhanced rents. Probably in the seventeenth century, the roof was raised and the new upper storey was given long bands of windows, probably to light the looms of silk weavers. The jettied range of houses in **All Saints Lane** is a later and smaller terrace with a single room on each of the two storeys (Figure 20).

The Weavers, 1-3 St Peter's Street, is another fifteenth-century example of a row of shops fronting halls, although here the framing is visible and has been ostentatiously restored in black and white. No. 3 has the typical arrangement of a shop with a passage beside it leading to a hall at the rear, with a jettied chamber over the shop and a garret, gabled at the front to provide for a window. No. 2 is separately constructed but repeats the arrangement, and is joined structurally to No. 1, which continues to the rear along the bank of the River Stour with a seventeenth-century extension; the gables belong to a remodelling of 1561 (Plate 65). The corner block comprising **8 and 9 The Parade** and **25-26 St Margaret's Street** is a medieval terrace with two storeys of jettied chambers built over shops, apparently divided bay by bay, and lacking open halls, so food must have been taken to the city's bakeries for cooking and the only warmth came from winter braziers; the roofs of the two ranges originally intersected at the corner and terminated in gables facing each way.

The lodgings built by Christ Church in

Prior Goldstone's time (1449-1468) at **1-3 Butchery Lane** and **41-44 Burgate** have a long history (Plate 68): a great stone house built here in the late twelfth century, once known as The Bull, was replaced in the middle of the fifteenth century by timber-framed shops built over the original undercrofts and with two jettied storeys of individual chambers over them (Figures 67 and 68); those at the west end were doubled in a front and a back range and probably heated by hearths set in brick chimney-stacks built against the rear wall, while the remainder comprised single chambers, bay by bay, storey by storey (Canterbury Archaeological Trust 1984). These groups of shops supporting jettied chambers, sometimes with halls at the rear, are typically urban; the medieval rural form of three-part hall-house aligned along the street is rare.

The Wealden at **3 St Radigund's Street** and the jettied **2 St Radigund's Street** lie in front of an earlier full Wealden hall-house (Figure 63) running back from the street in the usual urban way (Pantin 1962-3). This

Canterbury. 2-3 St. Radigund's Street.

Wealden is a reminder of how few of these distinctive houses are to be found in the larger towns of Kent, despite its reduced 'two-thirds', urban form. A full Wealden in the southern suburbs at **28 Wincheap**, now The Maiden's Head, with jetties on all sides must therefore have been built on an open site; it has an extended chamber end to contain one or two shops, and may have been built originally as an inn, as it had become early in the seventeenth century (Canterbury Archaeological Trust 1984). At **81 St Dunstan's Street** (Figure 62) is the restored services and jettied solar of another hall-house built in the rural way aligned with the street (Canterbury Archaeological Trust 1983), and the steeply pitched roofs of **92-94 Northgate** suggest much the same thing.

The arrangement of chambers over shops became universal in the later Middle Ages and has remained so. Consequently, such buildings are common everywhere in the centre of Canterbury that escaped bombing. Many fronts are jettied and gabled in the manner of the sixteenth and seventeenth centuries, although these often conceal earlier building behind. The most ostentatious façade of this period belongs to the refronting of the so-called **Queen Elizabeth's Guest House**, High Street, where two oriels with arched central lights recall 78 Bank Street, Maidstone, of 1611, and so does the pargeting above the second jetty; here, the plaster is raised into blocks to look like rusticated masonry and set off the sash windows beneath a parapet rather than a series of gables, evidence of the long period of decoration which gave the front its present appearance (Colour Plate 34).

Canterbury. 28 Palace Street, the side elevation.

Another spectacular jettied and also gabled house is **28 Palace Street**, built on a corner site in 1617 according to a date carved on the apex of the gable, with two jettied storeys of chambers and a jettied gable, large windows, originally oriels, extended by clerestories, and a jettied side which makes the house look as though it is falling over into King Street; this picturesque quality is enhanced by the white plasterwork once again raised into blocks suggesting rusticated masonry (Plate 90). **No. 68 Burgate** is a very small version of the same type, but with a close-studded and jettied chamber built over a shop (Figure 22i). **Nos. 13 and 13a St Peter's Street** again have a jettied upper storey and gables, here with surviving carved bargeboards, typical of about 1600, and there are visible remains of clerestory windows both here and at **Nos. 43 and 45**. The restored **Kingsmead House**, St Stephen's Street, gives some indication of their original appearance. **Nos. 1 and 2 The Borough** form another obscured house of this type. **St Dunstan's Street** is lined with jettied houses, particularly the west side, where there is a run of ten gables, broken only by a Georgianised house, and even the hipped ends of its triple roofs are clearly visible. These houses were built in ranges of three or four bays at a time, with a jettied upper storey and gabled garret, their main chambers lit by projecting bays or oriels, those of the **House of Agnes Hotel** once again containing arched central lights (Plate 92).

The introduction of brick to Canterbury owes much to the initiative of Archbishop Morton, but it took root only slowly. Its first major domestic use was probably in the **Roper Gateway**, St Dunstan's Street; this was completed between 1530 and 1560 with a four-centred arch and crow-stepped gable as the frontispiece to a large mansion belonging to the Roper family, who counted William Roper, son-in-law and biographer of Sir Thomas More, among their descendants (T. P. Smith 1990). For a century brick made little headway, and when it appeared it was often as nogging in framed buildings, as shown by the rear of a house in St Peter's Street dated 1620. Only in 1625 did the prominent shaped and pedimented gables of a house in Watling Street arrive; it was bombed, but its neighbour, **16 Watling Street**, survives as a teasing fragment of contemporary brickwork, laid in English bond with stone quoins and Doric entablature, but also with inserted sash windows and other alterations (Plate 42). It was built in 1625 as the town house of the Man family with a rectangular bay to the left, a canted bay to the right and a rectangular bay beside it for the entrance, all fitted out with mullioned and transomed windows; but in the nineteenth century all these had gone, leaving it with the appearance of a house of about 1700. It was only then that brick at last became really common.

The Red House, backing the later **St Peter's House**, just off St Peter's Street, set the pattern for the eighteenth century with red bricks chequered with black and a wooden bracketed cornice. **Nos. 72-74 Broad Street**, dated 1693, again have chequered brickwork; this never became very common, although it was taken up by **28 King Street**. Later brick houses such as **Barton Court**, Longport, and **Westgate House**, St Dunstan's Street, of 1760, are typical red brick double piles with block cornices; the former has a heavily rusticated doorcase and Venetian window over it, while **Hoystings**, Old Dover Road, is finished with arched windows with Gothic tracery and a Gothic doorcase to match. After this, stucco facing came into its own on larger houses, as can be seen nearby at **Delandale** in Old Dover Road, at **26 Castle Street**, and at **Westgate Court** and elsewhere in Linden Grove. Among smaller houses, especially the terraces of the inner suburbs, brick remained common, notably at **19-33 Old Dover Road**, the far larger houses at the start of **London Road**, in the engaging pair of doubled houses at **16-22**

Canterbury. 16-22 King Street.

King Street, and in such pretty enclaves as **Mill Lane** and **Pound Lane**, both dating from well into the nineteenth century. The

Canterbury. Mill Lane.

latter abut Sudbury Tower and the town wall, but respond to them not at all; for that and a response to other traditions of building one must turn to the crenellations and shaped flint gables of **Tower House**.

CHALK (2½ miles ESE of Gravesend): a small parish overlooking the Thames estuary. **Filborough Farmhouse**, which was associated with John Martyn 'of Fylbarowth' in 1489, has a hall with services and solar in the same range, and a later jettied cross-wing containing a chamber (Arnold 1895).

CHARING (5½ miles NW of Ashford): a street village built on the edge of the downland scarp where a route from Canterbury into the Weald crosses the Maidstone-Ashford road. The manor belonged to the Archbishops of Canterbury from ancient times, and, since it was a day's ride from Canterbury, Maidstone and Saltwood, it was a good stopping place. So here they built a **Palace** to accommodate them when touring their estates. The remains of an imposing gatehouse and precinct wall adjacent to the church, now with cottages built into its flint walls, open into a small courtyard, with a chamber block and chapel wing opposite (Plate 4), and the detached great hall of about 1300, now a barn, on the right. These works of Archbishops Winchester and Peckham are identifiable by the remains of traceried windows set in flint walling. Morton's and Warham's work undertaken about 1500 included a brick upper storey and a corridor linking the two buildings (Rigold 1969g). About 1545 Cranmer presented the Palace to Henry VIII, who used it occasionally and then leased it out; its conversion into a farm brought a plaque of 1556 and much ruination before Charles I finally sold it in 1629.

Beyond church and palace, the ancient market place leads to the High Street, which curves downhill towards the Maidstone-Ashford road. Beyond the top end of the High Street are bungalows set up by smallholders after the Great War. At the top of the street itself, a pair of nineteenth-century cottages revive the fashion for shaped gables; two early eighteenth-century brick houses follow, **Wakeley House** and **Ludwell House**, both double-piles with hipped roofs and five windows wide. Lower down, timber framing prevails, with seventeenth-century brickwork hiding the gabled front of the **Old Swan Hotel** and evidence of a Wealden hall behind weather-boarding on the east side; set back on the west, **Pierce House** has two close-studded gables with brick nogging, the forward one containing a porch and a doorway dating the front to about 1530 and hence with rows of arched lights rather than the oriels continued by clerestories of half a century later. Further down, there is a long jettied row, close-studded and with the remains of ground-floor arcaded shops at the south end. Beyond the main road comes another timber house, its close-studded gable fronting the street and showing the early seventeenth-century fashion for oriels continued right across each way by clerestories.

Outside the village, the brick encased **Payne Street Farm** in the far south of the parish had a recessed hall and a service and solar end jettied at the front and end in the Wealden way, and was then converted by the insertion of a floor into part of the hall to produce a smoke bay with a gallery at the rear, and, finally, a chimney-stack was built into the remaining space (Figures 12, 57 and 72) (Swain 1968). Other medieval houses include the remains of a Wealden at **Burleigh Farm** and **Wickens Manor**, named after a family of yeomen, but probably built by the Brents with an open hall in the fifteenth century; its present form dates from a marriage between the Brents and the Nevilles in 1513, commemorated by their arms carved over the porch, when, first, a smoke bay was created, and, much later, a new front was constructed with a jetty and ornamental framing with unusual diagonal studding on the porch, and a frieze of diamonds, curved in the main body of the house and underlying the now-blocked clerestories (Colour Plate 32). **Pett Place**, despite its present appearance, also began as a framed hall-house. It passed to the Atwaters and by marriage to the Honywoods and then the Sayers who altered and enlarged it in the sixteenth and seventeenth centuries, and then refronted it in dark red brick early in the eighteenth century, with two storeys of regularly placed sash windows and broad pilaster strips at the ends; only about 1875 were the Dutch gables added and the house extended to give it its present character. There is a **toll house** serving the road to Pluckley.

CHARTHAM (4¼ miles SW of Canterbury): a downland parish with its centre in a loop of the Great Stour. Facing the village green are **Bedford House**, a converted Wealden now with a full-length jetty and two gables, and **De l'Angle House**, which has a curious niche beneath its block cornice containing a bust of Charles II with his left hand raised in blessing. Outside the village is **Deanery Farm**, a possession of Christ Church; here Prior Henry of Eastry built a hall in 1303, with a roof comprising common rafters linked by pairs of rafters, and a detached kitchen joined it in the following year; in 1393-4 a chamber block was added to the hall, and these were refurbished about 1500 by Prior Goldstone II; at the Reformation they were handed over to the newly established Dean and Chapter of Christ Church Cathedral and allowed to fall into disrepair, eventually to be adapted and partly rebuilt. Meanwhile, a Wealden was built close by in 1496-7 for the tenant farmer, with a close-studded ground floor, and the unusually early feature of a queen-strut roof with clasped side-purlins (Figure 24) (Sparks and Parkin 1974; Canterbury Archaeological Trust 1982-3). Shalmsford Street, to the south-west, has several attractive brick houses.

CHART SUTTON (4½ miles SE of Maidstone): a small chartland parish with scattered farms below the scarp. Here, two early hall-houses have recently been accurately dated by dendrochronology: **Chart Hall Farmhouse** (formerly Chart Bottom Farmhouse) is an early Wealden with a surviving hall and service end whose timbers were felled in 1379-80 (Plate 58); **Old Moat Farmhouse** comprises a service wing whose timbers were felled in 1382, and a hall which was rebuilt in the sixteenth century (Howard *et al.* 1991).

CHATHAM (1 mile E of Rochester): a naval town on the east bank of the River Medway. Henry VIII's fleet is first recorded anchoring here in the last year of his reign. The anchorage rapidly grew in favour, and Chatham's fortunes rose accordingly. Despite the humiliating Dutch attack in 1667, the dockyard was developed in step with successful wars against the French. The **Commissioner's House** of 1703 is a fine double pile, built of brick and ornately decorated with a bracketed cornice. The twelve three-storeyed houses forming the **Officers' Terrace** were built in 1727-9 with the end and centre houses projecting and finished appropriately with battlements in the style then favoured by Vanbrugh (Plate 95). Outside the Dockyard several late Georgian terrace houses, particularly **Gibraltar Place** of 1794 in New Road, give the town some formal grandeur.

CHEVENING (3¼ miles NW of Sevenoaks): a parish extending from an estate village on the downland scarp across the River Darent to the wooded chartland. The main house, the mid-seventeenth-century **Chevening Park**, a large double pile, was given a Palladian guise between 1786 and 1796 by the architect James Wyatt working for the 3rd Earl Stanhope, and, surprisingly, accomplished in mathematical tile, not brick (Plate 84). One range of brick cottages in the adjacent village belongs to the seventeenth century, and sets the tone for the rest. Across the Darent at Bessels Green are several attractive cottages and the late Georgian **Bessel's House**, built as Providence House for Dr John Epps, the homeopathic physician and author of *Evidences of Christianity* *deduced from Phrenology,* with shallow full-height bay windows flanking a projecting porch carried on Greek Doric columns.

CHIDDINGSTONE (5¾ miles WSW of Tonbridge): a parish where the River Eden runs through the Wealden Vale with scattered farms and a short village street which continues as the private drive to **Chiddingstone Castle**. The Streatfeilds built it from the profits of their iron foundries in the seventeenth century as a large brick house with a hipped roof; it was known as High Street House until the architect William Atkinson recased it in sandstone about 1805 and gave it symmetrically placed Tudor Gothic windows with hoodmoulds, an embattled parapet, a central projecting entrance tower on the north side, and scattered towers elsewhere (Plate 99). On one side of the High Street is the churchyard, with the **Old Rectory** below it; here a framed house with the usual large hipped roof seems to have been modernised in the 1730s when it was tile-hung and given a symmetrical front with regularly placed sash windows on each storey and a pedimented centre. On the other side of the High Street is a long range of close-studded houses with prominent jetties and gables, many of which the architect Charles Rennie Mackintosh drew in 1910: No. 1, **Skinner's House**, is a late fifteenth-century hall-house with a rear aisle (Gray 1975) and a jettied cross-wing (Figure 18); No. 3, **Porch House**, has a recessed centre suggesting that it originally had the form of a Wealden, but this has been obscured by lavish additions, notably a full-height oriel set beneath a gable at the high end of the hall, and a projecting porch with a gabled room over it at the low end, dated 1637, and opening into an entry lobby with the chimney-stack behind it; **No. 4** has a symmetrical plastered front with the remains of a scheme of pargeting which included panels with serrated edges filled with upturned hearts or rings and bearing the date 1697 (Plate 36).

Just to the north of the Eden, at Somerden Green, is the **Old Workhouse**, a long framed building, with brick-nogging below and tile-hanging above, a central entry lobby and chimney-stack, which probably divided left and right for male and female paupers; the date 1601 in modern numerals probably refers to the date of the Elizabethan Poor Law rather than the date of construction, which, even so, is likely to be in the seventeenth century (Colour Plate 14). Further to the north is an oast-house, sensitively converted by Martin Quirk Associates with small windows. Three medieval houses at Bough Beech in the far north of the parish were taken down to make way for a reservoir in 1967 and removed to the Weald and Downland Open Air Museum at Singleton, and a fourth, **Hilders Farm**, is heavily disguised by a seventeenth-century refronting with symmetrically placed gables and, yet again, a lobby-entry plan (Plate 78). There is another medieval house to the south-west at **Hill Hoath**, and yet another to the south-east at **Watstock** with a single-bayed hall, a solid stud partition at the high end of the hall and a tall bay window, rising above the eaves, inserted when the hall was modernised and divided into two storeys. **Trugger's Oast**, to the south, has recently been attractively converted into a dwelling by the local architects Martin and Mitzi Quirk.

CHILHAM (5¾ miles SW of Canterbury): a downland parish centred on a strategically placed **Castle** built high above the Great Stour. In 1616 its partial rebuilding included a new house for Sir Dudley Digges. This has a curious plan, reflecting the octagonal keep of the medieval castle, with embattled ranges disposed around five sides of a hexagon (Figure 80); the front has a gabled porch and corner turrets, while the wings, cranking themselves round an open courtyard, have canted bays, large gabled dormers and groups of tall chimney-stacks (Colour Plate 78). Just outside the walls is a small square lined by framed houses with streets running downhill in all directions. Among at least four Wealden halls here are **Littlecroft** and **Burgoyne**, The Street; part of the recessed hall of the latter was built out with a continuation of the jetty when a floor was inserted at the high end and a smoke bay created in the remaining open half (Swain 1968). **Robins Croft**, opposite, another Wealden, now has a long jetty and evidence for oriels extended sideways by clerestories. By the church, the **Vicarage** is a typical early Georgian double pile of red brick with a hipped roof, distinguished by a Venetian window over the entrance. Beyond the hilltop village are a number of framed hall-houses, including **Bagham Farm, Monkton Manor** and one at **Mountain Street**, all with prominent end jetties, and **Hurst Farm**, with a great yawning entrance porch of stone acting as a buttress; here the unusually wide

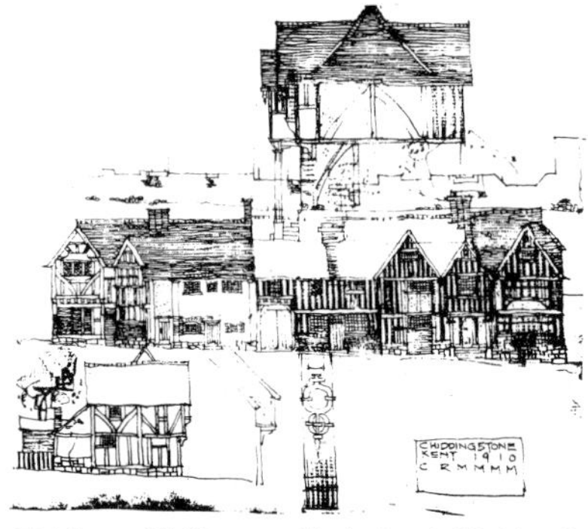

High Street, Chiddingstone. Charles Rennie Mackintosh's 1910 drawing of Nos. 1 (Skinner's House), 2 and 3 (Porch House), High Street.

No. 4 High Street, Chiddingstone. Charles Rennie Mackintosh's drawing of 1910 showing the pargeting.

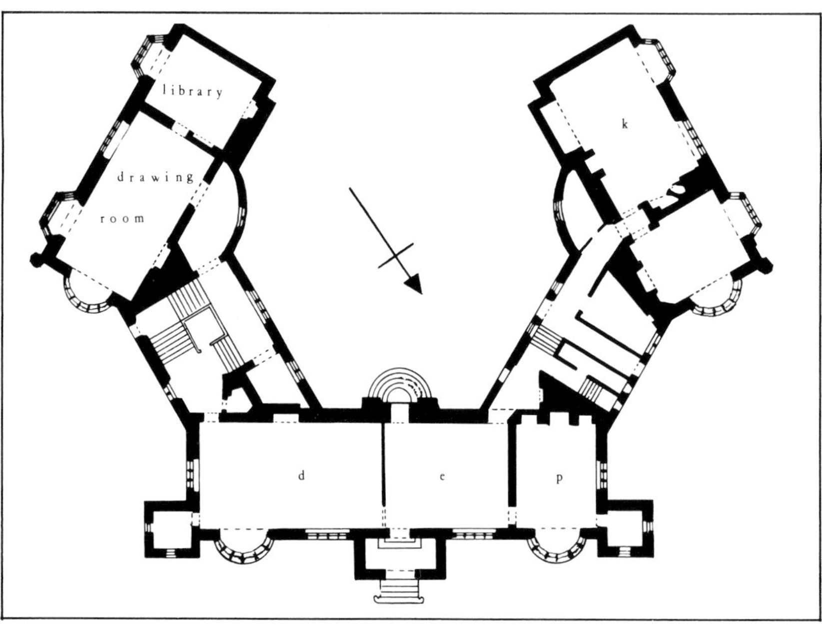

Chilham Castle. Plan of the house of 1616. (After Godfrey 1929a.)

Chilham. Monkton Manor.

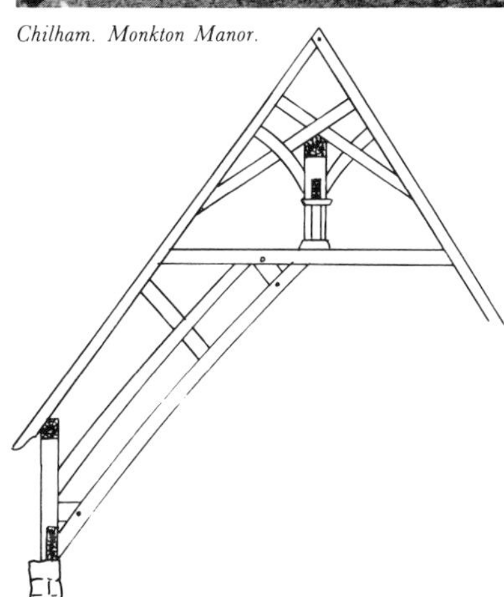

Hurst Farm, Chilham. Cross section of part of roof framing showing an early form of arch-bracing, here needed to span a wide hall. (After Bismanis 1987.)

hall (about 28ft. or 8.5m) is spanned by an arched collar with many secondary timbers and a crown-post supporting scissor-braces. There are more framed houses at **Dane Street**, and also **Young Manor Farm**, built in brick with an immense gabled roof for one of the Digges children.

CHISLET FORSTAL (6 miles NE of Canterbury): a parish of scattered farms on the edge of the marshes dividing Thanet from mainland Kent. When the hall of **Tudor House**, a solitary Wealden at Chislet Forstal, was floored over a new window was inserted in the form of a full-height canted bay and decorated with scrolls and dated 1637; unusually for a framed house, a lovely projecting brick porch with a shaped gable was also added, though later (Figure 27e).

CLIFFE (5 miles N of Rochester): a village built on the low chalk hills overlooking the marshes of the Thames estuary, particularly notable for **Manor Farm**, an early seventeenth-century, close-studded lobby-entry house with large oriel windows beneath the bracketed jetty and eaves, and a magnificent chimney-stack with four clustered octagonal shafts rising from a square base.

COBHAM (4¾ miles W of Rochester): a downland parish with two centres built along streets, Cobham proper and Sole Street. Among the several framed, weatherboarded and brick houses in the main street, **Mill Farmhouse** stands out for its attractive red brick façade enlivened with blue vitrified headers and a terracotta plaque with a scrolled pediment inscribed 'P WM 1712' (*see* Sole Place, Bobbing). Beyond all these is the Gothick **Rose Cottage** in one direction, and, in the other, **Owletts**, which was built in 1683-4 for Bonham Hayes (Arnold 1949), with a symmetrical façade and projecting wings at each end, and extended in this century by the architect Sir Herbert Baker who lived there. It was he who restored **Yeoman's House**, a Wealden at Sole Street. It was also he who suggested that Robert Weir Schultz should design **Scalers Hill** nearby for his friend A.W. Booth; this was built in 1899-1901 with a main block with three dormers projecting from a great hipped roof, and low wings, detailed in a simple but pleasing Tudor way (Ottewill 1979).

Cobham. Mill Farmhouse, the terracotta plaque.

The principal house, **Cobham Hall**, lies to the east in its own parkland. The Cobham estate also included lands in several parishes between here, the Thames and the Medway, and these were augmented by the inclusion of Rochester Priory after the Dissolution. This may have caused the ninth Lord Cobham to start building a new house here of brick in the 1550s. It included a hall range running north to south and a north range running eastwards, perhaps as the start of an intended courtyard which was not fully realised until some two centuries later. The second phase of building was undertaken by William Brooke, tenth Lord Cobham, whom Holinshed described as 'statlie augmenting' the house about 1582, works which continued after his death in 1597 under his son. These included the construction of a north and a south range running westwards from the hall range, possibly to form a second courtyard, which probably always remained open on the fourth side. The north range, among other things, was intended to provide accommodation for a visit by Queen Elizabeth which did not take place. In 1603 Henry Brooke, eleventh Lord Cobham, was arrested for his part in the plot to put Arabella Stuart on the throne. He forfeited the estate and it passed through the Crown to the Dukes of Lennox and Richmond. When the sixth Duke inherited

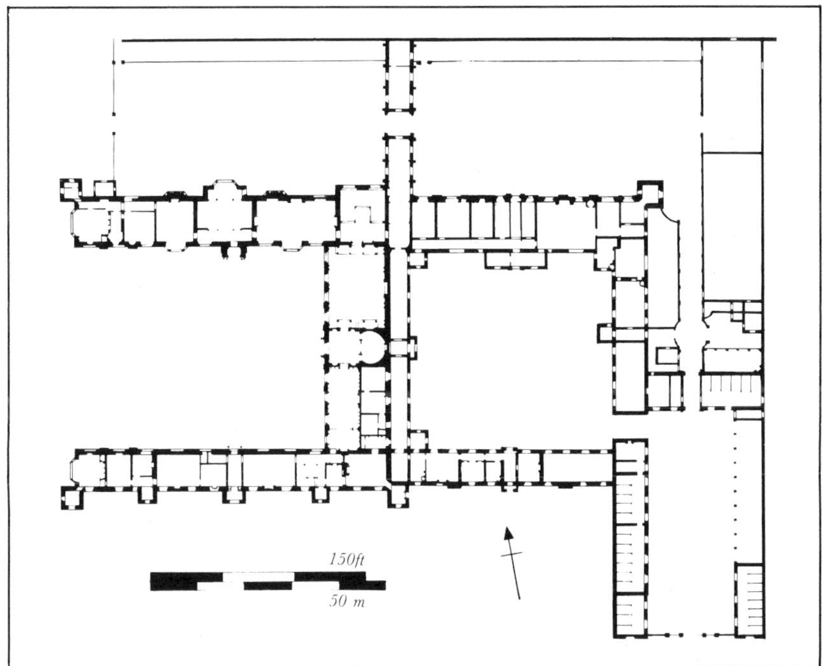

Cobham Hall. Plan, about 1830, showing the ninth Lord Cobham's central, hall range of the 1550s, as remodelled after 1661 and extended by a corridor along its eastern side during the works of 1801-31; the north-east range, also of the 1550s, rebuilt 1801-31, and the services and stabling block of the 1790s, completing the eastern courtyard; the tenth Lord Cobham's 'statlie augmenting' with the two west ranges, the southern one of about 1582-87, the northern one completed 1601; and the northward extension of the house during the 1801-31 works to include a porte-cochère *with a bridge over it linking the north-east tower to a raised garden. (After a drawing from the Repton office.)*

the estate in 1661 he employed the architect Peter Mills for the partial rebuilding of the hall range. By the 1720s the house had become run down and it was only in the 1760s that a long campaign of modernisation and change began for the third and fourth Earls of Darnley to whom the house had descended by marriage. Their works included neo-classical interiors designed by George Shakespear and James Wyatt. Finally the house reached its present form after a fifth campaign of building between 1801 and 1831 under James Wyatt and the Repton sons which included a new entrance on the north side in place of the original entrance into the hall range and a general enhancement of its Elizabethan style. The Park was reformed according to plans compiled by Humphrey Repton in a Red Book of 1790. This complicated building history has left a house full of puzzles still to be solved by reconciling its extensive documentation with the evidence of its fabric. It fully demonstrates the difficulty of trying to think of any building in the context of 'its own period'.

The surviving 1550s work includes a high plinth which runs along the north side of the much rebuilt north-east range to meet a stair tower with brickwork diapered with a pattern of crosses on its north face (Figure 28A). The better-preserved southern face of this range carries an unusual horizontal pattern of chevroned diaper (Colour Plate 43), and evidence for mullioned and transomed windows similar to the present later ones. Being at the high end of the hall, the range was probably devoted to chambers. In the interior of the recast hall range are the remains of mullioned and transomed windows and a moulded doorway on the eastern side of the cross-passage at the low end of the hall.

These early fragments pale before the two ranges which run westwards from the hall range to be marked at each end by prominent octagonal towers (Colour Plate 70). The earlier south wing has a stone doorway in the centre of the south side dated 1584 and there are rainwater heads dated 1587. The doorway is in a central projection, and between it and the two octagonal end towers are projecting garderobe blocks. These and the groups of paired octagonal chimney-stacks constitute a tellingly symmetrical façade, although this partly results from a later regularising of the fenestration and the removal of an off-centre stable block to the south. The regularity of the courtyard elevations of both this and the northern range was once again enhanced in the late eighteenth century by the removal of large staircase projections at the west ends and the substitution of pairs of chimney-stacks, and by alterations to the fenestration and the gables. The north entrance portal into the south range comprises a severely classical portico in dark stone, with a bay window above, canted out on a base enriched with a hugely overscaled egg and dart motif, a strange contrast between the sophisticated and the naïve. The north wing is dated 1595 on rainwater heads, and the last of its octagonal towers was built in 1601. It was designed to contain a Great Chamber, Lodging and Queen's Chamber on the upper floor, for the proposed visit of 1600. The magnificent stone portal on its south side may well have been removed here from the main entrance into the hall range, and does not quite fit the pedimented doorway into the wing which it shelters. An inscription beneath its pediment shows that it was intended to lead into a chapel. The portal, meanwhile, is dated 1594; the ground storey is supported by paired Roman Doric columns, which have been renewed, the second storey by enriched Ionic columns in the French style of Philibert Delorme, the attic by antae supporting baskets of fruit flanking the tenth Lord Cobham's achievement of arms (Colour Plate 37). The interior of this range is notable for a panelled ground-floor room with a chimney-piece in which a goddess — maybe Pomona — stands lightly clad before a Tournai marble background inscribed with a rustic scene of thatched cottages, and there are three more elaborate chimney-pieces upstairs as well as another in the hall range.

The renewed hall range of the 1660s has a grand centrepiece with a giant Corinthian pilastered portico, extended into the attic by antae. Later works continued the façade as far as the projecting ranges, raised it each side into a full third storey, and substituted sashes for the mullioned and transomed windows. The old hall became the Gilt Hall, and was given a sumptuous plastered ceiling with three shallow domes, further enriched during later works. Also of this period are the two staircases at either end of the hall range.

The third Earl of Darnley's programme of redecoration, executed by George Shakespear in the 1760s and 1770s, gave the Gilt Hall end galleries supported on Corinthian columns as well as gilded plasterwork; the decorative allusions to drama and music of Westmacott's chimney-piece of 1778, as well as the provision of an organ in one of the galleries, show that the room was now being used for concerts and, no doubt, dancing and other formal entertainment. Upstairs are several rooms with neo-classical plasterwork of this period, but beyond the Gilt Hall the conversion of the old screens passage into a two-part vestibule, divided by a kind of triumphal arch, and of the service rooms into a library, again of two parts, was James Wyatt's work for the fourth earl. He and Humphrey Repton began the reordering of the overall arrangements of the house in 1789-90 by demolishing the Elizabethan stable block to the south of the house and completing the eastern service courtyard with a south range in brickwork, passably Tudor in character.

In 1791 Humphrey Repton proposed a radical reordering of the park, with new vistas and drives, and also the provision of a new entrance on the north side of the house. These works were undertaken by his sons, together with Wyatt, from 1801, most notably with a *porte-cochère* set into a new single storeyed range which extends northwards from the line of a corridor running along the back of the hall range, complete with an entrance corridor at ground level and an open gallery above connecting an entrance in the north-east tower with a raised garden to the north of the house. At the same time the north elevation was regularised and made more imposing by the addition of projections, all in a convincing Elizabethan style, works which continued until 1831.

COLDRED (4½ miles NNW of Dover): a downland parish of a few scattered farms, and, by the church, **Coldred Manor Farm** (Colour Plate 77), a lobby-entry house built in rosy brickwork, asymmetrically planned with a single room to the left, two to the right, and a rear outshut *(see* Old Naccolt Farm, Brook).

COLLIER STREET (6½ miles SSW of Maidstone): a parish of scattered farms in the Wealden vale between the Rivers Beult and Teise. The close-studded **Saxonden** has a jettied cross-wing with a second jetty beneath the gable.

COOLING (4½ miles N of Rochester): a parish of scattered farms with John de Cobham's castle (licensed in 1381) strategically built on the low chalk hills overlooking the marshes of the Thames estuary. The irregular brick elevations of **Cooling Court**, which is dated 1700, are the result of a protracted series of building campaigns.

COWDEN (7½ miles W of Tunbridge Wells): the most westerly Wealden parish in the county, with a short village street and numerous scattered farms, many of them owing their existence to the profits made from iron foundries set up along the Kent Water. This still feeds what used to be hammer ponds which stretch along the Sussex border until it reaches Surrey. Opposite the Crown Inn at the start of the village street is a Wealden, underbuilt in brick and weatherboarded along the side. The houses further along were consumed by fire in the seventeenth century, and rebuilt with brick ground storeys and weather-boarded or tile-hung upper storeys and gables. In the lane opposite the church is a short terrace of similar nineteenth-century cottages, but notable for having the bricks of their ground storeys laid on their sides in what is called rat-trap bond. Of the framed houses outside the village, **Waystrode** is

Waystrode, Cowden. View as in 1893. (After Leveson-Gower 1895.)

demonstrably the earliest; it was mentioned in John Style's will in 1471 and has close-studding with small panels once enriched with curved diamonds between the ground-floor and upper windows commensurate with that date; projecting gables flank the main range, the left-hand one containing chambers, with a full-height projecting bay rising up to a jetty beneath the gable, the right-hand, lower one for services, and with a cusped bargeboard. **Basing** is also timber framed but now attractively tile-hung (Colour Plate 13); Richard and Elizabeth Knight rebuilt it at the end of the sixteenth century as a lobby-entry house with, apparently, the remains of an earlier house built into a rear service wing with a large kitchen in the ground floor. An upstairs chamber has their initials among painted texts based on *Proverbs* 21:13, and strapwork decoration (Figure 25). Downstairs is a stone chimney-piece carved with their initials and the date 1597, moved here from the altered **Scarletts Mill**, which they also built. Yet another framed house built on the proceeds of the iron industry is **Crippenden Manor**, which is dated 1607 on the sumptuous overmantel in the panelled hall (Leveson-Gower 1895). Among yet more framed houses is a small house with a cross-wing on the Hartfield Road, just north of the Kent Water, and **Bassett's Farm**, which is mostly encased in brick and, again, tile-hung, though with its gable end visibly close-studded and twice jettied, with bracketed oriels, extended by clerestories (Figure 30k).

CRANBROOK (6½ miles W of Tenterden): a prosperous Wealden parish of scattered farms with, at its centre, a once important market town given its charter by Edward III in 1332. Its fortunes rose with weaving until the Civil War, and continued in a modest way thereafter with, among other things, hop-growing. This kept it alive but did not spoil its original glories. So, like Headcorn and Tenterden, this is the epitome of what a country town should be: small, varied, yet all of a piece, thanks to an overriding sense of scale.

The High Street runs straight downhill, its timber and weatherboarding, tile-hanging, brick and stucco harmonising with a counterpoint of canted bays (Colour Plate 51). **The Studio** is a Wealden with a carriage entrance punched through its open hall and a large close-studded wing with curly bargeboards under the gable (Plate 64). At the bottom, a lane leads to the mellow brick **Museum**, and the jettied and weatherboarded Stone Street quickly narrows, miraculously to frame Union Mill in the distance (Colour Plate 6); it plunges down to cross a brook before rising up towards **Hill House**, whose fluted Corinthian doorcase shines out white from the red-brown tiles cladding the front. Nearly opposite, the tall chimney-stack inserted into a medieval hall-house adds its accent to the sails of the windmill, and **Rammells House** of 1882-3, opposite, shows the young Ernest Newton using brick to form notional pilasters with roughcast walls between them and roughcast again in the panels between the windows of a projecting polygonal bay. At opposite ends of the town are **Goddard's Green**, a wealthy clothier's house of at least two periods whose long close-studded, jettied front ends with projecting bays and gables, one of which has the date 1634 on a chimney-piece; and **Old Willesley** (Plate 60), a large Wealden hall, with gables added to the jettied ends, a canted bay added to the high end of the hall, and the framing rendered. Nearly opposite, a late Victorian house in the Old English style stridently proclaims its traditional credentials, a far cry from Norman Shaw's sensitive extensions of 1864-5 to Willesley Hotel (for the Royal Academician John Calcott Horsley) in the same style. Out in the Weald, more framed houses, notably **Old Cloth Hall**, part modern, part rebuilt in brick, and **Coursehorn**, are all hidden by brick and tile-hanging. **Glassenbury** grew in a different way, and now has a stretched appearance owing to its wide pediment spanning the five central windows, and long façade which reaches nine windows in all and ends in stone quoins. At Golford is a gabled **toll cottage** dated 1761 and with the usual projecting window for collecting tolls.

CROCKHAM HILL (6 miles WSW of Sevenoaks): a small village with sandstone houses built on the scarp of the chartland. Above it on the ridge and enjoying spectacular views towards the Weald are a handful of large half-timbered houses in the style of Norman Shaw, **Lewins** of 1876 by J. M. Brydon, **Heath House** and **Kent Hatch** of about 1882 among them; at Froghole, **High Quarry** of 1905 and **Acremead**, by Smith and Brewer, of 1906 continue the theme in sandstone.

Crockham Hill. Acremead, Froghole.

CRUNDALE (5½ miles NE of Ashford): a high downland parish of scattered settlements in the ancient Lyminge Forest. **Hunt Street Farm** is an early Wealden whose hall was floored over in the seventeenth century and extended forward with a new front framed in small squares, with a projecting square bay rising into a jettied gable; its deep windows on both of the new floors are flanked by the usual clerestories and the panelling between them is filled with a pretty pattern of brick nogging. **Winchcombe Farm** is a lovely mass of whitewashed gables and octagonally shafted chimney-stacks.

CUXTON (2¼ miles SW of Rochester): a suburb on the west bank of the Medway with an isolated hamlet in a fold of the downs at Upper Bush. **Upper Bush** itself is a late Wealden hall, close-studded with a coved overhang and a moulded, four-centred arch to the doorway, converted in one go with a chimney-stack backing the cross-passage.

Upper Bush, Cuxton. Elevation, showing its late 15th century Wealden form adapted by the insertion of a chimney-stack at the high end of the hall, initially with a single flue, later a second flue to serve the upper room created by inserting a floor into the hall, and further chimney-stacks built on to the house to serve the rooms in the jettied ends.

Just down the slope, **Barrow Hill House** (Figure 73) is a much earlier hall-house, that is of the fourteenth century and this time with an end-jetty, whose hall was partly floored over to make a smoke bay with a gallery connecting it to the chamber over the services; later, the remainder of the hall was floored over, a chimney-stack was built into the service bay and this end of the house was extended (Swain 1968).

DAVINGTON: a western suburb of Faversham on the further bank of the creek which originated when Fulk de Newenham founded a Benedictine Priory for nuns there in 1153; this was moribund before the Dissolution, and its church was taken over by the parish while the rest decayed. The west range of the cloisters was turned into a house in the seventeenth century with a framed upper storey and four (originally six) jettied gables

Davington. Davington Priory, the cloister.

to the front, all plastered, and a similar arrangement on the cloister side set above flint and stone chequered walls. In 1845 the stained glass artist Thomas Willement made additions to the south in brick and decorated the house in a medieval style.

DEAL. The old town, Upper Deal, is inland, with the original parish church standing among a handful of houses of the seventeenth and eighteenth centuries; the shaped gables of **Jenkin's Well**, dated 1694, are unusual for being paired at one end of a double pile.

Because The Downs offered a sheltered anchorage offshore, Deal was a favoured landing ground, and became a non-corporate Limb of Sandwich in 1229. As the harbour at Sandwich silted up, Deal's fortunes rose. In the seventeenth century a new town grew up along the beach where fishermen had their huts, and this was incorporated in 1699. These circumstances produced an unusual street plan, with Beach Street following the shore, High Street running parallel to it inland and the narrow Middle Street picking its way between them; across these run a number of lanes to produce an irregular, drawn-out grid, tightly packed with houses. Celia Fiennes said it was thriving in 1697, 'the buildings new and neate brickwork with gardens, I believe they are most masters of shipps houses and seamen or else those that belong to the Cordage and sail making, with other requisites to shipping' (Morris 1984, 123). Instead of grand terraces along the seafront (Deal never claimed to be a watering place), there are several groups of attractive houses with typical canted bays, often confined to an upper storey, and an irregular roofline of red tiles. The High Street has many similar groups, often with shops in the ground storey; **122 High Street** stands out as a double pile with block cornices over the windows in each of the three-storeyed bays, and pediments over the top ones; another double pile, **127 High Street**, is conspicuous for its yellow brick front with full-height shallow bowed bays. There are greater pleasures among the picturesque intimacies of Middle Street and the cross lanes. The sequence begins at South Street and the irregular pink stuccoed walls and red tiles of **Elizabeth Carter's House**, which this blue-stockinged classical scholar and famed translator in 1758 of Epictetus purchased out of the proceeds. It sets the scene for what

Deal. Middle Street.

follows. Beyond the blank interruption of a car park, Middle Street reaches **Queen Anne House**, truly named so far as its style goes, and a flurry of shaped gables which demonstrate that once, before these streets were completely filled with houses, the gables must have been far more visible than they are today (Figure 27j). Nowadays, it is not individual houses but the kaleidoscopic views of red brick, multicoloured stucco, plain and pedimented doorcases, and up-and-down rooflines marking three centuries of growth which are so endearing, view succeeding view all the way to **Alfred Square's** admirable terminus. Among the side streets, **Portobello Court, St George's Passage** and **Dolphin Street** have special charm, but none so singular as the contrast between the

Deal. 19 Farrier Street.

restored **19 Farrier Street**, the earliest type of house in these streets, complete with shaped gable, and **8 Farrier Street** and its neighbours, whose late Georgian taste is garnished with the seaside flavour of a ship's nameplate inscribed 'Esperanza'.

DODDINGTON (4¼ miles SSE of Sittingbourne): a wooded downland parish with numerous scattered farms. The medieval **Sharsted Court** has a mid-fourteenth-century crown-post roof, and comprised a hall with chamber and service blocks in the standard way; in 1711 these were regularised in an engagingly off-hand manner with an embattled brick front with a fine Corinthian doorcase for the entrance at one end of the hall range, and the projecting wings were given bracketed eaves and hipped roofs, the right-hand one with pairs of windows on each storey, the left-hand one with an extra window and a small hipped roof of its own; over the hall, a lantern with pairs of round arches and an ogee lead roof completes the ensemble. **Homestall**, meanwhile, is close-studded with a jetty, and the usual bracketed oriel windows of about 1600 extended by clerestories; its symmetry is broken by the chimney-stack, which heats only the right-hand end.

DOVER. Dover's ancient military significance is amply demonstrated by one of the finest royal castles in England. Yet its only asset, according to Defoe in 1724, was 'an ill repaired, dangerous, and good for little harbour and pier, very chargeable and little worth'; nevertheless, packets to France and the Low Countries used it, and so did freighters plying between New York, Virginia and Holland, among other things for the purpose of paying customs duty (Rogers 1971, 138-9). Dover is now *the* port for crossing the Channel, so it is little wonder that between 1940 and 1944 German batteries at Sangatte fired over two thousand shells at the town, punching great holes along the seafront. Mercifully, the white stucco curves of **Waterloo Crescent** survived (Colour Plate 96); their three ranges were built by the architect Philip Hardwick in 1834-8 to face the harbour with balconies running along the first floor and pilastered bows marking the ends of each block, but the continuation of the scheme inland is now a fragment. Further inland are several streets of later terraces, plainer as befits their more modest situation. The nineteenth century **Mill House** in Lower Road, Crabble, has its original tarred paper roof, an unusual survival.

EASTCHURCH (6½ miles NNW of Faversham): set on the clay slopes of northern Sheppey are the remains of the island's one important house, **Shurland**. Perhaps it was built by Sir Thomas Cheyney, cousin of Anne Boleyn, Lord Warden of the Cinque Ports and Henry VIII's Treasurer, to be ready for a royal visit in 1532, with brick ranges set round a courtyard, and a stone plinth on the surviving main front only. Its centrepiece is the gatehouse, with octagonal turrets prominently quoined in contrasting stone, but not otherwise projecting from the rest of the front, which has diapered brickwork; an off-centre archway leads into the courtyard, but all here is ruined except for the paired windows along the ground floor of the north range. For all its evident grandeur, the house is a mystery, despite features which can be associated stylistically with Knole at Sevenoaks, and Herstmonceux Castle in East Sussex.

EAST FARLEIGH (2 miles SW of Maidstone): a small village with scattered farms on the chartland south of the Medway. **Gallants Manor** comprises a three-part hall-house, now clad in stone except for the tile-hung end of the upper storey, and, beyond the service end, a practically detached wing, its framing still visible in the upper storey, which might have been a large kitchen.

EASTLING (4 miles SW of Faversham): a downland parish mostly built along a single street. To the south-west, **Tong House** is a Wealden hall, with a four-centred arch over the entrance and framing with widely curving down-braces, which form semi-ellipses in the jettied ends. The aisled hall of

Eastling Manor was rebuilt in 1616 as a large lobby-entry house, with close-studding but no jetties. Only the windows on the half-hipped end walls project as oriels, leaving the front unusually flat and only relieved by a projecting two-storeyed porch. Otherwise the severity of the decoration is moderated by central arched lights forming Ipswich windows in both storeys and the dormered garret at the front.

EAST MALLING (3½ miles WNW of Maidstone): a village built along a high street and a few side streets on the wooded lower slopes of the chartland, with yet more building at Larkfield along the London-Maidstone road, extending by speculative housing as far as the works at New Hythe on the west bank of the Medway. The principal house is **Bradbourne**, built around an older core with the finest quality brickwork in 1712-15 for Sir Francis Twisden with a U-plan, one of the wings being the main showpiece: it is in nine bays, three by three, with pairs of tall pilasters and a central pediment; tall sashes mark the ground floor, lower ones the second, and the entrance has a fluted Corinthian doorcase with French doors and an ornate radiating fanlight with a bracketed hood over it and a cambered head to the window above (Colour Plate 44). Here and even more in the ends of the wings facing the garden, bright red bricks accentuate the detailing; there are sunken panels above and below the windows in the ends and in the parapet, and a blind central bay beneath the chimney-stacks. In the centre of the village, a Wealden faces the brick **Court Lodge** across Church Walk. In Mill Street is another framed house, with a jetty and built in two sections. **Paris House**, The Rocks, has a regular brick front, described as new in 1714, oddly squeezed between two huge projecting chimney-stacks built of ragstone and rising up as though to support the corners of an overhanging hipped roof. **Clare House** is a picturesque villa completed outside the village in 1792 for John Larking, a wealthy timber merchant and owner of a paper mill: designed by Michael Searles with white stucco walls and low-pitched overhanging slate roofs, its cruciform plan comprises a circular staircase hall rising up to a glazed dome, with a circular library, an oval drawing-room, an octagonal dining-room and a rectangular domestic wing radiating from it; the library opens on to a semicircular arcade supported by widely spaced Roman Doric columns, and this carries a balcony for the ladies' boudoir above, since about 1840 shaded by a canopy with a fretted architrave and a copper tent roof (Bonwit 1987, 29-32). At Larkfield, the former Tudor Hall Cottages or **High Hall House** (now The Wealden Restaurant) is a prominent early Wealden with a pointed arch over the entrance and cusped tracery in a blocked chamber window (Figures 13 and 30c); similar arched doorways inside lead from the hall into the chamber and into a pair of service rooms and a passage leading to a lost external kitchen (Figure 22d). At Well Street, several framed houses include **The Barracks**, a hall-house, which appears to have been extended at both ends, notably to the north with a large cross-wing, jettied and gabled at the front, with cusped barge-boards, and to the south to provide an attached kitchen (Colour Plate 29).

East Malling. Clare House.

Clare House, East Malling. Elevation and sketch plan by Michael Searles. (After drawing in the RIBA Drawings Collection reproduced in Bonwit 1987.)

EAST PECKHAM (4½ miles ENE of Tonbridge): a large parish, with its church high up on the wooded chartland, but its centre and most of its scattered farms now below it in the vale among orchards on the north-west side of the Medway. A short way below the church are a Wealden hall and **Royden Hall**, a large brick house of 1535, improved by the antiquary Sir Roger Twysden and his son Sir William in the later seventeenth century, and heavily remodelled in 1875, leaving only the southern gabled end in anything like its original state. At **Hale Street** there is another Wealden, an early one, with a great pointed arch to its entrance. A further hall-house at **Peckham Bush** has an end jetty and a close-studded rear wing. Both **Kent House Farm** and **Bourne Place**, Barnes Street, have substantial chimney-stacks on their end walls and comparatively thin studding with no visible jetties, the one with a brick ground storey, the other with stone and a gabled wing; both appear to belong to the sixteenth century, but Bourne Place contains the remains of a fourteenth-century aisled hall. Opposite Bourne Place is another handsome house, tile-hung, and again with a wing under a half-hipped roof.

EASTRY (4½ miles WNW of Deal): a village built along the former Roman road between Dover and Minster, with numerous isolated settlements on the low chalkland overlooking the coastal flats. **Fairfield** (Colour Plate 56), formerly Christ Church Priory's secondary manor house, has an aisled hall of the usual two bays, extended by services and a chamber in further bays at each end; these are jettied at the front at the level of the top of the aisle wall, and rise into large hipped dormer roofs which embrace the ends of the main roof and reach the level of its ridge. Close studding and a four-centred arch over the entrance suggest that the end bays were built in the later fifteenth century; were the hall of the same date, it would be a remarkably old fashioned use of aisled framing (*see* Hogbrook, Alkham). Outside the village, **Heronden** and **Felderland Farm** are two-storeyed brick houses, the one of 1766 symmetrically fronted with a central entrance and five windows in the upper storey, the other similar but with six windows and a slightly off-centre entrance.

EAST SUTTON (5½ miles SW of Maidstone): a wooded parish with no discernible centre and numerous isolated farms running across the chartland ridge, down the scarp and into the Wealden vale. The rambling red-brick **East Sutton Park**, which Sir Edward Filmer purchased in 1610, is now a prison. He turned his attention to this house apparently after starting **Charlton Court**, which he already owned. Work here stopped in 1612, the date on a gable, leaving it as a two-storeyed block, perhaps as the south range of a projected square house, with waved rather than fully curved shaped gables at each end and, in a simpler form, over the projecting canted bays and triangular central bay of the front. The mullioned and transomed windows have heavily moulded surrounds joined by similarly moulded string-courses and eaves (Plate 5). The oldest of the numerous farmhouses in the parish is probably **Walnut Tree**, which was built of timber felled between 1393 and 1426 and is quasi-aisled with an arch-braced truss spanning the hall. The unusually ornate **Noah's Ark,** a hall-house built in the far south of the parish with timber felled between 1446 and 1481, has a jetty at the chamber end, where there appears to have been a privy jettied out from the upper storey (Plate 55). Most of the other framed farmhouses are Wealdens except for the latest ones. **Blue House**, Chartway Street, was built of timber felled between 1463 and 1493 and employs Kentish framing. **Parsonage Farm** has its timbers, felled between 1426 and 1461, plastered over and tile-hung at the sides; **Little Hearnden** is close-studded; **Barling Farm**, which has an unusually short chamber end, is also close-studded; **Street Farm**, Chartway Street, has coved eaves above the hall as well as the remains of close-studding where it has not been rebuilt in brick; **Divers Farm** has been entirely rebuilt in brick or hung with tiles; the close-studded **Luckhurst**, built of timber felled between 1484 and 1518, has an inserted canted bay at the high end of the hall, but lacks its intended chamber end and, considering the overall hipped roof, may never have had one (Howard *et al.* 1988, 1989 and 1990); it was modernised with a lobby-entry plan. Among the later framed houses, **Brissenden House** has end gables, a projecting bay for the hall window, close-studding yet again, but no jetties; the less austere **Moatenden** has a projecting close-studded central block with an oriel supported by a cove, and the usual clerestories beneath a jettied gable.

EASTWELL (2¾ miles N of Ashford): a deserted village, rare in Kent, with its few surviving houses around the wooded downland of Eastwell Park. Close to the ruins of the church and overlooking a reservoir, the former manor house, **Lake House** (Plate 47 and Figure 40), comprises the remains of an upper hall, built of flint late in the thirteenth century (*see* Old Rectory, Ickham), with stone traceried windows, now blocked, beneath a large hipped roof; all this has been patched and buttressed in brick with several nineteenth-century arched brick windows (Parkin 1968).

EDENBRIDGE (8¾ miles W of Tonbridge): a very long street village, now really a town, in the extreme west of the county, with a mill at the crossing of the River Eden, and several outlying settlements in the broad vale between the Weald and the scarp of the chartland. Near the bridge, the street widens into a triangle, and here the best framed houses are concentrated. **Tanyard House** and its neighbour both have the form of a hall and gabled cross-wing; beyond The Crown Inn, **Church House** has the same form but is encased in chequered brown and blue brick with two storeys of wide windows edged in red brick and with cambered heads, and the gable is hung with diamond-shaped tiles. On the other side of the triangle, a heavily disguised Wealden is now an inn, and down the lane leading to the church there is a 'two-thirds' Wealden. A doorway of **Taylor House** carries the arms of Sir William Taylour, Lord Mayor of London in 1469, but nothing else visibly of that date. In **Lingfield Road** are, first, a terrace of lightly framed houses with brick infilling and unpainted weatherboarding above, probably of the late eighteenth or early nineteenth century, and, a short way on, a terrace of two-up two-down artisans' houses with two sets of triple entrances, the central entrances providing access via passages through the terrace to the rear where earth closets were

Edenbridge. The Row, Main Street.

placed. **The Row** is a similar terrace in Main Street, far to the north (Plate 96). On the north-west fringe are the terraces of weather-boarded or tile-hung cottages of the London County Council's **Stangrove Park Estate**, built in 1959-61 along short streets leading to an open green, a good match for the town's traditional houses in concept, but lacking vitality in their isolation (Plate 22). A short way to the south of the centre, **2 and 4 Hever Road** have unusually sinuous down-braces. This way leads to **Delaware**, a symmetrical house of brick and tile-hanging, with a shell hood on richly carved brackets over the central entrance, end jetties, and four prominent gabled wings projecting from the rear. To the south in Mill Hill, the symmetrical front of **Eden House** is attractively finished with grooved weatherboarding in the form of rusticated masonry. Far beyond the village in this direction is the timber-framed **Gabriels Manor**, which has three prominent gables with highly decorated barge-boards rising to pendants beneath the ridges, all restored after a fire in the 1930s. Further on still, **Stanford's End** is marked by a pretty group of barns and oast-houses, with two hall-houses behind them, one with jetties at both ends and a projecting bay window in place of the former hall window, which rises into a small dormer, the other with a tile-hung upper storey; opposite, **Brookside** (formerly New Farm) is new by comparison, a lobby-entry house with recently exposed framing instead of its former tile-hanging, and an overall hipped roof covered in thatch, and a new thatched porch. Even further on, **Brook Street Farm** is a lovely brick and tile-hung house with half-hipped roofs over its wings, built beside ponds, perhaps from the profits of the Wealden iron industry.

EGERTON (6¾ miles WNW of Ashford): a chartland parish with a village street and many scattered farms. Among these are several hall-houses: **Groome Farm**, Newland Green, has an end jetty; **The Bedewell**, Lark Hill, has jetties at both ends; close by, a Wealden with a large hall window is all but hidden by ivy; **Island Farm** is another Wealden; and so is **Link Farm**, this time with jetties at both ends as well as the front, and a two-centred arch over the entrance, an early feature, but also close-studding, a late one. **Week Farm**, Bedlam Lane, is another Wealden, with Kentish framing in the upper storey, but underbuilt in brick and with two prominent dormers inserted above the hall. **Old Harrow Farm** (Colour Plate 74) is an ornate lobby-entry house of about 1600, close-studded and jettied, with bracketed oriel windows continued sideways by clerestories (*see* Yew Trees, Wye). A house at **The Forstal** is built in rat-trap bond.

ELHAM (6 miles NNW of Folkestone): a solidly built-up village overlooking the Nail Bourne, with several farms in the surrounding wooded downland. In the village, pretty tile-hung and brick houses front **The Square** by the church. Up in the High Street, **Abbot's Fireside** of 1614 has a long, close-studded front with a jettied upper storey and over-hanging eaves supported by grotesque brackets of a type found in Canterbury and Wye; the projecting bay windows of the ground storey may originally have been in the form of bracketed oriels, but the upper windows are flush with the blocked clere-stories which once ran from end to end. Up Cullings Hill, the **Manor House** is also close-studded and jettied, and has an oriel breaking the eaves as a dormer. To the south

Elham. Boyke Manor, Ottynge, showing the jettied post supporting the centre of the overhang.

at Ottinge, **Boyke Manor** is a Wealden, with original hollow-moulded mullions to its hall window, and, down a lane to its east, another Wealden, hidden behind a cladding of brick and tile-hanging, has an inserted chimney-stack with four circular shafts set on a square base and decorated by spiralling brickwork (Figure 26h).

ELMSTEAD (6½ miles ENE of Ashford): a heavily wooded downland parish of scattered farms. **Spong Farm** (Plate 73) was built with timber felled about 1520 as a three-part hall-house with a jetty along the entire front, extending as a gallery across the open hall to link the storeyed ends (Howard *et al.* 1991).

EYNSFORD (8½ miles SW of Gravesend): a village which grew where the Castle guarded a crossing over the River Darent. In the twelfth century, an upper hall was built within its walls (Figure 37). Among the village's pretty weatherboarded houses there is a Wealden and, facing the river, a house with a continuous jetty. In the surrounding downland, **Lower Austin Lodge** has the appearance of a medieval house which has grown through the addition of a parallel rear range and refronting in brick.

FARNINGHAM (7½ miles SW of Gravesend): a village built where the London-Maidstone road crosses the River Darent.

Just outside the centre in Sparepenny Lane, two neighbouring houses make a pretty contrast in Georgian taste: **Mount Pleasant**, which is of red brick and has an entrance with a bracketed hood symmetrically placed between the sash windows in the early eighteenth-century way; and **The Mount**, built about 1820 in yellow brick, with a prominent Roman Doric porch above a high basement and emphatic round-headed windows on the main and upper floors and also for a single dormer in the roof.

FAVERSHAM. Favourably sited at the head of a creek flowing into the Swale, Faversham was described as a royal town in a charter of 811. It achieved greater prominence in 1147 when King Stephen founded an abbey here which he intended to serve as a royal mausoleum, and this caused the town to extend along the bank of the creek down Court Street and Abbey Street. The harbour was the town's main commercial asset; Faversham became a Limb of Dover in 1229, and a charter of 1252 confirmed its already ancient privileges. Later specialities were its oyster fisheries, and also the manufacture of gunpowder. After the Dissolution many Flemish and Huguenot refugees settled here.

At the centre is the Market Place, lined with jettied and gabled houses, their frames mostly hidden and some comprising once open halls with crown-post roofs (Colour Plate 9). **Nos. 5 and 6** have a medieval stone arched doorway with an entry between a row of shops built over an undercroft with jettied chambers above them (Plate 66 and Figure 65); this leads to an open hall, possibly rebuilt in the fourteenth century but incorporating a thirteenth-century frame, unusually joined with iron nails, not wooden pegs, and further chambers and a large kitchen flank a courtyard at the rear (Faulkner 1969). **No. 10** carries the date 1570 in modern numbers, but has entirely appropriate grotesquely carved brackets to support oriels with not quite continuous clerestories beneath its jetties. Three main streets lead out from here. East Street leads to **Cooksditch**, fronted before 1790 by Stephen Gillow in white brick with a stone porch supported by Ionic columns, and continued by his widow in the 1790s with single-storeyed pavilions using the same Ionic Order for aedicules to embrace tripartite windows set beneath shallow relieving arches and pediments. Off East Street, Preston Street runs uphill, eventually to reach a group of Georgian houses, divided by the railway. West Street has several jettied houses and at **No. 121** plaster scrolls and swags with the date 1697 (*see* 78 Bank Street, Maidstone). Finally Court Street, with more close-studded and jettied houses, including **No. 25** (Plate 91 and Figure 87), probably built soon after 1608 for the shipmaster John Trowtes, with a shop, entrance and parlour across the front, and a kitchen and buttery running down the right-hand side (Laithwaite 1968). Court Street then leads directly into Abbey Street, where close-studding and jettying

Faversham. Abbey Street.

continue, often under a skin of brick and tile, and oriels sometimes extend downwards to become full canted bays. Occasionally there are gables, more often Georgian parapets and doorcases to complete a fashionable dress. **No. 80** formed part of the abbey gatehouse of about 1300, and was rebuilt about 1538-40. Richard Arden, mayor in 1547, bought the house in 1544-5 and was murdered here in 1559 by his wife and her lover; with its long windows, jetties, and exposed close-studding, it demonstrates the early appearance of the street. A large upper chamber with a crown-post roof flanks a chapel.

FAWKHAM (5½ miles SSW of Gravesend): a built-up downland parish. The medieval **Court Lodge** contains an early crown-post roof. Dean Bottom is a wonderfully concealed enclave, with a small weatherboarded cottage and **The Old Farmhouse**, a small Wealden which has lost its service end; it was modernised by partially flooring over the hall to form a small smoke bay with a gallery beside it leading from the upper storey at the

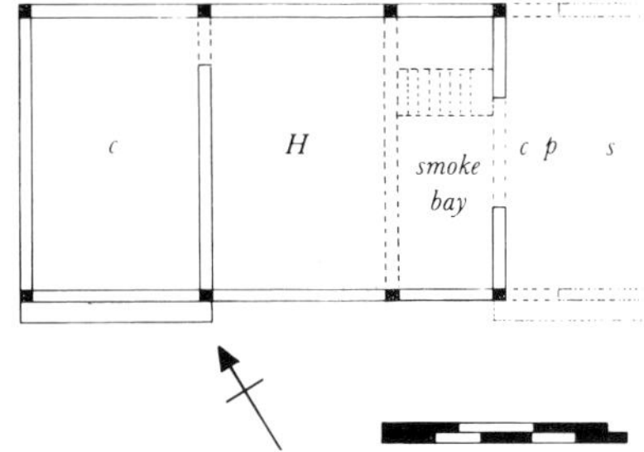

The Old Farmhouse, Dean Bottom, Fawkham. Plan of Wealden hall-house, showing position of inserted staircase running beside smoke bay, and position of removed service end. (After Swain 1968.)

chamber end to the lost services end, before a chimney-stack was eventually inserted into the bay (Swain 1968).

FOLKESTONE. The town had a chequered career in the Middle Ages, but became a Limb of Dover and gained a charter as a Cinque Port in 1313. Its importance lay in its fishing fleets, which specialised in catching mackerel for the London market. The arrival of the railway in 1843 and development by Lord Radnor at last brought prosperity; as the main embarkation point for soldiers going to the Great War, it was fully established as a ferry port second only to Dover. A few houses facing the churchyard, notably a fine red-brick early Georgian one, show the oldest face of the town; the best of the nineteenth century faces the sea. On the heights of the Leas, the stucco of **Albion Villas**, Tudor, Italianate and late Regency, came in 1843-4 with the railway. Below the cliff slope, the Italianate detailing and curving balconies of **Marine Parade** arrived five years later in 1848 (Plate 10), while its continuation in the taller and coarser **Marine Crescent** is as late as 1870. The westward continuation of **The Leas** on the cliff top brought long terraces facing the sea and short ones running inland in the 1850s, since the 1970s interspersed with lines of flats, built in concrete and staggered back, storey by storey. Down by the harbour, the old fishing village along **The Stade** was swept away between the world wars and replaced in 1935 by rows of gabled, brick, boarded and tile-hung cottages, a pretty but sober version of the Well Hall Estate, Eltham (London, Greenwich) of 1915. **The Durlocks**, a short way inland, was built at the instigation of Sir Philip Sassoon of Port Lympne, and more imaginatively laid out in 1919 by the architects Culpin and Bowers as a tiny garden suburb of weatherboarded cottages approached through a cement-faced arch with a shaped gable reminiscent of Sassoon's own house (Plate 107).

FORDCOMBE (3¾ miles WNW of Tunbridge Wells): a small parish above a crossing of the upper reaches of the Medway. The tile-hung **Fordcombe Manor** is notable for its cross-wing, which has a jettied upper storey and gable with bracketed oriels under each, dated 1622. Up the hill, the Viscounts Hardinge built a number of estate cottages,

Fordcombe. Fordcombe Place.

notably **Fordcombe Place**, a terrace of eight cottages built in 1831 of Wealden sandstone with projecting porches supported by brackets, and some pretty individual houses of brick and stone, one dated 1843, others with applied framing and tile-hanging. A small house with Kentish framing is said to be of 1511.

FORDWICH (2¼ miles NE of Canterbury): a small village on the south bank of the Great Stour, once belonging to St Augustine's, Canterbury, and serving as the city's port. It was an ancient burgh, later incorporated by Henry II, and a Limb of Sandwich, complete with mayor and Town Hall. **Watergate House** has a brick gable fronting the street with stucco quoins; opposite are the jetties of the **Manor House**, and, to the south, weatherboarding hides **The Maltings**, a Wealden, and brick hides a jettied house with a framed and jettied gable end. In **King Street**, three cottages dated 1736 have their brickwork still laid in old-fashioned English bond.

FRINSTED (4 miles S of Sittingbourne): a small downland parish with a few houses by the church, one of the mid-nineteenth century, stuccoed with low-pitched overhanging slate roofs and twin gables. Among the scattered farms is **Yoke's Court**, which has a single long brick range with mullioned and transomed windows beneath a hipped roof, suggesting a three-part services, hall and chamber arrangement, but on a large scale and fully storeyed from end to end.

Frinsted. Yoke's Court.

FRITTENDEN (9½ miles SSE of Maidstone): a small parish in the Wealden vale south of the River Beult, with a village street and numerous scattered farms, including the close-studded and jettied **Pond's Farm**, which has a lobby-entry plan.

GODMERSHAM (5½ miles NE of Ashford): a short village street with **Godmersham Park** on the flanks of the downs above the valley of the Great Stour. This was built for Thomas Brodnax, whose double inheritance and change of name to Knight brought the money to pay for it. The result is a handsome Palladian mansion with a slightly inset centre, pedimented doorcase and *oeuil-de-boeuf* windows for a mezzanine, and wings with pedimented windows in the ground storey, all of 1732, and low pavilions added at each end nearly fifty years later. On the main road to Ashford, **Bilting Grange** has the form of a symmetrical lobby-entry house, now underbuilt in brick and tile-hung above, but with rooms front and back on each side, making it a small double pile served by an immense central chimney-stack (Figure 26d) with a cluster of seven diagonally set shafts rising from the base (*see* Marle Place, Brenchley, of 1619).

GOODNESTONE (6½ miles WNW of Deal): a parish on open downland with an estate village built along a short street at its centre. The estate of **Goodnestone Park** was bought in 1700 by Brook Bridges, and he started a new house in 1704; this had two storeys and nine bays, the centre five projecting slightly beneath a wide pediment. Before 1790, a third storey was added and the pediment rebuilt. By 1838, a pedimented Greek Doric porch was added in stone, apparently by the architects Thomas Rickman and R. C. Hussey. A number of cottages with round-headed windows were built in the village street, elsewhere in the parish, and also in neighbouring Chillenden; one is dated 1706 (*see* the much later estate cottages on the Dering estate at Pluckley). The **Old Post Office** is an early hall-house with a jetty at the chamber end. Several houses have shaped gables, notably one in the village street, which has a pilastered gable end with a pediment perched at the apex (Figure 27s), and **Crixhall Farm**, where the curves are drawn out, the upper ones being ogee; here there are more round-headed windows typical of the estate. A curious double house at **Bonnington** comprises a close-studded range, with a three-part plan, jettied front and back and ending in an added brick shaped gable with double curves beneath a crowning semicircle (Figure 27f), and a second, detached range, originally a close-studded Wealden but now irregular in plan and mostly clad in brick. **The Dower House** is another extended Wealden.

Goodnestone (near Deal). Goodnestone Park.

GOODNESTONE (2¼ miles ENE of Faversham): a small parish on the banks of Faversham Creek with a street of scattered houses and, near the church, **Goodnestone Court**, a framed house plastered over, with an underbuilt jetty, notable for a small upper-storey cross-wing jettied out even further and with its close-studding and down-braces exposed; in its gable a three-light window with Perpendicular tracery in its arched head suggests that it might have been a private chapel (Figure 30d).

GOUDHURST (8¼ miles ESE of Tunbridge Wells): a Wealden parish, its centre spread around a hilltop church: 'this Goodhurst I went to' wrote Celia Fiennes in 1697, 'stands on a great hill and is seen severall miles...; its a pretty large place, old timber houses, but the extent of the parish is neare ten mile' (Morris 1984, 128). Much of the timber is now hidden. Dramatically placed at the top of the main street, the long jetty of **Church House**, weatherboarded below, tile-hung above, suggests a sixteenth-century framed house with a long history of change; it is completed by a block cornice and a large hipped roof which turns the corner by the church and merges with the hipped roofs of rear extensions to produce an irregular double pile. North of the church is a very long row of jettied cottages, brick below and tile-hung above; down the hill in the opposite direction, the same materials interspersed with weatherboarding disguise several framed houses, including a Wealden, in a number of styles. Just beyond the centre, **Pattenden** is an imposing close-studded Wealden with end jetties and obscured jetties at the rear as well (Plate 57 and Figure 51); it had belonged to the Pattenden family since the thirteenth century, and they may have built it in the later fifteenth century; but it passed to Sir Maurice Berkeley, standard-bearer to Henry VIII, Edward VI and Elizabeth I, and he must have inserted into the hall the four quarries of stained glass depicting a monkey drinking, a pomegranate crowned, and two roses crowned, which date from the period of Henry VIII's marriage to Catherine of Aragon (1509 to about 1533, *see* Cobb's Hall, Aldington), and this suggests when a floor was inserted into the hall (Cowper 1911).

Goudhurst, Twyssenden. The rear wing with its grandly designed stone entrance; the front range on the right-hand side has the form of a Wealden hall-house.

Further away, **Twyssenden** is another close-studded Wealden, modernised with large windows extending into clerestories, and with a bizarre rear wing, ambitiously built of Wealden sandstone and decorated with four giant Corinthian pilasters, too large for the space, and far too grand, not just for the doorway and elongated niches which they frame, but also for their inconsequential position. **Finchcocks** is both grand and consequential, built for Edward Bathurst after he inherited the estate in 1718 and finished about 1725; a four-square central block with a pedimented centre rising into an attic is completed with plain pilasters carrying stone triglyphs which stand out from the red brick façade, and framed by lower pavilions with their own order of pilasters — the baroque style of Vanbrugh, that is, without the fire of genius (Plate 87). The Culpepers built **Bedgebury Park** in a classical style some time beforehand from the profits of the Wealden iron industry; in 1836

Goudhurst, Bedgebury Park. The steeple to the right was added to the stable court in the middle of the 19th century.

Viscount Beresford, who had made his name in the Napoleonic Wars, eventually commanding the Portuguese army, retired here; at his death in 1854 the estate passed to his heir Alexander Beresford Hope who had also inherited a banking fortune. He devoted his time to sponsoring Gothic churches exemplifying the architectural ideals of the Ecclesiological Society *(see* Kilndown Parsonage). About 1854-5 he cased the house in Wealden sandstone, added a storey and projecting wings, and finished them all with double-pitched mansard roofs; these dour French classical lines are remarkable for coming from the hand of the architect Richard Cromwell Carpenter, a master of English Gothic.

GREAT CHART (2½ miles SW of Ashford): a chartland parish of outlying farms and a village built along a street with nineteenth-century shaped gables showing where the Tokes of Godinton improved their estate. **Court Lodge** is a large hall-house, built of stone in 1313, with a typical steeply pitched hipped roof carried by the earliest crown-posts to be dated (Plate 52). On the east side are two large windows; on the west the original tracery has been obscured or replaced by casements, but an arched porch indicates the early date of this remarkable house. **Godinton** lies in the centre of an extensive park; here, a framed house with a fourteenth-century open hall built around a small courtyard was modernised about 1628 for Captain Nicholas Toke with new brick elevations, enlivened with stone string-courses and window surrounds, and, notably, the shaped gables with quadrants linked by steps which were introduced to Kent at Knole in 1605. The close-studded **Singleton Manor** has projecting gabled wings and a two-storeyed porch. **Little Singleton Farm**, now clad with bands of rounded and straight tiles, looks like a modernised Wealden, and **Yardhurst** (Figures 12, 30e and 58) at Daniel's Water is a demonstrably grand Wealden, with jetties at each end as well as at the front (Figure 50), a close-studded front and a fine two-centred arched doorway; the interior (Figure 60) is complete with a fine panelled wall at the high end of the hall with a projecting spere before the chamber doorway (Rigold 1969g). **Handcock's Farm** is another Wealden, but with extensively weatherboarded Kentish framing.

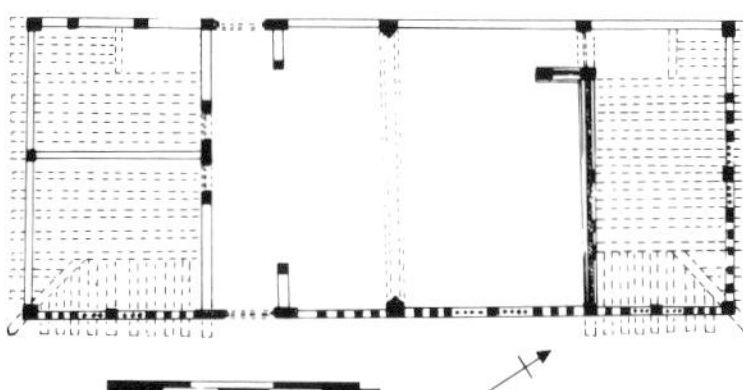

Yardhurst, Great Chart. Plan, showing the storeyed ends with jetties across front and both ends, thus requiring dragon beams to carry the internal ends of the joists round the corners; and also the screens shielding the hall from the front, back and chamber doors. (After Rigold 1969g.)

GREAT MONGEHAM (1 mile WSW of Deal): a small village on low chalkland dipping towards the coast. **Manor Farmhouse** of 1707 is a double pile, formally arranged with five windows and a central entrance set within a pilastered doorcase carrying a block cornice and pediment reflecting the block cornice beneath the eaves of the hipped roof. Opposite, the smaller **Brewery Farm** of 1735 has a doorcase with an open pediment carried on Roman Doric columns. Two cottages in the village have shaped gables.

GROOMBRIDGE (3½ miles WSW of Tunbridge Wells): a Wealden parish on the East Sussex county boundary with a pretty green sloping down to a stream. Philip Packer, whose father had bought the estate, rebuilt its most important house, **Groombridge Place**, at some time between 1652 and 1671 within a moated site. He used the cross-winged H-plan (Figure 75) popularised by Gervase Markham in *The English Husbandman* (1613, revised and enlarged 1635). The house is built in mellow red brick, laid in up-to-date Flemish bond with quoining to emphasise the wings and there is a hipped roof; across the front is a loggia with Wealden sandstone Ionic columns, symmetrically projecting in the centre to form a pedimented porch. This cleverly hides the entrance into the central hall, which is off-set to the right (Plate 75). This by now rather old-fashioned medieval arrangement was undoubtedly convenient, a point which Markham had emphasised. The great hall is entered through a small vestibule; to its right is the service wing with a kitchen, scullery, pantry and stairs for family and servants set behind the master's parlour, which occupies the front of the wing so that he could oversee the household affairs. The left-hand wing, beyond the high end of the hall, contains a withdrawing room and a closet or family parlour, these two rooms doubling as a suite of state rooms when guests were entertained, and also there are the principal stairs for formal occasions. The first floor contains a great chamber over the hall, a withdrawing room and parlour in the left-hand wing, and bedroom apartments in the right-hand wing. The top storey has a further great room in the centre, possibly used as a gallery, and more apartments in the wings. This double arrangement with twin staircases gave the family, servants and guests full privacy, and the central hall and great chambers had the advantage of light on both sides. The rear elevation still has the original wooden-framed mullioned and transomed windows (the front was given sashes later), and a huge stack, flanked by windows, rises up the centre to heat the hall and upper chambers (Maguire 1989). Outbuildings rise straight out of the moat, just as the previous house had done.

Opposite the entrance to Groombridge Place is the **Dower House**, much smaller, but also of brick with hipped roofs, and with two large wings with a central entrance squeezed between them. The chequered brickwork of **The Walks** provides a wonderful foil at the head of the green, and framed and weatherboarded houses run down each side. Up the hill, towards Tunbridge Wells, is the emphatically irregular Old English style of Norman Shaw's **Hillside** (Colour Plate 103), built in 1870-74 for David Livingstone's colleague, the African explorer and elephant hunter William Cotton Oswell, as a retirement home. It has Shaw's characteristic soaring brick chimney-stacks, applied black and white close-studding, and multicoloured, multi-shaped tile-hanging, a lesser version of what he had just completed at Glen Andred on the Sussex side of the border (Saint 1976, 31).

HADLOW (3½ miles NE of Tonbridge): a parish of orchards with a curving main street of pretty houses in the vale on the north side of the Medway. These rather pale beside **Hadlow Castle**, which Walter Barton May built in the 1820s for himself to his own design with J. Dugdale's assistance in the playful Gothick of the time, and in about 1838-40 turned into a landmark with the addition of a soaring tower, 170 ft. (52m) high, built by George Ledwell Taylor (Plate 100); this far more convincing Gothic was inspired by James Wyatt's Fonthill in Wiltshire, which had been jerry-built for William Beckford some forty years beforehand, and already had collapsed.

HAM (3¼ miles WNW of Deal): a parish of scattered settlements on low chalkland overlooking the east coast. **Finglesham** comprises a red brick rear pile with a three-tiered shaped gable, and a front pile built at least a century later in yellow brick with a shallow pediment embracing the whole plain façade; **Finglebury Farm** has a similar front, but with more assurance in its late Georgian detailing; and **Hilltop** has splendid shaped gables similar to Rushbourne Manor's at Hoath, although it is only a two-roomed cottage with garrets (Figure 27k). At **Marley**, the remnants of a handsome early seventeenth-century red brick house with plastered string-courses faces the remains of a large framed cottage, again single-storeyed with garrets, under a thatched roof.

HARBLEDOWN (1¼ miles W of Canterbury): a wooded parish outside Canterbury built up along the London road with a terrace of houses, notable for its cast-iron verandas. At the far end, the red brick **Hopebourne** faces down the street, its ivy-clad red bricks stopping at a wooden cornice and small, central pediment beneath an overall hipped roof. On the downs outside the village, **Havisham House** (formerly Michaels) was built in 1911-12 to M. H. Baillie Scott's designs with flint and red brick gabled blocks, lightly shaped over the porch, on the entrance front, with some waney framing in the upper storey, a variety of materials suggesting a house that grew over the years, and a symmetrical garden front marked on the ground floor by a pair of canted bays with flint and stone chequered parapets set between the arches of a veranda.

HARRIETSHAM (7 miles ESE of Maidstone): a parish between the scarp of the North Downs and the chartland with a main street cruelly divided by the Ashford road. Down the eastern stretch is the eye-catching

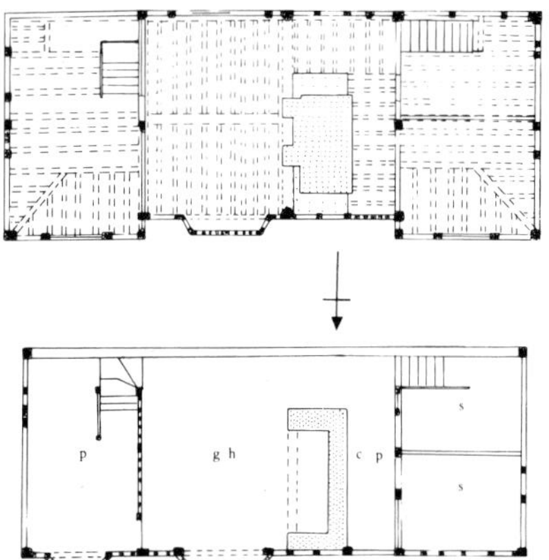

Old Bell Farm, Harrietsham. Plans of ground and upper floors, after conversion of medieval open hall by the insertion of a floor and a chimney-stack backing the cross-passage. (After Mercer 1975 [212].)

Old Bell Farm (Plate 62), a magnificently ornate Wealden, replete with close-studding, a canted bay rising into coved eaves for the recessed hall, moulded bressummers above the jetties, and a four-centred entrance arch with decorated spandrels and a moulded and embattled hood (Figure 22f), complete with an original nailed front door with alternating plain and moulded battens; inside, the triple doors in the screens passage remain together with a staircase made of solid timber blocks. Further down the street, warm red brick fronts mark a corner in the road, beyond which another Wealden hides beneath a modern skin. On the scarp of the North Downs, **Stede Hill** has a framed wing and a refaced late eighteenth-century front with a pedimented centre and pedimented Roman Doric porch. Beyond the scarp, **Harrietsham Manor** is the suburban view of what a traditional brick and half-timbered house should look like, and indeed buried in it are the remains of yet another Wealden.

HARTLEY (5¼ miles SSW of Gravesend): a built-up parish on wooded downland. The close-studded **Red Cow** (formerly Middleton) Farm has a restored full-height hall window, an entrance with a two-centred arch, and a cross-wing at the service end with Kentish framing.

HAWKHURST (8½ miles SSW of Tenterden): a Wealden parish with two centres, a small one around the church and The Moor, and Highgate to the north built around crossroads on the Cranbrook road, as well as numerous scattered settlements. By the church, **Church Court**, formerly The Workhouse, comprises a hall-house with Kentish framing underbuilt in brick, and a long wing added at one end. Facing The Moor, the mid-eighteenth-century **Wetheringhope** has a broad front with a curiously pinched pedimented Venetian window over its Doric porch, and, on the other side, the rather later, dour **Collingwood House**. The centre of Highgate is all red brick and weatherboarding. **Oakfield's** crisp early nineteenth-century detailing and large porch with coupled Ionic columns contrast with the red brick and pediments of **Marlborough House's** front of 1723; its rear wing was added in 1879-80 by George Devey for the MP Edward Hardcastle, a Yorkshire banker. Devey also extended **Chittenden** and **Chittenden Lodge**, opposite, for Hardcastle's unmarried daughters, by converting a hall-house with an end jetty into a more ambitious house in the Old English style, but left its original crown-post roof (Allibone 1991, 174-5). **Hawkhurst Place** also looks Victorian, but its close-studding, end-to-end jetty and triple gables belong to the sixteenth century. Further in this direction, **The Old Forge** of 1874 shows how well the Old English style which Devey did so much to introduce was taken up by Norman Shaw for what actually was, originally, a forge cottage, with a simple combination of jetty, weatherboarding, long sloping roof and tall stack (Saint 1976, 412). Nevertheless, this is clearly a contrivance, particularly when set against the artless unrestored close-studding, jettying, tile-hanging and traditional hipped roof of **Four Wents Cottage** or the long rose-red front of **Attwaters**.

HEADCORN (8¼ miles SSE of Maidstone): a township in the Wealden vale close to the River Beult, with a long main street full of framed houses, many hiding behind weatherboarding or tile-hanging, more facing the churchyard, and even more still among the many scattered farms in the rest of the parish. **Headcorn Manor** was built facing the churchyard, apparently after 1516, as the parsonage house. It is one of the grandest of Wealdens, close-studded with jetties to the ends and one side of the back (the other side may be older and has Kentish framing and no jetty), causing the hall to be recessed on both sides (Colour Plates 60 and 61). The windows have traceried cusped heads, and take the form of oriels in the upper storeys at each end of the front and full-height bays on both sides of the hall (Figures 30g and h). In the High Street, **Chequers** is another Wealden, with a jettied floor inserted across the hall, and a chamber at the service end under a slightly projecting roof. Next door, **Shakespeare House** may well have been a cloth hall; it has a prominent gabled wing facing the street, with two storeys of restored transomed four-light windows extended by clerestories of paired, arched lights; the upper storey was open to the roof, which, unusually, is trussed with arch-braced collars (Figure 17) rather than the usual crown-post or queen-struts and purlins, possibly to leave it free of framing timbers so that bulky goods such as bales of wool could be stored, but it is so ornately framed that it may well have had a formal use as well. **Nos. 1-4 North Street** also have an open upper storey and may have been built as a cloth hall about 1500. **Hawkenbury**, one of many medieval houses in the surrounding countryside, is an early Wealden with Kentish framing and a two-centred entrance arch, and another Wealden at **Hearsden Green** has an extended chamber end. The close-studded **Wick Farm** is a late Wealden which has lost its chamber end; again close-studded, **Tilden** has a jetty extending right across its front and along one end, and the remains of a framed and plastered firehood.

HERNE BAY (6½ miles NNE of Canterbury): a seaside resort on the north coast, laid out by Samuel Hacker in 1830-31 with a promenade and a parallel road inland. This never achieved great success, and the original aspirations for the resort can only be seen in two attractive groups of houses with bow windows facing the sea, individual houses at **27-35 Central Parade** (Plate 11) and, further west, a terrace at **101-109 Central Parade**.

HERNHILL (4½ miles E of Faversham): a small wooded downland parish with a centre built round a green. Among several attractive houses here is the **Manor House**, prettily sited beside the church with a framed cross-wing jettied at the front and side balancing an embattled square brick tower with a low central range with pointed windows; these and more Gothick detailing on the south side appear to hide a genuine medieval core.

HERSDEN (4½ miles ENE of Canterbury): a mining village beside the Canterbury-Minster road serving Chislet Colliery. It was laid out in a formal way by G. J. Skipper in the 1920s and built up with attractively detailed semi-detached brick cottages with canted bays in the Kent manner (Plate 16).

HEVER (7 miles WSW of Tonbridge): a Wealden parish of scattered farms with **Hever Castle** at its centre (Colour Plate 23). This is a toy, now even more toylike, a fortified manor house of Wealden sandstone set within a narrow moat, with a tiny 'village' clustering in its shadow. Sir John de Cobham, who was granted a licence to crenellate in 1384, gave the house its turreted exterior

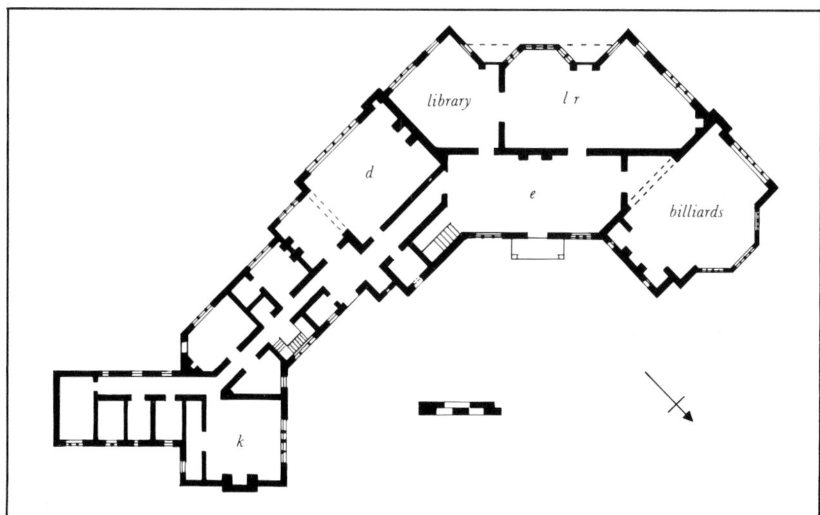

How Green House, Hever. Plan.

HORSMONDEN (7½ miles E of Tunbridge Wells): a Wealden parish with many scattered farms set among orchards and a large centre built around a green. **Wealden Cottage** at The Corner is just that, an early Wealden with a two-centred entrance arch, but curious for an unjettied service end, apparently an addition, which leaves the front recessed beneath deep eaves right to this end. **Westernhanger** is two-thirds of a Wealden, its hall floored over and jettied out even further than the jetty of the service end, which has been extended rearwards with a further jetty, and **Pullens Farm** comprises another two-thirds of a Wealden with a weatherboarded rear range built against it. There is a framed hall-house at **Smallbridge**, and **Spelmonden** is another with a sandstone ground floor, tile-hung above. **Grovehurst** also was built with an open hall but has been altered to take the form of a lobby-entry house with a cross-wing to the right. The front has a jetty with a moulded fascia, partly obscured by additions, and what originally was a central two-storeyed porch with a pendant at the apex of its gable; this is reflected by gables to the main front each side, one dated 1641 and both now tile-hung, the one on the right with the remains of oriel windows. The cross-wing is also jettied at the front, and close-studded, but ends in a hipped roof. Of the later houses, **Hale Farm** has a continuous jetty along the front and down one end, and the lovely **Broad Ford** is also jettied and gabled, the right-hand gable of the three projecting slightly and visibly independent structurally, even though the framing is entirely hidden under yellow painted rendering; in the centre a porch with an ogee doorway sets the tone for Gothick windows each side and elsewhere. The outer gabled bays have full-height canted bay windows with naïve arches bridging their leaded lights. The Capel Manor of 1859-62 has largely gone, but here the architects Michael Manser Associates built **Capel Manor House** about 1970 in the form of a single-storeyed glass pavilion framed with steel beneath a projecting reinforced concrete roof — a triumphant assertion of ideology over tradition.

Horsmonden. Wealden Cottage, The Corner.

with an entrance front, complete with drawbridge and embattled gateway. These and its later ownership by the Bullens, particularly as the birthplace of Anne Boleyn, so impressed the American diplomat William Waldorf (later Viscount) Astor, who had settled in England in 1890, that he purchased it in 1903 and employed the architect Frank Loughborough Pearson to convert the interior to suit his romantic ambitions. The framed courtyard was restored between then and 1907 and new interiors were fitted out in a swaggeringly Edwardian Elizabethan style. Astor was a great entertainer, but valued his privacy, so Pearson built the mock half-timbered village just outside the castle walls as lodgings (Plate 106), so that Astor could see his guests safely out of his house and into their rooms, before winding up the drawbridge and retiring for the night. Pearson also laid out the terraced gardens as a showplace for Astor's collection of antique monuments. Contemporary with Astor's grand works is **How Green House** (Colour Plate 104), which the architect Robert Weir Schultz built in 1904-5 for the coal merchant Mowbray V. Charrington in an Old English style, with a central hall flanked by canted, gabled wings forming a butterfly pattern and suggesting a bent Wealden, backing a drawing-room and library (Ottewill 1979; *see* The Dunes, Sandwich Bay). Away to the north-west is **Brocas Manor**, whose late open hall, built with timber felled between 1524 and 1557, was added to an earlier range (Howard *et al.* 1990).

HIGHAM (2¼ miles WNW of Rochester): a densely built-up village on the lower slopes of the North Downs. Dickens lived at **Gadshill**, a rather dour house of 1779, symmetrically designed with canted bays each side of a skimpy porch and a depressed Venetian window above.

HOATH (5 miles NE of Canterbury): a parish of scattered farms with a short curving village street on the chalkland between the north coast and the Great Stour. The red brick **Rushbourne Manor** is dated 1659 and still has a three-part arrangement of rooms with a parlour, hall, cross-passage and services, but the gables are shaped — convex, a step, concave, then a semicircle — and the porch reproduces these upper stages as well as having pilasters flanking the arched entrance.

HOLLINGBOURNE (5¼ miles E of Maidstone): a parish extending along a street up the scarp of the North Downs from the River Len. Among its many framed houses, **The Malthouse** was built in two sections at slightly different levels, with a continuous jetty and close-studding. Just below it, **Hollingbourne Manor** is a heavily detailed, red brick house of the late sixteenth century, the projecting three-storeyed porch squeezed between similarly detailed bays which rise above the two main storeys into large gabled dormers with squared-off heads; this range was to have been symmetrically flanked by similar projecting wings with massive chimney-breasts on their end walls, but apparently the northern one was hardly started, leaving the southern one forming an L-plan and facing a raised garden (Plate 74). Further down, **Godfrey House** is a conspicuously grand lobby-entry house, with an inscription over the entrance recording its construction in 1587 and restoration in 1859. It has a close-studded ground floor set on a stone plinth, and large panels above with slightly ogee down-braces. The entrance is in a two-storeyed porch which rises into a third storey with dragon-posts and jetties all round, and a further jetty beneath the gable; similarly jettied and gabled dormers rise above the large oriel windows in the single bay to the left of the porch and the two bays to the right. The tall chimney-stack has four octagonal shafts rising into a cluster of stars.

HORTON KIRBY (6½ miles SW of Gravesend): a downland parish with its centre beside the River Darent. The early brick house **Franks** was built by a London alderman Lancelot Bathurst and dated 1591, with gabled ranges set around a small courtyard (Colour Plate 67), and a fine classical arched entrance embellished with Tuscan columns, a triglyph frieze and segmental pediment.

HUNTON (4¼ miles SSW of Maidstone): a parish of orchards extending between the River Beult and the chartland scarp. The eighteenth-century **Hunton Court** is plain and built of rough-faced ragstone, with a pedimented centrepiece containing an elaborate doorcase with an open curved pediment over it on the main front, and asymmetrically arranged polygonal ends. **Stonewall Farm** is an unusually lavish framed house, with two projecting wings, one gabled at each end and dated 1634, with the usual close-studding, jettying and oriel windows extended by clerestories still current at this date; less usual is the studding of the gables, angled each side of the garret windows to be parallel with the rafters. Close by, a number of framed houses include a handsome close-studded Wealden with a roof gabled rather than hipped at each end.

HYTHE (4½ miles WSW of Folkestone): as its name suggests, Hythe was a port, originating when the Roman *Portus Lemanis* silted up; it was a possession of Christ Church but confirmed by charter as a Cinque Port in 1155. The noble parish church and a few houses beside it on the steeply rising hillside show this prosperity, but the sea has receded, and the shore is now marked by hotels, small houses and bungalows and Martello Towers, one of them converted to domestic use, its thick round brick walls drastically pierced by ungainly flat picture windows (Plate 14).

ICKHAM (4½ miles E of Canterbury): a small parish in the valley of the Little Stour with a short village street. **Old Rectory** has a front range of flint and chalk, with trefoiled windows, evidence of an upper hall or chamber block of about 1300 (*see* Luddesdown Court) which was built as Christ Church Priory's manor house; this was rebuilt by Prior Chillenden about 1400, and, in the eighteenth century, extended in brick at the rear with a pair of crow-stepped gables. A short way down the street are the shaped gables of **Treasury Farm House**, which rise with convex then concave quadrants, stepped between, and finish with a semicircle; set against the south-eastern one is a bold chimney-breast dated 1663. Further down the street, framed houses include **New Place**, a Wealden hall.

IGHTHAM (4½ miles ENE of Sevenoaks): a wooded chartland parish with large numbers of scattered houses, many of them modern, and a village centre with a tiny triangular green in a tight valley. Here, the highly restored **Town House** comprises a fifteenth-century hall and cross-wing, with a larger and later close-studded cross-wing at the chamber end. Opposite, the jettied range of a house constricting the highway brought a fine on its builder Thomas Skynner in 1555. A house just to the south was built in the unusual rat-trap bond. A short way to the north, **Ightham Court** has a symmetrical, three-storeyed façade with a full-height projecting centrepiece dated 1575; widely spaced, spindly orders of attached columns on tall plinths rise into a low fourth storey with columns lacking plinths and then a timid pediment, all detailed in plastered brickwork, and more notable for its early date than an understanding of classicism (Plate 41).

In the far south of the parish, **Ightham Mote** is that rare thing in Kent, a manor house with real gentry status (Colour Plate 4 and Figure 45). Its knightly owners are known from the middle of the fourteenth century, but the origins of the house are older than that, and its building history is both long and complicated. So it came to mix building materials — Greensand, timber and brick — in happy confusion, giving it a picturesque outline perfectly in keeping with its moated site tucked into a fold of the chartland. The earlier parts may be the work of Sir Thomas Cawne. They comprise an arched entrance of about 1340 in the west front which opens into a courtyard; the contemporary hall range lies opposite with an arched entrance and a five-light cusped window inserted about 1480. The entrance leads directly inside with no screens passage. Here, a great stone arch supports the centre of the roof whose timbers were felled between 1327 and 1361 (Figure 16). The solar has tie-beams in both directions carrying a crown-post at the intersection, and the timber for these was felled between 1321 and 1356, which must mean at the same time as the timbers of the hall roof. The timber of the old chapel roof was felled between 1333 and 1367, again within the same time span (Howard *et al.* 1988). The larger chapel, which fills the first floor of the north range, is the work of the minor courtier Sir Richard Clement, who, having purchased the estate, modernised the house in 1521-9. He rebuilt and refronted the private apartments beyond the high end of the hall with close-studding, large mullioned and transomed windows and lavishly carved bargeboards set beneath the two new gables of the solar and the chapel gallery. He fitted out his new chapel with modest furniture and a wagon roof, magnificently painted with royal arms and badges, including the Tudor rose and Aragonese pomegranate. These badges indeed mark most of his work, including the bargeboards, which also bear the fleur-de-lis of France, then still claimed by the English Crown. He reglazed the hall windows with glass which was painted with yet more badges demonstrating loyalty to his royal master (Starkey 1982).

KEMSING (3¼ miles NE of Sevenoaks): a long village strung out beneath the scarp of the North Downs. **St Clere**, the principal mansion, was built by the Parliamentarian Sir John Sedley about 1633 as a double pile, perhaps with Chevening Park in mind, but owes much of its present appearance to alterations late in the eighteenth century. At the hamlet of Heaverham, two thirds of a Wealden hall stand prettily beside the twin roundels of an oast-house; **Ivy Cottage** was built of local Greensand in 1759.

KEMSLEY (1¾ miles N of Sittingbourne): a model village serving Bowater's paper mill on the marshy banks of The Swale. It was built by the architects Adams, Thompson and Fry in 1925-6, with short terraces of plain, attractively detailed neo-Georgian cottages, spaciously laid out in formal rows with greens and crescents (Figure 95), and a social centre, but all rather too far apart to be cohesive (Plate 15).

KENARDINGTON (5½ miles ESE of Tenterden): a small parish on the clay ridge overlooking Romney Marsh. **Manor Farm** is a large, close-studded house with many diagonally barred mullioned windows, apparently built in the early sixteenth century with an L-plan, jettied along both outer sides; the northern range has a cross-passage with four-centred doorways dividing a hall and chamber from the services which extend into the western range. Maybe it is synonymous with **Place Farm**, which was built of timber felled in 1512/13 (Howard *et al.* 1989).

Kennington. Bybrook.

KENNINGTON (1¾ miles NNE of Ashford): a built-up village between the Great Stour and the North Downs. **Bybrook** is a fragment of a large brick house; what remains is the hall range, entered through a two-storeyed porch dated 1577 over the four-centred entrance and with a four-light transomed window in the upper storey, and this is balanced by a similar square bay which lights the high end of the hall, both of them projecting under hipped roofs. **Barton House** is a small early hall-house with an end jetty (*see* Old Kent Cottage, Newington).

KILNDOWN (7½ miles ESE of Tunbridge Wells): a Wealden parish with a small village centre and numerous scattered settlements among which **Riseden** has several framed houses. The **Parsonage** belongs to the True Gothic works inaugurated by Alexander Beresford Hope, founder member of the Cambridge Camden Society *(see* Bedgebury Park, Goudhurst); it was built in 1849-55 by the architect Richard Cromwell Carpenter, a devoted follower of Pugin *(see* St Augustine's, Ramsgate), with numerous trefoiled windows beneath hoodmoulds and a feeling for masonry, carried out in fine Wealden sandstone, which Pugin himself would have envied.

Kilndown. The Parsonage.

KINGSGATE (1¾ miles ESE of Margate): a small village high on North Foreland with a modern estate of seaside houses. **Sea Breezes** really is a breath of fresh air among the traditional gables and tile-hanging of Fitzroy Avenue; it was completed about 1939 to Brian O'Rourke's International Modern design with emphatically square lines, regularly spaced windows and a flat roof, but faced not in the hard, fragile cement of the era, but weatherboarding over a white-painted brick base, a happy compromise; at the front a matching timber porte-cochère on plain round piers, at the rear a veranda above a long band of Modernist windows.

Lamberhurst. Scotney Castle; the garden front of Salvin's house.

LAMBERHURST (6 miles ESE of Tunbridge Wells): a Wealden parish of framed and Wealden sandstone houses, which grew rich through iron, with a pretty village street crossing the River Teise. **Crown Cottage** is a small Wealden, and **Coggers Hall** a long close-studded house of about 1600 with a full-length jetty and evidence for large windows in the upper storey extended by clerestories. Away from the village, **Furnace Farm** conceals the remains of a Wealden hall behind brick and tile-hanging. **Scotney Castle**, a fragment of a moated castle with a picturesque tower, is evidence of Roger Ashburnham's fortifications late in the fourteenth century; the adjoining seventeenth-century house is itself a fragment of what was intended (Colour Plate 12). The later castle (Plate 105 and Figure 92) was built on the hill above by the architect Anthony Salvin for Edward Hussey in 1837-44, not as one of his sublime castles on the lines of Alnwick or Peckforton, but as a Tudor mansion, designed as an irregular double-pile with gables and mullioned windows and only a few turrets and embattled parapets scattered about (Allibone 1987).

LANGLEY (3¾ miles SE of Maidstone): a wooded chartland parish of scattered farms. **Corner Farm** is a fine, late Wealden, close-studded, with a restored hall window comprising two tiers of paired, four-light arched openings (Figure 30i), and an entrance at the service end with a four-centred head and moulded spandrels, and a plank door (Colour Plate 63 and Figure 22e). **Rumwood Court** is another late hall-house, much extended.

LEAVELAND (4½ miles S of Faversham): a wooded downland parish. **Leaveland Court** is jettied, with cross-wings, one gabled, one hipped, and a gabled two-storeyed porch.

LEEDS (4¼ miles ESE of Maidstone): a chartland village, famous for its picturesque castle, with an attractive winding village street climbing the sandstone hills, and many scattered farms. The lower half of the village starts with **Battel Hall**, an important early fourteenth-century stone house with a central hall and screens passage (Figure 44); beside the entrance is a laver with an ornate ogee arch, and the hall had a central transverse arch supporting its roof *(see* Ightham Mote); at the high end is a defensible great chamber built over a once vaulted undercroft with a projecting garderobe *(see* Old Soar, Plaxtol); the service rooms at the low end of the hall have been rebuilt (Rigold 1969d). Opposite are the five jettied gables of **Battel Hall Cottages**, not close-studded in the usual way, but with small panels filled with brick-nogging (Colour Plate 93). Beyond the church in Lower Street is **Manor House**, misnamed since Leeds Castle was the manor house, and in fact the gatehouse to the vanished Leeds Priory. The stone section to the right comprises a chamber lit by a pair of trefoiled lights with a straight hoodmould over them built on an undercroft, perhaps in the fourteenth century, to which a close-studded hall and jettied upper chamber were added, probably in the middle of the fifteenth century by Prior John Surrenden, to form two thirds of a Wealden hall; another foiled opening, framed in timber, gives access to the space over the screens passage (Parkin 1963). In Upper Street, **Vineys** is a full Wealden, again close-studded, and extended round the corner with a continuation of its jettied service end, and curious for the corbelled brick chimney-breast built under the eaves of the former open hall to back the cross-passage. **Lydian Farm**, opposite, has a symmetrical front and a tall seventeenth-century brick chimney-stack (Figure 26j).

LEIGH (2½ miles W of Tonbridge): an estate village on low sandy chartland north of the Medway, mainly built up by two landlords, Thomas Farmer Bailey and his successor Samuel Morley. Between them, they gave the village its rows of stone and brick or half-timbered and tile-hung cottages, grouped artfully together in little clumps and around tight squares. These exemplify the Old English style of the mid and later nineteenth century. Leigh lay within the large manor of Penshurst, but part of the village and the grounds of **Hall Place**, which lie immediately to the north of the High Street, were separated from it and by the later eighteenth century had passed to Robert Burges.

His widow sold this estate to the Baileys (or Bailys). They probably built **Park View Cottages** in High Street, with their pretty Tudor Gothic windows, in the 1820s. Thomas Farmer Bailey began the first major improvements to the village after he came of age in 1845. His architects were his cousin Charles Bailey and George Devey, architect to the Penshurst estate. It is hard to differentiate both their work and the work of local builders following their traditions. Bailey added two grand gateways to Hall Place in a Tudor Gothic style, and **West Lodge**, which is dated 1863 and bears the initials TFB together with the date in vitrified brickwork. Bailey probably also designed **Laundry Cottage** of 1855, and **Church Hill House**, which is dated 1856 both by a datestone and, once again, by vitrified headers which extend into the diaper-work of its attractive Tudor detailing. Maybe he also designed what were originally the four **Fleur-de-Lis Cottages** of 1855, now partly adapted as a public house. The **Stone House**, which was built as three cottages on the other side of the High Street in 1865 and carries the initials of Thomas Bailey's wife Gertrude, could also be his. Devey's work begins with his recasing of the sixteenth-century **Home Farm** in 1855, and **Home Farm Cottage** is again his. **Park House** was built to his design for the land agent to the estate in 1864, and there are further works within the grounds of Hall Place.

In 1870 Thomas Bailey sold the estate to Samuel Morley. He was the most substantial hosier in the country, and also a member of the temperance movement, the principal proprietor of the *Daily News* and, from 1868, Liberal MP for Bristol. His three-fold occupations, mercantile, political and philanthropic, were in the best tradition of nineteenth-century public life. After a false start when he employed Devey to patch up **Hall Place**, Devey produced a seriously intense yet gawky Elizabethan design in 1871 for a total rebuilding; completed in 1874, it was his most expensive work. The new house alone cost over £54,000, and the final total of all the works within its grounds came to over £70,000. Only part escaped demolition in the 1970s. Devey may also have designed **Institute Cottage**; its playful Tudor style gains from the irregular pieces of ragstone, said to be taken from the former Hall Place, laid in crazy patterns and punctuated by the occasional piece of dark ironstone. When Morley decided to build a convalescent home at Leigh for his hosiery workers in 1886, he turned to Ernest George. This is a finely detailed, half-timbered house in the Jacobean style, now forming one of the three sides of

Leigh. Forge Square: the range on the left is split into normal cottages, but the range on the right comprises four flats.

Forge Square, which is completed by an L-shaped range of seven cottages of George's design, with four of them built as flats. The framing both here and in the second group which George designed, **Leigh Square**, just a short way along the High Street, has far more of the decoratively panelled framing typical of the West Midlands than is normally seen in Kent (Colour Plate 106). Significantly, some of the ranges are shingled, perhaps because George was taking his inspiration from American 'stick' style houses, then being illustrated in England for the first time. George apparently went on to design **Oak Cottages** at the other end of the village, and the pair confusingly named **Oak Cottage** and **The Firs**. These repeat the crisply detailed timbering with prominent chimney-stacks which set the character of his first work here. Maybe he designed other groups of houses such as **The Bungalows**, and **Porcupine House**, built beside East Lodge (Allibone 1991, 163).

Leigh has a few older houses. **Old Chimneys**, overlooking the green, is a close-studded lobby-entry house of about 1600; **Great Barnetts** in Powder Mill Lane is of much the same date, but its framing is hidden by brick and tile-hanging; and **Paul's Farm** in Ensfield Road is a bit earlier, and has a full-length jetty broken by a two-storeyed porch, its framing also hidden, here by weatherboarding. The hamlet of Charcott is notable for **Margavan Cottage**, a Wealden, mostly tile-hung, and **Old Forge**, another tile-hung hall-house.

LENHAM (9 miles NW of Ashford): an attractive village in the vale below the scarp of the North Downs, full of good things built around The Square. In one corner, **Lenham Greengrocers**, a large Wealden whose service end extends far round the corner with a deep jetty, is reflected by another Wealden where the houses converge towards the east, this one close-studded with a projecting wing at the chamber end, and yet another Wealden is now brick-clad. In High Street is **Honywood House**, formerly High House, named after its builder Anthony Honywood, one of a well-established family known here and at Charing; it carries his initials and the date 1621. It has a lobby-entry plan, ornately treated with a symmetrical front emphasised by two canted bays rising from brick plinths each side of the entrance up to a jetty, to be continued as bracketed oriels in the upper storey which then rise into prominently jettied gables reflecting the larger jettied gables at each end of the house. The close-studding, the carving of the principal mullions of the windows and the moulding of the rest, and the continuation of the windows into clerestories give the house a lavish appearance (already established by Valence House, Sutton Valence, of 1598), which continues with the moulded base of the chimney-stack supporting four truncated octagonal shafts (Colour Plate 73).

LEYBOURNE (4¾ miles WNW of Maidstone): a small parish in the Medway valley, now heavily built up with housing to serve local industry, particularly paper-making. **Little Lunsford Farm** is a heavily restored hall-house with Kentish framing.

LINTON (3¼ miles S of Maidstone): a village of scattered farms among orchards, and a group of houses strung along the road descending the chartland scarp towards Staplehurst. To one side, overlooking the Weald, is the long expanse of **Linton Park**, begun in the 1730s and extended upwards and lengthwise, stuccoed and painted gleaming

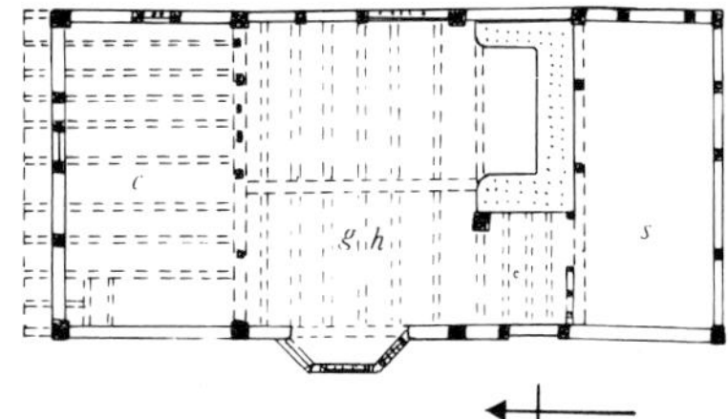

Old Vicarage, Linton. Plan, showing central open hall, with inserted chimney-stack blocking former cross-passage, inserted floor and added bay window, originally open service room, to the south, and added, storeyed chamber bay to the north with end jetty. (After Mercer 1975 [218].)

white. On the road itself, **The Old Vicarage** is a small hall-house with Kentish framing, jettied at its service end and extended at the chamber end. By the church and in a group down the hill are several estate cottages, mostly semi-detached pairs, built of white brick in the middle of the nineteenth century in a Tudor style and accented by vertiginously

Linton. Estate cottages.

tall chimney-stacks. On the chartland ridge to the west, **Westerhill Farm** is a Wealden well hidden by chequered brickwork in red and blue, and an upper storey with grooved, white-painted plaster looking like masonry; the eaves over the hall have been broken to let a tall gable rise against the roof. To its south, **Court Lodge**, which was built of timber felled between 1496 and 1531, has a continuous jetty (Howard *et al.* 1990).

LITTLEBOURNE (3½ miles E of Canterbury): a village with an attractive green lying on the west bank of the Little Stour, with a few farms among woods and orchards. Several houses in the village have shaped gables, particularly a row of single-storeyed cottages with double pediments, and so does **Higham Farm**. In a fold of the Downs to the north, just before the valley of the Great Stour, are **Elbridge House**, a double pile built about 1800 of buff brick with a wooden Tuscan porch in the centre and semicircular single-storey bays on the sides, and **Elbridge Farm**, a close-studded Wealden, lying opposite among the clustered roundels of an oast-house.

LOOSE (2 miles S of Maidstone): a tight cluster of houses on the steep slopes of the Loose Valley, where a stream cuts through the chartland and once turned numbers of watermills. **Church House**, a fifteenth-century close-studded hall-house with restored windows with plain diagonally set mullions, has an end jetty at the chamber end and a service block, which continues as a rear wing. **Rook House**, possibly also a hall-house, has a jettied wing, and the remains of windows extended by clerestories. **Wool House** comprises a fifteenth-century, close-studded range of two storeys, with long bands of windows in the upper storey, reputedly used for washing wool, and an adjacent cottage with the remains of coloured pargeting on its projecting wing (Plate 35). **The Old Vicarage** is a much altered but typical early seventeenth-century, timber-framed, lobby-entry house, similar to the Chequers Inn, with jettied upper storey and twin jettied gables above that. **Florence Cottage** is an attractively weather-boarded house, probably late medieval or of the sixteenth century. **Vale House**, a small eighteenth-century double pile, is the one notable brick house, sited just to the west of Thomas Telford's bridge of 1829, which dramatically spans the valley.

LUDDESDOWN (5 miles WSW of Rochester): a downland village with a few scattered farms. **Luddesdown Court** has the form of an upper hall, built soon after 1200 of flint with Caen stone quoins and window openings, with a perpendicular solar wing completing an L-plan (Figure 39); inside is an early fourteenth-century chimney-piece, an uncommon survival, with chamfered imposts rising into corbels which support the lintel, which is made from individual stones joggled together in the typical manner of the time.

LULLINGSTONE (6½ miles N of Sevenoaks): a small parish overlooking the River Darent, best known for its Roman villa (Figure 2). Shortly to the south is **Lullingstone Castle**, with a fine gatehouse (Colour Plate 36), built in diapered brick as early as 1497, and finished with embattled parapets and octagonal turrets (T. P. Smith 1990); the medieval and Tudor house lies concealed behind a symmetrical eighteenth-century refronting with three-storeyed wings and a recessed two-storeyed centre.

LYDD (10½ miles SE of Tenterden): an ancient town which received a charter from Edward I, but became isolated in the wastes of Dungeness after the great storm of 1287 shifted the mouth of the River Rother. A long high street, the churchyard and a vast empty green, The Ripe, are lined by attractive framed, weatherboarded, brick and rubble houses, with one or two grand ones, such as **Tourney Hall**, and **Skinner House** (formerly The Rectory) of 1695. Beyond, a great shingle bank juts out into the English Channel, marked by a series of lighthouses, the base of the earliest, designed by Samuel Wyatt in 1792, now a house, and also by a nuclear power station. This was a place for fishermen's huts, but following the First World War squatters took advantage of

Lydd. Houses made from disused railway coaches on Denge Beach; in the background is Dungeness nuclear power station, the base of Samuel Wyatt's lighthouse of 1792, also converted to a house, and the second lighthouse of 1904.

disused railway carriages which could be brought here on the now closed line from Appledore, and converted these into houses. Other, more amenable houses followed, all bungalows, mostly weatherboarded and of the simplest kind, giving a short stretch of Denge Beach the appearance of an American shanty town (Colour Plate 107).

LYDDEN (4¼ miles NW of Dover): a small village where the Roman road crosses a fold of the North Downs. On the hill a pair of single-storeyed flint cottages with a heavy thatched roof is typical of many which labourers built in great numbers in poorer counties than Kent during the eighteenth and nineteenth centuries on waste land immediately beside the road (Plate 13).

LYMINGE (5¼ miles NW of Folkestone): a plain downland village with one framed house, the close-studded and jettied **Old Robus**, and a few outlying settlements. **Sibton Park** has a plain early nineteenth-century front of white brick.

Lympne. Lympne Castle, view over the roofs towards Lorimer's new courtyard.

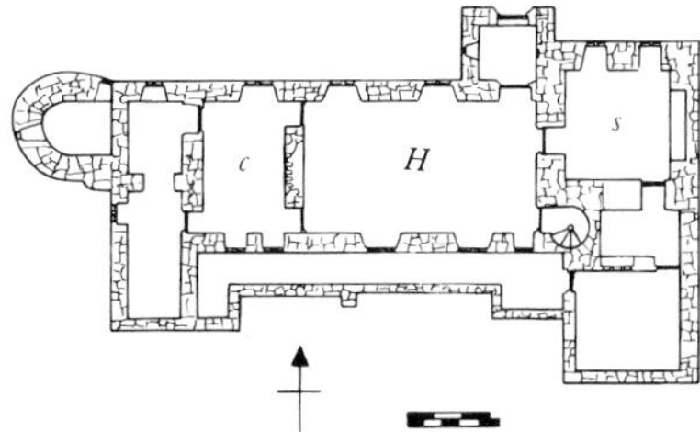

Lympne Castle. Plan. (After Rigold 1969e.)

LYMPNE (6¾ miles W of Folkestone): a village perched on the clay ridge overlooking Romney Marsh and the site of the Roman *Portus Lemanis*. **Lympne Castle** dominates the ridge; it was customarily granted to the Archdeacons of Canterbury, and started, probably in the thirteenth century, with a stone tower; a hall and chamber block were added to these to form a fortified manor in the third quarter of the fourteenth century; possibly Archdeacon Chichele (brother of the Archbishop) added the D-shaped tower to the chamber block. All of this fell into decay and became no more than a farmhouse after the Reformation, but was sold, eventually to become a modern home with Sir Robert Lorimer's restoration and extension for F. J. Tennant (the son of Sir Charles Tennant, a chemical manufacturer, and brother of H. J. Tennant; *see* Great Maythem, Rolvenden) in 1906-12 (Rigold 1969e). At the centre, a hall entered through a two-storeyed porch is marked by a pair of traceried two-light windows; the high end leads into chambers, a solar with a crown-post roof and tower rooms; to the north are Lorimer's extensions, a courtyard of cottages (Figure 4). More credible as a modern home is **Port Lympne**, built about 1912 for Sir Philip Sassoon to the west on an equally imposing site overlooking the marsh (Plates 17 and 104). He was MP for Hythe, Lord Haig's secretary, a protagonist of the Royal Air Force, connoisseur and socialite. These pursuits needed an imposing house, and the architect Sir Herbert Baker did not let him down. Chips Channon called it 'a triumph of beautiful bad taste and Babylonian luxury'. The house has an H-plan with shaped gables to the wings, front and back, in Baker's best Cape Dutch style, but one still appropriate to Kent. The house nestles into the steep hillside and extends down the slope with terraces embraced by colonnaded quadrants added in the 1920s by Philip Tilden (who later rebuilt Chartwell for Churchill, a frequent visitor to Port Lympne), and Tilden also added the Moorish patio on the uphill side of the house — 'the epitome of all things conducive to luxurious relaxation after the strenuousness of war', he said. Sassoon entertained the statesmen involved with negotiating the Versailles Treaty here; later it became almost a second home for the RAF flyers based at Lympne aerodrome, and, after Sassoon's death in 1939, they occupied the house for the duration of the Second World War.

LYNSTED (3 miles ESE of Sittingbourne): a parish on the dip slope of the North Downs, full of orchards which evidently brought prosperity to numerous farms. Possibly no other parish in Kent has so many fine houses dating from before 1650, yet the important Lynsted Lodge, Christopher Roper's Elizabethan country seat, has largely disappeared, and the village centre is almost inconsiderable, with just a few framed and brick houses to set the tone for the rest. One of these, **Anchor House**, was bombed in the Second World War, but retains a large round-headed entrance and a close-studded cross-wing with clerestories beside the upper window. Another house, again close-studded, has a dragon-post with jetties across the front and side, and also a thatched roof.

Just beyond the village is **Lynsted Court**, a lavish close-studded hall-house, extended at each end by jettied cross-wings, with a jettied two-storeyed porch projecting even further than the service end wing, against which it abuts; this wing is notable for its double-curved down-braces and the separate roof over the oriel with an original cusped bargeboard which contrasts with the wavy bargeboard of the main gable above (Plate 32). Close to the old London-Dover road is **Claxfield Farm**, the one obvious Wealden hall, close-studded but with curved down-braces unusually visible on the outside. **Tudor Cottage** was built about 1515 with a floored hall and smoke bay and given a parlour a generation later (Howard *et al.* 1988, 1989). **Sunderland** belongs more firmly among the new generation of houses with floored-over halls, and is notable for close-studding, a full-length jetty turning round both ends, and a four-centred entrance leading to a cross-passage backed by a chimney-stack, all happily untouched by restoration (Plate 70). Restored, and later in date by virtue of its small-panelled framing, **Ludgate** has a symmetrical arrangement of rooms flanking a central chimney-stack, lit by deep, four-light windows almost linked across the entire front of the house by clerestories hard under the jetty; oddly the entrance is not into a central lobby, but at the right-hand end. The full lobby-entry plan appears in the otherwise similar **Cherry Gardens** and at **Millhouse**, which has a close-studded ground floor and small panels with ogee down-braces above, as well as a prominent jettied porch, projecting well forward, and a rear wing.

Lynsted. Bumpit; trompe-l'oeil *wall-painting in emulation of panelling.*

Significantly hiding behind a comparatively plain exterior is **Bumpit**, a possibly medieval house which Sir John Roper rebuilt in 1587. The Ropers were an old Kent family, staunchly Catholic in later years; nevertheless John Roper was knighted for services to Queen Elizabeth. He gave the house framed walls, modestly panelled rather than close-studded, but loyally carved the tie-beam below the southern gable with Tudor roses alternating with naïve triglyphs, and dated it on the head of one of the supporting posts; inside, however, the house is lavishly decorated with wall paintings (one dated 1605) depicting the Roper arms and religious symbols which suggest that the adherents of the old faith may have celebrated Mass here, but the royal crest over a fireplace again shows their loyalty to the Crown. By 1643, when William Hugesson (of Provender at Norton) rebuilt **Bogle**, loyalty to the Crown implied opposition to Parliament, and he was one of Kent's ineffectual supporters of Charles I. Brick was then becoming as cheap as timber-framing, and here the two materials are combined in a singularly attractive house with a long panelled and brick-nogged elevation terminating in plain gables, entirely of brick and carrying chimney-stacks; a narrow two-storeyed porch projects from the centre, with a third chimney-stack not quite aligned and serving the rooms on the right-hand side (Plate 79). What Kent could achieve in brick was shown within a century by the house opposite, a small, symmetrical double pile with panels of vitrified bricks framed in red.

MAIDSTONE. Although the county town, Maidstone is very much second to Canterbury, and throughout the Middle Ages was little more than several other small towns, Smarden, for instance, or Headcorn. Even so, the archbishops had a palace here at least from the fourteenth century, and Archbishop Courtenay established a well-endowed college of priests next door in 1395. Thanks to Maidstone's central position in Kent, lying beside the Medway in the long vale beneath the scarp of the North Downs, its market prospered, and the town was eventually incorporated in 1549, just as its ecclesiastical importance was failing. In 1697 Celia Fiennes found 'a very neate market town..., its buildings are mostly timber worke... [and the] very pretty houses about the town look like the habitations of rich men...' (Morris 1984, 124). Defoe noted that all of Kent's wealth passed through the market, much of it *en route* to London, in particular, red cattle, timber, corn, hops, apples and cherries, Wealden paving stone, and white sand for glass-making; in all, it was 'a very agreeable place to live in, and where a man of letters and of manners, will always find suitable society...' (Rogers 1971, 130-33). With the increase of hop-growing in the vale after the Middle Ages, Maidstone's manufacture of linen thread gave way to brewing, and, by the nineteenth century, this and its county status at last began to tell.

The best thing about the **Archbishop's Palace** is its site, overlooking a bend in the river (Colour Plate 2), and superior by far to other palace sites at Charing, Otford, Knole, and even Canterbury itself. The windows on this side all belong to a reconstruction of 1909, and the other side is evidently an Elizabethan reconstruction, a symmetrical façade with a centrepiece and three-storeyed gabled ends, added after the Astley family had taken over the palace following the Reformation. The earliest recognisable part of the interior, a solar chamber, has timbers felled about 1315-1344, but other medieval parts belong to the fifteenth century (Howard *et al.* 1989). Archbishop Courtenay's **College** is far more redolent of archiepiscopal splendour: the **Master's House**, the part of the college belonging to the first campaign of building in 1396-8, is fully two-storeyed with an upper hall, gabled at one end as now, but the only details belonging to this period are the cusped, slightly ogee windows on the ground storey and in the gable, leaving much of its original form unclear (Plate 48).

Medieval buildings are not particularly evident elsewhere in town, although a number of framed buildings, for instance at the corner of High Street and Gabriel's Hill, are built on stone undercrofts in the medieval way. In St Faith's Street, a Wealden hall survives at **Tudor Cottage**, with services and solar at one end, the hall at the other, and lacking a full chamber end as so often happens in towns. Other houses with exposed framing are later, notably the gabled pair in **King Street**, the long jettied range on the corner of **Lower Stone Street** and **Knightrider Street**, and, most importantly, **45 Earl Street** (Plate 82); this is a tall lobby-entry house, built on a high plinth of ragstone with shallow two-storeyed bays flanking the central entrance and rising up to a jetty which supports a blind garret beneath a pair of gables, all backed by a second range gabled at each end and forming a double pile; the small-panelled framing and queen-strut roof suggest that it must belong to the earlier seventeenth century.

Before the century was out it was common practice to hide timber frames beneath plaster, and brick was even better. This is evident in several jettied houses in **Gabriel's Hill** and **Week Street**, and, splendidly, at **78 Bank Street** (Colour Plates 8 and 33), where the jettied first storey is a *tour de force* of pargeting and fenestration: a large oriel window has Corinthian columns set into its corners and an arched light at its centre supported by carved terms to form a so-called Ipswich window (after the much later windows of Sparrow's House in that town); beneath the window is a pargeted frieze with foliage and Tudor roses, the date 1611 and the initials 'G I L'; flanking it, beneath an upper jetty, are two more pargeted panels, with the Prince of Wales' feathers on the left, the royal arms on the right, framed by two more columns, free-standing and Ionic this time, which carry the ends of the upper jetty. By the end of the century, restraint was the order of the day; even so, the pargeting of **55-57 Week Street**, which is dated 1680, is hardly discreet (Plate 37): here the two upper floors have a pair of large aligned sash windows with plastered panels between them; each panel is marked out with Ionic pilasters enriched with swags; from the pilasters in the wide central panels hang great swags with voussoirs of notional arches above them, and the lower panel also contains the initials 'S B' and the date; meanwhile the narrower outer panels bear urns with pairs of fleurs-de-lis below, and diamonds set within wreaths above. **Nos. 31 and 33 Earl Street** show the later modernising trend of a house built early in the seventeenth century, for Andrew Broughton, with projecting wings terminating in shallow, full-height canted bays of the Kent type; the house was divided in two and brought up to date a century or so later with a plaster skin, sash windows and a double porch with fanlights and a bracketed hood. Opposite, **38 Earl Street** shows how this might have been done from scratch using yellow brick enlivened with red, and a judicious use of keystones and a block cornice beneath a low-pitched hipped roof. **Grove House** at the top of Week Street, is a fine mid-eighteenth-century town house of three storeys, brown brick with red brick for the openings, and a nice contrast in windows, round-headed with white keystones for the first two floors, cambered for the attic; the slightly projecting centre has a gleaming Tuscan porch.

On the fringes of the town are two contrasting houses. To the north, **Old Farm House**, Chatham Road, is a late Wealden with visible down-braces and close-studding.

Mote Park, Maidstone. View from the south-east about 1911. (From a sale catalogue in Kent Archives Office, Maidstone.)

To the east, the 1st Earl of Romney's **Mote Park** stands in extensive parkland, its crisp walls of fine Portland ashlar a stranger to Kent as much as its pure lines. Built in 1793-1801 to the designs of Daniel Asher Alexander, architect of great warehouses for the London Dock Company, lighthouses for Trinity House, Dartmoor Prison and, shortly, Maidstone Gaol, it looks severe if not utilitarian. The garden front is furthest from his other works, with an Ionic colonnade set between two-storeyed segmental bows, above which are segmental relieving arches embracing the Diocletian windows at each end of the attic storey (Colour Plate 88 and Figure 84).

MARDEN (6¾ miles SSW of Maidstone): a parish of scattered settlements in the Wealden vale along the eastern arm of the River Teise. There is a heavily restored Wealden at **Chainhurst** and a later farmhouse beside a pond, jettied along its considerable length, close-studded in the upper storey, and symmetrical in all but the position of its chimney-stacks. In the attractively curving village street, there is another Wealden, its close-studded upper storey standing out among the weatherboarding.

MARGATE: the first Thanet village to become a sea-bathing resort, particularly by exploiting a local Quaker's invention of the bathing machine in 1753. Before then the town comprised a harbour, a point of embarkation for Holland, and a few streets

Margate. King Street.

running along a valley inland. Its flavour can still be tasted along **King Street**, where a pair of brick and flint houses of the early eighteenth century have shaped gable walls; they are joined by later houses towards the harbour, and in the other direction by a close-studded and jettied house, **The Museum** (Plate 69), of the early sixteenth century, with a three-part plan of services, hall and chamber, bracketed oriels below the jetty and slightly projecting windows above, though without the usual clerestories, and projecting eaves with brackets (*see* Sunderland, Lynsted). The early popularity of bathing gave Margate Hawley Street, Hawley Square and Cecil Square rather than a promenade. **The India House**, Hawley Street, was built in brown brick in 1767, apparently as a copy of a house in Calcutta, with the unusual arrangement enforced by the slope of the road of an entrance into the upper storey, which has two windows fringed in red brick flanking a slightly projecting centre containing an Ionic doorcase with an oval attic window beneath an embattled parapet. The terraces in Cecil Square are of red brick, in Hawley Square of yellow, with a castellated house on one corner.

MATFIELD (5¼ miles ENE of Tunbridge Wells): a Wealden parish with scattered farms and a small village with a pretty green. Here, an attractive group of tile-hung cottages face the village pond, and just beyond them comes the imposing baroque front of **Matfield House**, built in 1728 for Thomas Marchant; it has a sandstone basement and pinkish grey bricks above with dark red bricks to articulate the windows, band-course and parapet, the projecting centre and giant end pilasters which carry a section of white-painted entablature; the centre has round-headed windows and a doorcase with Tuscan pilasters echoing the main ones (Colour Plate 83); all in all the design is comparable to Finchcocks at Goudhurst, but its smaller size increases the tension between its parts necessary to the baroque style. Just round the corner is a long tile-hung house with a tall chimney-stack and Victorian two-storeyed porch, evidence of the conversion of a hall-house to a lobby-entry plan.

MEREWORTH (6½ miles WSW of Maidstone): a heavily wooded chartland parish with a pretty village street. **Mereworth Castle** stands for the place as the most famous surviving exemplar in England of Andrea Palladio's Villa Rotunda, adapted here by the architect Colen Campbell, and roofed in 1723, so becoming a powerful ideological salvo fired against the weakening forces of Hawksmoor's and Vanbrugh's 'licentious' baroque style, not to mention anything so English as the everyday houses of the locality. Campbell built it for John Fane, who fought with distinction under Marlborough, and much later became seventh Earl of Westmorland. The four elevations are similarly arranged with porticoes set before the central rotunda, which is slightly pointed and carries the flues from the fireplaces up to a central stack in the form of a lantern. Unlike Palladio's original, the plan is not identical in each quarter, but maintains an axiality only from front to back with an entrance vestibule leading to a salon under the rotunda and a gallery with a luxuriously plastered ceiling along the further side; to left and right are suites of rooms; modest newel staircases lead to four suites of bedrooms in the attic, and to service rooms in the basement, and servants' rooms in the mezzanine (Figure 83). A pair of flanking porticoed pavilions were added, perhaps to provide further accommodation when Fane received his peerage in 1736; one contains a grotesque room decorated with shells (Colour Plate 85).

At the western end of the parish, and built before the baroque style had taken root, **Yotes Court** demonstrates the early achievement of Renaissance classicism inaugurated by Inigo Jones; built for James Masters and dated 1656 and 1658, it has an H-plan with a double pile at the centre, stucco quoins and plain architraves for the windows, a band-course and eaves cornice beneath hipped roofs (Colour Plate 79). This essay in plain, proportioned regularity is worlds away from the playfully naïve classical details still strewn with great abandon about many contemporary houses. To its south there is a late Georgian octagonal house of stone with quoins and band-courses, and a central chimney-stack.

MERSHAM (3½ miles SE of Ashford): a parish of scattered settlements on low chartland crossed by the East Stour River, with a spread out village centre. Christ Church Priory built **Court Lodge** (Colour Plates 3 and 59 and Figure 8) beside the church as a manor house in the middle of the fourteenth century when the demesne was probably already let out to a tenant, with a two-part plan comprising an open hall and a storeyed bay for services and a solar, visible on the outside in the large cusped two-light hall window with a foiled hexagon in its head at one end, the arched entrance at the low end of the hall, and the trefoiled two-light solar window at the further end, all set into sandstone walls beneath a tall hipped roof with tiny gablets which acted as vents for the smoke from the open fire. On the edge of the village, **New House** has a long early eighteenth-century front of red and grey chequered brickwork with a block cornice and hipped roof; **Glebe House**, opposite, has a more vigorous façade with sunken panels beneath its sash windows; and **Stonegreen Hall**, to the south of the village, is of the same type, but altogether more competently treated, and, unusually, extends to the rear in a lower wing with different details as though it was meant to be separate; perhaps this was the framed part apparently refaced in brick in 1712. On the further edge of the parish, **Mersham-le-Hatch** is an early house of Robert Adam's, a large double pile with a central pedimented projection, linked by low corridors with niches containing statues to end pavilions, themselves small double piles (Plate 88); all this was started in 1762 to a remarkably self-effacing Palladian design for Sir Wyndham Knatchbull and completed after his death for his uncle Sir Edward Knatchbull in 1766 with little of that sense for the antique which was to imbue Adam's Brasted Place twenty years later.

MILSTEAD (3 miles S of Sittingbourne): a wooded downland parish, with a village centre at a crossroads. In one corner stands **Milstead Manor**, close-studded with a long jettied front, a central gabled porch, and gabled ends continuing backwards as wings. **Hoggeshawes**, to the south, is an early Wealden with a simple arched entrance (Figure 22c), and the jettied wings underbuilt in brick; the massive chimney-stack (Figure 26k) carries a plaque dated as late as 1700, making this one of the last of Kent's large hall-houses to be modernised. **Lion Farm**, north of the village, is another hall-house, but with end jetties.

MILTON REGIS (½ mile N of Sittingbourne): hardly more than a suburb now, but once served by a market and a port through which oysters were sent to Billingsgate. Opposite the framed Court House is a narrow Wealden with a single bay for its hall, typical for a built-up town; further down the High Street is the decorated front of No. 77, the **Post Office**, with two storeys of jetties, large bracketed oriels and panelled framing with inset squares linked by short arms (Plate 34); opposite, a plainer jettied range with a pargeted upper storey has a four-centred entrance inscribed 'THOMAS 1536 BRADBURY' (Figure 22h).

MINSTER-IN-THANET (4½ miles WSW of Ramsgate): a large parish stretching up into chalkland from the marshes on the north bank of the River Stour, with a village centre close to the ruins of the early grange of St Augustine's at Canterbury, recently converted into an abbey (Figure 3). Typically, several houses have shaped gables. Outside the village, **Wayborough Manor** is a large sixteenth-century house with a flint and brick ground storey, close studding above and wings at the rear with fewer studs and curved down-braces. Close to Pegwell Bay, **Sevenscore** is an attractive brick house of the early eighteenth century with a block cornice and hipped roof, only one pile deep, but with rear extensions.

MONKS HORTON (7¼ miles WNW of Folkestone): a downland parish of scattered settlements. The ruins of the Cluniac **Horton Priory**, which was founded in the early twelfth century, were built into a new

Monks Horton. Horton Priory.

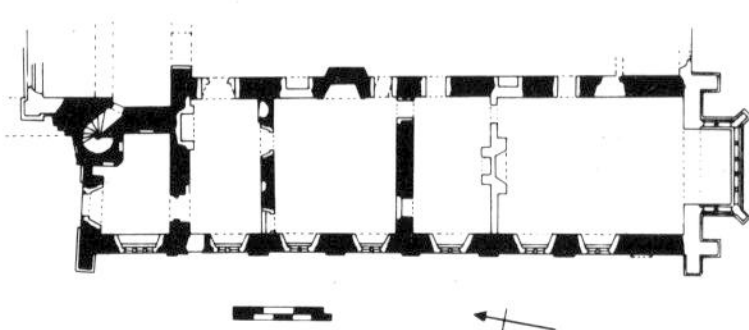

Horton Priory, Monks Horton. Plan showing the remains of the buildings along the west range of the cloister in solid, and their conversion into a house by the architect George Hornblower in 1913-14 shown in outline. (After Oswald 1929b.)

house in 1913-14, keeping a fragment of the west front of the church, and continuing along the west range of the cloisters by using the buttressed wall and the two storeys of mullioned, two-light cusped windows which had been inserted in the fourteenth century. **Kite Manor** is a close-studded Wealden with a two-centred entrance, largely underbuilt in brick and jettied at a higher level than the end ranges when the hall was floored over and given a new window in the form of a large gabled dormer, coved out at eaves level and dated 1574.

MONKTON (6 miles W of Ramsgate): a large parish on the north bank of the River Stour with a number of brick houses, some with shaped gables, along the street from Sarre to Minster. **Cleve Court**, high on Thanet's downland, has an opulent early eighteenth-century brick front with a bracketed hood to its central entrance, a Venetian window in the storey above and symmetrically placed sash windows edged in red brick, with cambered heads and stucco keystones.

NETTLESTEAD (5 miles WSW of Maidstone): a small parish on the chartland slopes rising from the Medway valley, with the principal settlement around a green, well to the south of the parish church. Beside the church is **Nettlestead Place**, a fragment of a medieval house belonging to the Wharhole and then the Pympe family, which was built into a neo-Tudor house in 1922 designed by

Nettlestead. Nettlestead Place: the medieval range.

Morley Horder. The most spectacular survival is an undercroft of about 1250, two bays by four, with sturdy circular columns supporting quadripartite rib-vaults (Colour Plate 55 and Figure 43); the range rises above this with a series of two-light windows with Perpendicular tracery of no earlier than 1400-10, separated by rectangular projections which might have contained garderobes. A fourteenth-century gatehouse with Kentish framing has windows with surviving traceried heads.

NEWINGTON (3 miles WNW of Folkestone): a parish with a short village street lying just below the scarp of the North Downs and now all but submerged by the works for the Channel Tunnel. One wing of **Pound Farm** comprises a thirteenth-century upper hall, and to this were added a hall and cross-wing in the usual medieval way. Nearby is one of the smallest Wealden halls (Figure 56), just 15ft. (4.55 m) square, its service and chamber ends adding a further 6 and 7ft. (2.12 and 1.82 m). Outside the village, **Old Kent Cottage** (formerly Frogholt Cottage) is a similarly small hall-house (Plate 56), its plain collared roof without crown-post or plate, perhaps owing to cheap rather than primitive construction; it has an end jetty at the high end with an upper storey rising into the roof as little more than a loft, and a rebuilt service end which lacked an upper floor (Parkin 1986).

NEWNHAM (4¼ miles SW of Faversham): a downland parish with a village street set in a tight valley. First comes a **Wealden** with a jettied floor inserted across the hall, then the formal late eighteenth-century **Parsonage Farm**, and next **Calico House**, a close-studded hall-house, modernised and jettied in the sixteenth century, but now underbuilt in brick and extended to the west, and — the great surprise — plastered and painted in 1710 with naïve floral patterns including what appear to be large egg-cups of wilting tulips (Colour Plate 35); the chamber at the east end has painted walls too (Plate 38). At Seed, the heavily restored **Foxenden** has two jettied projecting wings with hipped roofs rising to the apex of the main roof, and an inserted projecting block with oriel windows rising into jetties and a gable dated 1604; the ground storey is close studded as is the central block, the upper storey otherwise being large-panelled with double-curved down-braces; beside the central block, the roof sweeps down to first-floor level, suggesting that this was originally a late example of an aisled hall (*see* Fairstead, Eastry, and Hogbrook, Alkham).

NEW ROMNEY (12 miles SSE of Ashford): one of the original Cinque Ports, planned in the later tenth century to take advantage of the sheltered waters at the mouth of the River Rother, which once flowed between Romney Marsh and Dungeness. The town was one of the few to oppose William the Conqueror, and was consequently slighted and became part of the Archbishop of Canterbury's large, prosperous manor of Aldington. After the great storm of 1287, when the Rother changed its course and reached the sea at Rye, the harbour started to silt up and the town slowly decayed. Strong evidence of a number of houses built before this is their lower level, for instance several in the High Street including **Nos. 28 and 30**, which comprised a hall and cross-wing, **3 and 4 West Street** (Plate 46 and Figure 61), built of stone rubble with a central hall and rear aisle entered from a two-centred arched doorway (Figure 22a), and fragments in the rear part of the **Assembly Hall** in Church Approach, which had an undercroft with a hall above (Parkin 1973). In the High Street is **Electric House**, a fifteenth-century hall-house; opposite, **Priory House** has a long, symmetrical red brick front with a bracketed hood to the central entrance and sash windows.

Nonington. St. Alban's Court; the garden front (copyright Jill Allibone).

NONINGTON (7¼ miles ESE of Canterbury): a parish of built-up streets on undulating downland with **St Alban's Court** on a hill nearby. This was built for Walter Oxenden Hammond, a landowner and enthusiasiastic watercolourist, by his friend, the architect George Devey, who also enjoyed painting in watercolours. Designed in 1875 around three sides of a courtyard (Figure 93) with the gabled outline that Devey had already established at Betteshanger some twenty years beforehand, and finished about 1879, the house has about it a regularity in massing and detail in contrast to the lack of cohesion induced by the youthful prolixity of his earlier house (Girouard 1971, 103-7; Franklin 1981, 158 and 194). There are a lodge and gardener's cottage on the estate, and, between 1872 and 1886, Devey also designed eight double estate cottages in and around the village in his Old English style with oriels, timber and plaster, tile-hanging, gables and tall chimney-stacks all to the fore. This work was continued by James Williams into the 1890s with the pair now called Gooseberry Hall Cottage. Some houses were remodelled: **Southdown Cottage**, for instance, began as an early hall-house with an end jetty, now much extended (Allibone 1991, 100-103, 158).

NORTHBOURNE (2¾ miles W of Deal): a nucleated village on undulating downland. At one end, **Flint House** is a pretty double pile built in two parts, indeed with a flint front trimmed with brick and stone, and brick sides. Down the street, **Vine Farm** is all of brick, laid in English bond, with a central two-storeyed porch squeezed between two projectings wings to form an E-plan, all under hipped roofs; the four-centred doorway and the timber mullioned and transomed windows have flat hoodmoulds over them, carried out in plaster in the centre, and in bright red brick in the wings; the details but not the plan are reminiscent of Yoke's Court at Frinsted and suggest a building date early in the seventeenth century.

NORTON (3 miles W of Faversham): a parish of orchards on the fertile dip slope of the North Downs. **Provender** was occupied by William Hugesson, also of Lynsted, in the early seventeenth century, but who built this heavily restored large, close-studded house is unclear. It comprises a main range with a central entrance beneath a small gable and two further gabled bays flank it; the house continues to the left, where a separate, apparently later, jettied and gabled block projects forward to form an L-plan. Just beyond, a framed cottage with a thatched roof has the appearance of a hall of the smallest kind with a service room and solar.

NURSTEAD (3¾ miles S of Gravesend): a small downland parish lacking a centre. **Nurstead Court** contains the surviving half of a large aisled hall-house built about 1314 as a manor house by Sir Stephen de Gravesend or one of the de Gravesend Bishops of London, with low flint walls and tall cusped hall windows breaking through the eaves into dormers (Figure 30a). Huge circular timber arcade-posts with foliated capitals divided the immense hall from its aisles and from the two end bays which were without upper floors, even at this date. The columns in the centre of the hall carry moulded braces which form a pointed arch, supporting a cranked tie-beam with a curtailed king-strut and a strutted collared roof above (Figures 10, 13, 21, 33 and 35). The service end and the lower half of the hall were demolished in the late 1830s, but the high end survives, and so does the room beyond it, which was probably an antechamber leading to an attached bower or chamber block, perhaps in the form of an 'upper hall', of which only the stone footings remain (Cherry 1989).

OFFHAM (6¾ miles WNW of Maidstone): a wooded chartland parish with a village street and a long green. Two lovely Queen Anne houses face it, both symmetrical with five windows across the front: **Manor House**, with a pedimented doorcase, bright red brick surrounds to the windows and a gabled roof

Offham. Quintain House and the quintain (or tilting post).

with a dentilled cornice; and **Quintain House** (so named after the quintain or tilting post for horseplay, opposite on the green), of chequered red and vitrified brick, with a cove beneath a hipped roof; between them is a modest, ragstone cottage with external, brick chimney-stacks rising up the gabled ends.

ORLESTONE (5 miles SSW of Ashford): a parish on the wooded clay hills overlooking Romney Marsh. **Court Lodge** is notable for a long, close-studded and jettied range, perhaps a cross-wing to a hall in the position of the rendered range beyond it, with a large chimney-breast built out from the opposite side. **Capel Farm** comprises a brick lobby-entry house attached to a second house, close-studded with a jettied cross-wing, which appears to be entirely modern. At Ham Street, a number of framed houses, some jettied along the front, include **The Old Bakery**, a Wealden with large panelled framing and a jetty along the end of the service end as well as the front.

OSPRINGE (1 mile WSW of Faversham): a parish of orchards on the dip slope of the North Downs with a village street running into the old London-Dover road. The chief medieval building is the **Maison Dieu** whose sixteenth-century framed upper storey has curved down-braces meeting to form flat arcs. **Queen Court** is a close-studded Wealden.

OTFORD (3 miles N of Sevenoaks): a parish on the River Darent where it cuts into the scarp of the North Downs. Shortly after Archbishop Bourchier had completed his palace nearby at Knole, his successor Archbishop Warham began another here on a similarly large scale by transforming the manor house; it was occupied by 1518, but, unlike its predecessor, did not outlast the Reformation. Only ruins of one of the four brick ranges survive in a row of cottages and part of a tower gateway. At the further end of the village is **Broughton Manor**, which has a prominent jettied and close-studded gable with cusped bargeboards.

OTHAM (2 miles SE of Maidstone): a chartland parish of scattered settlements among orchards. Three framed medieval houses are important in different ways. **Stoneacre** has a fifteenth-century hall and cross-wing at the chamber end, extended by the architect Aymer Vallance in 1920 during his restoration, when he also added a north wing with ornate diamond-patterned small framing, dated 1546 and 1629, brought from the demolished North Blore Place, Chiddingstone. **Synyards** is a large Wealden of similar date, close-studded at the front and sides but panelled at the rear; the hall was floored over by 1603, and, later, the roof was also floored and given a prominent dormer dated 1663 in its gable. **Wardes** is another Wealden, but of great significance for its early form: its original part, probably of the late fourteenth century, comprises a hall of two equal bays with moulded arched braces supporting the tie-beam and a slender crown-post with a carved base and capital (Figure 54); two-centred back and front doorways provide access at the low end but apparently there was no service bay, only a chamber bay at the other end, which is jettied front and back and along the end (or was this a services and solar bay?). At all events, to these a separately roofed close-studded service bay, jettied at the front, was added to complete the Wealden pattern, and this was also jettied along the end where it extends into a wider, Tudor range projecting at the rear (Figure 55). **Gore Court** is an irregular gabled house, its framing concealed by rendering and said to bear the date 1577.

OTTERDEN (6 miles SSE of Sittingbourne): a wooded downland parish of scattered settlements. **Otterden Place** is a winged brick house of two storeys, possibly built by Sir Anthony Aucher whose support of Henry VIII was well rewarded with pickings from Kent's dissolved monasteries; but in 1802-4 the house was transformed by the architect William Pilkington for Granville Wheler with Tudor style canted bays, mullioned and transomed windows and an embattled parapet.

PATRIXBOURNE (3 miles SE of Canterbury): a downland parish of orchards. The red brick **Hode Farm** is extremely long, with a crow-stepped gable at one end, quoined in stone and enriched with vitrified brick diaper forming the date 1566 (Figure 27a), and a shaped gable at the other end dated 1674. Another shaped gable in the village comprises a small pediment set on ogee curves (Figure

Patrixbourne. Highland Court.

27o). The pedimented façade of **Highland Court** is an impressive stranger to Kent, added in gleaming white stone about 1904 to an insignificant earlier house by the racing motorist Count Zborowski in a tasteful French classical style reminiscent of the architect Jacques-Ange Gabriel; it now overlooks the traffic racing along the A2 motorway.

PENSHURST (4½ miles WSW of Tonbridge): a chartland parish by the upper reaches of the Medway with a picturesque village and many scattered settlements. How much **Penshurst Place** (Figure 46) owes to Stephen de Penchester, who died in 1299, is unclear, but the centrepiece is largely if not entirely the creation of Sir John de Pulteney, a renaissance prince out of his time, whose fabulous wealth served king and Church as well as himself; he was a City Draper, four times Lord Mayor of London in the 1330s, and founder of a chantry, a college and a friary. He was granted a licence to crenellate Penshurst in 1341, but built a manor house, albeit embattled, with little other fortification beyond an apparently isolated gatehouse (Colour Plate 58). At the centre is a hall, large, complete but for a louver in the roof, and a classic of its type; windows with rich Decorated tracery (Plate 45) are matched by a heavily moulded false-hammerbeam roof; arch-braced collars support purlins and short crown-posts beneath an upper tier of collars (Colour Plate 28 and Figure 15). Pulteney could have employed the best royal craftsmen for these, perhaps William Ramsey III for the masonry and William Hurley for the roof, which is of chestnut, although the evidence is only circumstantial (Harvey 1984, 154-5 and 242-5). Beyond the hall, three doorways in the screens passage lead to service rooms, a newel staircase at the high end, soon to be replaced by a grander one, led to a solar chamber over an undercroft, and also to the parapet; another newel beside the contemporary north porch again leads to the parapet, but, oddly, not to the room over the porch. Pulteney died in 1349, apparently of the plague, and the house came into the hands of Sir John Devereux, warrior, governor of Calais, and Warden of the Cinque Ports; he was granted a further licence to crenellate in 1392, and this may account for the building of eight towers, including the Garden Tower, and a curtain wall. He died in 1393, so these works may only have been accomplished by Henry IV's third son, John of Lancaster, Duke of Bedford and Regent during Henry VI's minority, who bought the estate in 1430. Although preoccupied in France, he added a new, even larger hall, the so-called Bedford Building. It has curiously French-looking inset traceried windows within deep external reveals. In 1552 the estate was granted to the Sidneys, later Earls of Leicester and Viscounts De L'Isle and Dudley of the first creation, and they transformed much of the house, apart from the original hall (Figure 46). This process continued into the nineteenth century when Sir John Shelley Sidney, to whom the estate had descended by marriage, employed the architect John Biagio Rebecca to rearrange the circulation, to reface half the west front and the north front west of the King's Tower in a dull Tudor Gothic, and to build a new range east of the King's Tower. Following Rebecca's death in 1847, George Devey refurbished the Buckingham or Bedford Building for the second Baron De L'Isle and Dudley, and added new stables, laundry and outhouses (Allibone 1991, 152; Binney and Emery 1975).

Aristocratic ownership of Penshurst and its estates was unconducive to yeoman wealth, and no small medieval houses survive. Yet, just beside the churchyard there is the close-studded and jettied **Church House**, resplendent with cusped bargeboards (Plate 31), and, far outside the village at Poundsbridge, the heavily restored, timber-framed **Picture House**, which has similar bargeboards on one of the two gabled wings; these project far beyond a central gable where the date 1593 is inscribed in immense letters and 1669 in far smaller ones beside a monogram. A tall framed house to the south of the village is notable for small panelled framing and a bracketed oriel extended by clerestories beneath a jettied gable dated 1610. After that date comes the regularity of **The Rectory's** brick refronting, and an attention to style which produced the minimally Palladian villa-like front of **Colquhoun House**; its slightly projecting centre is pedimented, the sides rising as though into a second pediment behind the first. The nineteenth century brought, first, **The Yews**, a double pile of fine Wealden sandstone with a Doric porch and a low upper storey. Then came a dramatic change in style introduced by the architect Decimus Burton's **The Grove** of 1828-30, a *cottage orné* with exaggeratedly cusped bargeboards. This was followed with true innovation by the young George Devey with the cottages of **Leicester Square** (Plate 101). These continue the style of Church House forward to the village street with the happy mixture of stone, close-studding, tile-hanging and tall chimney-stacks which was to become the trade mark of the Old English style late in the 1860s. Devey's cottages, however, were designed in 1848 and bear the date 1850. Their appearance of almost natural growth from Church House had to await a visit from the young Norman Shaw ten years later and his vigorous if not hectic use of the style *(see* Hillside, Groombridge) before it became popular. Meanwhile, Devey went on to work for the first and second Barons De L'Isle and Dudley, allowing local inspiration to lead him in 1867 to **The Cottage**, Rogue's Hill, a rather more obviously Victorian reworking of tradition, this time of the Wealden theme; his hand appears in similar vein elsewhere on the estate in groups of cottages, designed up to 1877, for instance at Ennisfield and Cinder Hill. He also worked for Lieutenant General Sir Henry Hardinge, Governor General of India, later Viscount Hardinge *(see also* Fordcombe), on his South Park estate, adding a lodge; and for James Nasmyth (astronomer, engineer and inventor of the steam hammer) at **Hammerfield**; and at

Penshurst. The Cottage, Rogues Hill.

Swaylands, first for Edward Cropper, then for G.J. Drummond (Allibone 1991, 153, 162, 174).

Close to Chiddingstone there is a small estate house, symmetrically designed in a neo-Elizabethan style; more interestingly, there are two oast-houses converted by Martin and Mitzi Quirk (Colour Plate 111), a small one in the angle of the road with two roundels and an external timber staircase, and a larger one to the south-west (which the architect Charles Rennie Mackintosh painted in 1910 when he drew many of the houses in Chiddingstone) which has four roundels, and small, well-placed windows designed to avoid breaking the essential shape of the building.

PETHAM (4 miles S of Canterbury): a wooded downland parish with its centre lying in a valley below the Roman Stone Street. Despite their obvious charms, it is unusual in Kent for small cottages to have the significance of **Dormer Cottage**, which is an extremely rare survivor of the earliest kind of small house once common in much of England, but long superseded in Kent (Colour Plate 45): although one end has been rebuilt, it apparently comprised a single aisled bay for the hall, extended by cantilevered half bays like Kentish barns under the hipped ends of the roof for a service room and chamber, all of them without an upper floor (Figure 34); the framing is primitive, the rafters simply being collared for support, and this suggests a building date before the end of the thirteenth century (*see* Canon Cottage, Wingham), even though primitive methods may be due to its small size rather than such an early date; a framed and plastered firehood, itself a rare survivor, and upper floors have been inserted (Parkin 1982). Just down the hill is **Cotterell Court**, a close-studded Wealden with a jettied chamber end but curtailed at the other end, leaving space for only modest service rooms; surviving windows have hollow-moulded mullions (Figures 22g and 30j); when the house was modernised, chimney-stacks were inserted with pretty circular shafts embellished with rings (*see* Old Manor House, Wye). Almost next door is **Old Hall**, formerly Thatched Cottage, again a hall-house, although with a very low hall and a cross-wing at the service end to provide the necessary height for a solar; its modernisation brought a canted bay window to the front of the hall, which rises into a gabled dormer to light the new upper storey. Just up the hill is another framed house, now tile-hung, but evidently jettied and at least as early as the sixteenth century. Towards the church is **China Court**, built with an open hall and an end jetty from timber felled between 1506 and 1541, and therefore a late example of the type, and still with Kentish framing (Howard *et al.* 1988). **Stone Street Farm**, up on the Roman road, is a modest framed medieval house underbuilt in brick and tile-hung, and modernised to give it a lobby-entry plan. Close by, in a hollow below the road, is **Dane Chantry**, another lobby-entry house with a long history. Its origin seems to have been in the mid-thirteenth century when the lord of the manor of Deepdene or Deepdane founded a chantry in Petham; the chapel built of flint and attached to the present house may date from then, going by its king-strut roof; the mouldings of the doorway into a crypt or undercroft suggest that this was an addition, and the upper part of the chapel has been much rebuilt in brick. The house itself has a medieval crown-post roof but has been rebuilt; this took place in 1638 according to a dated post and may be attributed to a yeoman, Sawkins of Lyminge, who had bought the house in 1625. He gave the house a nearly symmetrical lobby-entry plan and refronted it with a panelled frame, brick-nogged, a jettied upper storey with oriels to both floors, the upper ones continued by clerestories, all very much in the style achieved by Yew Trees at Wye twenty years beforehand. **Kenfield Hall** is a fine two-storeyed double pile, built of brown brick enlivened with red about 1700, with a garden front of five bays, the centre three projecting slightly under a pediment, a theme picked up by a central pedimented doorcase entrance and a pair of pedimented dormers projecting from the hipped roof. **Swarling Farm**, meanwhile, is a more urban version of the same idea, a three-storeyed double pile, built, perhaps rebuilt, in brown brick some three-quarters of a century later with all the severity of the later eighteenth century, only relieved by a copybook doorcase with a pedimented fanlight.

PLATT (5¾ miles ENE of Sevenoaks): a heavily wooded chartland parish with a web of lanes at its centre. Here, as early as 1933, the Modern Movement architect Colin Lucas built **The Hopfield** as a weekend cottage for himself; it is a cement-rendered box, painted white, with an external staircase, a long window, balcony and a flat roof, an 'honest' expression of how new materials and functional planning could exemplify International ideals (Colour Plate 108).

PLAXTOL (6½ miles E of Sevenoaks): a heavily wooded chartland parish with a straggling village and numerous outlying farmhouses. **Ashenden**, beside the church, is a Wealden of about 1500 with a Georgian front. To the south is a group of cottages built in rat-trap bond. Beyond the church, up Sheet Hill, weatherboarded cottages give way to individual framed houses, and one or two of ragstone. **Bartons Farm** is a hall-house with a jettied cross-wing, built from timber felled between 1373 and 1408, and refronted in ragstone in the mid-eighteenth century. The close-studded **Jordans** (formerly Sheet Hill Cottage) was rebuilt in the first half of the sixteenth century with a crown-post roof and perhaps a smoke bay, but was soon, if not originally, given a lobby entry and brick chimney-stack, making it similar to Cobb's Hall, Aldington, so it is an early example of this plan (Plate 77). The close-studded **Nut Tree Hall** has a jettied front with gabled cross-wings; William Hubble built the wing at the high end of the hall about 1480; the house was restored and extended at the rear in 1905 by the architect Charles Harrison Townsend. **The Grange** has an unusual arrangement of round-headed windows closely flanking the entrance, itself with a round-headed window, and a bull's-eye window over it — early eighteenth-century baroque on a small scale. **Spoute House** is a hall-house with Kentish framing of two builds, whose jettied service end was built first with timber felled between 1414 and 1449, the hall and chamber end being added later with timber felled between 1435 and 1470 (Plate 61); meanwhile, to the north at Claygate Cross, the similar **Clakkers Hall** was built with timber felled between 1442 and 1477 (Howard *et al.* 1988 and 1990). Nearby is another hall-house, now mostly cased in brick. Far out to the east is **Old Soar**, whose aisled hall has been replaced but whose solar wing remains as an exemplar of its type and the most important fragment in the parish (Colour Plate 52 and Figure 36). It served a sub-manor created by the Archbishop and probably takes its name from an old local family called Hore. Built about 1290 of ragstone with galletting decorating the mortared interstices between the blocks of stone (Plate 24), it comprises a tunnel-vaulted undercroft and a large chamber over it with Y-tracery in its end windows and recesses in the inner arches to take hinged shutters; there is Y-tracery again in the east window of a small chapel, which projects from one of the corners on the further side from the demolished hall, and is balanced by a garderobe projecting from the other corner; this has a latrine built against the outer wall venting outwards through a large pointed arch (Plate 54). The chamber roof is supported by tall crown-posts (Figure 12), among the earliest recognised, which have straight braces rising from them to carry the collars and the crown-plate. The similarity of the solar block to contemporary 'upper halls' such as the one at Westdean Rectory, East Sussex, is remarkable, and, if nothing else, suggests that upper halls may have been as much grand chambers in concept as semi-public rooms. The hall was replaced by a symmetrical red brick house with five sashes and a hooded doorway with Gothick tracery in the fanlight. A short way to the south is **Broadfield**, a mid seventeenth-century framed house, refaced with a handsome red brick front with vitrified headers, and dated 1700 over the central doorway, together with the initials of Robert Baldwin, a maltster who came from a local family of yeomen known

Plaxtol. Rats Castle.

here for five hundred years. Further east still is **Rats Castle**, a fifteenth-century hall-house inscribed with the initials of Stephen Chilman, who modernised it in the seventeenth century. On the west side of the parish is the minor courtier Lord Barnard's **Fairlawne**, which may have started as a courtyard house, but by the early eighteenth century had gained a fairly regular two-storeyed main block, partly of brick, partly ragstone, with a parapet and prominent belfry and cupola, offset to the left of the main front. This now has a new cornice and a porte-cochère, and there is a three-storeyed extension to the left.

PLUCKLEY (5½ miles WNW of Ashford): a wooded parish on the lower slopes of the Weald, and, unusually in this part of Kent, it developed as a single estate. It belonged to St Augustine's, but after the Dissolution passed to the St Leger family and then to the Derings. Near the centre stood **Surrenden Dering**, which Sir Edward-Dering had built of brick with an H-plan and numerous shaped gables in the 1630s. In the middle of the nineteenth century Sir Edward Cholmeley Dering altered it, adding several groups of arched windows set beneath relieving arches (*see* the earlier groups of round-headed windows at Goodnestone). He believed that these brought him good luck, but his house was largely burnt down in 1952. Nevertheless, his lucky windows are ubiquitous in the parish on houses, old and new. The most unusual of these is **Rooting Manor**; it was in the hands of an eponymous family by the 1360s, and it was probably then that they built the hall, which might have been aisled or supported by base-crucks like those of Hamden at Smarden. This has been replaced by a brick range with lucky windows, but the rather later, structurally separate cross-wing remains, and it is remarkable for the decorative use of curved braces to form arcs beneath the ogee braces supporting the crown-post in its gable end (Figures 12 and 23) (Rigold 1967). Here again there are groups of lucky windows. Among other medieval houses to be so graced is **Cooper Farm**, an early hall-house with an end jetty, modernised with a two-storeyed canted bay added to the hall and the lucky windows set in a brick extension. **Dowle Cottage**, Dowle Street, has a similar form made the more visible following a restoration which brought it back to single occupation after having been split into three cottages, although the door derns are not original here; it too had a canted bay inserted into the hall at the time it was floored over (Colour Plate 19). **Jennings**, again, is an end-jetty house, but a later one built with timber felled between 1490 and 1525 (Howard *et al.* 1989). **Gore Court** is an early Wealden with massive door derns forming a two-centred arch; here the hall has again been modernised by the addition of a great bay window, coved beneath its upper storey and jettied beneath its gable, and lucky windows have been inserted in the upper storey at each end. At **Chambers Green**, two apparently similar houses with lucky windows face each other at the crossroads: both are faced in ragstone and have triple dormers in their hipped roofs; nevertheless, one was built as a semi-detached pair of cottages, presumably by Sir Edward, and given its lucky windows as an original feature (Plate 8), but the other is a heavily disguised timber-framed three-part house of the fifteenth or sixteenth

Pluckley. Dowle Street Farm.

century. The red brick **Dowle Street Farm** is much later than most of these, being a small double pile with heavy eaves to its hipped roof and triplets of lucky windows beneath segmental relieving arches.

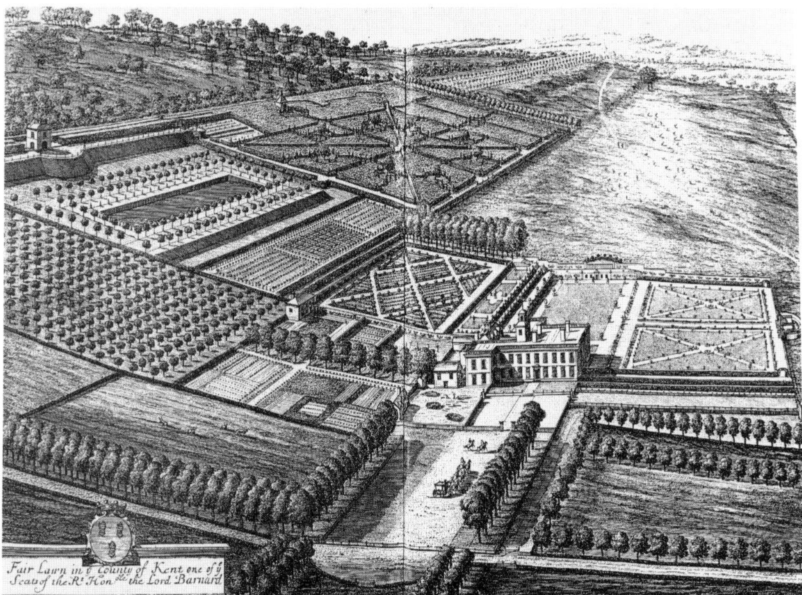

Fairlawne, Plaxtol. Panorama about 1700. (After Knyff and Kip 1707.)

PRESTON (6½ miles ENE of Canterbury): a parish of orchards overlooking the Little Stour. Near the church is an endearingly thatched cottage, its overhanging roof almost hiding the low plastered walls. **Perry Farm** is more usual, a brick house of about 1700 with shaped gables comprising two tiers of quadrants and semicircular pediments.

RAMSGATE. The harbour in the lee of the North Foreland cliffs gave Ramsgate its status as a Limb of Sandwich, though it was used mainly for fishing. In the late seventeenth and early eighteenth centuries many houses were built in the **High Street** and in **Paradise** with shaped gables. Then in the later eighteenth century sandy beaches encouraged sea-bathing and brought more and more visitors; the town developed and so did the harbour, which was the point of embarkation for troops going to Waterloo. Already the first patriotically named terraces were transforming the cliffs on each side (Colour Plate 95). **Nelson Crescent** started the process on the West Cliff in 1798-1801, and this was continued by **The Paragon** (the painter Vincent van Gogh lived here briefly) in 1816 with typical tent-roofed balconies (Colour Plate 16), and then in 1826 by **Royal Crescent** with pilaster strips between the houses and a low pediment over the two central ones; the next twenty years saw the building of similar terraces in **Liverpool Lawn**, ending with **West Cliff Terrace**, now with two storeys of arcaded balconies. Before this comes **The Grange**, which the Gothic Revivalist Augustus Welby Northmore Pugin built for himself in 1843-4 as the first part of his quasi-monastic settlement, St Augustine's, which also included a church, cloister, sacristy and school; the house is unassuming, apart from its embattled tower from where Pugin watched out for fishing boats caught in stormy weather (Colour Plate 100). Patriotism went further on East Cliff with **Kent Place**, tucked above the harbour, **Albion Place** perched above by 1817, leading to the long curve of **Wellington Crescent**, which was going up two years later with verandas supported by a Doric colonnade (Plate 97); in the centre there is a break for a street called **The Plains of Waterloo**, though it is more of a tunnel than a plain, so close and high are its facing terraces. This leads on to

Ramsgate. La Belle Alliance Square.

La Belle Alliance Square, where some of the houses have bays with round-headed windows supporting their balconies, and three-light windows above, oddly inset beneath basket arches (Colour Plate 98). So much for the terraces. Two houses at opposite ends of the town embrace it chronologically: to the west, **Chilton Farm** has the traditional shaped gables of east Kent, with quadrants, ogees and a pediment to each (Plate 80); to the east, **East Court** (Plate 103) has a late Victorian view of tradition, magnificently expressed by the architect Sir Ernest George in 1889 with grey-green tiling to match the sea, and quirky jetties, oriels, gables and tall, red brick chimney-stacks for contrast (*see* his estate cottages at Leigh).

RINGWOULD (2¾ miles SSW of Deal): a downland parish with a small group of red brick houses close to the church. Set back from these are the yellow bricks of **Ringwould House**, built for the Reverend John Monins of Ringwould in 1813 to a characteristically self-effacing design by the architect John Soane; it lacks his usual quirkiness: plain pilaster strips articulate the entrance front into three, with the centre rendered and painted, and emphasised by a porch with smaller, paired pilaster strips and a doorway squeezed between them, typical of his desire to reduce classical detail to plain geometrical shapes (Plate 89).

ROCHESTER. The Roman *Durobrivae* was strategically sited on the road from London to Dover where it crossed the Medway. In 604 St Augustine confirmed the site's importance by ordaining one of his missionaries as Rochester's first bishop. The cathedral was built beside the old Roman road, which became the **High Street**. Here, typically of medieval towns, the oldest surviving buildings are undercrofts, but the overall character is of eighteenth-century façades, mostly with shops at ground level, mingling red and yellow brick with stucco, gables with wooden eaves cornices or plain parapets. Here and there, something older is expressed by jetties and framed gables, or by weatherboarding. The timber-framed **Nos. 150-154** have the small panelling, bracketed oriels and jetties to both upper floors and three front and single end gables typical of the early seventeenth century (Plate 93). **Eastgate House** (Colour Plate 89), opposite, again has bracketed oriels, jetties and gables facing the street, but the front, which faces sideways on to a small yard, is of bright red brick and has a projecting two-storeyed porch with a pilastered and pedimented door surround, flanked by two projecting timber-framed polygonal bays with brick-nogging and three storeys of mullioned and transomed windows; just before the angle with the street rises a brick stair-turret with deeply moulded windows beneath four-centred arches with hoodmoulds and capped by a small gable. The house is clearly of some importance and was meant to show it; the arms of Sir Peter Buck, Clerk of the Acts in the Navy Board, and the date 1590 on a chimney-piece suggest the reason why. For the rest, **No. 42**, dated 1778, is distinguished by stucco loops at second-floor level with swags hanging from them, and, at the end of the street, the stuccoed late eighteenth-century **Berkeley House** is set back, its pedimented Corinthian porch echoed by projecting pavilions forming a small courtyard. **Star Hill**, which runs out of High Street, was laid out about 1790 with standard first-rate terraces of the London type (Colour Plate 94), before the discontinuous houses of Chatham begin, and a number of houses of the seventeenth and eighteenth centuries line the low road as well. In Maidstone Road, **Restoration House** has an E-plan, sixteenth-century in origin, but refronted in brick in the seventeenth, with shaped gables, unusual this far west, to the pilastered three-storeyed porch and on the left (Figure 27i). Within the cathedral precinct, **Minor Canon Row** is a three-storeyed terrace of seven houses, built in 1736, still with projecting wooden hoods over the entrances and flush-framed sashes (casements in the top floor), but with parapets instead of eaves cornices.

ROLVENDEN (2¾ miles WSW of Tenterden): a Wealden parish in the vale of the River Rother with a memorable curving village street of weatherboarded houses; as William Cobbett saw in 1823, 'Here the houses have gardens in front of them as well as behind; and there is a good deal of show and finery about them and their gardens' (1912, 230). One is a large **Wealden** with a jettied floor inserted into the hall; a secondary settlement at Rolvenden Layne has two more medieval houses, **Wesley House**, Maythem Road, which has a jetty at the chamber end and a tall, close-studded bay with two storeys of windows rising into a gable, added when the hall was floored over, and its neighbour, which is similar but underbuilt in brick and lacking an inserted bay. Among the outlying houses, **Pyx's Farm**, now a pair of tile-hung cottages, was built about 1600 with three close-studded gables, the outer ones jettied forward on brackets, their ties decorated with guilloche mouldings, and the eaves finished with gently cusped bargeboards. The principal house is **Great Maythem** (Colour Plate 20), built in 1721 as a double pile, which Sir Edwin Lutyens entirely transformed in 1907-09 for the MP H. J. Tennant (son of Sir Charles Tennant and brother of F. J. Tennant, *see* Lympne Castle). He encased the house in dove grey brick with vermilion window surrounds, added a storey, and extended it each side into lower, winged pavilions; the axial entrances front and back have stone doorcases, rusticated at the front, carrying open segmental pediments, and the windows have cambered heads, except in the attic, and once had louvered shutters; over all this, hipped roofs and tall chimney-stacks do not quite bring the house to life as they do at his contemporary Wittersham House and at The Salutation, Sandwich, which he built a couple of years later.

ST NICHOLAS AT WADE (6 miles WSW of Margate): a parish occupying the chalkland at the western end of Thanet with a nucleated village and a few settlements close to the marshes. Its houses are pre-eminent for their shaped gables: **Old Cottage** and **1 and 2 Shuart Lane** have two tiers of quadrants and semicircular tops (Figure 27h), while **Shuart** has stepped convex and concave curves beneath pediments (Figure 27p).

SANDGATE (2 miles W of Folkestone): now a suburb of Folkestone, overlooking the Channel from the last throw of the Greensand hills. Hiding among the fashionable houses of Radnor Cliff Crescent are the white roughcast walls of **Spade House**, which the architect Charles Francis Annesley Voysey designed for H. G. Wells as a seaside retreat, and extended in 1903; it has the architect's characteristic battered buttresses, long, low runs of windows set in plain stone reveals, with bays and dormers to provide accents, and sweeping tiled roofs penetrated by roughcast chimney-stacks (Colour Plate 24). All this was high fashion at the turn of the century in its vision of plain, uncluttered forms as opposed to the vulgar opulence and knick-knackery of much Victorian taste, and far less to do with a re-affirmation of local building traditions on the one side or, on the other, a vision of a future modern style than some critics have claimed.

SANDHURST (7 miles SW of Tenterden): a Wealden parish overlooking the vale of the River Rother with two separate streets of houses and scattered settlements. These include **Field Green House**, a mid-eighteenth-century double pile with chequered brickwork and red window heads and an egg-and-dart cornice which breaks upward at the centre, with a gabled dormer set back from the parapet above; and, opposite, a large rectangular oast-house which has been attractively converted to domestic use. **Sponden** is a framed hall-house with end jetties.

SANDWICH (4 miles NNW of Deal): once Kent's second town in size, and the most important Cinque Port. The Roman port of Richborough silted up in Saxon times, allowing Sandwich to develop on the sandy shore of the Wantsum, the stretch of water which divided Thanet from the mainland. Much of the wool from Kent's monastic estates was exported to Flemish and Italian weavers from here, and the town became an entrepôt for wine. Christ Church Priory, which owned the Hundred of Sandwich, benefited from this. The town grew, both inland and along the shore with suburbs east and west. Henry II gave Sandwich a charter in 1155, and it remained one of England's principal ports until the early fifteenth century. Richborough's loss was eventually Sandwich's loss too as the quixotic River Stour piled silt up here as well, leaving Kent's seaports, particularly Deal, better placed to profit, but also leaving Sandwich with its medieval pattern of streets and a strong image of its past unchanged (Plate 2). Only immigrant clothworkers from France and Holland kept the town going in the century after 1560. Visiting in 1697, Celia Fiennes found 'a sad old town all timber building, but its so run to decay that except one or two good houses its just like to drop down...' Defoe agreed, only remarking that it still sent two members to Parliament (Morris 1984, 123; Rogers 1971, 136-7).

Fragments of the town's earliest stone houses built slightly inland from Strand Street show the pre-1300 shoreline; these follow the usual pattern of thirteenth-century building with halls and private chambers built over undercrofts which were in commercial use. The flint walls of **3 Kings Yard** behind 11 Strand Street are the remains of just such a building of about 1230, with a single lancet lighting a chamber, and a pair lighting the hall (Plate 50); at **27 Strand Street** are the remains of another, built over a vaulted undercroft; and further flint walling at **39 Strand Street** has part of the arched doorway of a similar building; the shafted doorway of a rather later house of this type at **Paradise Row** is a further indication of the houses which once lined Strand Street before it was realigned closer to the river. There is more evidence of stone houses at **50 St Peter's Street**, and, possibly some of the flint walling of **Pellicane House** (formerly Flint House), High Street (Colour Plate 27), and also **Horns Pond House**, Delf Street, indicate the former existence of yet more of these houses; both have been much rebuilt with yellow bricks made from river mud, yet Pellicane House seems to have a medieval tiled roof. Possibly it was the great storm of 1287 which made it imperative for Strand Street to move forward, and all the oldest framed houses are here; many others inland and to the east and west were destroyed when the town was left in flames after the French raid of 1457. Among the oldest survivors is **The Long House**, Strand Street, which was built in the later thirteenth century for John Pickenot, cellarer to Christ Church, but it was almost entirely rebuilt in the sixteenth century with a jetty along the street and refronted two centuries later. By the fifteenth century, **39 Strand Street** had been rebuilt with an open hall fronted by a shop with two jettied storeys above it; in 1606 further chambers were built at the rear over its thirteenth-century undercroft. There are further halls fronted by shops and jettied chambers at **3, 5 and 7 Strand Street** (Plate 26), at **38 King Street** and **7 Potter Street**, and the remains of other medieval framed houses brings their total to around thirty (Parkin 1969a, 1984). The tradition of building shops with jettied chambers over them continued well after Sandwich was in decline; this is particularly evident in Strand Street, where the King's Arms has this form and is dated 1592, and there are more examples, many hiding behind plaster, in Delf Street, Fisher Street, Harnet Street, King Street, New Street and St Peter's Street. Brick has obscured much more, and little brickwork belongs obviously to a first build. **Old Dutch House**, 62 King Street, may owe its origin to the influx of Protestants from Holland; its white painted brickwork detracts from the usual quality attending most of Kent's naïvely classical fronts of the later seventeenth century, and it has probably lost its crowning gables; there is a shaped gable at the rear. Its neighbour, **64 King Street**, which has a plain gable to the front, is probably a refronting, but **52 King Street** is what it appears, a delightful late eighteenth-century double pile of three storeys, executed in dark grey brick with red brick window surrounds and quoining, with a wooden block cornice beneath a low-pitched hipped roof. **Blenheim House**, Delf Street, is a seventeenth-century lobby-entry house refronted in brick and renamed in 1709, five years after the famous battle (by a grateful Dutch immigrant?). From this time until well into the nineteenth century dozens of houses, old and new, received fine new copybook doorcases, ringing a number of changes on a theme of pilasters, plain or fluted, flat block cornices or pediments, these broken or closed, and an array of semicircular or elliptical fanlights.

At the end of Upper Strand Street is the gatehouse of **The Salutation** (Plate 86 and Figure 82), which Lutyens designed in his best Queen Anne style for Henry Farrer in 1911; the house is all the better for its compact shape (*see* Great Maythem, Rolvenden), but the quirky arrangement of sash windows in the gatehouse leaves a more indelible mark on the town than the house itself. The Lutyens styles reappear at Sandwich Bay, an estate on the coast which the Earl of Guildford developed just before the Great War between two golf courses. Kentish vernacular is revived in one or two half-timbered houses and in the shaped gables of **Beadles. Rest Harrow** has low white painted walls and slated mansard roofs with two tiers of prominent dormers; **White Hall** has a long frontage almost entirely filled by small-paned windows with thick white glazing bars, and these, rather than the dun-coloured plaster rendering, presumably give it its name (Plate 12); **Bay House** has the long, easygoing lines of Lutyens' earlier houses, but little of his finesse; and, finally, **The Dunes** reworks his butterfly plan (taken from Papillon Hall, Leicestershire; also *see* How Green House, Hever), and does so with some *élan*, although now spoiled by modern plate-glass windows.

SARRE (6¾ miles WSW of Margate): a small parish on the chalkland at the western end of Thanet with its centre on the Roman road from Canterbury. Shaped gables with stepped quadrants and semicircular tops are much in evidence here; one on **Lamb's Cottage** is dated 1691 in the brickwork, and the gables of **Elleswood** are dated 1739 (Figures 27c and d).

SEAL (2 miles ENE of Sevenoaks): a parish at the foot of the chartland with a built-up street of brick and tile-hung houses. **Stonepitts** has a winged Elizabethan plan with small gabled blocks abutting larger ones and numerous stone mullioned and transomed windows, but the house was heavily modernised after 1928 by the architect G. L. Kennedy.

SELLINDGE (6 miles ESE of Ashford): a parish of scattered settlements on low chartland. Trapped between the Folkestone road and the new motorway, **Somerfield Court** was built about 1700 in red brick with two storeys of blandly proportioned windows beneath an overhanging hipped roof: the best thing about the house is its central pedimented porch with corner pilasters and round-headed front and side openings.

SELLING (2¾ miles SSE of Faversham): a wooded downland parish of scattered settlements, and a centre at Hogben's Hill, where there is a group of brick cottages with thin framing and brick-nogging in the upper storey built around a courtyard. Nearby is a small *cottage orné*, a lodge of Lees Court (*see* Sheldwich), with an immense thatched roof supported on knotted tree trunks (*see* Thatched House, Wateringbury). **The Oast**, Rhode Common, may be a modernised

Wealden, now largely plastered. Opposite, **Rhode Court Farm** is a restored sixteenth-century house, close-studded and jettied to the front and sides, with large clerestoried windows on the left. To the north-west is a close-studded lobby-entry house and **New House Court,** a close-studded hall-house with Kentish framing in the upper storey, and a later jettied cross-wing. Further north is a hall-house with jettied, close-studded wings, and **Well House**, which was built with an open hall and a single aisle.

SEVENOAKS. A small town climbing a spur of the chartland. To the east lies Knole, which grew in importance once Archbishop Bourchier had purchased the manor in 1456. His predecessors had had an interest in the town before then as witnessed by the arms of Archbishop Chichele (1414-43) together with those of Warham (1502-32) on a chimney-piece in **63-65 High Street**, apparently a much altered hall and cross-wing occupied by the archbishop's reeve. At **21-25 London Road** are the remains of another hall-house, but all else belongs to the town's continuing prosperity after the Sackvilles made Knole their home. **The Chantry** established an affluent tone with its projecting wings embracing a small courtyard in front of the house, still with mullioned and transomed casement windows, bands between the storeys and a block cornice beneath the eaves of flared hipped roofs. **The Red House**, which was built in 1686 for John Couchman

Sevenoaks. Old House, High Street.

of Tooting, lacks wings and is more refined (Plate 94), while **Old House**, built a bit later, has a tight centrepiece with a pilastered doorcase and round pediment flanked by circular windows, a similarly flanked sash above, and a deep pediment continuing the block cornice of the main façade. Similar details appear outside the town at **Bradbourne Farmhouse**, a double pile with a formal front and an irregular back (Figure 81). A later and smaller double pile is the painted **Old Vicarage**, which has a rusticated door-case with Doric pilasters and a hood. Giant pilasters articulate the ragstone front of **Manor House**, built about 1800 with a slightly inset centre from which a spindly porch projects, and, at the other end of the town, **The Vine** takes Kent's canted bays and marries them rather unsuccessfully to a late Georgian façade. Shaped gables were

Lime Tree Walk, Sevenoaks. Panorama drawn by its architect, T. G. Jackson.

attractively revived in 1878-9 when the architect Sir T. G. Jackson and his father built cottages for working men in **Lime Tree Walk** (Colour Plate 105), using double curved gables like those which James Pennethorne added to St Julian's, Underriver. There are more shaped gables at **Lynch House**, built with hard red brick in 1899 to designs by Niven and Wigglesworth.

Knole, meanwhile, is out of sight but not out of mind. Thomas Bourchier started work soon after 1456 and was able to occupy his new house eight years later (Figures 47 and 74). At the centre is a hall with a courtyard before it, approached through a tower gate-house (Colour Plate 7), and a second court-yard at the rear, flanked by service rooms. The palatial scale of these works was modestly executed with two-light windows and embattled parapets. Archbishops Morton and Warham made additions, but it was left to Sir Thomas Sackville, Earl of Dorset, to transform the house after 1603 (Colour Plate 68), long after Queen Elizabeth had granted it to him in 1566. He refurbished the interior and added the outer court, which is again fairly plain, but has an impressive four-square turreted gatehouse and shaped gables in the form of quadrants, a step, and a crowning semicircle.

SHELDWICH (2½ miles S of Faversham): a downland parish with several attractive houses strung along a green and scattered settlements. **Cobrahamsole Farmhouse** is a three-part farmhouse with rear wings (Plate 25) and an added brick front dated 1741 and 1743. A much altered hall-house at **North Street** has cross-wings slightly higher at one end, slightly lower at the other. Nearby is a toll house serving the Faversham-Ashford road. Further north, the medieval part of **Copton** is fragmentary; this was a manor of Christ Church, with a stone house, built possibly as early as 1200 with a hall and cross-wing at the high end, both with scissor-braced common-rafter roofs, and bailiff's quarters added at the low end; but little of

Sheldwich. Cobrahamsole Farmhouse; the screens passage, with modern trompe-l'oeil *painting in a blocked service doorway.*

these is visible behind the Georgian and Victorian rebuilding except a length of flint walling and a typical hipped roof with a gablet (Ashenden-Bax 1980). On the road to Selling **Oast Cottage** is a hall-house with Kentish framing and an end jetty, and nearby is a Georgianised framed house with an attractive Roman Doric porch. By contrast, **Lees Court** is utterly atypical of Kent; teasingly associated with Inigo Jones, it shows how his innovations could become the point of departure, probably for a City mason of the utmost imagination. Yet who built the house for Sir George Sondes is unknown and even when this was done is uncertain; Sondes complained about the expense of the house in 1655 as though it had just been completed, but, despite strong City connections, he was a royalist who had been imprisoned between 1645 and 1650, and his fortunes only improved after the Restoration. The use of giant Ionic pilasters to embrace the two storeys of his house shows how far classicism was understood by the middle of the seventeenth century, despite the lack of any strong central emphasis or a feeling for proportion in the façade as a whole (Colour Plate 38). The oddly overhanging roof may well be an eighteenth-century restoration which removed a balustraded parapet, and a fire about 1913 caused further changes as well as destroying the sumptuous interior.

SHEPHERDSWELL (5½ miles NW of Dover): a downland parish with a built-up centre. In a lonely position on the Downs, **West Court Farm** comprises a framed hall-house abutting a three-storeyed brick tower dated 1587, perhaps part of an extensive rebuilding campaign which got no further.

SHIPBOURNE (3¼ miles N of Tonbridge): a wooded chartland parish with a few houses including some estate cottages scattered around an open green. **The Wood House** has far more than local interest: it was designed by Walter Gropius in 1937, following his flight from Nazi Germany, in a style that combines the flat roofs, long bands of windows and free planning on many levels of the Modern Movement, but with the use of natural materials rather than white-painted cement-faced concrete; the cedar weatherboarding which gives the house its name also gives it a Scandinavian flavour rather than a Kentish one (Colour Plate 109). Before it was complete, Gropius had moved on to the United States, taking its style with him, and leaving his former partner Maxwell Fry to finish the work.

SHOREHAM (4¼ miles N of Sevenoaks): a secluded village built on each side of a crossing of the River Darent. **Holly Place**, on the west side, is a hall-house with a jettied cross wing at the service end. Just across the river are **Riverside House**, built in 1774 in red brick chequered with vitrified headers,

Shoreham. Water House.

and, beyond a pretty flint cottage, is **Water House**, again symmetrical, but stuccoed; Samuel Palmer stayed here when he was painting his famous views of the Shoreham landscape between 1827 and 1833.

SHORNE (3¼ miles SE of Gravesend): a wooded parish on the dip-slope of the North Downs with a village street lined with brick and weatherboarded houses running down towards the marshes of the Thames estuary.

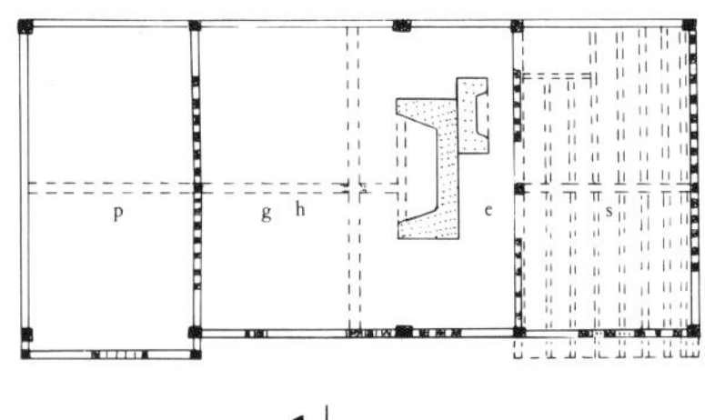

Little St. Katherine's, Shorne. Plan of Wealden hall-house after insertion of chimney-stack in two stages, the first backing cross-passage to heat the hall, the second largely blocking cross-passage to heat the service rooms. (After Mercer 1975 [231].)

Little St Katherine's, a close-studded Wealden, is the most visible of the village's framed houses of the fifteenth and sixteenth centuries.

SISSINGHURST (6 miles WNW of Tenterden): a Wealden parish with a pretty street of tile-hung and weatherboarded houses. The great red brick tower of **Sissinghurst Castle**, rising from the trees around it, has become a symbol of the Weald itself. Its setting is the creation of Vita Sackville-West and Harold Nicolson who purchased the ruins of an Elizabethan courtyard house in 1930 and restored it as their home. The house itself was started by the Bakers, a wealthy Cranbrook family of ironmasters, who had purchased the manor about 1490 and started the brick entrance range; some forty-five years later, the lawyer Sir John Baker completed its gatehouse with an arched entrance set between two gabled towers on the front, each containing brick traceried windows, and flanked by twin chimney-stacks rising into octagonal shafts on the back (Colour Plate 10). Sir John, meanwhile, did well from the Tudors: he served Henry VIII as ambassador to Denmark, as speaker of the House of Commons and as attorney general, lining his pocket at the same time, and then became Chancellor of the Exchequer, under Edward, Mary and Elizabeth in turn, a remarkable feat of survival. His son, Sir Richard Baker, succeeded in 1558, and began to spend his father's fortune on the courtyard house of which only the great tower and a few other fragments survive; an engraving shows projecting bays, gables and tall chimney-stacks, all complete to receive Queen Elizabeth during her Progress through the Weald in 1573. The surviving tower only shows the halting classicism of the period: the arch on the courtyard side and the window above are flanked by pilasters carrying entablatures executed in plastered brickwork (Plate 40); but otherwise it is remarkably plain despite the picturesque qualities of the attached polygonal staircase turrets (Colour Plate 66). The decay of the family fortunes through espousing the Royalist cause and the eventual decay of the house has a poignant ending because Vita Sackville-West was a direct descendent of the Bakers.

SITTINGBOURNE. A small town built up along the old Dover road at the head of Milton Creek. **No. 49 High Street** stands out from a few surviving Georgian houses for its stuccoed front with twin bows containing large, three-light sashes with fans enriching the cambered relieving arches over them, and a central Doric porch carrying a cast-iron balcony.

SMALLHYTHE (2 miles SSE of Tenterden): a parish on a clay eminence with a street running down to the Rother Levels where once there was a harbour, hence the name. This served Tenterden, which became a Limb of Rye in 1449, and was also an important centre of shipbuilding until the channel silted up in the later sixteenth century. A disastrous fire swept the street in 1516, immediately causing Archbishop Warham to instigate the rebuilding of the church, notably in brick with crow-stepped gables, the first in Kent. Two framed houses came

Smallhythe. Photographed nearly a hundred years ago: beyond the church is, first, The Priest's House, then the roof of Smallhythe Place.

soon afterwards, the so-called **Priest's House** and **Smallhythe Place**. These modern names are without significance, and the houses owed their undoubted status to wealth encouraged by the port. Both are close-studded and jettied along their fronts as an advertisement of their full upper storeys, uninterrupted by an open hall, a real innovation at the time. This was made possible at Smallhythe Place by a smoke bay, soon filled by a chimney-stack, and by a chimney-stack at The Priest's House from the very start (Colour Plate 65); both are multi-flued and served back-to-back hearths in the single-storeyed halls and the parlours which backed them in the two houses.

SMARDEN (8 miles W of Ashford): a Wealden parish of scattered settlements in the vale of the River Beult, centred on a market town licensed by Edward III in 1332, and now just a small village. Its former wealth shows in numerous fine houses. The village street starts with **Chessenden** (formerly Smarden House), a lavish Wealden, jettied at both ends as well as to the front, close-studded in the centre and made grander when the hall was floored over and given a

Sittingbourne. 49 High Street.

canted bay at its upper end with two storeys of windows and a jettied gable with a further window to light the garret formed in the roof (Colour Plate 48 and Figure 51). A short way along comes **Dragon House**, a hall with a projecting jettied wing at the chamber end, perhaps once containing a shop, which has a jettied half-hip, and a frieze of dragons carved on its fascia (Plate 29). The mid-fifteenth-century jetties of **Churchgate House** mark a divide in the street filled by the churchyard. One way immediately leads to **Hartnup House** (Figure 26i), built as yet another hall-house, with a doorway carved with the roses of York and Lancaster in the spandrels of its arch, indicating a date before 1485, and a large jettied cross-wing at the service end, close-studded in the ground storey, the rest modernised with brick-nogging and a tall canted bay rising into a jettied gable and inscribed with Dr Matthew Hartnup's name and the date of his third marriage, 1671, to Joanna Newenden (Mills 1932). **The Cloth Hall** (formerly Turk Farm), next door, is another Wealden, close-studded and extended into a tile-hung gable at one end; far more interestingly, the other end has a hoist and two doorways, one in the jettied first storey, the second above it opening into the roof, both protected by an overhanging extension of the roof. These must be taking-in doors for bales of wool, unusually clear evidence of the cloth industry which gave the Weald its late medieval prosperity. Another overhanging roof-end appears outside the village at **Langley**, where the upper taking-in door has been replaced by a window and weatherboarding conceals the rest. Among other outlying framed houses are **Westhoy**, a close-studded Wealden with coved eaves, notable for a surviving louvered opening to one of its service rooms, **The Fleece House**, an early hall with a restored window, a two-centred entrance and a jetty at the service end, **Fullers Farm** and **Littlegates**, two more hall-houses with end jetties, the aptly named but otherwise similar **Thatched House**, and **Watch House**, where the front jetty runs from end to end and a single chimney heats both the chamber and the single-storeyed hall (*see* Smallhythe). **Marley Farm**, opposite, contains the remains of a framed and plastered firehood. Smarden's prize is **Hamden**, though brick hides its framing and only the low sweep of its roof and the massive derns forming a two-centred arch for its entrance give a clue to its origin (Colour Plate 5 and Figure 12). This was probably towards the middle of the fourteenth century, after one of the Hamdens had cleared this part of the Weald for a farm and established the family's wealth soundly enough for a John Hamden to endow the parish church in 1361 with an annual income of six shillings. What was built was a large hall, over 21ft. (6.5 m) wide, which is not in itself rare, but unusually was aisled at each end and had its central truss supported on base-crucks from which a spectacular arch springs across the hall (Figure 14). This avoided the encumbrance of arcade-posts

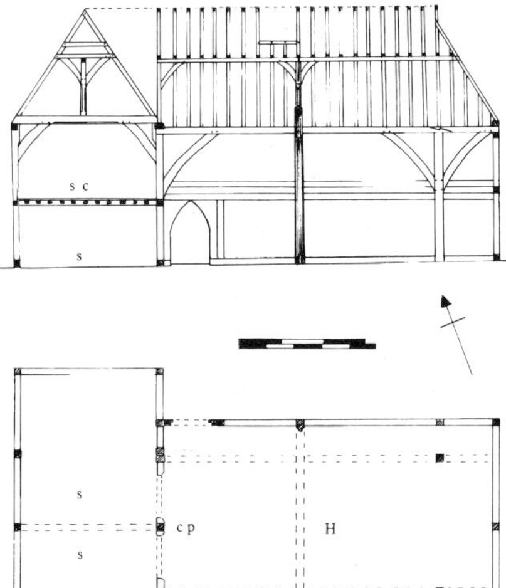

Hamden, Smarden. Plan and longitudinal section, showing possible cantilevered high end, which may have contained a chamber, open to the roof. (After Rigold 1967.)

and gives the hall a magnificence unparalleled in Kent, and not attained in the base-cruck halls of Sussex. The arrangements at the high end of the hall are unclear, but it may have ended in a cantilevered bay, typical of large Kentish barns and also found at the primitive level of Dormer Cottage at Petham; the low end, meanwhile, was in the form of a storeyed cross-wing, part of which survives behind the brick casing.

SNODLAND (4¾ miles SW of Rochester): a large, industrial village with much speculative housing beside the Medway where it breaks through the North Downs. **Mulberry Cottage**, a heavily restored Wealden with a long band of windows at one end, which may be evidence of a shop, and a second, close-studded Wealden in **Constitution Hill** provide a welcome contrast; at **Paddlesworth** a derelict house of about 1700 like a small version of Somerfield Court at Sellindge is flanked by barns and faces an equally disused church.

SOUTHFLEET (3 miles SW of Gravesend): a downland parish with a pronounced centre at crossroads by the church. Here, **Church Cottages** form a Wealden, and there is a second one in **Red Street**, which has close-studding only in the upper part of the hall bays and a cove beneath the eaves. Rather earlier than either is **The Old Rectory**, which was built of flint, perhaps for Thomas of Alkham after 1323, with a hall and cross wings, the southern one possibly being an earlier chamber block or 'upper hall'; the windows have cusped tracery (Colour Plate 54).

STAPLEHURST (8 miles S of Maidstone): a Wealden parish (Colour Plate 1) with a long village street built along the Roman road running southward from the River Beult. **Loddenden Manor** (Plate 72), at the top end, was never a manor, despite its name and size, but owes the grand effect of its close-studding and fully jettied front to the Usbornes, a family who farmed the Weald on a big scale and added the profits of tanning to their wealth. Thomas Usborne is the likely builder, perhaps in 1566; a chimney-stack economically planned with back-to-back hearths serves a single-storeyed hall, where cooking was originally done, as well as the chamber or parlour beyond, and the two chambers above (Cowper 1911). Half way down the street are **Crown Cottages**, also close-studded and jettied, and possibly not much later; each of the three is double-fronted with two rooms per floor (Colour Plate 92). Just opposite the church is **Kent Cottage**, a low hall-house with chamber and service ends, the latter built as a wing with timbers felled about 1394 (Howard *et al.* 1991). At the south end of the street, is **Fuller House**, close-studded, jettied and twice gabled, with triangular-headed windows, self-consciously Tudoresque, taking the place of Georgian sashes which had themselves replaced the original; the chimney-stack has an unusually crenellated top (Figure 26c). Outside the village, there is another rich collection of framed houses: **Coppwilliam**, in Marden Road, was built with timbers felled in 1370/71 (Howard *et al.* 1991) as a low hall with a rear aisle; **Little Pagehurst** is a Wealden, and **Harts Heath Farm** two thirds of a Wealden (Plate 59); **Husheath**, of about 1600, is fully jettied along the front and at each end, with oriels lighting the upper chambers over the hall and in the high end, which rise into jettied gables, the end one so large as to have the form of a cross-wing; and, finally, **Great Pagehurst**, now obscured by tile-hanging, is dominated by a magnificent chimney-stack with four octagonal shafts becoming star-shaped at their crowns (Figure 26g).

STONE (4½ miles W of Gravesend): a built-up downland parish overlooking the Thames, in the shadow of cement works. **Stone Rectory** is a mid eighteenth-century triple pile, each pile marked by a hipped roof, with an attractive staircase with twisted balusters.

STONE IN OXNEY (5¼ miles SE of Tenterden): a parish of scattered houses at the east end of a clay island rising above the Rother Levels. Close to the church is **Tilmenden**, a small Wealden with a bracketed oriel perching beneath the eaves.

SUNDRIDGE (2¾ miles W of Sevenoaks): a wooded parish of scattered settlements stretching up the chartland. Among several brick houses built along the Sevenoaks road is **Old Hall**, a close-studded Wealden with a restored hall window beneath coved eaves (Vallance 1925). In complete antithesis, **Combe Bank** is a Palladian mansion built by the architect Roger Morris for Colonel John Campbell, 4th Duke of Argyll. The design is heavily based on Lord Burlington's Tottenham

Park, Wiltshire, of 1721, and probably followed it closely in years as well; it comprises a four-square main block of two storeys with projecting corner turrets, a storey higher, and a front porch joined to the turrets by colonnades, and a projecting pedimented rear (Colour Plate 86).

SUTTON VALENCE (5¼ miles SE of Maidstone): a wooded parish with a long High Street running along the scarp of the chartland and scattered settlements above and below it. Among the plaster, tile-hanging and weatherboarding of the High Street, exemplified by **Ye Olde Poste House**, are two Wealdens, close together, one the Swan

Sutton Valence. Valence House.

Inn. The plain, plastered frame of **Valence House** emphasises the complete symmetry of its lobby-entry plan; a balustraded porch rises into a second storey with a three-light window, the central light arched forming an Ipswich window *(see* 78 Bank Street, Maidstone, of 1611), beneath a bargeboarded gable; this pattern of windows and gables is repeated in the body of the house, which has a projecting bay each side with two storeys of Ipswich windows, and a jettied gable. The date 1598 carved on a finial makes this the earliest rigidly symmetrical lobby-entry house *(see* Honywood, Lenham, and Bishops Farm, Boughton Monchelsea, for two others nearby), but the Ipswich windows appear to be later insertions. **Linden House** was built of brick early in the eighteenth century, and there are similar houses in the lower street; **Tudor Cottage** may be earlier than the sixteenth century; **Spring Cottages** are inscribed 'J. Higgens Builder 1854' and mix red and yellow bricks in a way typical of that date; meanwhile **Motto House** is inscribed with no less than five improving texts. South of the village, below the scarp, **Hennikers** hides an early open hall built of timber felled about 1356-91 behind tile-hanging (Howard *et al.* 1988) which was modernised with a lobby-entry plan; a nineteenth century oast adjoins to the south (Plate 6). Further south at Farthing Green, **Greenways Farm** is another early hall-house, with Kentish framing and an arched doorway. Yet another framed house opposite has an end jetty.

TENTERDEN. Unlike other Wealden towns, Tenterden enjoyed the benefits of proximity to the sea and a good harbour on the River Rother at Smallhythe. In 1332 Edward III confirmed its role as a trading town by licensing a market, and in 1449 the town became a Limb of Rye. The resulting wealth gave the parish church its magnificent tower, built leisurely in the second half of the fifteenth century to overlook the High Street, and arguably the finest in all Kent (Plate 1). Although the harbour silted up rapidly in the later sixteenth century and the Wealden cloth industry had become a shadow of its former self a hundred years later, Tenterden continued to attract trade and is still recognisably a town, unlike Smarden. William Cobbett called it 'a singularly bright spot' in 1823: 'It consists of one street, which is, in some places, more, perhaps, than two hundred feet wide' (1912, 230) — just right for a flourishing market.

The town's houses confirm this ancient and continuing prosperity. More or less opposite the church, **Tudor Rose Tea Rooms** is evidently a Wealden, large, close-studded and late, probably contemporary with the church tower, and modernised by a jettied floor inserted into the hall and continuing the line of the jettied ends, but happily lacking a chimney-stack breaking through the hipped roof. More close-studding just doors away, and several steeply pitched hipped roofs attest to the town's early wealth; **Pittlesden Gatehouse**, 91 High Street, is an earlier and far smaller version of the standard three-unit hall-house, complete with Kentish framing and a hipped roof, which may have been one of three gatehouses to a large mansion. The way timber-framing continued here is evident in the number of later houses which are still framed but endeavour to disguise what had become an unfashionable building material with mathematical tiling. Among the earlier of these houses is **19-21 High Street**, which has two storeys of sash windows over its shop fronts and a hoist serving a full-height loading bay on one side, showing that it was used as a workshop as well; the illusion of red tiles looking like brickwork is completed by wooden quoins and a modillion cornice, but round the corner ordinary tile-hanging begins (Colour Plate 47). The same pattern appears again in a row of four jettied houses, now **Halifax Property Services**, although here the tiles are brown and the jetty is marked by a fascia patterned with grooves; beneath the jetty the doorways have moulded architraves with imposts and keystones and the walls are faced with plaster channelled to look like masonry to complete the deception. **No. 16 High Street** carries the deception into the nineteenth century with a yellow tiled façade which successfully turns at each end, and a spindly porch with fanlight and open pediment complete its pursuit of elegance. Mathematical tiles were used to good effect from about 1700 onwards in numerous houses just beyond the centre. **Yew Tree House** and **Miriam House**, East Cross, a terraced pair, have a brick ground storey, tiled above, and a bracketed hood to one house, a fanlight and a spindly porch to the other. **East Hill House** follows the

Tenterden. East Hill House.

established pattern with bright red mathematical tiles for the front and plain overlapping tiles for the sides of its two piles; but makes a show of its own with an unusually wide front door set within a pilastered doorcase carrying a pediment on a modillioned frieze, over which comes a Venetian window with a rusticated arch, and, finally, an *oeuil-de-boeuf* with spiralling tracery just below a typical modillion cornice. **Nos. 7-13 Smallhythe Road** were probably built well over a century later, perhaps as late as 1840, with yellow tiles, partly painted white, over a boarded ground storey, grooved to look like masonry blocks. This pattern was already established by **Craythorne House**, newly built in 1790, a double pile with a copybook Doric doorcase flanked by typical canted bays rising up all three storeys. A house attached to a tower in **East Cross** does much the same in a very modest way, but the plain rendered front of **White House** appears to be covering nothing less common than ordinary brick, and its pilastered three-light windows, arched in Venetian form on the ground floor, and pedimented Ionic doorcase stand out with some *élan*.

Not all of Tenterden's houses are dressed to seem what they are not. **Nos. 8-11 East Cross** are simply tilehung, but rise to three-storeyed canted bays, pilastered doorcases with fanlights and pediments, wooden quoins at each end and, typically, a modillion cornice. **Westfield House** displays the taste of 1700 with a real sense of occasion in the well-proportioned but modest detailing dressing the front of its two piles; all of these could have appealed to Lutyens, and so would the two large, quite plain chimney-stacks marking the line of the spine wall which rise above the hipped roof. There is nothing modest about its neighbour, **Westwell**, which is markedly more baroque as well as larger: the three central windows are flanked by ovals and grouped more closely than the outer pairs, and, over the pilastered and bracketed doorcase and hood of the entrance, Doric pilasters rise each side of the central window to the level of a full-length cornice and support a small broken pediment which carries the date 1711 (Colour Plate 82). No other eighteenth-century house in Tenterden touches this display, although there are several attractive ones down Smallhythe Road such as **Chestnut House, The Cedars,** which has a bow window at the back with an unusual embattled parapet, and **Morghew**, which has Tenterden's standard canted bays and a modillion cornice, but also a rusticated Venetian window over its copybook doorcase; **Heronden**, meanwhile, shows just how severe Georgian taste could become by 1818 when reduced to plain lines executed in yellow brick.

The outlying countryside is full of good houses too, starting with **Knock Farm**, where a jetty heaves its way uphill and downhill across a chamber bay, up a step and across what was possibly a recessed Wealden hall, to reach the long service end; Kentish framing suggests an early fifteenth-century date, although the entrance has a four-centred head, and the modernisation included inserted windows extended by clerestories. The lobby-entry plan was apparently first used in the late sixteenth century for the wonderfully rustic **Briton House** at St Michael's, whose close-studding and clerestoried windows appear through the leaves of encroaching creepers (Colour Plate 72). The much altered and extended **Finchden Manor**, Leigh Green, is again close-studded, and also jettied and gabled, and carries the date 1658. Opposite, **Priory Farm** was built perhaps thirty or forty years beforehand with small panelling filled with brick-nogging and a lobby-entry plan based on a tall chimney-stack with oversailing courses (Figure 26b). The prize among these lobby-entry houses nevertheless goes to **Brunger Farm** (Colour Plate 76), again at Leigh Green, whose licheny brickwork carried up to crow-stepped gables, even for its segmentally arched porch, gives it instant appeal *(see* School Farm, Ash). Tenterden's more simple traditions come to the fore at **Goods Hill Cottages**, a weatherboarded terrace with the plainest of Venetian windows beneath yet another modillion cornice, and in the plain Georgian façades of **Kench Hill** and **Homewood**, the latter dated 1766, which are as alike as peas in a pod.

TEYNHAM (3½ miles WNW of Faversham): a fertile parish of orchards on the dip-slope of the Downs overlooking the marshes of the Thames estuary. Lambarde recognised this, calling the locality 'the cherry garden and the apple orchard of Kent'. The demolition of Newgardens is therefore all the sadder since its reputed builder was Richard Harrys, Henry VIII's Fruiterer and, in 1533, the first man to grow cherries in Kent. **Lower Newlands** is one of Kent's later aisled hall-houses (Plate 51), built about 1385 (Howard *et al.* 1988) with a down-swept main roof extending over the aisles and two higher, jettied cross-wings *(see* Fairfield, Eastry). **Bank Farmhouse** shows the more normal Wealden way of achieving the same thing, but it is later in date, close-studded, and now partly tile-hung and brick-nogged; the **Old Post Office** at **Teynham Street** is another Wealden. More timber framing appears at **Home Farm, Deerton Street**, an early sixteenth century house with a wing at the front of about 1600, jettied between the storeys and again beneath the gable, and

Teynham. Frognal Farm, the framed western range.

Teynham. Frognal Farm, the brick eastern range.

windows once extended by clerestories. This kind of framing was still in use in 1668, witness the four jettied gables of **Frognal Farm**, one of them filled with decorative crosses and circles, once covered over with grooved plaster in imitation of rusticated masonry; this house Janus-like was made to face the other way as well, with the addition of a second pile hardly more than forty or fifty years later, which has a fashionable brick façade with sash windows, a lovely doorcase with a broken scrolly pediment on brackets, and a block eaves cornice to welcome the eighteenth century.

THANINGTON (1½ miles SW of Canterbury): a parish of orchards in the valley of the Great Stour. The remains of **Tonford Manor** show little more than the lower levels of the flint and stone turreted walls of a gatehouse and hall with a small courtyard between them, built by Henry VI's Comptroller and Treasurer Thomas Browne, with a licence to crenellate in 1449. The north-west front has flint towers diapered with red brick, and the courtyard was faced in brick (Plate 39). The hall had a hammerbeam roof made of chestnut, and this survives within the eighteenth-century house built into the ruins.

THROWLEY (3½ miles SSW of Faversham): a wooded downland parish of small settlements. **Church Cottages** were probably built in the sixteenth century with a continuous jetty along the front. Among a number of attractive cottages at **Throwley Forstal** is at least one hall-house. **Snoad Street Farm**, though unfortunately painted, is an early seventeenth-century brick house, still with a medieval three-part plan although fully storeyed, with a full-height gabled porch and deep windows continued by clerestories with boldly moulded hoodmoulds. **Belmont** was built for George Harris, veteran of the American War of Independence, who retired here in 1787 to recuperate before going on to fight in India, eventually to be made a general and, in 1815, created Baron Harris. His architect was Samuel Wyatt, who reconstructed a previous house and, very unusually in such grand circumstances, faced it with mathematical tiles *(see* Chevening Park); it is in his typically spare neo-classical style, with domed bows turning the corners of the garden front, and a camellia house at one side, tall pilasters framing its windows (Colour Plate 46). Perhaps contemporary is

Throwley. New York.

New York, a pair of cottages which the architect John Plaw designed in an American style, that is with verandas on three sides carried on shallow arches, and published in his *Ferme ornée* in 1795.

TILMANSTONE (3¾ miles W of Deal): a downland parish with a leafy built-up street. A tiny two-roomed cottage with a loft nevertheless has shaped gables at each end with quadrants, and semicircles above a step. **Church House** is a brick lobby-entry house dated 1702, and, though larger, lacks gables of any kind.

TONBRIDGE. A crossing point over the Medway gave the town its name; this was guarded by a castle, and a town grew up along the street running northwards from the river. **Tonbridge Castle** was slighted in 1646, and the house built beside the gatehouse became the country home of the playwright and theatre designer Samuel Beazley (Colour Plate 22); he also became architect to the South Eastern Railway *(see* Ashford New Town), and died here in 1851. In the **High Street** a number of framed houses were built on undercrofts in the common medieval way, with shops at ground level and chambers above, for instance at **Moss Bros** and its neighbour, **The Chequers.** The **Portreeve's House** in East Street may also have been first built in the Middle Ages, but its prominent gabled end, with bracketed oriels extended by clerestories beneath jetties, is a seventeenth-century addition. Two houses at the top of the High Street are now part of Tonbridge School: **Ferox Hall**, which was built in red brick in 1755 with giant corner and central pilasters and a projecting porch supported by Roman Doric columns, and, opposite, a pretty weatherboarded house with sash windows and canted bays. South-east of the town is **Somerhill**, part of the castle demesne, which came by marriage to the 4th Earl of Clanricarde about 1603. He put in hand the construction of a new house which was being finished about 1613; it has an H-plan (Figure 76) devised by the surveyor John Thorpe, with a centrally placed hall in the advanced manner of Charlton House (now Greenwich, London) and at precisely the same time; but Somerhill's main accents come from traditional canted bays and gables (Colour Plate 11), and it lacks Charlton House's copybook mannerist centrepiece, and has instead a round-arched entrance set between Doric pilasters and a frieze of triglyphs beneath an embattled parapet. In 1697 Celia Fiennes remarked on its 'good sizeable roomes leading one out of another in visto's thro' the house, something like our new way of building' (Morris 1984, 128); that was perceptive, but she failed to elaborate on the disreputable owners of the house: it had passed to Lady Muskerry, a jolly woman who called herself Lady Purbeck following her marriage to the son of a bastard son of a real Lady Purbeck; ugly and deformed, she enjoyed dancing in public, earning the name 'Princess of Babylon'; at the death of her husband in a duel, she married Robert 'Beau' Feilding; surviving her, he in turn was tricked into marrying Mary Wadsworth, a prostitute impersonating a rich widow, and then bigamously married the Duchess of Cleveland.

TONGE (2 miles E of Sittingbourne): a fertile parish of orchards and open fields overlooking the marshes of the Swale. Between orchards and marsh are the brick walls of

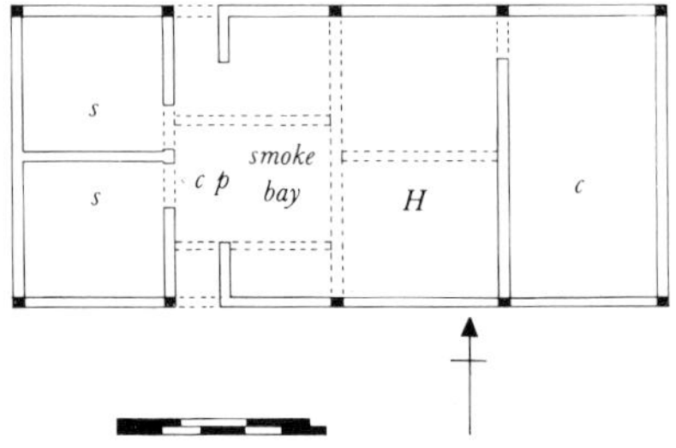

Tonge Corner, Tonge. Plan, showing position of inserted smoke bay in hall and gallery. (After Swain 1968.)

Tonge Corner, hiding a medieval hall-house which lacked jetties, and was progressively modernised, first by forming a smoke bay over part of the low end of the hall with a floor inserted across the high end, joined to the floor over the services by a gallery at the front and a more extensively floored space at the rear, and, later, by building a chimney-stack into the bay, completing the upper floor, encasing the house in brick and giving it sash windows (Swain 1968). Inland, **Bunce's Farm** is a Wealden with an inserted floor higher than its jettied ends, sitting out in the open fields. Nearby, the mixture of

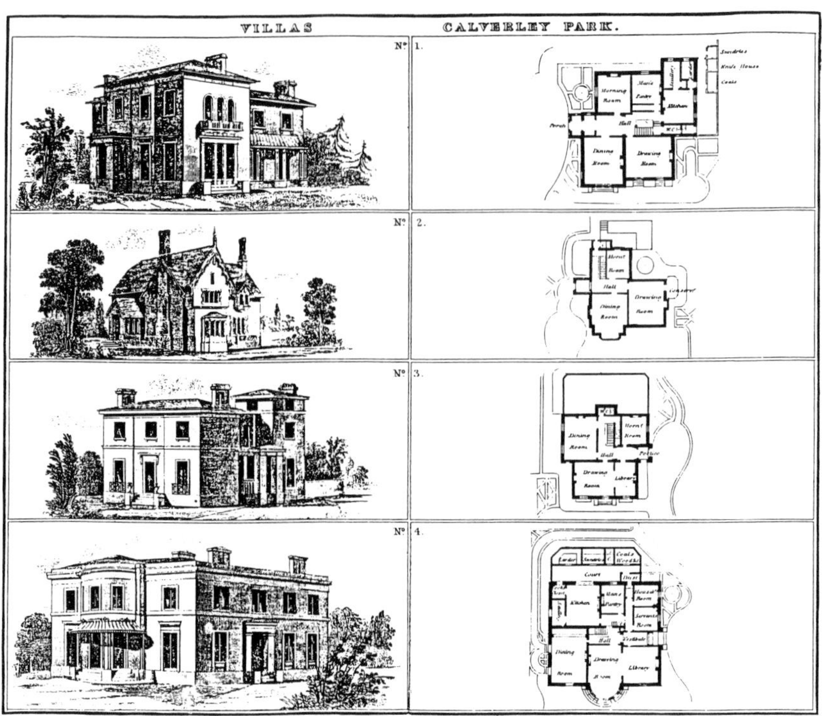

Views and plans of four villas built to Decimus Burton's designs in Calverley Park, Tunbridge Wells. (After Britton's Topographical Sketches of Tunbridge Wells.)

flint and ragstone, brick and close-studding of **Bax Farm** belongs to what was probably the service wing of an H-plan house, which once had a central hall range and a balancing wing; the date 1567 over a doorway is probably good for the crow-stepped gable (Colour Plate 69 and Figure 27b) and the breasts of the two prominent chimney-stacks, but their shafts have been renewed. Already on the lowest downland slopes are the brick walls of **Woodstreet House**, which was built about 1776 for John May of Sittingbourne with a lovely dove-grey brick front with twin red brick canted bays of the Kent kind, symmetrically arranged each side of a polygonal entrance porch with an ogee-headed doorway reflected by an ogee-headed sash above set under a relieving arch. At the southernmost tip of the parish, the derelict **Newbury Farmhouse** has an ancient form of aisled hall with passing-braces and a plain collared roof without crown-posts or plates, the form of framing which was current in the thirteenth century but died out soon afterwards, and attached to it is a stone chamber block.

TUNBRIDGE WELLS. Only the extraordinary whim of fashion could have created a town in the densest part of the Wealden heights with no obvious ancient route to the outside world. Lord North's discovery of the chalybeate springs was therefore less important than the realisation of how profitable their exploitation could be. Nevertheless, it was only after the Restoration that Tunbridge Wells attracted large crowds. At first, visitors stayed elsewhere, but cheap lodgings were erected in great numbers before the end of the seventeenth century. The Wells attracted all sorts, but, despite the fashionable Pantiles, where visitors could stroll up and down and, indeed, engage in less reputable pursuits, Tunbridge Wells was not to become a town until 1828 when John Ward employed the youthful architect Decimus Burton to lay out the Calverley Estate. It was to be developed with 'edifices suitable to the reception of genteel families', as Colbran's guide of 1840 reported. The railway arrived in 1845, and since then Tunbridge Wells has changed from a fashionable resort into a refuge of disgusted conservatism and changed again into a commuter town, partly dependent on London, partly competing with London.

The Pantiles lies at three levels, winding away from the chalybeate spring, with its famous colonnaded shops on the west side; on the east, beyond the lime trees and balustrades, are terraces of stuccoed houses and hotels at a lower level. Above the colonnades, the houses are characterised by weatherboarding, grooved to suggest masonry, and by canted bays rising to plain eaves cornices, the stock-in-trade of small Kent towns in the eighteenth and nineteenth centuries (Colour Plate 15). Nearby at **6 and 7 Cumberland Walk** the same taste appears again in two houses of about 1830, No. 7 embraced by giant pilasters with the ammonite capitals used as a trademark in Lewes and Brighton by the architect Amon Wilds; **8 Cumberland Walk**, rather later, is faced in flint cobbles with yellow brick trimmings and a fretted, cast-iron balcony rising up to second-floor level (Colour Plates 90 and 91). After the brick and bracketed bow windows of **Bedford Terrace** come the stucco and bow windows characterising the best houses in **Mount Sion** and also porches, those at **Nos. 19-21** with deeply fluted columns, typical of the oddities in the late Georgian style of the 1830s. More contemporary bow windows appear in **Grove Hill Road**. Burton's **Calverley Park Crescent** picks up the arcades of The Pantiles, slender, here, and gracefully curving in front of what had been designed to be shops, but soon were converted to domestic use; above, the fine sandstone ashlar of the terrace rises three storeys into an accented parapet in the centre and at each end (Plate 98). The villas of **Calverley Park** follow what Nash had inaugurated at Regent's Park, but handsomely executed in Wealden sandstone with variations on an italianate theme of bows, bays and balconies, done with telling panache (Colour Plates 25 and 99). When **Camden Park** was started twenty years later, stucco and a heavier touch were the rule, but the original scheme was never completed. In **London Road**, the varying taste of Tunbridge Wells from its beginnings in the late seventeenth century can be seen in several individual houses, for instance the tile-hung **Thackeray's House**, and a few terraces of distinction. There are several imposing Victorian villas along Pembury Road, one in Sandown Park,

Tunbridge Wells. Pembury Grange, Sandown Park, when new, from a photograph in Devey's collection (copyright RIBA).

Pembury Grange (formerly Calverley Grange), being in George Devey's picturesque Old English style, with brick diapering, half-timbering and plaster enlivening its gabled elevations; he built it in 1869-71 for Neville Ward, and extended it in 1881 (Allibone 1991, 160, 175).

TUNSTALL (1¼ miles SSW of Sittingbourne): a downland parish of orchards with an attractive winding village street. **Tunstall House** was built of warm brick, probably in the middle of the seventeenth century, with large wooden framed mullioned and transomed casement windows set under wide relieving arches on its two storeys which are continued into small gables; the old arrangement of services, hall and chamber evidently still survived here, and the gabled, full-height porch is therefore offset towards the service end, its entrance marked by a Doric pilastered

doorcase, arched and completed with a pediment. **Hales House** is a plainer and reduced version, gabled only over the porch and over a slightly projecting bay at the high end of the hall.

ULCOMBE (6½ miles SE of Maidstone): a wooded chartland parish with a street of houses. Descending Knowle Hill are: **Knowle Hill House**, a small double-pile refronted in 1736 in brown brick with plain pilasters and bands dividing it into panels; **Upper Knowle Hill Farmhouse**, which has an uncommon arch-braced gable (*see* Shakespeare House, Headcorn), but the rest of its framing is hidden by tile-hanging; and the former rectory, now **Lower Knowle Hill Farmhouse**, timber-framed and also tile-hung, with large gabled cross-wings, a projecting gabled bay in the centre serving the hall and, off-centre, a small gabled porch. Further down, a Wealden is again tile-hung along the upper storey with a length of close-studding under the eaves. **King's Manor Farm** has a prominent gabled wing, close-studded and twice jettied, with an oriel in the upper storey, once extended by clerestories.

UNDERRIVER (2 miles SE of Sevenoaks): a wooded chartland parish of scattered settlements below the scarp. **St Julian's** was built in 1818-20 to the designs of J. B. Papworth and enlarged in 1835-8 for John Charles Herries, statesman, financier, and economist; later he became MP for Harwich and, briefly and unsuccessfully, Chancellor of the Exchequer. His house is ideally placed on the scarp with long views over the Weald, just like the views from another house built a century later for an unsuccessful Chancellor — Chartwell. The architect of the later works was James Pennethorne, who provided a gabled triple pile with bargeboarded gables down each side, the northern ones now replaced, and three Jacobean shaped gables across the front, no doubt based on Knole, which is just over the hilltop. Beneath these gables are three symmetrical bays with chamfered corners, with triplets of Tudor four-centred lights, to each of the two storeys.

WALMER (1¾ miles SSW of Deal): like Deal, a Limb of Sandwich, but part of the borough of Deal since 1935; it was never of much consequence but for **Walmer Castle**. This was one of Henry VIII's fortifications defending the anchorage of The Downs, and now the official home of the Warden of the Cinque Ports; it was converted for domestic use about 1730 by the first Warden, the Duke of Dorset, and given an appropriately embattled domestic range; the Duke of Wellington, a later Warden, thought it was 'the most charming marine residence he had ever seen', and it was further enlarged by George Devey in 1863 to provide extra bedrooms for the second Earl Granville, with a shaped gable and a picturesque tower (Saunders 1969; Allibone 1991, 163). The fortifications of **Walmer Court** are of an earlier period; its ruined flint walls just outside the churchyard belong to a semi-fortified house with a first-floor hall and chamber built over an undercroft (Figure 38), probably in the third quarter of the twelfth century by the Aubevilles, sub-tenants of the Archbishop (Rigold 1969b); this soon fell into ruin, eventually to be replaced in the early nineteenth century by a three-storeyed double pile with canted bays rising symmetrically through two storeys beside the entrance porch (Colour Plate 53). Among a number of other Georgian houses nearby, **275 Dover Road** stands out as a large Gothic *cottage orné* with two gabled cross-wings and, running between them, an impossibly large triple-arched veranda, reminiscent of James Hall's fantastic illustration of a 'Wicker Cathedral' or 'Gothic Hut' of 1797 (Colour Plate 102).

Walmer Castle. View after conversion to a house before Devey's enlargements.

WAREHORNE (6½ miles S of Ashford): a small parish on the clay ridge overlooking Romney Marsh. **Leacon Hall** stands out for its prominent site and ideal shape: it was built in 1708 for Thomas Hodges as a double pile, with red and vitrified bricks with bright rubbed brick heads to the sash windows of the ground floor and a wooden block cornice giving it the easy appearance that Lutyens strove to recapture two centuries later (Colour Plate 81).

WATERINGBURY (5½ miles WSW of Maidstone): a chartland parish of orchards with a built-up centre including a Wealden hall-house at the crossroads. Thomas Style's **Wateringbury Place** was built in 1707 with the full range of Kent's warm-tinted bricks to enliven a façade articulated by giant Ionic pilasters with a projecting centrepiece, and finished by a bracketed frieze with a panelled parapet above it. **Thatched House** is one of a small group of early nineteenth-century *cottages ornées* in Kent with an overhanging thatched roof supported by rough trunks (*see* Lees Court lodge, Selling).

WESTBERE (3¾ miles NE of Canterbury): a small parish squeezed between the Roman Sarre Wall and the Great Stour. The towny **Westbere House** was built early in the nineteenth century of brick, now painted to resemble stone, with a thin, pedimented Ionic doorcase and elliptical fanlight in the centre, and a mansard roof behind the parapet, which rises slightly at each end for canted bays facing outwards.

WEST CLIFFE (2¾ miles NE of Dover): a small downland parish close to South Foreland. **Wallets Court** was built for Matthew Gibbon in 1627 in red brick, now largely painted, with four carved pilasters on tall plinths articulating the right-hand side of the front (Plate 43) and three more, rather shorter, more widely spaced pilasters doing the same for the left-hand side; the naïvity of this attempted classicism appeared close to London in 1634-5 at 66 Crooms Hill, Greenwich, and probably as late as 1698 at Vicarage House, Wingham; a canted bay on the left-hand return has two storeys of windows with brick mullions and transoms, two lights deep, below, three lights above, with a kind of crude pediment over it, but the rest of the windows are inserted sashes.

WESTERHAM (5¾ miles W of Sevenoaks): the westernmost parish of Kent, hence the name, stretching from the scarp of the North Downs across the vale and up into the chartland, with a long built-up street, once the centre of a thriving market town. The street starts with **Quebec House**, built mostly of brick with some ragstone in the lower stages as a double pile with triple gables to front and back, and along both sides (Plate 83). The angled parapets and ball finials of the gables, and the flat hood-moulds over the windows suggest a date before 1650, but these belong to a rebuild of an earlier house, and there has been much rebuilding of the front since then. The house is famed as the home of James Wolfe from soon after his birth until he was eleven when his family moved to Greenwich. Across the road, **Grosvenor House** has a wide façade of vitrified brick trimmed with bright red brick and ending in giant pilasters supporting a deep cornice. A short way up the hill, **Darenth**, a Wealden with a built-out wing for a shop, comes before the green and its rustic weather-boarding and tile-hanging. **Squerries Lodge** contains fragments, including a cusped, traceried window, of a thirteenth-century stone house, perhaps with an upper hall or chamber. On toward Surrey come **49-51 High Street**, a hall-house with a jettied cross-wing at the service end, which was modernised, first by forming a smoke bay, then by inserting a chimney-stack and completing the upper floor over the hall (Colour Plate 64). Behind the town is **Squerries Court**, a large, rather plain house built for the merchant who gained a monopoly of trade with Guinea, customs farmer and royalist Sir Nicholas Crisp, soon after he purchased the estate in 1680; it is a triple pile, with the centre of both front and back slightly projecting beneath a pediment, above which is the usual low-pitched hipped roof with large chimney-stacks, attractively panelled (Plate 85). Looking out from a wonderful position on the chartland scarp is Sir Winston Churchill's **Chartwell**, recast by the architect Philip Tilden in 1923; the original house is still visible in the centre of the entrance front, and everything that happens about it is curiously haphazard, although, from some angles, the conjunction of stepped gables and turreted weathervane is very pretty (Plate 18).

WEST FARLEIGH (3 miles WSW of Maidstone): a chartland parish of woods and orchards above the Medway valley. **West Farleigh Hall** has a long, brown brick façade, dated 1719 on a rain-water head, and articulated into three groups of three windows by very slender Doric pilasters; these stand out in bright red brick, as do the window surrounds, the panels between them, and a dentil cornice below a panelled parapet; in the centre, a later porch projects on columns with anthemion capitals carrying a broken pediment. **Court Lodge** produces an opposite effect through similar means; its dour façade comes from a tightly articulated front of about 1800 with pilasters rising between each window from pedestals at ground-storey level through two upper storeys to anthemion capitals set immediately beneath the eaves with no entablature, and the central porch has sternly unfluted Doric columns.

WESTGATE ON SEA (2 miles W of Margate): a Thanet seaside resort built up in the last two decades of the nineteenth century. It owes its origin to H. D. Mertens who owned land here and in 1868 commissioned a local architect, Charles N. Beazley (presumably a descendant of Charles Beazley, architect of Hollingbourne House, and cousin of Samuel Beazley of Tonbridge) to develop it for him. The railway duly arrived, linking Herne Bay with Margate, but little else. Mertens sold out to a Mr W. Corbett, who saw roads laid out and a sea wall built, drainage laid and gasworks and waterworks established. John Taylor, who had built Birchington's first bungalows, built a few here. One of these was purchased by Erasmus Wilson, a successful doctor who prescribed daily baths and promoted the benefits of a bracing climate; Westgate, he claimed, was the healthiest place within easy reach of London. Fashionable doctors started to send their patients there in droves. Beazley laid out two of his projected squares, Adrian and Ethelbert Squares, and built terraces and rows of villas, the latter of white brick, gabled, Gothic and grim. By 1880, Westgate was the venue for London society, with aristocrats and artists mingling with medicos and their patients. The promenade was purposely not joined to Margate's, and nice distinctions between the two places were duly observed; indeed, Westgate prided itself on its freedom from Margate's 'hawkers, niggers, hurdy-gurdies and the general rowdy element that is so great a draw back to some of our English watering-places'. That was the year when **Waterside** was built, a small hotel which Ernest George designed as a large villa in the fashionable 'Queen Anne' style. Its neighbour, **Exbury**, followed almost immediately: who designed it for Algernon Bertram Mitford, diplomat and friend of the artist James Whistler, with a distinctly Japanese-looking veranda, remains unknown, but it could have been Beazley. He was now converted to 'Queen Anne', and designed other houses along the front, combining bay windows and verandas, gables and dormers into a happy holiday style (Girouard 1977, 186-9).

Westgate. Waterside and Exbury.

WEST MALLING (5¾ miles WNW of Maidstone): a chartland parish of orchards with a large centre built along the wide High Street. Many of the best houses are here, starting at the top end by the church with **Street House** and a series of later Georgian houses in glowing brick or plaster, sometimes grooved to suggest masonry, and this is also how the village ends in Swan Street with **Went House**. Behind an encroachment into the High Street lie two medieval houses: **Prebendal House**, behind Harrington's, is of stone and the twelfth-century windows, shafted with scallop capitals, survive from its upper hall; the other is the usual sort of framed hall-house with curved up-braces and, at the high end, a cross-wing, jettied and gabled to protrude over the pavement. Beyond, at **St Leonards**, a later, close-studded house was built in two sections with projecting gabled bays at one end, and an end gable at the other with a large window and clerestories. At the Royal Air Force station, on the chartland to the south, there are symmetrically arranged barracks facing a square (Plate 21) and two-storeyed houses regularly laid out along streets named after warplanes based here: the Spitfire, Hurricane, Mosquito, Beaufighter and Lysander.

West Malling. RAF married quarters.

WEST PECKHAM (5½ miles NE of Tonbridge): a chartland parish of scattered settlements. **Duke's Place** is said to have been the preceptory of the Knights Hospitaller who were granted land in the parish in 1337, but nothing belongs to that date. The oldest part of the splendid timber house is the northern portion of the rear range, which was probably built in the middle of the fifteenth century as a *camera* or lodging, associated with a hall; it has an elliptical head to its entrance, a jettied upper storey and a crown-post roof. Its southern extension comprises a wider range with a smoke bay, perhaps serving as kitchen. The main house, attached to the north, is in the form of a large ornate Wealden with gabled ends. The still open hall was built about 1500 on a grand scale with overhangs front and back (Figure 59); the entrance has a fine arch with Tudor roses in the spandrels; the canted bay window at the high end is an addition, probably repeated at the back, but now removed, with two tiers of cusped and traceried lights (Figure 30f). The two storeyed ends are later and structurally separate. Twin doorways with moulded surrounds lead to the service end, and doors with grotesques serving as chamfer-stops above them lead into the chamber end; it has oriels with clerestories added to both floors and a stone chimney-surround with a moulded flat arch. On the other side of the parish, the long, yellow brick façades of **Hampton's** were built about 1813 for the Dalison family to designs by the architect Robert William Jearrad, and perhaps completed in 1820 with a porch carried by pairs of Greek Ionic columns and similar pairs carrying a veranda across the garden front (Plate 9). **Oxon Hoath**, first built in the seventeenth and eighteenth centuries, was recast for the Francophile furniture collector Sir William Geary in a French Empire style with a central domed roof by the architect Anthony Salvin about 1846-7, and given a pair of Tudor style lodges dated 1846 (Allibone 1987, 92 and 172-3).

Duke's Place, West Peckham. Detail of mask chamfer stop at upper end of hall.

WICKHAMBREAUX (4¼ miles E of Canterbury): a small parish of orchards and meadows lying in the angle between the Great and Little Stour, with a memorable village complete with church, green, Georgian houses and watermill. Nevertheless, the chequered flint and ragstone walls of **The Old Post Office** are medieval, as a pair of cusped windows beneath the eaves demonstrates, but rebuilding with Tudor brickwork has given the house stepped gables at each end, and a pair of projecting bays added to the front again rise into stepped gables, the larger bay serving as a porch for a brick arched entrance; the one jarring feature is an overlarge bay window which served the post office. **The Old Rectory** is a solid double pile built in brown brick in the first half of the eighteenth century with bright red surrounds to the windows, a fine doorcase with a hood carried by *putti*, a prominent wooden block cornice and a hipped roof with three dormers, the central one emerging from a heavy brick surround carrying an open pediment. **Wickham Court**, which faces the top of the green, is plainer by far, right down to its gleaming white Roman Doric porch. A gabled cottage on the opposite side of the green is dated 1736.

WILLINGTON (2 miles ESE of Maidstone): a built-up suburb of Maidstone beyond Mote Park, with quarries and orchards on its further side. On the edge of the park and reached from School Lane are two Wealdens, **The Bothy House** and **Raigersfield**, both with Kentish framing and four-centred entrance doorways.

WINGHAM (3½ miles E of Canterbury): a downland parish, once the Archbishop of Canterbury's richest manor, with a built-up village on the Sandwich road, almost a town, which Henry III licensed to hold a market in 1252. In 1283 Archbishop Peckham founded a prebendal college for a master and six canons here, and houses for them had been built by 1287 in Canterbury Road. These include the adjacent **Old Canonry** and **Canon Cottage**; both are built on undercrofts, and these are certainly original, but there is a structural break between the two parts of the building, and the framing of the Old Canonry, which has a close-studded gable facing the street and an upper floor jettied to the front and down the side, is late medieval; the framing of Canon Cottage (Figure 19) is earlier and harder to assess: it has a large two-centred doorway (Figure 22b), possibly of about the 1280s, and a jetty along the street, carrying a comparatively low upper storey which rises into the roof space; this is simply framed with lapped collars bracing the common rafters, pair by pair, and there are no longitudinal timbers, such as a crown-plate or purlins, at all. This may be due to the small size of the building and the need to keep the roof free of encumbering tie-beams and crown-posts, or

Wingham (from left to right). The Dog Inn, Canon Cottage, and The Old Canonry, Canterbury Road.

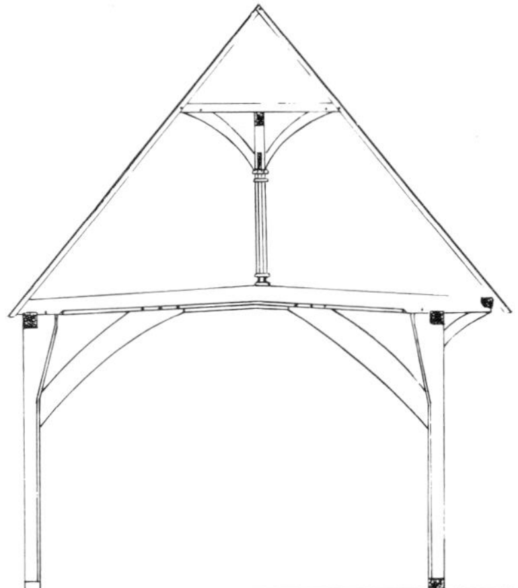

Raigersfield, Willington. Cross section through open hall of Wealden house, showing lack of alignment between framing below and above tie-beam. (After Mercer 1975 [225].)

it may be due to the primitive framing techniques available in the 1280s (Parkin 1979). If it is the latter, the jetty is contemporary with the oldest examples known in Essex, at Priory Place, Little Dunmow (Hewett 1966). Undercrofts and further remains of more canon's houses appear at the Dog Inn and the Red Lion, which face Canterbury Road before the right-angle bend into the High Street. Then come rows of brick and plastered houses: **No. 40** is a Wealden, the hall now disguised by a jettied floor inserted across it, **Nos. 54-55** comprise another concealed Wealden, with jetties at the ends as well as the front, and **No. 28** is yet another. **Nos. 56-60** include the remains of an aisled hall (Parkin 1977). The red brick

Wingham. Vicarage House, High Street.

Vicarage House has Doric pilasters mounted on a string-course and brackets naïvely articulating its upper storey and bears the date 1698 (could it be 1628?) *(see* Wallets Court, West Cliffe). There are a few shaped gables in the High Street and again near the church at **Wingham Court**, where the plastered front ends in a brick gable. Opposite, **Delbridge House** is a double pile of about 1700 with a well-proportioned front of red brick enhanced by a pedimented Corinthian doorcase and bracketed eaves. Another shaped gable at **Wingham Well Farmhouse** (Colour Plate 41) is notable for double pediments, the lower one open, the upper one rising directly above it (Figure 27r); nearby, **Wingham Well House** is yet another Wealden, also with jettied ends, and, close by, is a fully jettied house with a thatched roof.

WITTERSHAM (4 miles S of Tenterden): a parish occupying the west end of the Isle of Oxney, with a cluster of attractive houses by the parish church. Set back a little is **Wittersham House**, which Lutyens remodelled in 1907 for the cricketer, lawyer and statesman, the Hon Alfred Lyttleton, for whom he had already built a holiday home in Lothian; it is in a bland, wide Georgian style with a long porch supported by paired Roman Doric columns stretching the length of a pedimented centrepiece. At the far end of the village is the framed **Stocks Mill House**, with curiously paired gables at one end of the front.

WOMENSWOLD (8 miles NW of Dover): a small downland parish with a pretty group of mid eighteenth-century brick cottages by the church. **Denne Hill** is the work of Major Edwards Dyson; in 1875 he inherited a fortune made from his family's Halifax woollen mill, as well as the estate, to add to another fortune, based on the law, which had come with his marriage in 1854. In 1871-3, that is before the estate was his, he was spending his wife's money on the new house. The architect was George Devey. He produced a symmetrical entrance front with shaped gables, both curved and pedimented, emulating the Dutch or Queen's House at Kew, although broader and lower, and with the irregular outline more typical of him for the other elevations and the service wing (Allibone 1991, 97-9, 163).

WOODCHURCH (3¾ miles ENE of Tenterden): a large parish extending from the clay ridge overlooking Romney Marsh down on to the levels, with several outlying settlements and a centre built around a green. Overlooking it is **Hendon Place**, a fine Wealden, close-studded with ochred plaster infill, and always lacking its chamber end if the overall roof, hipped at both ends, is reliable evidence (Colour Plate 62). A near neighbour has a similar roof, but is fronted in lovely red and dove-grey brick. **Little Robhurst Farm** is another two-thirds Wealden, this time an early one, reduced at the service end and underbuilt in brick; **Great Engeham** is yet another Wealden, complete this time, but with a low-pitched roof, designed, perhaps, to be slated rather than tiled. The lonely **Shirley Farm** is another three-part Wealden, also with an end jetty, and again underbuilt in brick.

WOODNESBOROUGH (4½ miles NW of Deal): a downland parish of orchards with a built-up centre. A number of houses have shaped gables, including **Church Farm** and a group of cottages nearby; **Poulton's Farm** was given comparatively plain ones with double curves rising to semicircular pediments when the framed centre was extended in the late seventeenth century by the addition of brick cross-wings. **Rose Cottage**, near Ash at Combe, has shaped gables of 1723.

WORTH (3 miles NW of Deal): a small coastal parish; at the centre of the small village are the shaped gables of **Worth Farm** (Figure 27g), which is dated 1675, and **Barton House** overlooking the village pond.

Worth. Yew Tree Cottage.

Nearby, **Yew Tree Cottage** is small, weatherboarded and single-storeyed beneath a heavy thatched roof. On the main road, **Upton House** has a Doric porch and a low pediment over its central three bays suggesting a building date about 1800. There are more shaped gables at **Hacklinge**, including a pair on a cottage dated 1738.

WOULDHAM (3 miles SW of Rochester): a downland parish which stretches down to the marshy east bank of the Medway. The weatherboarded **Scarborough Farm** is a hall-house with an end jetty. **Starkey Castle Farm** is a good deal less usual, a hall-house built of ragstone and flint, possibly about 1380 by Richard Bysets who possessed it in Edward III's reign, with a service and solar block and attached garderobe and privy *(see* Old Soar, Plaxtol); a doorway in the hall probably led to a chamber block at the high end whose foundations have recently been uncovered (Colour Plate 26 and Figures 30b and 41). Richard III's chief baron of the Exchequer, Sir Humphrey Starkey, who owned the house towards the end of the fifteenth century, not only gave it its present name, but apparently also floored over the hall and added a chimney-stack at the rear (Swain 1966).

WROTHAM (6 miles NE of Sevenoaks): a parish lying between the North Downs and the chartland, with a small village just below the scarp. **Ford Place** is the remaining wing of an Elizabethan mansion (Colour Plate 39), built of brick perhaps about 1589 with a stepped gable at one end, and three shaped gables for dormer windows added on the north side perhaps about 1605 (these dates were once inscribed on chimneybreasts); brick mullioned and transomed windows characterise the surviving original parts, with a long plastered hoodmould at first-floor level echoed by a moulded frieze beneath the parapet; inside is the modified crown-post roof of a former house. **Nepicar House** was extended at the front in red brick chequered with vitrified headers about 1700 to become a double pile and given a fine doorcase with a shell hood on carved brackets.

Wrotham. Nepicar House.

WYE (3¾ miles NE of Ashford): a large parish at the southern end of the valley cut by the Great Stour through the North Downs, with a large village, once a market town, built around the parish church and the college founded in 1432. Bridge Street runs from **Mill House**, a small double pile with a pedimented doorcase, uphill past the steeply pitched roof of a well-concealed Wealden, which was jettied at both ends as well as at the front, to **134-140 Bridge Street**, where the remains of a continuous jetty along the front belongs to a framed house of the sixteenth century, made the more credible by the grotesque brackets *(see* Tudor House, Canterbury) which support the jetty and, removed from their original positions, the pedimented doorhood. In Church Street, the plain brick front of **Little Lords** faces the three-storeyed canted bays and pedimented doorcase and central window of **Swan House**; **Old Manor House** is now marked by little more than a pleasing chimney-breast rising into octagonal shafts which then become round *(see* Cottrill Court, Petham). Behind the street, **Old Vicarage House** has a lobby-entry plan and three prominent gables across the front, still with curving bargeboards and pendants at the ridges, but the band of windows below them has been blocked, the framing below the upper jetty is now clad in tile leaving only a few carved brackets visible, and the ground storey has had its jetty underbuilt in brick. To make up for this crude treatment, one of Kent's grandest lobby-entry houses survives in Scotton Street: **Yew Trees** bears the date 1605 on a lead rainwater-head attached to an end wall in a way suggesting that it may be an addition; the house is sumptuously finished in small panelled framing filled with brick-nogging (Plate 28) in the upper storey, and all in accord with a date of 1605; the front jetty has a moulded fascia and there is a similarly moulded eaves cornice; console brackets, distinctly later in style than the grotesques in Bridge Street, support the jetty and the oriels which rise over canted bays in the ground storey to reach the eaves, and pairs of clerestories fill in much of the rest of both storeys, making the house into a significant stylistic landmark. Outside the village, **Olantigh** retains its eighteenth-century portico, but otherwise is an Edwardian version of the original, built in 1910-12 to the design of A. Burnett Brown and E. R. Barrow.

YALDING (5¾ miles SW of Maidstone): a large parish of hamlets and scattered farms in the vale of the Medway below the chartland scarp, with a pretty village built up along a winding street leading to the medieval Town Bridge over the River Beult and continued on the further side as The Lees. Red brick prevails, but there are two Wealdens, one showing its framing, the other dressed in black weatherboarding. The major house, **Court Lodge**, was built towards the end of the seventeenth century as a double pile with keystones over the mullioned and transomed casement windows, a band between the storeys and a moulded wooden cornice and a projecting centre marked out with quoins to match the ends of the front, all picked out in white; here the lavish decoration comes to an end because, instead of a pediment, the centre is crowned by a plain gable, and the entrance has the simplest of hoods. Across the road, **Holborough House** has detailing rather later in style, but it was clearly built in two stages and probably hides the remains of an earlier house; on the right-hand side, the red brick façade is built on a stone plinth, and decorated with vitrified headers, panels between the two storeys of sash windows, a doorcase with a shallow bracketed hood, and a wooden block cornice; to the left, a modern but matching projection obscures the ground storey, the windows above have narrow side lights and dripmoulds, and the similar cornice comes at a lower level beneath a steeply pitched roof which looks suspiciously medieval. Just before Town Bridge is a cottage with turned balusters at the front of its porch. On the further side, **The Lees** has rather more weatherboarding and tile-hanging by way of contrast. The entrance to the village from the crossing over the Medway by way of the medieval Twyford Bridge is marked by two small houses placed close to the road like a gateway, a lobby-entry house to one side, with channelled plaster made to look like masonry, a brick house on the other painted to look like plaster with three of the shallowest of bows hardly projecting from the wall. Of the outlying hamlets, Benover stands out for the modestly named **Norman Cottages**, in fact a major timber-framed house of about 1600-1650 with a symmetrically planned front dominated by large gabled cross-wings and a smaller gabled centrepiece filling the gap between them (Colour Plate 49); an unknown hand executed these with immaculate symmetry, all but the entrance, and a show of close-studding, jetties with moulded fascias at first-floor and gable level, bracketed oriels beneath them extended to the full length of the façade by clerestories, and, finally, carved bargeboards with pendants and finials at the gable tops; at the back, the cross-wings extend to embrace a small courtyard. More ordinary rural wealth, that is by the high standards of Kent, gave **Burnt House** a hall spanned by base-crucks *(see* Hamden, Smarden), and jetties extending both of the storeyed ends. The truly named **Glass House** was originally close-studded like Norman Cottages and again had full-length clerestories extending its oriels, but it was more modestly designed about a lobby-entry plan and is now finished with a tile-hung upper storey above the front jetty (Figure 26e). Among the many solitary houses in the parish, **Bow Hill House** stands out for its gabled front finished with canted bays on the ground floor, and prominent lancet windows with intersecting tracery giving it a distinct Gothick character.

Glossary

AEDICULE — a surround to an opening, usually comprising two columns or *pilasters* supporting a *pediment*

AISLE — secondary space running along the length of a building, usually divided by an *arcade* from a primary space, or nave

AISLE-TIE — *tie-beam* spanning an *aisle* and connecting a *wall-post* to an *arcade-post*

ANTA — a square *pilaster* at either side of a doorway or the corner of a flank wall

ARCADE — row of *posts* or piers, usually supporting arches

ARCADE-POST — one of a series of structural *posts* dividing, for example, the main part of a building from an *aisle*

ARCH-BRACES — pair of touching curved *braces*, usually supporting a *tie-beam* or *collar*, which together form an arch

ARCHITRAVE — lowest, structural part of an *entablature* forming a *lintel*, or similarly formed surround to an opening

ASHLAR — masonry comprising large blocks with square edges and a flat face

ATTIC — top *storey*, set above *cornice* in classical building

BALUSTER — supporting *post* of handrail

BARGEBOARD — board fixed beneath eaves of *gable* to protect *rafters* from weather

BASE-CRUCK — one of a pair of short *crucks* which rise only a short way into the roof of a building and are linked by a *tie-beam* which carries a superstructure to support the upper part of the roof

BATTER — inward inclination of wall

BAY — vertical section of building, often divided by structural members; or projecting part of building usually containing a window

BEAM — structural horizontal member, usually of timber, spanning part of a building

BOND — pattern in which long sides and short sides (stretchers and headers) of bricks are laid

BOW WINDOW — projecting curved window

BOWER — archaic word for *chamber* or private room

BOX-FRAME — timber frame comprising horizontal and vertical timbers, forming the walls of a building and directly supporting the roof

BRACE — triangulating piece, usually in a timber frame

BRACKET — supporting piece, sometimes grotesquely carved, sometimes given a compound curve as in a console bracket

BRESSUMMER — horizontal, intermediate structural timber, sometimes supporting ends of floor *joists* or chimney

BRICK-NOGGING — brick infilling in a timber-framed wall

BRIDGING-PIECE — horizontal timber spanning a building, for instance to support a series of floor *joists*

BURGAGE PLOT — long, narrow plot of land, running back from main town street, usually to a back lane, often in possession of a *burgess*

BURGESS — free citizen of town with full municipal rights

BUTTERY — a bottle store, from Fr. *bouteillerie*, hence a service room for liquid foodstuffs

CANTED — angled

CAPITAL — decorative top of *post* or column

CASEMENT — vertically hinged opening window

CELLAR — bottle store, latterly in a basement or fully underground

CHAMBER — private room

CHAMFER — flattened edge

CHIMNEY-HOOD — wide funnel-shaped chimney, usually made of timber and plaster, synonymous with *firehood*

CLERESTORY — upper window, sometimes as a continuation of a deeper window

CLOSE-STUDDING — *studs* set about as closely together as their own width

CLOSET — small private room, often for storage or the intimate conduct of bodily functions

COLLAR — horizontal timber, usually joining a pair of *rafters* some way below their apex

COMMON RAFTER — one of a series of similarly sized *rafters* not forming part of a roof *truss*, ie not a *principal rafter*, which is usually larger and part of a roof truss

CORBEL — piece of stone or timber projecting from wall, usually to support an arch, *post* or *beam*

CORNICE — horizontal projection, particularly the topmost part of a classical *entablature*, designed to stop rain from running down the face of a building

COURSE — continuous layer of stones or bricks

COVE — curved piece, usually joining a wall to ceiling, or acting as a canopy

CROSS-PASSAGE — passage running across house, usually adjacent to a *hall*, between front and back entrance doors

CROWN-PLATE — timber running down the length of a roof, carried by a series of *crown-posts*, to support the *collars* linking pairs of *rafters*

CROWN-POST — timber post rising centrally into roof space from a *tie-beam* to support a longitudinal timber or *crown-plate*

CROW-STEP — stepped *gable*

CRUCK — curved timber, used in pairs to form a bowed A-frame which supports roof of building independently of walls

DAIS — raised floor, usually at high end of *hall* further from entrance

DAIS-BEAM — decorative beam fixed to wall at high end of hall as an alternative to a cove

DAUB — mixture of earth, clay, sand and binding material such as cowhair or straw, often used on base of *wattles* to fill panels of timber-framed wall

DIAPER — decorative pattern of squares or lozenges

DIOCLETIAN WINDOW — semicircular window rising from a flat base with two symmetrically placed *mullions*, as in the Baths of Diocletian, Rome; also known as a thermal window

DORMER WINDOW — window projecting from roof, and having a roof of its own

DOUBLE-PILE PLAN — plan of house usually formed by two clearly identifiable contiguous ranges

DOVETAIL — reversed wedge-shaped timber joint designed to withstand tension, for instance between a *tie-beam* and a pair of *wall-plates*

DOWN-BRACE — subsidiary timber set into the lower angle of a frame to strengthen it — typical of *Kentish framing*

DRAGON-POST — *post* at corner of a building bearing a projecting diagonal *beam*, usually in association with *jetties* on adjacent sides

DRIPMOULD — projecting moulding designed to throw rainwater off face of building

DUTCH GABLE — shaped *gable* with curved sides and pedimented top

EAVES — overhanging edge of roof

EMBATTLED — indented top, usually of wall, originally for purposes of defence, latterly for decoration

ENTABLATURE — classical *lintel*, comprising an *architrave*, or main structural element, decorative *frieze*, and *cornice*

FINIAL — ornamental finishing of apex, for instance of *post* or *gable*

FIREHOOD — wide funnel-shaped chimney, usually made of timber and plaster, synonymous with *chimney-hood*

FLAG — large paving stone, or stone roof *tile*

FRIEZE — horizontal band of decoration

GABLE — triangular upper part of wall rising into end of roof

GALLERY — upper balcony or passage

GALLETING — insertion of chips of stone into mortar between larger stones for decorative effect

GARDEROBE — archaic word for *privy*

GARRET — upper room, often in roof space

GIANT ORDER — classical order of column or *pilaster* rising two or more *storeys*

GRUBENHAUS — German for sunken house; a form of Anglo-Saxon building characterised by a floor sunk to a depth of about 3ft. (1 m) below ground level

GUILLOCHE — classical ornament of plaited bands

HALL — large public room, often open to the roof and containing a hearth, used as a main living room in the Middle Ages; latterly, also an entrance vestibule

HALL-HOUSE — house whose main room is an open *hall*

HAMMER-BEAM — one of a pair of cantilevered *beams* which project from opposite walls to support a timber roof

HEARTH-PASSAGE — *cross-passage* partly backing chimney-stack with hearth in adjacent *hall*

HIP — slanting outward angle of roof, the opposite of a valley, the inward angle

HOODMOULD — projecting moulding over an opening or other feature of a building which needs protection from rainwater

IMPOST — horizontal moulding carrying the springing of an arch

IPSWICH WINDOW — *mullioned* and *transomed* window in which the central light is arched, as at Sparrow's House, Ipswich, but probably a debased form of a *Venetian* or Serlian window; typical of the seventeenth century

JETTY — projecting *joists* extending a floor beyond wall below

JOIST — horizontal supporting member, usually of timber, to carry a floor

KENTISH FRAMING — form of timber framing comprising large panels with their lower corners characteristically triangulated by curved *down-braces*

KEYSTONE — centre stone or *voussoir* at head of arch

KING-STRUT — vertical roof timber supporting the apex of a pair of *rafters* or a *collar* below the apex

LANTERN — opening, usually in roof, to let in light

LAP-JOINT — joint between two timbers in which the thickness of each one is halved to allow them to fit or lap over each other

LATH — thin strip of wood, sometimes used as base for plaster

LAVER — small basin containing washing water

LIGHT — individual vertical compartment of a window

LIGHT WELL — vertical opening, such as between flights of stairs, to let in light

LINTEL — flat structural top of an opening

LOBBY-ENTRY PLAN — plan of house in which entrance is into a lobby which gives access to two flanking rooms and backs on to a chimney-stack set between them

LOFT — low upper room, open to roof

LOUVER — ventilation opening, usually slatted to reduce entry of rain and light

MANSARD ROOF — roof with a double *pitch*, the lower one steeper than the upper

MATHEMATICAL TILE — facing *tile* with upper part indented so that lower, visible part looks like a brick

MODERN MOVEMENT — style of architecture based on an ideological belief in the unadorned use of such modern building materials as reinforced concrete, steel and plate glass to produce Utopian buildings

MODILLION — small bracket in the shape of a console, usually placed regularly along underside of Corinthian *cornice*

MORTAR — mixture of sand and lime and sometimes clay used to bind bricks or stones together

MORTISE — hole in framework usually designed to receive a *tenon*

MULLION — vertical framing member of an opening such as a window

NEWEL — stair which winds round a central newel-*post*

NOGGING — infilling of a frame, usually comprising brickwork

OAST — kiln house

OEUIL-DE-BOEUF WINDOW — oval window set horizontally

OGEE — double convex concave curve

OLD ENGLISH STYLE — romantic style developed in the nineteenth century and based on the traditional buildings of the past

ORIEL — projecting window, often bracketed out from wall

OUTSHUT — part of building beneath a low continuation of downward slope of roof

PANTRY — from Fr. *panetrie*, a bread store, and hence a store for flour, bread and dry foodstuff

PARAPET — top of wall, sometimes when projecting above roof

PARGETING — plastering, or patterning in plasterwork

PARLOUR — private room, descended from *chamber*, latterly not for sleeping

PASSING-BRACE — *brace* which, in one or two lengths, passes across the principal transverse members of a timber-framed building from an *aisle-post* on one side to a roof *rafter* on the other

PEDIMENT — formalised classical *gable*

PENDANT — hanging decorative feature

PILASTER — flat projection with form of a column, used to decorate and articulate wall or pier

PITCH — angle at which roof slopes upwards from the horizontal

POST — principal vertical structural timber

PRINCIPAL RAFTER — stout *rafter* forming a structural part of a roof *truss*

PRIVY — small private room, particularly for the intimate conduct of bodily functions

PURLIN — longitudinal roof timber designed to support *rafters*

QUEEN-STRUT — one of a pair of struts which rise, usually from a *tie-beam*, to support the ends of a roof *collar*

QUOIN — projecting corner stone

RAFTER — roof timber, generally running from eaves to ridge, on to which roof covering is fixed

RAIL — horizontal timber, such as in wall or door

REVEAL — the inward-facing planes of an opening

RIB-VAULT — vault articulated at *bay* intervals and at the intersections of its parts by projecting ribs

SASH WINDOW — window whose opening is usually filled by a pair of vertically sliding glazed frames

SCARF-JOINT — joint connecting the ends of two timbers together

SCISSOR-BRACES — pair of *braces* which cross over each other, like a pair of scissors, below the apex of a roof

SCULLERY — small service room

SEMI-DETACHED PLAN — plan of pair of houses joined together, usually so that the plan of one is a mirror image of the other

SERLIAN WINDOW — see *Venetian window*

SERVICE ROOM — room used to store goods, usually food, and prepare food for cooking

SHAPED GABLE — *gable* with curved and stepped sides

SHOP — room or building used for manufacture or sale of goods

SHORE — part of timber frame acting as a buttress

SILL — base, for instance of wall or window

SLATE — specific type of impermeable metamorphic stone which can be split into thin layers, usually for covering roofs, occasionally imported into Kent in the Middle Ages, but mostly after about 1800

SMOKE BAY — *bay*, or part of bay, of *hall-house*, open from ground to roof for purpose of removing smoke from open hearth

SOLAR — upper *chamber* in medieval dwelling

SOLE-PLATE — a timber serving as a *sill*-beam

SPANDREL — space above arch beneath level of its top

SPERE — short partition, often fixed to a *truss* adjacent to a *cross-passage*

STOREY — space between two floors

STUD — secondary vertical timber

TENON — projecting piece of timber designed to fit into *mortise* to form a joint

TERRACE — row of joined houses, often similar and designed as a whole

THATCH — roof covering of straw, reed or other vegetable matter

TIE-BEAM — transverse *beam* linking tops of two walls, designed to counter outward thrust of roof above

TILE — flat baked clay or split stone slab used for roof, floor or wall covering

TIMBER FRAME — structural part of timber house

TRACERY — decorative stonework or timberwork filling top part of opening such as a window or *spandrel* of arch

TRANSOM — horizontal bar set across an opening such as a window

TRIGLYPH — stylised beam-end, in form of tripled bars, decorating Doric *frieze*

TRUSS — transverse *timber frame* designed to support a roof at *bay* intervals

UNDERCROFT — large basement room on which a building is founded

VAULT — arched ceiling, usually of stone

VENETIAN WINDOW — symmetrical tripartite window, the central *light* arched and wider, often decorated with classical features

VOUSSOIR — wedge-shaped stone forming part of an arch

WALL-PLATE — longitudinal timber framing top of wall

WALL-POST — *post* which forms structural part of a wall

WANEY — rough edge of a timber, usually resulting from not planing away bark

WATER TABLE — level in the ground to which water naturally rises

WATTLE — interlaced twigs used as a base for daub to fill the intervals of a *timber-framed* wall

WEALDEN HALL — *hall-house* common in Kent and Sussex (not just the Weald) characterised at front by *hall* recessed between *jetties* of flanking *bays* and under overhanging roof

WEATHERBOARDING — overlapping horizontal boards making a weatherproof covering

WIND-BRACE — *brace* joining *purlin* and principal *rafter* of roof to counteract effect of wind pressure, and often to decorate roof as well

WING — projecting end of building

BIBLIOGRAPHY

Airs, M. R.	1972	*The manor house, Headstone, London Borough of Harrow.* English Heritage, London Division, unpublished report
	1975	*The making of the English country house 1500-1640.* London: Architectural Press
	1983	Timber-framed buildings, *The buildings of England: London 2: South,* B. Cherry and N. Pevsner, 104-12. Harmondsworth: Penguin Books
Alcock, N. W., and M. W. Barley	1972	Medieval roofs with base-crucks and short principals, *Antiquaries J.,* 52, 132-68
Allibone, J.	1987	*Anthony Salvin.* Columbia, USA: University of Missouri Press
	1991	*George Devey, architect, 1820-1886.* Cambridge: Lutterworth Press
Arnold, G. M.	1895	Filborough Farmhouse, East Chalk, Gravesend, *Archaeol. Cantiana,* 21, 161-71
Arnold, R.,	1949	*A yeoman of Kent.* London: Constable
Arschavir, A.	1956	False fronts in minor domestic architecture, *Trans. Ancient Monuments Soc.,* new ser., 4, 110-22
Ashenden-Bax, M.	1980	Copton Manor, Faversham, in Wade 1980, 16-21
Aston, T. H.	1958	The origins of the manor in Britain, *Trans. Royal Hist. Soc.,* 5th ser., 8, 59-83
Baker, A. R. H.	1964-5	Open fields and partible inheritance on a Kent manor, *Econ. Hist. Rev.,* 2nd ser., 17, 1-23
	1976	Changes in the later Middle Ages, *A new historical geography of England before 1600,* ed. H. C. Darby, 186-247. Cambridge: University Press
Barley, M. W.	1961	*The English farmhouse and cottage.* London: Routledge and Kegan Paul
	1963	A glossary of names in houses of the 16th and 17th centuries, in Foster and Alcock 1963, 479-501
	1967	Rural housing in England, in Thirsk 1967, 696-766
	1979	The double-pile house, *Archaeol. J.,* 136, 253-64
	1986	*Houses and history.* London: Faber and Faber
Binney, M. and A. Emery	1975	*The architectural development of Penshurst Place.* Dunstable, ABC Historic Publications
Bismanis, M. R.	1987	*The medieval English domestic timber roof,* American University Studies Series 9, vol. 25. New York, Peter Lang
Blair, J.	1984	Some developments in English domestic planning, 1100-1250. Paper presented to 13th Annual Symposium of Soc. of Archit. Hist. of Great Britain, Domestic Architecture in Britain 1100-1660. Victoria and Albert Museum, 3 March 1984
Bonwit. W.	1987	*Michael Searles: a Georgian architect and surveyor.* Architectural History Monographs 3. Leeds: Society of Architectural Historians of Great Britain

Burchess, M. and K. Crawley	1983	The hall-house at Romden, in Wade 1983, 5-10
Canterbury Archaeological Trust	1977-78	*Annual Report*
	1979-80	*Annual Report*
	1980-81	*Annual Report*
	1982-83	*Annual Report*
	1983-84	*Annual Report*
	1988	*Interim Annual Report*
	1989	*Interim Annual Report*
	1990	*Interim Annual Report*
Cherry, M	1989	Nurstead Court, Kent: a re-appraisal, *Archaeol. J.*, 146, 451-64
Clifton-Taylor, A.	1972	*The pattern of English building,* 3rd edn. London: Faber and Faber
	1983	Building materials, in Newman 1983, 27-33
Cobbett, W.	1912	*Rural rides,* Everyman's edn. London: Dent
Colvin, H. M.	1978	*A biographical dictionary of British architects, 1600-1840.* London: John Murray
Coutin, K.	1990	The Wealden House, in Warren 1990, 73-86
Cowper, H. S.	1911	Some timber-framed houses in the Kentish Weald, *Archaeol. Cantiana,* 29, 169-205
	1915	Two Headcorn cloth halls, *Archaeol. Cantiana,* 31, 121-30
Cronk, A.	1978-9	Oasts in Kent and E. Sussex, *Archaeol. Cantiana,* 94, 99-110; 95, 241-54
Currie, C. R. J.	1983	Timber supply and timber building in a Sussex parish, *Vernacular Archit.,* 14, 52-4
Davie, W. and E. G. Dawber	1900	*Old cottages in Kent and Sussex.* London: Batsford
Du Boulay, F. R. H.	1958	Archbishop Cranmer and the Canterbury temporalities, *Eng. Hist Rev.,* 67, 11-36
	1962	Gavelkind and knight's fee in medieval Kent, *Eng. Hist Rev.,* 77, 504-11
	1964-5	Who were farming the English demesnes at the end of the Middle Ages?, *Econ. Hist. Rev.,* 2nd ser., 17, 443-55
	1966	*The lordship of Canterbury.* London: Thomas Nelson
Exwood, M.	1981	Mathematical tiles, *Vernacular Archit.,* 12, 48-53
Faulkner, P. A.	1958	Domestic planning from the 12th to 14th centuries, *Archaeol. J.,* 115, 150-83
	1966	Medieval undercrofts and town houses, *Archaeol. J.,* 123, 120-35
	1969	No. 6 Market Square (Faversham), *Archaeol. J.,* 126, 249-52
	1970	Some medieval archiepiscopal palaces, *Archaeol. J.,* 127, 130-46
Fisher, F. J.	1935	The development of the London food market, 1540-1640, *Econ. Hist. Rev.,* 5, 46-64
	1961	Tawney's century, *Essays in the economic and social history of Tudor and Stuart England,* ed. F. J. Fisher, 1-14. Cambridge: University Press
Fletcher, J. M.	1980	A list of tree-ring dates for building timber in S. England and Wales, *Vernacular Archit.,* 11, 32-8
Fletcher, J. M. M. Bridge and J. Hillam	1981	Tree-ring dates for buildings with oak timber, *Vernacular Archit.,* 12, 38-40
Fletcher, J. M. and P. S Spokes	1964	The origin and development of crown-post roofs, *Med. Archaeol.,* 8, 152-83
Foster, I. Ll. and L. Alcock	1963	*Culture and environment, essays in honour of* Sir Cyril Fox. London: Routledge and Kegan Paul
Franklin, J.	1981	*The Gentleman's Country House and its Plan.* London: Routledge and Kegan Paul
Girouard, M.	1971	*The Victorian country house.* Oxford: Clarendon Press
	1977	*Sweetness and light: the 'Queen Anne' movement, 1860-1900.* London, Oxford University Press
Godfrey, W. H.	1929a	Chilham Castle; the house, *Archaeol. J.,* 86, 304-6
	1929b	Monks Horton Priory, *Archaeol. J.,* 86, 314-16
Gravett, K. W. E.	1971	*Timber and brick building in Kent.* London and Chichester: Phillimore
	1981	The Clergy House, Alfriston, *National Trust Studies,* ed. G. Jackson-Stops, 103-108. London: National Trust
Gray, H. L.	1915	*English Field Systems.* Cambridge, Mass.: Harvard University Press
Gray, P. J.	1975	Skinner's House, Chiddingstone, *Arch. Cantiana,* 91, 179-82
Gregory, M.	1963	Wickham Court and the Heydons, *Arch. Cantiana,* 78, 1-21
Harris, J.	1969	Cobham Hall, *Archaeol. J.,* 126, 274-6
Harris, R. (ed.)	1987	*Weald and Open Air Museum Guidebook.* Chichester: the Museum
Harvey, J.	1984	*English medieval architects: a biographical dictionary down to 1540,* revised edn. Gloucester: Alan Sutton
Hasted, E.	1797-1801	*History and topographical survey of the County of Kent,* 2nd edn., twelve volumes. Canterbury: W. Bristow
Hatcher, J.	1977	*Plague, population and the English economy, 1348-1530.* London: Macmillan

Hawkes, S. C. 1969 Early Anglo-Saxon Kent, *Archaeol. J.*, 126, 186-92

Hayes, D. 1981 Some hall-house plans in E. Kent, in Wade 1981, 24-30

Hewett, C. A. 1966 Jettying and floor-framing in medieval Essex, *Medieval Archaeol.*, 10, 89-112

1980 *English historic carpentry.* London and Chichester: Phillimore

Hillam, J. and J. M. Fletcher 1983 Tree-ring dates for buildings with oak timber, *Vernacular Archit.*, 14, 61-2

Hilton, R. H. 1949 Peasant movements in England before 1381, *Econ. Hist. Rev.*, 2nd ser., 2, 2-43

Horsman, V. 1988 Eynsford Castle: a reinterpretation of its early history in the light of recent excavations, *Archaeol. Cantiana,* 105, 39-57

Howard, M. 1987 *The early Tudor country house: architecture and politics 1490-1550.* London: George Philip

Howard, R., R. R. Laxton, C.D. Litton and S. Pearson 1988 Tree-ring dates, *Vernacular Archit.*, 19, 47-9

Howard, R., R. R. Laxton, C. D. Litton, N. Cooper and S. Pearson 1989 Tree-ring dates, *Vernacular Archit.*, 20, 42-3

Howard, R., R. R. Laxton, C. D. Litton, and S. Pearson 1990 Tree-ring dates, *Vernacular Archit.*, 21, 40-2

1991 Tree-ring dates, *Vernacular Archit.*, 22, 43-4

1992 Tree-ring dates, *Vernacular Archit.*, 23, 57

Kelsall, A. F. 1974 The London house plan in the later 17th century, *Post-Med. Archaeol.*, 8, 80-91

Kenyon, G. H. 1967 *The glass industry of the Weald.* Leicester: University Press

Kerridge, E. 1953-4 The movement of rent, 1540-1640, *Econ. Hist. Rev.*, 2nd ser., 6, 16-34

Kidner, R. W. 1963 *The South Eastern and Chatham Railway.* Lingfield, Surrey: The Oakwood Press

Kipps, P. C. 1929 Minster Court, Thanet, *Archaeol. J.*, 86, 213-23

Laithwaite, M. 1968 A ship-master's house at Faversham, Kent, *Post-Med. Archaeol.*, 2, 150-162

Lambarde, W. 1970 *Perambulation of Kent.* Bath: Adams and Kent

Laxton, R. R., C. D. Litton and W. G. Simpson 1984 Tree-ring dates for buildings in eastern and midland England, *Vernacular Archit.*, 15, 65-9

Leggett, P.A., F. A. Hibbert, M. K. Hughes, J. M. Fletcher and R. Morgan 1982 Tree ring dates for buildings with oak timber, *Vernacular Archit.*, 13, 48-9

Leveson-Gower, G. 1895 Three ancient houses in the parish of Cowden, *Archaeol. Cantiana,* 21, 103-8

Lloyd, N. 1931 *A history of the English house.* London: Architectural Press

Lucas, H. S. 1930 The Great European famine of 1315, 1316 and 1317, *Speculum,* 5, 343-77

McGrail, S. (ed.) 1982 *Woodworking techniques before AD 1500,* British Archaeol. Reps, International Ser. 129. Oxford: BAR

Maguire, A. A. 1989 *Country House Planning in England from c.1660 — c. 1700.* Unpublished PhD thesis, Courtauld Institute, London

Maitland, F. W. 1897 *Domesday Book and beyond.* Cambridge: University Press

Mason, R. T. 1969 *Framed buildings of the Weald,* revised edn. Horsham: Coach Publishing

Mason, R. T. and R. H. Wood 1968 Winkhurst Farm, Bough Beech, *Archaeol. Cantiana,* 83, 33-7

Meates, G. W. 1980 *The Lullingstone Roman villa.* Maidstone: Kent Archaeol. Soc.

Melling, E. 1961 *Kentish sources: 3. Aspects of agriculture and industry.* Maidstone: Kent County Council

1965 *Kentish sources: 5. Some Kentish houses.* Maidstone: Kent County Council

Mercer, W. E. R. 1975 *English vernacular houses.* London: HMSO

Mills, H. L. 1932 The dating of timber-framed houses in the Weald, *Archaeol. Cantiana,* 44, 120-28

Morris, C. (ed.) 1984 *The illustrated journeys of Celia Fiennes.* London: Macdonald

Munby, J., M. Sparks and T. Tatton-Brown 1983 Crown-post and king-strut roofs in south-east England, *Med. Archaeol.*, 27, 123-35

Newman, J. A. 1980 *The buildings of England: West Kent and the Weald,* 2nd edn. with corrections. Harmondsworth: Penguin

1983 *The buildings of England: North East and East Kent,* 3rd edn. Harmondsworth: Penguin

Newman, J. A., G. Allan, and R. Wood 1988 Nos 79-80 High Street, Gravesend, *Trans Assoc. for Studies in the Conservation of Historic Buildings,* 13, 51-57

Orme, B. J. 1982 Prehistoric woodlands and woodworking in the Somerset Levels, in McGrail 1982, 79-84

Oswald, A. 1933 *Country houses of Kent.* London: Country Life

Ottewill, D.	1979	Robert Weir Schultz (1860-1951): An Arts and Crafts architect, *Archit. Hist.* 22, 88-115
Pantin, W. A.	1961	Medieval inns, *Studies in building history,* ed. E. M. Jope, 166-91. London: Odhams Press
	1962-3	Medieval English town-house plans, *Med. Archaeol.,* 6-7, 202-239
Parker, J. H.	1853	*Some account of domestic architecture in England, Vol. 2.* Oxford: J. H. Parker
Parkin, E. W.	1962	The vanishing houses of Kent, 1: Durlock Grange, Minster-in-Thanet, *Archaeol. Cantiana,* 77, 82-90
	1963	Leeds Priory Gatehouse, *Archaeol. Cantiana,* 78, 142-6
	1966	The vanishing houses of Kent, 6: The old cottage at Upper Hardres, *Archaeol. Cantiana,* 80, 53-61
	1968	The vanishing houses of Kent, 8: Lake House, Eastwell, *Archaeol. Cantiana,* 83, 151-61
	1969a	Perambulation of Sandwich, *Archaeol. J.,* 126, 220-21
	1069b	The Old Rectory of St Alphege, Canterbury, *Archaeol. Cantiana,* 84, 201-10
	1970	Cogan House, St Peter's, Canterbury, *Archaeol. Cantiana,* 85, 123-38
	1971	Cobb's Hall, Aldington, and the Holy Maid of Kent, *Archaeol. Cantiana,* 86, 15-24
	1972	No. 17 Palace Street, Canterbury, *Archaeol. Cantiana,* 87, 183-90
	1973	The ancient buildings of New Romney, *Archaeol. Cantiana,* 88, 117-28
	1975	The Old Chantry House, Bredgar, *Archaeol. Cantiana,* 91, 87-97
	1976	Ratling Court, Aylesham (Nonington), *Archaeol. Cantiana,* 92, 53-64
	1977	Wingham, a medieval town, *Archaeol. Cantiana,* 93, 61-80
	1979	The Old Canonry and Canonry Cottage, Wingham, *Archaeol. Cantiana,* 95, 197-204
	1981	A unique aisled cottage at Petham, *Collectanea Historica: essays in memory of Stuart Rigold,* ed. A. Detsicas, 225-30. Maidstone: Kent Archaeological Society
	1984	The ancient Cinque Port of Sandwich, *Archaeol. Cantiana,* 100, 189-216
	1986	Newington, near Hythe, *Archaeol. Cantiana,* 103, 167-89
	1989	Barham: the old aisled house, *Archaeol. Cantiana,* 107, 225-33
Peake, W. B.	1920	*Luddesdown Court, Kent: the story of a Kentish manor.* Privately published
Percival, A.	1966	The Dutch influence on English vernacular architecture with particular reference to East Kent, *Blackmansbury,* 3, 1, 2-58
Postan, M.M.	1944	The rise of a money economy, *Econ. Hist. Rev.,* 14, 123-34
	1966	Medieval agrarian society in its prime: England, *Cambridge Hist. of Europe,* vol. 1, ed. M. M. Postan, 2nd edn., 553-. Cambridge: University Press
Quiney, A. P.	1979	*John Loughborough Pearson.* New Haven, Conn., and London: Yale University Press
	1984	The lobby-entry house: its origins and distribution, *Archit. Hist.,* 27, 456-66
	1986	*House and home: a history of the small English house.* London: BBC Publications
	1990	*The traditional buildings of England.* London: Thames and Hudson
Rackham, O.	1972	Grundle House: on the quantities of timber in certain E. Anglian buildings in relation to local supplies, *Vernacular Archit.* 3, 3-8
	1976	*Trees and woodland in the British landscape.* London: J. M. Dent
	1982	The growing and transport of timber and underwood, in McGrail 1982, 199-218
Rigold, S. E.	1962	*Temple Manor, Strood,* Ministry of Housing and Public Works Guidebook. London: HMSO
	1963	The distribution of the 'Wealden' house, in Foster and Alcock 1963, 351-4
	1967	Fourteenth-century halls in the E. Weald, *Archaeol. Cantiana,* 82, 246-56
	1969a	Timber-framed buildings in Kent, *Archaeol. J.,* 126, 198-200
	1969b	Walmer Old Manor House, *Archaeol. J.,* 126, 215-17
	1969c	Maidstone: the archiepiscopal precinct, *Archaeol. J.,* 126, 252-4
	1969d	Battell Hall, Leeds, *Archaeol. J.,* 126, 255-6
	1969e	Lympne Castle, *Archaeol. J.,* 126, 260-62
	1969f	Charing Palace, *Archaeol. J.,* 126, 267
	1969g	Yardhurst, Daniel's Water, *Archaeol. J.,* 126, 267-9
	1971	Eynsford castle and its excavation, *Archaeol. Cantiana,* 86, 109-71
	1973	Domestic buildings, *The rural landscape of Kent,* ed. S. G. MacRae and C. P. Burnham, 184-90. Wye: Wye College
Robson, J.	1988	Some farms in Aldington, in Wade 1988, 4-14
Rogers, P (ed.)	1971	*A tour through the whole island of Great Britain,* by Daniel Defoe. Harmondsworth: Penguin
Saint, A.	1976	*Richard Norman Shaw.* New Haven, Conn. and London: Yale University Press
Sandall, K.	1975	Aisled halls in England and Wales, *Vernacular Archit.,* 6, 19-27
	1986	Aisled halls in England and Wales, *Vernacular Archit.,* 17, 21-35
Saunders, A. D.	1969	Walmer Castle, *Archaeol. J.,* 126, 215
Sheail, J.	1972	The distribution of taxable population and wealth in England during the early 16th century, *Trans. and Papers Inst. of British geographers,* 55, 120
Slane, P.	1984	*Bayleaf Farmhouse.* Unpublished dissertation: Thames Polytechnic, School of Architcture and Landscape

Smith, J. T. 1955 Medieval aisled halls and their derivatives, *Archaeol. J.*, 112, 76-94

1958 Medieval roofs, a classification, *Archaeol. J.*, 115, 111-49

1970 The evolution of the English peasant house to the late 17th century: the evidence of buildings, *J. British Archaeol. Assoc.*, 3rd ser., 33, 122-47

Smith, T. P. 1979 Refacing with brick-tiles, *Vernacular Archit.*, 10, 33-36

1990 The Roper Gateway, St Dunstan's Street, Canterbury, *Archaeol. Cantiana,* 108, 163-82

Sparks, M. J. and E. W. Parkin 1974 The Deanery, Chartham, *Archaeol. Cantiana,* 89, 169-82

Starkey, D. 1982 Ightham Mote: politics and architecture in early Tudor England, *Archaeologia,* 107, 153-63

Stephenson, D. 1971 Balcony railings in Kent, *Archaeol. Cantiana,* 86, 173-91

Swain, E. R. 1963 A timber-framed building in Tonbridge High Street, *Archaeol. Cantiana,* 78, 169-73

1964 A hall-house at Upper Bush, Cuxton, *Archaeol. Cantiana,* 79, 149-57

1966 Starkey Castle, Wouldham, *Archaeol. Cantiana,* 81, 118-25

1968 Divided and galleried hall-houses, *Med. Archaeol.*, 12, 127-45

Thirsk, J. 1961 Industries in the countryside, *Essays in the economic and social history of Tudor and Stuart England,* ed. F. J. Fisher, 70-88. Cambridge: University Press

1967 *The agrarian history of England and Wales, vol. 4, 1500-1640.* Cambridge: University Press

Thompson, F. M. L. 1968 The second agricultural revolution, 1815-1880, *Econ. Hist. Rev.*, 21, 62-77

Titow, J. Z. 1969 *English rural society, 1200-1350.* London: Allen and Unwin

Vallance, A. 1925 An old timber house at Sundridge, *Archaeol. Cantiana,* 37, 167-75

1942 Anchor House, Lynsted, *Archaeol. Cantiana,* 55, 53-6

Wade, J. (ed.) 1980 *Traditional Kent buildings,* No. 1. Maidstone: Kent County Council Education Committee

1981 *Traditional Kent buildings,* No. 2. Maidstone: Kent County Council Education Committee

1983 *Traditional Kent buildings,* No. 3. Maidstone: Kent County Council Education Committee

1985 *Traditional Kent buildings,* No. 4. Maidstone: Kent County Council Education Committee

1986 *Traditional Kent buildings,* No. 5. Maidstone: Kent County Council Education Committee

1988 *Traditional Kent buildings,* No. 6. Maidstone: Kent County Council Education Committee

Warren, J. (ed.) 1990 *Wealden Buildings: Studies in Kent, Sussex and Surrey.* Horsham: Coach Publishing

Whinifrith, J. 1980 The 'Priest's House' at Smallhythe: a false identification?, *Archaeol. Cantiana,* 94, 363-6

Wood, M. 1947 *Old Soar, Plaxtol, Kent,* Ministry of Public Buildings and Works Guide. London: HMSO

1965 *The English medieval house.* London: J. M. Dent

Index